T0396172

Critical Perspectives on Counter-Terrorism

This volume examines the rationale, effectiveness and consequences of counter-terrorism practices from a range of perspectives and cases.

The book critically interrogates contemporary counter-terrorism powers from military campaigns and repression through to the prosecution of terrorist suspects, counter-terrorism policing, counter-radicalisation programmes, and the proscription of terrorist organisations. Drawing on a range of timely and important case studies from around the world including the UK, Sri Lanka, Spain, Canada, Australia and the USA, its chapters explore the impacts of counter-terrorism on individuals, communities and political processes.

The book focuses on three questions of vital importance to any assessment of counter-terrorism. First, what do counter-terrorism strategies seek to achieve? Second, what are the consequences of different counter-terrorism campaigns, and how are these measured? And, third, how and why do changes to counter-terrorism occur?

This volume will be of much interest to students of counter-terrorism, critical terrorism studies, criminology, security studies and International Relations.

Lee Jarvis is a Senior Lecturer in International Security at the University of East Anglia. He is author of *Times of Terror: Discourse, Temporality and the War on Terror* (2009), and co-author of *Terrorism: A Critical Introduction* (2011).

Michael Lister is Reader in Politics at Oxford Brookes University. He is co-author of *Citizenship in Contemporary Europe* (2008) and co-editor of *The State: Theories and Issues* (2005).

Series: Routledge Critical Terrorism Studies
Series Editor: Richard Jackson
University of Otago, New Zealand

This book series will publish rigorous and innovative studies on all aspects of terrorism, counter-terrorism and state terror. It seeks to advance a new generation of thinking on traditional subjects and investigate topics frequently overlooked in orthodox accounts of terrorism. Books in this series will typically adopt approaches informed by critical-normative theory, post-positivist methodologies and non-Western perspectives, as well as rigorous and reflective orthodox terrorism studies.

Terrorism and the Politics of Response
Edited by Angharad Closs Stephens and Nick Vaughan-Williams

Critical Terrorism Studies
Framing a new research agenda
Edited by Richard Jackson, Marie Breen Smyth and Jeroen Gunning

State Terrorism and Neoliberalism
The north in the south
Ruth Blakeley

Contemporary State Terrorism
Theory and practice
Edited by Richard Jackson, Eamon Murphy and Scott Poynting

State Violence and Genocide in Latin America
The Cold War years
Edited by Marcia Esparza, Henry R. Huttenbach and Daniel Feierstein

Discourses and Practices of Terrorism
Interrogating terror
Edited by Bob Brecher, Mark Devenney and Aaron Winter

An Intellectual History of Terror
War, violence and the state
Mikkel Thorup

Women Suicide Bombers
Narratives of violence
V.G. Julie Rajan

Terrorism, Talking and Transformation
A critical approach
Harmonie Toros

Counter-Terrorism and State Political Violence
The 'War on Terror' as terror
Edited by Scott Poynting and David Whyte

Selling the War on Terror
Foreign policy discourses after 9/11
Jack Holland

The Making of Terrorism in Pakistan
Historical and social roots of extremism
Eamon Murphy

Lessons and Legacies of the War on Terror
From moral panic to permanent war
Edited by Gershon Shafir, Everard Meade, and William J. Aceves

Arguing Counterterrorism
New perspectives
Edited by Daniela Pisoiu

States of War since 9/11
Terrorism, sovereignty and the war on terror
Edited by Alex Houen

Counter-Radicalisation
Critical perspectives
Edited by Charlotte Heath-Kelly, Lee Jarvis and Christopher Baker-Beall

Critical Perspectives on Counter-Terrorism
Edited by Lee Jarvis and Michael Lister

Critical Perspectives on Counter-Terrorism

Edited by
Lee Jarvis and Michael Lister

LONDON AND NEW YORK

First published 2015
by Routledge
2 Park Square, Milton Park, Abingdon, Oxon OX14 4RN

and by Routledge
711 Third Avenue, New York, NY 10017

Routledge is an imprint of the Taylor & Francis Group, an informa business

© 2015 selection and editorial matter, Lee Jarvis and Michael Lister; individual chapters, the contributors

The right of the editors to be identified as the authors of the editorial material, and of the authors for their individual chapters, has been asserted in accordance with sections 77 and 78 of the Copyright, Designs and Patents Act 1988.

All rights reserved. No part of this book may be reprinted or reproduced or utilised in any form or by any electronic, mechanical, or other means, now known or hereafter invented, including photocopying and recording, or in any information storage or retrieval system, without permission in writing from the publishers.

Trademark notice: Product or corporate names may be trademarks or registered trademarks, and are used only for identification and explanation without intent to infringe.

British Library Cataloguing-in-Publication Data
A catalogue record for this book is available from the British Library

Library of Congress Cataloging-in-Publication Data
Critical perspectives on counter-terrorism / edited by Lee Jarvis and Michael Lister.
  pages cm – (Routledge critical terrorism studies)
  Includes bibliographical references and index.
  1. Terrorism–Prevention. 2. Terrorism–Prevention–Government policy.
  I. Jarvis, Lee, 1979– II. Lister, Michael, 1976–
  HV6431.C7626 2014
  363.325'16–dc23   2014019029

ISBN: 978-0-415-85547-1 (hbk)
ISBN: 978-0-203-72197-1 (ebk)

Typeset in Times New Roman
by Wearset Ltd, Boldon, Tyne and Wear

For our siblings

Greg, Kerri

and

Sarah

Contents

Notes on contributors xi
Acknowledgements xvi

Introduction: the ends of counter-terrorism 1
LEE JARVIS AND MICHAEL LISTER

1 'There's a good reason they are called al-Qaeda in Iraq. They are al-Qaeda ... in ... Iraq.' The impossibility of a global counter-terrorism strategy, or the end of the nation state 11
BOB DE GRAAFF

2 Counter-terrorism: the ends of a secular ministry 41
CHARLOTTE HEATH-KELLY

3 Spatial and temporal imaginaries in the securitisation of terrorism 56
KATHRYN MARIE FISHER

4 Counter-terrorism as conflict transformation 77
LAURA ZAHRA McDONALD, BASIA SPALEK, PHILLIP DANIEL SILK, RAQUEL DA SILVA AND ZUBEDA LIMBADA

5 Contemporary Spanish anti-terrorist policies: ancient myths, new approaches 91
AGATA SERRANÒ

6 'I read it in the FT': 'everyday' knowledge of counter-terrorism and its articulation 109
LEE JARVIS AND MICHAEL LISTER

Contents

7 **Prosecuting suspected terrorists: precursor crimes, intercept evidence and the priority of security** 130
   STUART MacDONALD

8 **Banishing the enemies of all mankind: the effectiveness of proscribing terrorist organisations in Australia, Canada, the UK and US** 150
   TIMOTHY LEGRAND

9 **Britain's Prevent programme: an end in sight?** 169
   PAUL THOMAS

10 **How terrorism ends: negotiating the end of the IRA's 'armed struggle'** 187
   PAUL DIXON

11 **From counter-terrorism to soft authoritarianism: the case of Sri Lanka** 210
   NEIL DeVOTTA

   Index 231

Contributors

Raquel Da Silva is a second year full-time doctoral researcher at the Institute of Applied Social Studies, at the University of Birmingham. Her research is related to armed political struggle in Portugal (1970–1987) and explores the perspectives and experiences of its participants and the social and political conditions that helped create and sustain violent organisations, in order to try to prevent the creation of such conditions in the future through making policy recommendations.

Neil DeVotta is an Associate Professor in Politics and International Affairs at Wake Forest University. His research interests include South Asian security and politics, ethnicity and nationalism, ethnic conflict resolution, and democratic transition and consolidation. He is the author of *Blowback: Linguistic Nationalism, Institutional Decay, and Ethnic Conflict in Sri Lanka* (Stanford: Stanford University Press, 2004) and editor of *Understanding Contemporary India, 2nd edition* (Boulder: Lynne Rienner Publishers, 2010). His current work focuses on democratic regression and authoritarianism.

Paul Dixon is Professor in Politics and International Studies at Kingston University having taught previously at the universities of Ulster, Leeds and Luton. He is the author of *Northern Ireland: The Politics of War and Peace* (Palgrave 2nd edition 2008) and with Eamonn O'Kane *Northern Ireland Since 1969* (Pearson, 2011). Dr Dixon is also the editor of *The British Approach to Counterinsurgency: From Malaya and Northern Ireland to Iraq and Afghanistan* (Palgrave, 2012). He has published numerous articles on the Northern Ireland conflict in *Journal of Strategic Studies, Political Science Quarterly, Political Studies, Journal of Peace Research, Political Quarterly* and *Democratization*. He is writing a book on the Northern Ireland peace process and his research interests also include British public opinion and military intervention, counterinsurgency and conflict management.

Kathryn Marie Fisher is a Visiting Assistant Professor in the Department of Political Science at Ohio University in Athens, Ohio. She was recently awarded her PhD in International Relations from the London School of Economics and Political Science and holds an MA in International Affairs from the American University in Washington. Her research interests and recent publications focus largely on the relational and consequential intersection of identity, securitisation and counter-terrorism.

Bob de Graaff is a historian by training. He was the Netherlands' first professor for terrorism and counter-terrorism at the University of Leiden (Campus The Hague), where he established the Centre for Terrorism and Countertrerrorism (CTC). Currently he is professor for intelligence and security studies at both the University of Utrecht and the Netherland Defense Academy in Breda. His current research interest is: state and on-state intelligence organisations as learning organisations.

Charlotte Heath-Kelly holds concurrent postdoctoral fellowships at The University of Warwick, based in the Institute of Advanced Studies and the department of Politics and International Studies (PAIS). Her monograph, *Politics of Violence: Militancy, International Politics, Killing in the Name*, has been shortlisted for the 2014 Susan Strange book prize by the British International Studies Association. She has published widely on issues of violence, memory and critical security studies in journals such as *Security Dialogue* and the *British Journal of Politics and International Relations*.

Lee Jarvis is Senior Lecturer in International Security at the University of East Anglia. His books include *Times of Terror: Discourse, Temporality and the War on Terror* (Palgrave, 2009); *Terrorism: A Critical Introduction* (Palgrave, 2011, with Richard Jackson, Jeroen Gunning and Marie Breen Smyth); *Cyberterrorism: Understanding, Assessment and Response* (Springer, 2014, co-edited with Tom Chen and Stuart Macdonald); and, *Counter-Radicalisation: Critical Perspectives* (Routledge, 2015, co-edited with Christopher Baker-Beall and Charlotte Heath-Kelly). His research has been published in journals including *Security Dialogue, Political Studies, Millennium: Journal of International Studies, International Relations, Terrorism and Political Violence* and *Critical Studies on Terrorism*.

Timothy Legrand is Lecturer at the National Security College at the Australian National University and adjunct research fellow at the ARC Centre of Excellence in Policing and Security at Griffith University. He is the co-editor, with Allan McConnell, of *Emergency Policy* (Ashgate, 2013), and the author of articles published in *Policy Studies* on policy transfer and evidence-based policy. His interdisciplinary research traverses political science, public administration and criminology and investigates policy learning, emergency policy-making, critical infrastructure protection and the application of counter-terrorism laws.

Michael Lister is Reader in Politics at Oxford Brookes University. He joined the Department in November 2007, having previously been Lecturer in Politics at the University of Surrey and an ESRC/Office of the Deputy Prime Minister (ODPM) Postdoctoral Research Fellow at the University of

Birmingham. He is the co-author with Emily Pia of *Citizenship in Contemporary Europe* (2008) and co-editor with Colin Hay and David Marsh of *The State: Theories and Issues* (2005). He has published research in journals including *Political Studies, Government and Opposition, Comparative European Politics, British Journal of Politics and International Relations, Citizenship Studies* and *Contemporary Politics*.

Zubeda Limbada works for Birmingham City Council and has over 10 years of local government experience around policy and project management and the preventing violent extremism (PVE) strands. She developed an operational accredited mentoring programme on behalf of statutory agencies and partners for individuals vulnerable to violent extremism during a two year secondment with West Midlands Police counter-terrorism unit. Alongside an international team, Zubeda is a co-director of ConnectJustice, an organisation which researches, evaluates, trains and facilitates communities and states experiencing social and political conflicts. Zubeda is an alumni of the USA Dept of State 'International Visitors Leadership Programme' (IVLP), alumni of the Wilton Park British–German Forum, Oxford University Young Muslim Leadership Programme and the British Council (Africa) Interaction programme. She speaks and writes extensively on communities, community-policing, trust and confidence and extremism. She graduated from The University of Manchester with a BA in Politics and Modern History and an MA in Middle Eastern Studies. Her co-authored chapter has been submitted in a personal capacity and remain her personal views and not representative of any organisation.

Laura Zahra McDonald Co-Director of ConnectJustice, an organisation specialising in research, training and facilitation with communities and states experiencing conflict, and Visiting Lecturer and Research Advisor at the University of Cambridge, Laura's academic and activist interests centre on the intersection of equalities, securities and justice. After studying Social Anthropology with sub-honours in Arabic and Middle Eastern Studies at the University of St Andrews, she completed her PhD at the Centre for Women's Studies, University of York, exploring women's conversion to Islam and the subsequent relevance of Islamic feminism to their experience of gender, ethnicity, faith and nation. Her postdoctoral work at the University of Birmingham has contributed to a body of research on the development of Muslim community and state engagement in the context of security and conflict. Laura strives to connect academic research with community activism and practitioner perspectives, focusing on the development of research and best practice for achieving state and community securities. Since 2001 much of this work has been shaped by the impact of the War on Terror and debates around multiculturalism, minorities and diversity. Laura lectures to academic, policy and practitioner audiences internationally, and has designed and delivered extensive community training around topics including gender and youth issues, community safety and violent extremism.

Stuart Macdonald is Associate Professor in Law and Deputy Director of the Centre for Criminal Justice and Criminology at Swansea University. His work on counter-terrorism laws and policy has been published in a number of leading international journals including *Studies in Conflict and Terrorism*, the *Cornell Journal of Law and Public Policy* and the *Sydney Law Review*. His recent project on security and liberty was funded by the British Academy, and he has held visiting scholarships at Columbia University Law School, New York, and the Institute of Criminology at the University of Sydney.

Agata Serranò is doing a PhD on Analysis and Prevention of Terrorism at the King Juan Carlos University (Spain). She obtained a Master's Degree in Analysis and Prevention of Terrorism in 2008 from the same university. In 2006 she was awarded the Italian 'Nicola Calipari' prize and carried out research on international terrorism at the University of Jaén (Spain). In 2009 this research was published in Italy by Giuffré under the title: *Rational weapons against contemporary terrorism*. The book was a 2010 finalist for the international 'G. Falcone P. Borsellino' scientific prize, awarded by the Carlo Cattaneo University (Italy). In 2011 she was awarded the 'Antonio Beristain' prize by the Basque Institute of Criminology (Spain) for research on victims of ETA's terrorism. From 2011 to 2013 she was a Research Fellow at the King Juan Carlos University working on the European project 'Assessing support initiatives for victims of terrorism in the United Kingdom and Spain: Lessons for the European Context', in collaboration with the Centre for the Study of Terrorism and Political Violence (University of St Andrews, UK).

Phillip Daniel Silk is a teacher, researcher and 20-year veteran of local, campus and federal law enforcement in the United States. In 2002 he was part of the first permanent staff at the newly re-opened US Embassy in Kabul, Afghanistan; he has also been a captain with the Athens-Clarke County (Georgia) Police Department, where at various times he commanded a community policing unit, internal affairs, training and vice. He currently works for the University of Georgia, where he manages police training and teaches in the Criminal Justice Studies Program. As a Fulbright Police Research Fellow, Dan studied outreach between Muslim communities and British police in 2009, and a similar topic was the subject of his PhD dissertation. Dan has continued to conduct work in this area, and recently served as the lead editor on the new book *Preventing Ideological Violence: Communities, Police, and Case Studies of "Success"* which was published by Palgrave Macmillan in early 2013. Dan has been called on to present or consult on a variety of related law enforcement topics throughout the world, most recently for the United Nations at conferences in Amman, Jordan and Ouagadougou, Burkina Faso.

Basia Spalek is professor within the Department of Criminology and Sociology at Kingston University. Basia has extensive research, evaluation and consultation experience on issues of social and community cohesion and integration, counter-terrorism, policing multicultural and multi-faith societies and community-based approaches to security. Basia has written, edited and co-edited nine books and has written over 30 research papers. Basia has also led many international, national and local research projects and consultations for work funded by the ESRC, AHRC, Unison, West Midlands Police, the Crown Prosecution Service, the Department for Communities & Local Government, the Office for Security and Cooperation in Europe (OSCE), the Institute for Strategic Dialogue (ISD) and others. Alongside an international team, Basia is co-director of ConnectJustice, an organisation which researches, evaluates, trains and facilitates communities and states experiencing social and political conflicts. Basia is an alumni of Wilton Park forums on violent extremism; she is also a regularly invited international speaker at academic, policy and practitioner conferences on community policing, trust and confidence, community based approaches to security and counter-terrorism. Basia is also a trainee psychotherapy practitioner, working with the voluntary and statutory sectors to provide wide-ranging therapeutic interventions.

Paul Thomas is Professor of Youth and Policy at the School of Education and Professional Development, University of Huddersfield, UK. Paul has carried out empirical research into the local mediation and implementation of national Prevent and wider ethnic cohesion/integration policies in the north of England over a number of years. In 2009, Paul gave expert witness testimony at the House of Commons on the Prevent strategy as part of the Communities and Local Government Select Committee Inquiry into Prevent. In 2012 he published his book *Responding to the Threat of Violent Extremism – Failing to Prevent* (Bloomsbury Academic).

Acknowledgements

The idea for this edited collection initially emerged within a workshop that took place at Swansea University in the summer of 2010, titled 'Anti-terrorism, Citizenship and Security in the UK'. The workshop was funded by, and formed part of, a larger ESRC project of the same title (reference RES-000-22-3765), which we gratefully acknowledge. We would also like to thank all those who attended the original workshop for their participation and expertise.

We would like also to thank Richard Jackson for his enthusiasm for this project, and we are delighted to see the book published in the Routledge Critical Terrorism Studies series that he edits. We are grateful, too, for all the support we have received for this collection of essays from Andrew Humphrys, Annabelle Harris and Hannah Ferguson at Routledge.

Finally, as always, we reserve our greatest thanks for our family and friends for their continuing support and encouragement.

Introduction

The ends of counter-terrorism

Lee Jarvis and Michael Lister

The seed of this edited collection was sown at a workshop we organised at Swansea University in the summer of 2010. That workshop was funded by an ESRC project, 'Anti-Terrorism, Citizenship and Security in the UK' (RES-000-22-3765) on which we were both working and centred on three overarching sets of research objectives that, in our mind, merited further academic analysis. The first of these ambitions was to better understand the drivers and roots of contemporary counter-terrorism powers: both in a British and a comparative context. Second, the workshop set out to explore the varying impacts of counter-terrorism powers on individuals and communities of different social, political and demographic backgrounds, experiences and statuses. And, third, it sought to locate contemporary counter-terrorism measures within relevant historical and political backdrops. These backdrops included, but were not limited to: the current terrorism threat; prior counter-terrorism strategies; political and legislative techniques and procedures within other policy areas (for example, criminal justice); and broader geopolitical dynamics of the post-9/11 period. As explored now below, this book both continues and expands these interests, bringing together a range of geographical and historical case studies of counter-terrorism, written from a diversity of conceptual and political standpoints, and from a spread of academic disciplines.

The chapters that follow all share two features. The first is some form of critical interrogation of counter-terrorism discourse and/or practice. Critical, here, is approached in a broad sense, to refer to a determined, unrelenting questioning of the purposes, scope, conduct, consequences and justifications of counter-terrorism powers that are (typically) instituted by national governments. As the chapters that follow demonstrate, such powers have implications for everyday life and community relations, for instance, that are every bit as profound as any impact they may or may not have upon national security. Counter-terrorism powers also, importantly, rely upon claims about the nation (and security thereof) that must be subject to critique, not least given the vast resources expended upon this contemporary security challenge (Mueller and Stewart 2011). Critical inquiry of this sort, we argue, is vital when such powers are visible and the subject of widespread public debate, perhaps even anger. It is, however, perhaps more vital still when security practices go uncontested or even unseen, either because of general support or a sense of 'war on terror' fatigue as the years since 9/11 begin now to spread into decades (Heath-Kelly *et al.* 2014). In short, while a variety of political, normative and methodological commitments are evident in the chapters that follow, they all work to problematise, make strange, or render visible the politics of contemporary counter-terrorism.

The second point at which these chapters coalesce is in their more specific interest in the 'ends' of counter-terrorism. By this we mean three things. The first is the *ambitions* of counter-terrorism initiatives of different states, whether stated or otherwise. Key questions here include: what do particular counter-terrorism powers seek to achieve, and, is it possible to discern different or competing motivations behind contemporary powers in this area? Similarly, do the ambitions of national counter-terrorism frameworks change over time – for example, following ceasefires or military victories – and, if so, from where do these changes come, and are they significant? Moreover, how do counter-terrorism powers overlap and interweave with other areas of public policy, including criminal justice initiatives against other actors, or priorities surrounding community cohesion? The chapters that follow explore these questions in relation to a wide range of countries including Australia, Canada, Italy, Spain, Sri Lanka, the United Kingdom, and the United States of America. These case studies include some of the most notorious and bloody confrontations with 'terrorism' of the twentieth and twenty-first century, spanning so-called 'old' and 'new' terrorist groups (compare Neumann 2009; Jackson *et al.* 2011: 165–167). In doing this, the chapters also engage with a wide menu of counter-terrorism activities that have been employed by these and other states. These include powers of proscription, by which terrorist organisations are outlawed; counter-radicalisation programmes; counter-terrorism policing; the prosecution of suspected terrorists; military power; institutionalised repression; and negotiations aimed at ending armed struggle.

Staying with the 'ends' of counter-terrorism, this collection also engages with the *consequences* of counter-terrorism powers at various levels of social, political and everyday existence. In other words, what do counter-terrorism initiatives do in practice, above or beyond any explicit or implicit ambitions beneath them? On this second theme, our chapters investigate the differing impacts of counter-terrorism powers on specific individuals and communities. This includes drawing on empirical research into localised understandings or experiences thereof. Other contributions investigate the consequences of conflicts with terrorism on formalised or elite political processes more specifically – including their impact upon liberal democracies (UK, US, Italy, Spain and so forth) or illiberal democracies (or soft authoritarian) states (as in Sri Lanka). Important within this are the implications of counter-terrorism for the relations between different parts of the body politic, not least those between executives, judiciaries and civil societies which are at the forefront of several of our contributions.

Finally, the 'ends' of counter-terrorism also has *temporal* connotations, signalling moments of climax, conclusion or termination in these struggles. Several of our contributors speak also to this theme, including by asking whether mechanisms and frameworks instituted under the post-9/11 war on terrorism, earlier 'troubles', or civil wars signal permanent developments within the political and judicial systems of Western states. Whether and why changes within counter-terrorism regimes, logics and apparatuses take place is also of crucial importance here, as, indeed, are invocations or articulations of time itself in the legitimisation of counter-terrorism powers. This is, not least in the use of historical analogies to justify such powers, or in the securitising language of claims made about national emergency or exceptional circumstances. Chapters such as Fisher's (this volume) here make an important contribution to the growing interest in the role that time plays in counter-terrorism discourse (for an overview, see Holland and Jarvis forthcoming) and in the construction of international politics more widely (for instance, Hom 2010; Solomon 2013).

Aims of the book

Our motivation for assembling this collection is a shared conviction that reflection on the ends of counter-terrorism, understood in the multiple sense adumbrated above, is both important and timely. This is, not least, because executive changes within many of the war on terrorism's most enthusiastic supporters have stimulated reflection on precisely these kinds of question around the workings of counter-terrorism powers. In the United Kingdom, for instance, the 2010 general election that saw the formation of a Conservative-Liberal Democrat coalition government was followed by a rethinking of the necessity and importance of existing counter-terrorism powers. This process led to the Home Office counter-terrorism review of 2011, the Protection of Freedoms Act 2012 (which reduced and removed some counter-terrorism measures), and a subsequent revised release of the UK's overarching counter-terrorism strategy: CONTEST (Home Office 2011). In the United States, the Obama administration has been arguably far less successful in reversing core elements of the war on terror paradigm, despite ongoing rhetorical efforts to distance itself from its predecessor. Indeed, many critics have identified considerable rhetorical, material and strategic continuity between the Democrat Obama and the Republican Bush (McCrisken 2011; Jackson 2011; Bentley and Holland 2014). The rationale for this book is that sufficient time has now elapsed within the post-9/11 struggle against terrorism and extremism to make possible the exploration of logics, rationales and consequences outlined above. In the process, our aim is to evaluate and debate questions relating to the effectiveness, legitimacy and longevity of counter-terrorism in contemporary context, and in historical and comparative perspective. Doing so, we suggest, both contributes to and grounds a broader discussion of what counter-terrorism is, what it does, and what it should do.

In doing the above, this book attempts to speak to the rapid recent growth of scholarship on (counter-) terrorism that has been documented at length in a number of places now. Some of the most important contributions to this broad literature have been overviews of the politics of counter-terrorism (e.g. Crelinsten 2009; English 2009) that draw on a wealth of historical research and stand, in the process, as a warning against the presentism that dominated the breathless rush to analyse 9/11, al Qaeda and so-called 'Islamist terrorism' from 2001 onwards. Several studies focus more specifically on the thorny issue of international cooperation in this area of public policy (Romaniuk 2010; Rees 2006); while others detail the dynamics of particular case-studies, whether country-specific (e.g. Geltzer 2010; Hewitt 2007), strategy-specific (Toros 2012; Silke 2011; Spalek 2012; Baker-Beall et al. forthcoming), or comparative (Art and Richardson 2006; Alexander 2002, 2006). Also of relevance are explorations of the processes through which terrorism campaigns or organisations cease to exist, including excellent studies by Cronin (2009), and – at the level of the individual 'terrorist' – Horgan (2009). Other studies still, finally, offer conceptual food for thought for dynamics such as those discussed in this book, with their primary focus on (re)theorising counter-terrorism practices, their implications, and discursive or political legitimation (Jackson 2005; Bigo and Tsoukala 2008; Jarvis 2009; Neal 2010; Poynting and Whyte 2012).

This book attempts to add to this rich and growing literature in a number of ways. Most obviously, by bringing together a range of authors on counter-terrorism from different disciplinary backgrounds – including International Relations, Political Science, Political Sociology, Public Policy, History, Criminology and Law – it seeks to facilitate new ways of thinking about the various ends of counter-terrorism strategies, and their differences across time and space. This heterogeneity means, of course, that there is as much disagreement as consensus in the pages that follow. This, in our view is both a strength of the book and a reflection of the complexities of contemporary confrontations with terrorism.

Perhaps more important, though, is this book's effort to problematise absolutely fundamental issues around what counter-terrorism actually is, and what functions it performs, whether intended or otherwise. This, we believe, offers something different to the more traditional focus of much literature in this area that tends to concentrate on what makes counter-terrorism work more or less effectively: a concern that is shared by advocates and critics of counter-terrorism alike. Whilst concerns of efficacy such as this are explored in several of the following chapters, this volume focuses more keenly on the broader question of how, more than 10 years into a war on terror, we can think about counter-terrorism. Is it best conceptualised as a temporary response to surges of unconventional violence, or does it constitute a more permanent form of government or politics? Is counter-terrorism aimed at securing the nation or citizens therein (from the threat of terrorism), or is its purpose to secure national identity by helping to distinguish 'us' from the 'terrorist' other? Ultimately, we believe there is perhaps too little reflection on the aims, consequences and temporalities of counter-terrorism powers, and the interaction between these dynamics. Our hope is that the chapters collected here begin to address this.

Chapter summary

In Chapter 1, Bob de Graaff critically engages with the efforts to find an effective global counter-terrorism strategy. His overall argument is that such a strategy has thus far proved to be problematic and is probably impossible and may even be counterproductive. Al Qaeda, de Graaff argues, remains a strong and vital presence. Part of its strength derives from its combination of global and local elements; its ability to fight both the 'near enemy' and the 'far enemy'. Global, or Western, attempts to pursue a global counter-terrorism strategy, de Graaff argues, have been blighted by a range of problems. A more appropriate response, he suggests, would be one which was sensitive to local contexts and grievances. The outlines of something like this (an approach of 'leading from behind' through a 'tailor-made micro approach') can be identified in Obama's more recent counter-terrorism strategy but this too is not without problems. The West may struggle, de Graaff suggests, to find victory in the global counter-terrorism fight, but by avoiding the mistakes of a totalising, but ultimately 'un-strategic', campaign, it may be able to deny victory to Al Qaeda and its associates.

In Chapter 2, Charlotte Heath-Kelly engages a question of fundamental importance in relation to counter-terrorism, yet one too infrequently asked: what, precisely, does counter-terrorism (seek to) do? Taking inspiration from continental political theorists including Lacan and Žižek, Heath-Kelly pulls our attention to the ritualistic and symbolic aspects of political life, arguing that counter-terrorism is concerned with the continued performance of political authority. For her, terrorism constitutes a problem to the state's political authority not because of the threat it poses to human life, which is far lower than other types of harm. Rather, because terrorism represents an attempt to disrupt the existing order by articulating a vision of a radically different politics. This is why, she argues, counter-terrorism policies now supplement moments of extraordinary force with more pervasive, pre-emptive strategies that are designed to target, suppress and remake those individuals who are deemed a risk to the status quo. To illustrate, Heath-Kelly connects the Italian dissociation process of the 1980s with contemporary counter-radicalisation programmes at work in the UK and elsewhere. These, as she argues, target those 'at risk of being risky', prohibiting the circulation of dangerous ideas as much as actual, corporeal, violence.

Chapter 3, by Kathryn Marie Fisher, pulls our attention to the ways in which counter-terrorism powers are legitimated within political discourse and the identity claims enacted therein. Focusing on the United Kingdom's efforts to counter different forms of terrorism from the 1960s onwards, the chapter concentrates in particular on the importance of assertions about time and space in the (re)production of the British self and terrorist other over this period. Drawing, in part, on postcolonial theory, Fisher reveals how the use of 'international' as a prefix for terrorism has been central to differentiating contemporary forms of terrorism from prior – and ongoing – threats which could equally have been described thus. This prefix, she argues, has helped construct 'Islamic' types of terrorism as both more foreign and more threatening to the British self than 'Irish' terrorisms.

In Chapter 4 Laura Zahra McDonald *et al.* distinguish between hard and soft approaches to counter-terrorism. Noting the problems of labelling involved in all designations of 'terrorism' and 'counter-terrorism', they argue that 'hard' strategies such as stop and search and detention without charge are frequently made possible by the demonisation or dehumanisation of 'terrorists'. This, in turn, leads to a lack of questioning into the root causes of terrorism, and, indeed, potentially thorny issues around state culpability. This team of researchers ask whether an alternative approach to counter-terrorism might be possible; one that is centred around conflict transformation and procedural justice. Such an approach – the shoots of which might be identified in community policing – for them opens space for state and non-state actors to work through their differences, thereby reducing the potential for extreme forms of violence. Drawing on their own empirical research from the ConnectJustice project, the authors conclude their discussion by highlighting the importance of credibility, consent and trust within such approaches and the need for new forms of partnership between state and citizen.

Chapter 5, by Agata Serranò, points to what she sees as two 'myths' in counter-terrorism. With particular reference to Spain and its struggle with ETA, the first myth identified is what she refers to as the 'myth of the exclusivity of the state', where the state is seen to be the only legitimate player in counter-terrorism. She contrasts this with an ideal type of the socialisation of the fight against terrorism, pointing to the key role played by societal groups in Spain, particularly those of the victims of terrorism. The second myth which Serranò seeks to tackle is the myth of 'peace as the end of violence', where peace is something that automatically comes about when violence and killings come to an end. Yet, the chapter argues, the cessation of direct violence does not automatically end indirect and structural violence which can hinder democratic culture and the enjoyment of civil rights and freedoms. Invoking Galtung's distinction between positive and negative peace, Serranò argues whilst the end of violence is a first and essential step in ending terrorism, that counter-terrorism should aim for a more positive peace, which allows for respect for justice, human rights and democracy. Crucially, this also involves facing up to past injustices.

Chapter 6, by Lee Jarvis and Michael Lister, explores how potential subjects of counter-terrorism powers understand and evaluate their necessity and legitimacy. More specifically, by drawing on focus group research from the UK, they investigate how public or 'vernacular' conceptions of counter-terrorism are formed, and demonstrate the importance of four key sources of knowledge therein: personal experiences, whether direct or vicarious; media sources, including the news media and popular entertainment; exemplary events, and especially high profile government errors; and, paradoxically, public beliefs about their own ignorance and therefore inability to assess government policy in this area. The chapter argues that vernacular conceptions of counter-terrorism are often highly individualised and personal. Whilst this might pose reason for optimism amongst critics of seemingly hegemonic counter-terrorism discourses (given that such discourses may be less hegemonic than frequently assumed), it also, they argue, potentially militates against large-scale public opposition to contemporary counter-terrorism logics, frameworks and measures.

Chapter 7 by Stuart Macdonald turns our attention to the Pursue strand of the UK's counter-terrorist approach, which seeks to reduce the threat of terrorism by disrupting organisations and their operations. Focusing on prosecution as one mechanism to this end, Macdonald explores two related concerns. The first is the swathe of precursor offences that have been introduced in the UK in relation to terrorism: offences that criminalise preparatory actions which might lead to terrorism, such as training for terrorism or dissemination of terrorist publications. The expansive reach of such offences, Macdonald argues, raise fundamental questions of necessity and justifiability. This is, not least, because of their sweep such that it is now an offence, for example, 'for an individual (D1) to intentionally encourage someone else (D2) to cause someone else (D3) to publish a statement which indirectly encourages someone else (D4) to instigate someone else (D5) to commit an act of terrorism'! The second half of Macdonald's chapter turns to the use of intercept in terrorist prosecutions, and the continuing ban on such material in legal proceedings despite its growing use for intelligence and investigation purposes. Bringing these two issues together, Macdonald argues that they illustrate a prioritisation of national security concerns in the counter-terrorism arena that extends beyond any desire to prosecute those engaged in terrorism related activities.

Tim Legrand, in Chapter 8, focuses on powers of proscription as one particular, and often overlooked, dimension of the counter-terrorism menu of contemporary Western states. Proscription powers are those that work to outlaw an organisation from a particular territory, often rendering illegal membership thereof. Focusing on the Anglosphere countries of Australia, Canada, the UK and US, Legrand's discussion does two things of importance for any critical assessment of proscription regimes. The first is to explore the emergence of these powers by locating them historically (pointing to centuries of outlawing 'enemies of the state') and comparatively by tracing evidence of policy transfer in this area between these states. The second thing Legrand does is to subject these powers to critical examination, in which three arguments are made. First, that the effectiveness of proscription is difficult to evaluate given the lack of reliable data in this area. Second, that proscription regimes suffer from a quite profound lack of democratic oversight from judiciaries, legislatures or other bodies. And, third, that these powers have potentially unwanted implications upon individuals, communities and organisations designated or suspected of being 'terrorist'.

In Paul Thomas' Chapter 9, it is argued that Prevent, the counter-radicalisation policy introduced by the British Government in 2007, should be brought to an end. After reviewing the development of the policy, particularly through its revisions in 2011, he argues that Prevent is conceptually misguided and inherently flawed such that it stands in contradiction to other policy areas such as community cohesion. Thomas goes on to argue that through a lack of clarity in aims and purpose, issues with implementation (primarily through security services) and its focus on terrorism and extremism from within the

Muslim community alone (ignoring, for example, far-right extremism) Prevent has produced a number of negative outcomes. These include the securitisation of Muslims, which has damaged the human intelligence that is so important to counter-terrorism, and the essentialisation and reification of Muslim identities, thus preventing more intersectional and nuanced forms of identity. This leads Thomas to argue that Prevent as a distinct policy should end and that attempts to deal with extremism and violence should draw on and work with constructive and non-stigmatising community cohesion practice.

In Chapter 10, Paul Dixon, takes aim at the debate around when, and whether to talk to terrorists. After discussing this debate in general terms, which he argues is divided between Neoconservatives who argue that the only proper position is to nearly never talk to terrorists, and Conciliators, who view negotiations with terrorists as one way to end violent conflicts, he goes on to consider the peace process in Northern Ireland. Dixon describes this as 'the hard case' for those opposed to negotiations with terrorists as it appears to show a successful instance of so doing: one that has led to a peace process and a significant reduction in violence. Dixon contends that the Neoconservative argument that the Northern Ireland case fits the 'no negotiations' prescription is flawed. He argues that the view that the IRA had been defeated, through measures such as 'the dirty war' and that the peace process was thus a process of negotiating the IRA's surrender is problematic. Rather, Dixon contends, the IRA had not been defeated and the situation prior to the peace process was one of stalemate. This lead to a process marked by tortuous negotiations, which Dixon suggests, probably did violate democratic norms, particularly around the issue of ceasefires. Yet the 'pragmatic realism' that marked the negotiations, Dixon argues, is what led to the peace process in Northern Ireland and he argues that we risk learning the wrong lessons about negotiations and counter-terrorism if we ignore this.

In Chapter 11, Neil DeVotta writes about the legacy of counter-terrorism in Sri Lanka. He begins by noting that after Sri Lanka gained independence in 1948, it was considered to be a potential postcolonial success story. Yet, he argues, the years since have proved this not to be the case. The chapter outlines how the experiences of counter-terrorism to combat the LTTE have led Sri Lanka to shift from a liberal democracy, to an illiberal democracy and presently to a form of soft authoritarianism under the present Rajapaksa regime. After reviewing the conflict in Sri Lanka, and the controversial measures undertaken to end it in 2009, DeVotta argues that these counter-terrorism measures have been turned towards the perpetuation of government power. Thus, linking to debates about exceptionalism, he argues that the Sri Lankan case evidences the challenges of disengaging from institutionalised extraconstitutional and extrajudicial processes that counter-terrorism frequently brings about. Sri Lanka, DeVotta argues, is at present marked by cultures of immunity, corruption and a weakening of the rule of law. As well as arguing that the road back to democratic norms is a long one for Sri Lanka, DeVotta's chapter also stands as a salutary lesson about the long term implications and consequences of the shifts in legal, cultural and political norms that counter-terrorism may bring about.

References

Alexander, Y. (ed.) (2002) *Combating Terrorism: Strategies of Ten Countries*. University of Michigan Press.
Alexander, Y. (ed.) (2006) *Counterterrorism Strategies: Successes and Failures of Six Nations*. Washington, DC: Potomac Books.
Art, R. and L. Richardson (eds) (2006) *Democracy and Counterterrorism: Lessons From the Past*. Washington, DC: United States Institute for Peace.
Baker-Beall, C., C. Heath-Kelly and L. Jarvis (eds) (forthcoming) *Counter-Radicalisation: Critical Perspectives*. Abingdon: Routledge.
Bentley, M. and J. Holland (eds) (2014) *Obama's Foreign Policy: Ending the War on Terror*. Abingdon: Routledge.
Bigo, D. and A. Tsoukala (eds) (2008) *Terror, Insecurity and Liberty: Illiberal Practices of Liberal Regimes after 9/11*. Abingdon: Routledge.
Crelinsten, R. (2009) *Counterterrorism*. Cambridge: Polity.
Cronin, A. (2009) *How Terrorism Ends: Understanding the Decline and Demise of Terrorist Campaigns*. Oxford: Princeton University Press.
English, R. (2009) *Terrorism: How to Respond*. Oxford: Oxford University Press.
Geltzer, J. (2010) *US Counter-Terrorism Strategy and al Qaeda: Signalling and the Terrorist World-View*. Abingdon: Routledge.
Heath-Kelly, C., L. Jarvis and C. Baker-Beall (2014) 'Editors' Introduction: Critical Terrorism Studies: Practice, Limits and Experience', *Critical Studies on Terrorism*, 7 (1), pp. 1–10.
Hewitt, S. (2007) *The British War on Terror: Terrorism and Counter-Terrorism on the Home Front Since 9/11*. London: Continuum.
Holland, J. and L. Jarvis (forthcoming) '"Night Fell on a Different World": Experiencing, Constructing and Remembering 9/11', *Critical Studies on Terrorism*, DOI: 10.1080/17539153.2014.886396.
Hom, A. (2010) 'Hegemonic Metronome: The Ascendancy of Western Standard Time', *Review of International Studies*, 36 (4), pp. 1145–1170.
Home Office (2011) *CONTEST: The Government's Counter-Terrorism Strategy*. London: The Home Office.
Horgan, J. (2009) *Walking Away from Terrorism: Accounts of Disengagement from Radical and Extremist Movements*. Abingdon: Routledge.
Jackson, R. (2005) *Writing the War on Terrorism: Language, Politics and Counterterrorism*. Manchester: Manchester University Press.
Jackson, R. (2011) 'Culture, Identity and Hegemony: Continuity and (the Lack of) Change in US Counterterrorism Policy from Bush to Obama', *International Politics*, 48 (2/3), pp. 390–411.
Jackson, R., L. Jarvis, J. Gunning and M. Breen Smyth (2011) *Terrorism: A Critical Introduction*. Basingstoke: Palgrave.
Jarvis, L. (2009) *Times of Terror: Discourse, Temporality and the War on Terror*. Basingstoke: Palgrave.
McCrisken, T. (2011) 'Ten Years on: Obama's War on Terrorism in Rhetoric and Practice', *International Affairs*, 87 (4), pp. 781–801.
Mueller, J. and M. Stewart (2011) *Terror, Security and Money: Balancing the Risks, Benefits, and Costs of Homeland Security*. Oxford: Oxford University Press.
Neal, A. (2010) *Exceptionalism and the Politics of Counter-Terrorism: Liberty, Security and the War on Terror*. Abingdon: Routledge.

Neumann, P. (2009) *Old and New Terrorism: Late Modernity, Globalization and the Transformation of Political Violence*. Cambridge: Polity.

Poynting, S. and D. Whyte (2012) *Counter-Terrorism and State Political Violence: The 'War on Terror' as Terror*. Abingdon: Routledge.

Rees, W. (2006) *Transatlantic Counter-Terrorism Cooperation: The New Imperative*. Abingdon: Routledge.

Romaniuk, P. (2010) *Multilateral Counter-Terrorism: The Global Politics of Cooperation and Contestation*. Abingdon: Routledge.

Silke, A. (ed.) (2011) *The Psychology of Counter-Terrorism*. Abingdon: Routledge.

Solomon, T. (forthcoming) 'Time and Subjectivity in World Politics', *International Studies Quarterly*, DOI: 10.1111/isqu.12091.

Spalek, B. (ed.) (2012) *Counter-Terrorism: Community-Based Approaches to Preventing Terror Crime*. Basingstoke: Palgrave.

Toros, H. (2012) *Terrorism, Talking and Transformation: A Critical Approach*. Abingdon: Routledge.

1 'There's a good reason they are called al-Qaeda in Iraq. They are al-Qaeda ... in ... Iraq.'[1]

The impossibility of a global counter-terrorism strategy, or the end of the nation state

Bob de Graaff

Introduction

In this chapter I argue that a global grand strategy against the jihadist insurgency of al Qaeda and its affiliates is impossible and could even be counterproductive. The traditional world order, based on the Westphalian system of sovereign states, is not facilitated to successfully counter a transnational insurgency, which can act simultaneously at or switch flexibly between the supra-state and the infra-state level. Having no strategy at all may therefore be the best option, apart from using as little violence as possible.

Al Qaeda, a continuous and growing threat to the world order

To begin with, al Qaeda has gathered great strength over the past years after it initially seemed to be cornered in the aftermath of the so-called 9/11-attacks. 'Nous sommes tous Américains' (We are all Americans) was the heading of the French newspaper *Le Monde* the day after the terrorist attacks of September 11, 2001 in New York and Washington DC. This sense that the whole world was in this together was also reflected in the invocation, for the first time in the history of NATO, of Article 5 of the alliance's Charter and the perhaps somewhat theatrical willingness of PLO's Yasser Arafat to donate blood for the victims. Suddenly, the United Nations developed into more or less a world legislature in the fight against terrorism; resolutions were accepted that had to be laid down in the national legislation of the Member States. These reactions showed that henceforth it would be the world against the terrorists.

That this instantaneous solidarity was not converted into actual joint action in all areas was initially mainly attributed to US President George W. Bush. In response to the 9/11 attacks he opted for a US military *Alleingang* in Afghanistan, where only a coalition of the willing was tolerated by the US authorities. Subsequently he took the decision to start a war in Iraq, which relationship with the President's declared 'war on terror' was obscure to the rest of the world.

Almost a dozen years since the 9/11 attacks, on 20 April 2013, *Le Monde* ran another article, this time under the heading: 'En Europe, le terrorisme revient à l'ordre du jour' ('In Europe, terrorism is back on the agenda'). It was published in the aftermath of the bombings at the Boston Marathon, but in a more general way it reflected the belief that 12 years after the events of '9/11' al Qaeda and its affiliates have not been decisively beaten. In fact, al Qaeda's scope is expanding into the Levant and both North and Sub-Saharan Africa. The Afghan hosts of al Qaeda, the Taliban, have returned to their home country and their insurgency shows no signs of abating.[2] And Iraq has seen a strong resurgence of terrrorist and insurgent violence after the full withdrawal of US troops in 2011, causing a significant increase in the number of civilian deaths (*The Economist* 2013c; J.D. Lewis 2013). Never before in its 25-year history did the terrorist network of al Qaeda and its affiliates hold sway over more territory than today, while the number of its recruits is also vaster than ever before. The number of deaths caused by al Qaeda attacks has increased considerably. And Westerners living in regions where jihadism is strong are at greater risk of terrorist attacks than on any occasion (Jones 2013; The Quilliam Foundation 2013; Farrall 2011; Farrell and Giustozzi 2013; Gartenstein-Ross 2011: 133; Simcox 2013; *The Economist* 2013c).

After trying to convince the public at large for many years that al Qaeda and especially 'al Qaeda Core' were moribund (Ackerman 2013a; Voice of America 2013; Dilanian 2013; Simpson 2013; Danner 2005; Watts 2012; Roggio 2013b; Taylot 2013; Hoffman 2013: 635–636), all of a sudden almost two dozen American embassies and many other western legations from Yemen to Pakistan had to be temporarily closed in early August 2013 because of an alleged conference call among al Qaeda's top 20, during which its leader Ayman al-Zawahiri named Nasir al-Wuhayshi, head of the al Qaeda branch in Yemen, as his second-in-command. Also participating in this call would have been al Qaeda leaders from Iraq, North Africa, Uzbekistan and the Sinai Peninsula, as well as Pakistan's Taliban and Nigeria's Boko Haram (Rosner, Mendelbaum and Schweitzer 2013). Even if ultimately untrue, the fact that so many authorities initially believed in the story is proof of the regained strangth of al Qaeda and its ilk. Similarly, Somalia turned from an unqualified success for US counter-terrorism efforts in 2012 into another nightmare caused by Islamist insurgents, with the major terrorist group's (al-Shabaab) operational readiness intact (Lynch 2013). In the single weekend of 21 and 22 September 2013 at least 60 people were killed in Nairobi, nearly 80 in Pakistan and over 60 in Iraq as a consequence of al Qaeda related terrorist actions (The Weekly Number 2013). This weekend exemplified that even when al Qaeda and its affiliates manifest themselves more or less locally they may, especially if local initiatives are consciously or unconsciously aggregated, create a global effect (Mishal and Rosenthal 2005).

Whether it is the jihadists operating in Syria, the January 2013 attack on the Amenas gas facility in Algeria or the September 2013 attack on the Westgate shopping mall in Nairobi, all of these offences were carried out by multinational forces, evidence again that al Qaeda has created and sustained a pan-Islamist militancy that operates across national boundaries and policies (Riedel 2013e).

One has to conclude that al Qaeda is in scope and techniques the largest insurgency ever and has proven to be a game changer that opened up a whole new era of conflict. One can distinguish between state confirming types of terrorism of the past and the present, which attack(ed) the state but did not discuss the principle that the world order should be based on nation states, and state denying types of terrorism. Al Qaeda and its affiliates certainly belong to the second category. They are not only a threat to the existing world order, but also to the state as the main political unit (Stivachtis 2009). As the American author on military strategy Philip Bobbitt writes: nation states are by definition unable to solve problems that present themselves as global. 'Those states that do so will be tarred as imperial...' (Bobbitt 2008: 504). Meanwhile nothing can keep al Qaeda and its terrorist and insurgent actions from simultaneously operating at the transnational and the local level, aspiring to establish a boundary-crossing *khalifate*, based on the community of Muslims (*ummah*) (Meleagrou-Hitchens 2011: 65).

The call for a global grand strategy to thwart al Qaeda

Several authors have demanded the development of a grand strategy in the war against terror or the so-called global counterinsurgency, realising that, by its very nature, transnational terrorism demands a broad international response and recognising that counter-terrorist strategies so far have been mainly formulated at the nation-state level. Among them are such prominent and influential spokesmen as the counterinsurgency expert David Kilcullen, the counter-terrorism expert Bruce Hoffman and the former head of GCHQ and first Permanent Secretary and Security and Intelligence Coordinator in the Cabinet Office Sir David Omand (Omand 2005; Kilcullen 2009: 14 and 296–298; Rich 2003: 39; Biddle 2013; Cardash *et al.* 2013: 1 and 5; Hoffman 2009: 369–370 and 372; Pearlstein 2004: 98; Watts 2009: vii and 5–6; Reed 2006a: 89–90; Reed 2006b: 2 and 13; Rees 2006: 128–129; Zimmerman 2013: 1 and 4; McDougall 2010; Drezner 2006). As recent as August 2013 the former Director for Administration and Information in the United Nations Counter-Terrorism Committee Executive Directorate (CTED) of the Security Council, Howard Stoffer, called for a UN Global Counter-Terrorism Coordinator to make the counter-terrorism efforts by the different UN organs and inter-governmental organisations more effective. The General Assembly did adopt a Global Counter-Terrorism Strategy in 2006 demanding tougher law enforcement and a comprehensive set of other measures to reduce the likelihood and consequences of terrorist attacks, but according to Howard the piecemeal and scattered approach by the UN has made this strategy largely futile (Stoffer 2013).

As the UN Global Counter-Terrorism Strategy is no more than a chimera any global strategy that could be developed should include the ideas and interests of the United States, the worldwide leader in counter-terrorism efforts, whose population continues to perceive preventing terrorism as the top priority of their country's foreign policy and, like President Bush in 2001, as 'America's defining mission for the foreseeable future' (quoted in Smith 2008: 61; cf. Gallup

2013). Therefore this contribution will mainly use examples from the US, where stubs of a global strategy were developed, to demonstrate that any global counter-terrorism strategy is deemed to be fruitless.

The first question to be addressed is: what do we understand by 'grand strategy'? A grand strategy is meant 'to coordinate and direct all the resources of a nation, or band of nations, towards the attainment of the political object of the war' (Liddell Hart 1967: 322; cf. Biddle 2005). Strategy is thus considered to be the brains, which direct the muscles of a nation or groups of nations and makes war effective. If grand strategy integrates all necessary means to pursue states' ultimate aims, dictated by their national interest, this is true *in extremis* for a counterinsurgency strategy as best-practice counterinsurgency encompasses, in the words of one of its proponents, David Kilcullen: 'political, security, economic, and information components. It synchronizes civil and military efforts under unified political direction and common command-and-control, funding, and resource mechanisms' (Kilcullen 2009: 112). How daunting the integration of different policy elements may be is illustrated by the case of Afghanistan, for which Kilcullen found the already excessive demands of a counterinsurgency strategy still insufficient. According to Kilcullen Afghan strategy had to 'integrate counterinsurgency with nationbuilding, border security, and counternarcotics' (Kilcullen 2009: 113). It is clear that if these are only the demands for countering jihadist insurgency in one nation, how much more demanding a global counterinsurgency strategy must be. However, not only is a global grand strategy still lacking more than a decade after '9/11', there is so far even considerable uncertainty about the elements that should constitute such a master plan.

To begin with, in order to draw up a (grand) strategy one needs to know the *end goals*. The end goals in the war on terror which have been formulated by the US authorities thus far have been either vague or farfetched (Reed 2006a: 21, 25, 44–45, 78–79). The 2003 *National Strategy for Combating Terrorism* essentially stated that there will be no defining moment indicating victory. Instead, the war on terror would be an open-ended effort 'to compress the scope and capability of terrorist organisations, isolate them regionally, and destroy them within state borders' (National Strategy 2003: 12). Several writers have maintained that this point of departure is the starting point of eternal war (de Graaff 2013). Such a lack of an end vision manifested itself likewise in the subtheatres of what was to be the war on terror. It took for instance two and a half years of war before the US government finally, in November 2005, published its *National Strategy for Victory in Iraq*.

Another problem is that, in spite of the high expenditure on counter-terrorism measures (the wars in Afghanistan and Iraq alone will finally account for approximately five trillion dollars (Bilmes 2013; cf. Kilcullen 2009: 25)), very little is actually known about the *effectiveness* of both counter-terrorism and counterinsurgency strategies and the ways to measure success (Connable 2012; Lum *et al.* 2006; de Graaff and de Graaf 2010).

Authors who have compared national counter-terrorism policies agree that a common or similar definition and perception of the terrorist threat is the cornerstone of international cooperation against terrorism (Ganor 2005: 278–279; Foley 2013: 322). The 2002 *National Security Strategy* of the US noted: 'The enemy is not a single political regime, or person, or religion, or ideology. The enemy is terrorism' (National Security Strategy 2002: 5). However, many others were of the opinion that the fight against terrorism was handicapped by defining a tactic, terrorism, as the *opponent*. Moreover, not only is terrorism a tactic that can be used by many groups for a broad array of purposes (cf. Rabasa 2011: 62), it can also be perceived in a wide variety of ways: as a crime, as a threat to the political or democratic order, as warfare, as a societal problem, as a security issue along with others. The way one defines terrorism, indicates in whose remit countering it belongs: law enforcement, the intelligence and security services, the armed forces, the ministry for foreign affairs and so on. Terrorism thus challenges governments' lack of interoperability and interdisciplinarity and thus far records of interagency cooperation repeatedly remain poor (Corum 2007: 113; US Senate 2012; Gill and Wilson 2013: 169; Watts 2009: 2, 9, 12–14; Gerges 2011: 11–12). The understandable ensuing risk is that every designated part of the government, whether it is the armed forces or law enforcement or any other government organisation, shows an interest in only its own battles and loses sight of the overall strategic context (Corum 2009: 117). If it has up to now been difficult to create a common understanding and approach at the national level, this problem was further compounded at the international level by the fact that the term 'terrorism' has been stretched rather far in some countries, to include non-terrorist 'crimes' like opposition or information leaking (e.g. Schneider 2013; Schmidt and Moynihan 2012; Secrecy News 2013; Michaels 2013; *Courrier international* 2013; Megenta 2011).

And finally, just as any other type of policy, counter-terrorism is interest-driven (Kofas 2013). However, as terrorism and counter-terrorism touch upon the national interest of states the internal contradictions of such policies may be even greater in this case. The diverging positions of different countries vis-à-vis Hezbollah are a case in point. After extensive pressuring by Israel and the United States the EU finally designated the armed wing of Hezbollah as a terrorist group in the summer of 2013. Turkey, however, declared immediately that it was not going to follow suit (*Today's Zaman* 2013). Another example of the dominating role national interests play when it comes to counter-terrorism is the position of Saudi Arabia in US foreign policy. Although Saudi Arabia has been a main provider for the ideology if not the resources of al Qaeda, it nevertheless remains a fundamental ally of the United States. Seen from the perspective of counter-terrorism alone it would be difficult to understand why Saudi Arabia would be treated differently by the US than Pakistan, a country with which the US maintains a rather uneasy partnership in the fight against terror (Aid 2012: 8; Miller *et al.* 2013; Allen 2006; Ali 2002: 294; Gold 2004; Graham 2004; Stern 2012; Schwarz 2004; Quitta 2013; Ehrenfeld and Jensen 2013; for a different view see: Awhad Asseri 2009). Even putting these two examples aside, the amalgam of countries fighting terrorism still seems rather diverse in their objectives. Just think of the United States, Russia, Israel and Egypt and it will be apparent that they do not share the same ends (Wolton 2005: 242). The willingness to invest in counter-terrorism measures depends on a country's own historical and current experiences of terrorism (Meijer 2012: 166–169). Not every country has been equally affected by terrorism and consequently not every country is willing to sacrifice freedoms and citizens' rights in equal degree as countries that for obvious reasons are the frontrunners in the fight against terrorism (cf. Scoop 2013). This distinction was illustrated by the uneasiness that entered into US–German relations upon the disclosures about US electronic eavesdropping in Europe (e.g. Travis *et al.* 2013; Nielsen 2013; Augstein 2013; SpiegelOnline 2013; Erlanger 2013b; Brinkbäumer 2013; Jordans 2013).

Furthermore, governments can decide that cooperating or negotiating with certain terrorist groups is more in their national interest than fighting or ignoring them. Cases in point are the US support to the mujaheddin in the 1980s, Israel's initial support to Hamas as a counterweight to the PLO, the support by the Algerian Département du Renseignement et de la Sécurité for Islamist militants over the past 20 years, the interrelation between the National Intelligence and Security Agency of Somalia and al-Shabaab and, along NATO's borderline, the Turkish authorities' support for jihadiist groups fighting the Kurds in Syria (Keenan 2009, 2010, 2012, 2013; Schindler 2012; Ghosh 2013; Herridge 2013; Somalia 2013; Deutsche Welle 2013b). But even within the United States the interest-drivenness has manifested itself, e.g. when just because of the financial implications US authorities refused to call the killing spree by Major Nidal Hasan in Fort Hood in November 2009 an act of terrorism; instead they called it 'workplace violence' (Herridge and Browne 2013; Goldman 2013).

Because of the multifacetedness of the term 'terrorism' it had to be refined in successive US strategic blueprints. The US *National Military Strategic Plan for the War on Terrorism* for instance defined the enemy as 'a transnational movement of extremist organisations, networks, and individuals – and their state and non-state supporters – which have in common that they exploit Islam and use terrorism for ideological ends' (US Department of Defense 2006: 4). Actually, however, the war on terror was from the beginning mainly a war against al Qaeda and its affiliates, even though President Bush had farther reaching ambitions when he stated shortly after 9/11: 'Our war on terror begins with al Qaeda, but it does not end there. It will not end until every terrorist group of global reach has been found, stopped, and defeated' (quoted in Biddle 2013: 7; Tertrais 2004: 32). President Bush's successor, Barack Obama, had apparently more modest ambitions focusing mainly upon so-called al Qaeda Core or al Qaeda Central in Afghanistan and Pakistan, which he has tried to eliminate by drone attacks, further distinguishing among the affiliates between those that have the intent and capability to strike on US territory (mainly Al Qaeda in the Arabian Peninsula, AQAP) and those that do not and only need monitoring (Kagan 2013). I will therefore focus on al Qaeda as well, including its affilates and adherents, as the main opponent in the fight against terrorism, leaving out other terrorist organisations like Hezbollah, which has been in existence for a longer time and was in a more or less old-fashioned way still partly state-supported (by

Iran), but may be as broad in its scope as al Qaeda, having spread its operations over Africa and even into Latin-America (Levitt 2013; Wege 2012; Keating 2013; Adamu 2013; Derrick 2013; Noriega 2013; Sklarz 2013; Lewis 2013).

The most far-reaching strategic question of all in accordance with Carl von Clausewitz is to establish *the kind of war* on which one embarks, 'neither mistaking it for, nor trying to turn it into, something that is alien to its nature' (quoted in Crumpton 2012: 309) Let us therefore turn to the opponent – al Qaeda and its affiliates – and the kind of fight it prefers.

The enemy

According to one of the great students of political Islam, the Frenchman Olivier Roy: 'It is probably a paradox of globalization to gear together modern supranational networks and traditional, even archaic, infrastate forms of relationships (tribalism, for instance, or religious schools' networks)' (quoted in Bobbitt 2008: 64). This is the essence of the al Qaeda network of networks: it is globalised and decentralised at the same time, or as some would have it: glocalised (cf. Crelinsten 2009: 47; Hansen 2013: 139–40).

Contemporary jihadist terrorism crosses national boundaries. The lesson many terrorism fighters learned from '9/11' was, as former CIA operations officer Henry Crumpton wrote, that 'at an operational, even tactical level, the battlefield was now global. An enemy group could plot and plan on one side of the planet and execute on the other side in days, if not hours. In cyberspace, impact could be measured in seconds' (Crumpton 2012: 280). The more capricious the threat became the more difficult it became for terrorism fighters to understand what they were doing. As a CIA analyst wondered in despair:

> We're fighting the War on Terror. What does that actually mean? How do you specifically go about that day to day? Like, when we were fighting the Cold War, we were more sure then, I think. There was a country that we could point to and we knew we were fighting. Now it's like networks, there doesn't seem to be countries anymore with this, and it's really hard to know what winning this war would look like.
>
> (quoted in Kelly 2013)

The wars in Afghanistan and Iraq solved little. In the aftermath of the US invasion of Afghanistan, al Qaeda and the Taliban traded Afghanistan for Pakistan as their primary safe haven. Europe and the United States got their share of homegrown terrorists who were inspired by the al Qaeda ideology and strategists who told them, by way of Internet and social media, that they would be much more effective causing trouble at home singlehandedly than by flocking to jihadi struggles elsewhere. (e.g. Cloherty 2012; Simcox and Dyer 2013a; Brinkman 2013; Shane 2013b; Gorman 2013; Hustadt 2013). Al Qaeda and its ilk have however been even more successful in establishing themselves in so-called failed or failing states, where they sometimes have more power and influence than the government in whose jurisdiction they work, thereby forcing counter-terrorists again and again to either endure or counter them in areas beyond the reach of effective governance (Panetta quoted in Ackerman 2013b; cf. SpiegelOnline 2012). They branched out to Yemen, Somalia, Algeria, Libya, Syria, Sinai and Lebanon (Roggio 2013a; Barnard and Schmitt 2013; Riedel 2013d; AP 2013). Over the past years terrorism in Africa has become a serious growth business (Kitfield 2013; cf. Akwagiram 2013). With the number of failed states on that continent one is perplexed at the opportunities that offer themselves to jihadists looking for either safe havens or areas to pick a fight.

Over the years the strategy of al Qaeda regarding the West has remained the same: bleeding the US 'until bankruptcy' by forcing them to enormous expenditure on counter-terrorism measures (cf. Gartenstein-Ross 2011: 8–12, 68–69, 152, 165; Bobbitt 2008: 75, 78; Hoffman 2013: 640; Reed 2006a: 36, 44, 79–80; Kilcullen 2009: 29). At an operational and tactical level they have been rather flexible. Guerrilla warfare is their main instrument to realise their goals, but they may resort to terrorist activities. And the near enemy, the regimes in the Islamic world, is their primary target, but if necessary they will hit the far enemy as well (Jones 2013: 4).

All the same or all different?

This duality of al Qaeda and its affiliates has resulted in confusion and continuous debate among both experts and policy-makers who find it hard to deal with a phenomenon that is essentially glocalised. The branching out of al Qaeda into new territories has prompted concepts like 'terrorism belt' (Mac Donald 2010) or 'arc of instability' (Alexander 2012), emphasising the contiguity of seemingly similar expressions of terrorism and insurgency. It has also contributed to the idea that violent (Islamist) groups form part of a single global phenomenon that can be addressed by a common approach, as summarised in the words of British Prime Minister David Cameron when he lumped together North-African and Asian extremism: 'This is a global threat and it will require a global response' (*Guardian* 2013a; cf. Dowd and Raleigh 2013). A similar way of blending all expressions of Islamist extremism can be seen in phrases like 'Africa's Afghanistan' (e.g. Baroud 2012; Hackensberger 2012) or the 'Taliban of Timbuktu' (Bennoune 2013), applied to the situation in Mali. The idea of contiguity also evokes thoughts of what was once thought to be an outdated domino-theory: outside action against Islamic extremism in one country is needed in order to prevent its success in adjacent nations (e.g. Colebatch 2009; Haddick 2009; Hall 2013; Parker 2013a). The actual events of the Arab Spring underlined the feasibility of such dramatic domino effects and French President François Hollande's move to send troops to Mali originated in his fears that the extremist turmoil there may cross the country's borders, and eventually the Mediterranean (*Washington Post* 2013a).

This tendency to conceive of almost all violent Islamist groups as local or national manifestations of a global jihadi or al Qaeda network (*Wall Street*

Journal 2013) and to configurate counter-terrorism strategy as 'a single conflict against a single, united and uniform foe' (Burke 2011: 260) has been criticised as a 'de-contextualized approach' (Dowd and Raleigh 2013; Gerges 2011: 146, 193). Furthermore, this position has been commented upon because stressing the global nature of al Qaeda and its associates threatens to play into the hands of the terrorists, who like to be seen as an imposing monolithic actor (Burke 2013).

Quite the opposite is a 'de-globalized approach', which stresses that violent Islamist groups operate (almost) solely within the local and national contexts of their origins (e.g. Homeland Security News Wire 2013d; Johnston 2013: 128; Whittington 2013): in Syria the jihadi insurgents fight the Alawite government and the Kurds; in Mali the government and the Tuaregs; in Iraq the Shiite government; and al Qaeda in the Arabian Peninsula opposes the House of Saud and the Yemeni government. 'Localists' can claim that even organisations like Al Qaeda in the Maghreb, AQIM, and al-Shabaab, which are feared in the West for their transnational threats, have concentrated 90 to 95 per cent of their attacks locally (Dowd and Raleigh 2013). An exponent of this de-globalised view is the former member of the French intelligence service DGSE (Direction Génerale de la Sécurité Extérieure) and connaisseur of the Arab world Alain Chouet, who states that AQIM consists for 99.9 per cent of Algerians, of criminals rather than terrorists, and that every AQIM operation is intricately tied in to the vicissitudes of the Algerian politics (Chouet 2013: 226–227, 329). Another one would be Mark Sageman, the champion of the concept of 'leaderless jihad', who maintained that the Madrid and London bombings of 2004 and 2005 occurred without any al Qaeda Core influence, contrary to the evidence gathered by a host of other authors (cf. Celso 2012; Jones 2011: 41–42).

The degree to which it has become problematic to designate a domestic or a foreign origin and influence to indidividual terrorist behaviour was maybe best epitomised by the case of the brothers Tamerlan and Dzhokhar Tsarnaev, who were responsible for the bombings at the Boston marathon. Experts and other commentators tumbled over each other to characterise their action as either some kind of school shooting by social losers and loners or as Islamist influenced radicalisation and terrorism, executed by two boys of whom the oldest, Tamerlan, was inspired by the writings of Anwar al-Awlaki, the US Islamist preacher who had been killed in 2011 by an American drone, and who had connections with terrorist fighters in the North Caucasus. Things were even further complicated when it turned out that Tamerlan seemed to have been inspired by extremist right-wing literature as well (Bullough 2013; Shane 2013a; Schmitz 2013; the Clarion Project 2013; Buruma 2013; Hinnant 2013; Killough and Cruikshank 2013; Al-Shishani 2013a; Herszenhorn 2013; Nimmo 2013; Satter 2013; Barry 2013; the Jihad and Terrorism Monitor 2013). It shows that lone wolves are rarely lonesome. They are encouraged by messages on the Internet to do their act at home, 'coz the frontline has come to you', as the 'Lone Mujahid Pocketbook' article in the Spring 2013 edition of AQAP's *Inspire* stated (Brunker 2013; CNBC 2013; Homeland Security News Wire 2013b; Carafano *et al.* 2012 and 2013; Simcox and Dyer 2013b).

The Arab Spring offered another opportunity for both indigenous Muslim extremists and al Qaeda-like organisations from abroad to reach the man on the Arab street, this time no longer, or at least less, hindered by interdiction by repressive regimes (Dickey 2011; AP 2012; Maher and Neumann 2012: 15–18; Zelin et al. 2013; Mond 2013). The regime change in some Arab countries may have caused a (temporary) change in direction in jihadist violence against the West. As long as there were nearby enemies in the Middle East in the form of dictators backed up by the West, it was necessary to engage the far enemy (the US) on its home turf. Since those dictators have left jihadists can concentrate on winning the state in the Middle East and removing Western influences from the Arab world. This change coincided with Osama bin Laden's sudden exit as leader of al Qaeda and his repacement by the Egyptian Ayman al-Zawahiri. Whereas Osama bin Laden concentrated in his speeches on the 'far enemy', Al-Zawahiri hardly ever does so (Al-Shishani 2013b). It seems the latter is more interested in expanding the presence of extremist Islamists in Africa and Asia, concentrating on the 'near enemy' than in attacking the West. A decrease in the threat to the US home territory may, however, well go hand in hand with an increase in the risks run by Westerners and their interests in regions where jihadists are active.

A SWOT-analysis of al Qaeda

After all these years of fighting al Qaeda and its affiliates and associates, 'the most lethal and effective enemy of the United States since the end of the Vietnam War' (Zimmerman 2013), the US and other Western authorities keep wondering: 'They're coming after us, but who are they now?' (Frantz 2002; cf. Aid 2012: 25–26, 71, 75, 91, 94; Burke 2011: 372; Simcox 2013: 8; Reed 2006b: 7; Zimmerman 2013: 1; *The Economist* 2013a).

Today al Qaeda incorporates a core, presumably mainly tied up in the Afghanistan-Pakistan border areas, and affiliates, of which the most important ones are:

- al Qaeda in the Arabian Peninsula (AQAP), which after al Qaeda Core came under increasing pressure from drone and other attacks in Afghanistan and Pakistan became responsible for attacks against the United States (Farrall 2011).
- al Qaeda in Iraq (AQI).
- Jabhat al Nusra in Syria.
- al Qaeda in the Maghreb (AQIM) and its splinter organisation Movement for Tawhid and Jihad in West Africa (MUJAO) and;
- al-Shabaab in Somalia.

More loosely connected than the affiliates, which have sworn loyalty to al Qaeda's leadership, are: Ansar al-Dine in Mali and Boko Haram in Nigeria.

Since the Arab Spring additional al Qaeda organisations have sprung up, such as Ansar al Sharia in Egypt, Yemen, Libya and Tunisia. Moreover, there is a coalition of partners of al Qaeda, such as the Taliban, the Islamic Movement of Uzbekistan, the Islamic Jihad Union, the Tehrik-e Taliban (Pakistani Taliban), the Haqqani Network, Lashkar-e Taiba and Abu Sayyaf, to mention only the most well-known. Altogether it looks like a motley variety of 'non-state actors operating as transnational networks within a galaxy of like-minded networks' (Sullivan 2006: 6). Al Qaeda has become a hydra with constantly changing heads. Meanwhile, the threat from al Qaeda Core has diminished, partially by drone harassment (e.g. AP 2012).

Yet as bin Laden once said: the term 'core' or 'central al Qaeda' 'was coined in the media. Consultation among brothers in any region will take place internally, though they will also consult with "Central al Qaeda"' (Joscelyn and Roggio 2013). After Bin Laden's death in 2011 this is in substance still the case. In each region an *emir* and a *shura* council are responsible for the conduct of operations. They report more or less regularly to the central group. While the affiliates have a large degree of latitude in their day-to-day business operations outside their own turf, questions of cooperation with other groups, mergers or splits, or the use of new tactics and means require a more explicit consent from the Core (Farrall 2011: 134–135; Joscelyn and Roggio 2013; Gartenstein-Ross 2013; Allam and Barron 2013; Thiessen 2013; Coren and Walter 2012; Hoffman 2013: 638–639). Even some crucial operations such as hostage-taking in Northern Africa were submitted for decisions by the core (Joscelyn 2013a). Of course, as in any organisation orders from the core are not always obeyed, as was shown by the case of Abu Bakr al-Baghdadi, the leader of al Qaeda in Iraq, who openly defied al-Zawahiri's course on Syria, or that of the long-time terrorist commander Mokhtar Belmokhtar, breaking away from AQIM (Atassi 2013; Watts 2013; Karouny 2013; *The Economist* 2013b; Al-Shishani 2013b; Hoffman 2013: 639; Farrall 2011: 135; Nelson and Sanderson 2011: 12–13).

Although the glocal approach seems to fit al Qaeda and its ilk like a glove, the ambiguous nature of the movement has it challenges for them as well. Al Qaeda has for example been ambivalent about the question whether to operate in small entities or to unite in order to confront opposing national regimes. However, as the international scene develops, they have been quick to adapt their tactics. For years they urged, especially, their Western followers to operate in small cells or even as loners who by a myriad of small attacks would be able to tie Gulliver down. However, after the outbreak of the Arab Spring al Qaeda spokesmen have encouraged Muslims, e.g. in Egypt, to unite and confront their 'heretic' regimes in 'an open war' or 'jihad' (Barnett 2013). Syria and Somalia have offered radical Muslims in the West new opportunities to participate in a major 'Muslim battle' similar to previous opportunities in Afghanistan, Bosnia and Chechnya, fuelling fear among Western authorities that, if they survive, they may return radicalised, possibly armed with chemical weapons, and willing to promote terrorist attacks in the West (Cardash, Cilluffo and Marret 2013; Hegghammer 2013a and 2013b; Reuters 2012; *Guardian* 2013b; Gertz 2013; Deutsche Welle 2013a; *Copenhagen Post* 2013; Valenta 2013; Europol 2013: 22). Every form of expansion of their efforts not only enforces a tendency of the al Qaeda affiliates towards (re)bureaucratisation, but also makes them more visible and surveillable, which offers opportunities for counter-terrorism strategies, both at a national level and guided by international cooperation.

What has the West done so far?

Against the backdrop of all the failures of the West to tackle al Qaeda conceptually one may wonder whether there have been any real life counterinsurgency or counter-terrorist successes against this transnational phenomenon. A substantial part of the US counter-terrorism effort since 9/11 has been directed at preventing another similar attack at the homefront by tying al Qaeda and its brand down in the Middle East and South Asia. Although no other '9/11' has manifested itself so far, many efforts to manufacture a global counter-terrorism approach have been counterproductive as they had the effect of inciting local or regional groups to intensify and internationalise their fight (Scahill 2013: 220, 225, 228–229, 353, 518–519; Ali 2002: 292–293; Johnsen 2013; Nevin 2003; Muñoz 2011: 25; Hoffman 2009: 360–361; Kilcullen 2009: 15). In the words of Barack Obama, when he was still a presidential hopeful condemning the war in Iraq, this had sparked new insurgencies, increased the pool of terrorists and alienated America, while sapping the morale and the finances of the American people (Bowden 2012: 80).

It is axiomatic for insurgents and most terrorist groups to subordinate global goals to local objectives (Perry and Gordon 2008: 21). However, as Obama understood, when international or global forces make themselves felt, whether by occupation, intervention or drone attacks, insurgents' motives begin to prioritise removing foreign forces and influences, *inter alia* by acts of (suicide) terrorism (Pape and Feldman 2010; Ahmed 2013; Jenkins 2012: 3). A good case in point is the Haqqani network, 'a group that existed in the netherworld between an insurgent group and a criminal cartel, and lived unmolested in Pakistani territory', but became 'one of the greatest threats to U.S. forces in Afghanistan' and beyond (Sanger 2013: 6; Warrick 2011: 112, 196) after the US government started stirring this hornets' nest in an effort to make this group weak enough to be dealt with by the Pakistani forces. The internationalising or even globalising effect of outside interventions on insurgent groups explains also why there seemed to be a symbiotic relationship between NATO's expanding campaign in Afghanistan and the number of suicide bombings. Or why the US and the France have become the most significant foreign enemies for jihadist groups. Or why al-Shabaab attacked the Westgate Mall in Kenya's capital Nairobi in September 2013, since Kenya was the main contributor to the African forces fighting in Somalia (Garfield and Boyd 2013; Erlanger 2013a; Youssef 2013; RT 2013a; Tawil 2013; Reuters 2013b; *Guardian* 2013c; Raghavan 2013). And finally, that is why interstate intervention usually leads to the prolonging of internal conflicts (Hironaka 2005: 25).

(Western) military interventions or civil war situations allow Islamist extremist groups to fight alongside national resistance groups and to impose their politico-religious narrative on the national struggle. This is happening today in Syria, where al Qaeda oriented groups and the resistance joined forces in the Islamic State of Iraq and the Levant and another al Qaeda affiliate, the Al Nusrah Front (Gertz 2013; Star et al. 2013; Riedel 2013b; Barfi 2013; Joscelyn 2013c; Reuters 2013b; Homeland Security News Wire 2013c; SpiegelOnline 2013; The Lon War Journal 2013; Hubbard 2013), as well as in Mali, where Mokhtar Belmokhtar's al Qaeda-group joined forces with Mali's Movement for Oneness and Jihad in West Africa (MUJAO) in order to fight the French presence in Mali (Tope 2013; Jacinto 2013).

What should the West do?

The British South Asian correspondent Jason Burke has aptly described that the hodgepodge of conflicts merged under the headings of the war on terrorism, the long war or the global counterinsurgency actually takes place at multiple levels:

> At the local level, they were a mass of private battles, fratricidal skirmishes, communal clashes, often sparked by specific incidents of misgovernment or injustice, some pitting village against village, neighbourhood against neighbourhood, tribe against tribe. At the next level, the wars were often about participation of a particular group in politics at a provincial or a national level.... Only at the final level, the biggest scale, could some of these conflicts be integrated into an overarching cosmic conflict pitting the West and its allies against radical Islam.
> (Burke 2011: 495–496)

Among Islamist terrorists a divide can be observed between globalists and localists (Kurzman 2011: 59; Rogers 2013). Al Qaeda subsidiaries like AQIM and al-Shabaab have been divided and split exactly on the question of the strength of their connections with al Qaeda Central, the emphasis on being a part of a global movement not excluding the focusing on Western targets ('the far enemy') instead of being an organisation adapting to local needs, attacking local targets ('the near enemy') (Dowd and Raleigh 2013; Selected Wisdom 2013a, 2013b). Quite often globalists and localists are operating in the same geographical area, such as AQIM (global) and MUJAO (local) in the Maghreb, al-Shabaab (global) and Hizbul Islam (local) in Somalia, Boko Haram (local) and Ansaru (global) in Nigeria. Furthermore, given al Qaeda's command structure it is not unthinkable that at some point in time al Qaeda Core may outsource international attacks to groups that hitherto have been active only locally.

Part of the oscillating between global and local is tactical. Al Qaeda affiliates have learned over the past decade that they had better shed their foreign character, adapt to local circumstances, exploit local grievances, set up local services and thus endear themselves to the local population as their membership is mostly local. A good example is al Qaeda in the Arabian Peninsula, which gained a central position in Yemen. According to one of the experts on this organisation, the Near Eastern studies scholar Gregory Johnsen at Princeton University, AQAP 'has done a very good job of tailoring a narrative to fit the Yemen context. So they put themselves on the right side of nearly ever issue from local corruption, to the Israeli–Palestinian conflict to flooding in Hadramaut' (Homeland Security News Wire 2013a). AQIM also showed an awareness that they needed to move more gradually, compromise for the moment and provide services to the population (McLaughlin 2013). The insurgency in Russia's North Caucasus, which once attracted considerable numbers of fighters from Arab countries, became more and more dominated by local grievances, such as poverty, unemployment, corruption, violation of human rights and the hegemony of the Russian authorities (Al-Shishani 2013a). Even the fighting in the area that was once associated with 'al Qaeda Core' and its global terrorism, Afghanistan–Pakistan, has become 'a much more regional and domestic conflict' (Bezhan 2013; Semple 2013).

It is an illusion to think that, because the world has globalised, there are no historical and cultural differences. Being as it is, there can be no global rules in the fight against present day terrorism (Burke 2011: 499). In stead of a 'one size fits all' approach strategies are needed that take the local context and regional exigencies into account. However, recognition of this fact poses no less complicated problems. 'Effective responses (...) require excellent knowledge about local populations and their politics, the sort of understanding that too often eludes the US government and military', thus claimed former CIA analyst Michael Shurkin (Schmitt 2013b). Well-intentioned efforts by foreign entities to raise their cultural awarness often fall short in the light of counter-terrorism demands (e.g. Patton 2010), as was perfectly illustrated by an evaluation of foreign aid in Afghanistan. An effective aid programme, both military and civilian, in that country proved difficult,

> because the Afghans themselves have different views of what Afghanistan is and should be. Intense rivalries among Afghans do not make it easy to pursue Afghan solutions to Afghan problems. Furthermore, on some issues, traditional Afghan sentiments clash with policies favored by the United States and the European nations.... The issue of women's rights is a prime example, as is the role of Islam.
>
> (Muñoz 2011: 24)

However, before one concludes that everything is turning local, it is worth noting that the reverse may also occur. For instance, AQIM moved from an Algerian domestic issue to a regional Sahelian problem to an African menace and ultimately to a threat to international peace and security, but it cannot be ruled out that it will slide back to its former position (Mohamedou 2013). Boko Haram ('Western education is sin'), which has been attacking schools and churches for years, demanding the implementation of sharia law across Nigeria and killing several thousands along that road, has recently been seen scaling up its targets by attacking and abducting Westerners, warning France of retaliation because it 'declared war on Islam' by invading Mali and sending fighters to the Maghreb (Barrett and Ibrahim 2013; Pratt 2012; Zenn 2013; Ilias 2013; Gambrell 2013; Defence IQ 2013). Scaling up may result from strength or unity, but also from weakness and internal disputes, as was the case with al-Shabaab's attack on the Westgate Mall, many experts believe (e.g. McGregor 2013b). Anyway, scaling up to the global level remains a possibility and for some an ambition. In the words of al Qaeda specialist Thomas Joscelyn in testimony for the US House Subcommittee on Terrorism, Nonproliferation and Trade, in July 2013: 'While the affiliates have varying degrees of capabilities, and devote most of their resources to fighting "over there", history demonstrates that the threat they pose "over here" can manifest itself at any time.' (Joscelyn 2013b).

Is the US approach changing?

But recently a change for the better may have been set in US strategy. Thus far the US goverment has vis-à-vis the terrorist movement deliberately restrained from the containment and deterrence strategies which were rather successful during the Cold War. It turned to a strategy of rollback and pre-emption (Bamford 2004: 268; Daalder and Lindsay 2003: 10, 121, 125; Tertrais 2004: 39). There was a very strong tendency in the US and in general in the West's counter-terrorism policies not to look weak. However, by doing so they have helped to grow the monster they were afraid of (Kolko 2002: 149). They have also raised the expectations that they will bring about their own defeat or at least withdrawal from the Islamic world, as happened before when they withdrew from Lebanon in 1984, from Somalia in 1993–1994 and from Iraq in 2011. The French announcement that their troops would stay in Mali for only a limited time had a similar effect. All the insurgents or terrorists have to do is to wait out the 'occupying' forces (RT 2013a; *Washington Post* 2013a; Ward 2013; Dreyfuss 2013; Sen 2013; CTV News 2013).

Under President Obama a change of policy took place, set in motion with the *U.S. National Strategy for Counterterrorism* of June 2011, which promised to be 'more focused and specific' than previous ones and which subsequently may have been reinforced by war-wariness among the American people, the US financial problems and prioritising other threats like cyber attacks, organised crime and China (Susskind 2013; Mueller 2013; Hayden 2013; Pellerin 2013; Crelinsten 2009: 30). In early 2013 the Obama administration stated that 'Building Partnership Capacity', would be a fundamental element of this new strategy (Morgenstein 2013). There would be no more big footprints, but instead the US would rely on other nations' capabilities to tackle their local and regional terrorism problems and to support them in a less conspicuous way in their fight against transnational forms of terrorism (Schmitt 2013b). Countries like the Philippines, Georgia, Colombia and Uganda have received security assistance from the United States. In his major speech at the National Defense University on 23 May 2013 Obama showed himself acutely aware of the dangers of US invasions, which 'lead us to be viewed as occupying armies, unleash a torrent of unintended consequences, are difficult to contain, and ultimately empower those who thrive on violent conflict'. Putting more boots on the ground would, according to the President, lead to 'more U.S. deaths, more Black Hawks down, more confrontations with local populations, and an inevitable mission creep in support of such raids that could easily escalate into new wars.' (White House 2013).

> Beyond Afghanistan, we must define our efforts not as a boundless global war on terror but rather as a series of persistent, targeted efforts to dismantle specific networks of violent extremists that threaten America. In many cases, this will involve partnerships with other countries.... Where foreign governments cannot or will not effectively stop terrorism in their territory, the primary alternative to targeted lethal action would be the use of conventional military options.... We cannot use force everywhere that a radical ideology takes root.... So the next element of our strategy involves addressing the underlying grievances and conflicts that feed extremism, from North Africa to South Asia.
>
> (*Washington Post* 2013b)

This is the new US 'comprehensive strategy', a mix of targeted killings, conventional wars and partnerships.

There is a certain wisdom in a tailor-made micro approach, by which the US supports partners with assistance in special forces, air support, intelligence, logistics and training (Watts 2013; Hoffman 2009: 362; Manea 2013). As Kilcullen states: 'Effective counterinsurgency requires indigenous security forces who are legitimate in local eyes, operate humanely under the rule of law, and can effectively protect local communities against insurgents.' (Kilcullen 2009: 112; cf. ibidem: 271) Another reason to applaud such a policy would be that in as far as extreme Islamists view their fight as a cosmic war there seems to be only one advice to take the fuse out of it: refuse to fight in it (Aslan 2009: 11; cf. Robb 2007: 171).

However, this policy of leading from behind has problems of its own. To begin with, many of the states upon which the US wants to rely as a partner in the fight against terror have appalling human rights records when it comes to fighting 'terrorism' (Morgenstein 2013). This problem would increase even further if the US would try to engage European states in their strategy, as the latter have already objected to certain human rights aspects of the counter-terrorism policy of the United States itself.

Another issue finds its roots in the weaknesses or corruption of the local security structures. The US authorities rightly fear that their intelligence, expertise and weapons will end up in the hands of the terrorists or insurgents. For exactly this reason they have already refrained from cooperating, e.g. with the authorities in Nigeria, which has the largest standing army in Sub-Saharan Africa (Barrett and Ibrahim 2013; Riedel 2013c; Parker 2013b; Blair 2013; Hansen 2013: 141). A certain degree of governance should be present in order to make external security assistance workable (Rubin 2013).

How difficult it is to find the right size of training and resourcing can be learned from the experiences in Mali before French troops arrived on the scene in January 2013. For many years the US trained Mali's military as part of a $500 million counter-terrorism programme in order to assist the authorities in this poor African country who were not able to face the insurgents' threat solely. Mali, at the end of 2002 still characterised as 'almost an ideal democracy' by former CIA Director James Woolsey (Woolsey 2002), was according to the US State Department 'a leading regional partner in U.S. efforts against terrorism' (Masters 2013). However, members of the official Mali elite forces, trained by the US, defected to the rebels, and it was American-trained captain Amadou Sanogo who toppled the democratically-elected government in a coup that created such a chaos that half of the country fell into the hands of insurgents. Amanda Dory, US Deputy Assistant Secretary of Defense for Africa, had to admit that the US level of resourcing had not been commensurate with the threat (Polgreen 2013; Schmitt 2013a). Previously the examples of Afghanistan, Columbia and the Philippines had already demonstrated how consuming providing training and resources of police and armed forces may be (Muñoz 2011; Cragin 2011: 118). Today Niger, still an island of stability in the midst of unrest in Mali, Libya and Boko Haram's activities in northern Nigeria, has only a poorly equipped military of 5,200 troops, which would be incapable of heading a serious extremist threat. The urge for Niger's government to spend more money on countering the terrorist threat at the expense of social expenditure is as much a recipe for raising the risks of instability as for reducing them (McGregor 2013a; Africa Report 2013).

As American international relations scholar Mary Haybeck concluded: no al Qaeda affiliate or partner has been deposed by local forces alone; in all cases outside intervention was needed (Habeck 2012). However, outside forces can do little to enhance political legitimacy of the governments in the weak states where al Qaeda and its associates seek to enhance their influence (cf. Riedel 2013a). Moreover, limiting terrorist and insurgent organisations to operate on their national soil may drive them to attack abroad, as was shown by al-Shabaab's attack in Kenya. And, incidentally, al-Shabaab struck at the Westgate Mall to punish Kenya not only for its role in the African Union force operating in Somalia, but also because of the growing American support for the Kenyan security forces (Kulish, Mazzetti and Schmitt 2013).

Everywhere the US decides to show a military presence after a while the question will arise that the *Tala'i' al-Khurasan*, al Qaeda's journal of the jihad in Afghanistan, stated in June 2009 on its cover: 'Humiliating Withdrawal or Disastrous Occupation?' And once the outside pressure is eased or removed, the jihadists recover quickly. Even the idea, uttered by some, of cutting the ties between al Qaeda Core and its affiliates, associates and Western adherents, a kind of quarantining (Kilcullen 2009: 15), makes no sense in the interconnected world of today (cf. Meleagrou-Hitchens 2011: 8). Just like an all-out war with big footprints would be unwise, a range of 'limited wars' would be 'a fools strategy at best' (Webb 2013).

Finally, there has been a remarkable one-sidedness in American counter-terrorism strategy and that is the dominant use of military means. Fighting power, however, is but one of the instruments of a grand strategy (cf. Adoyl 2013). Defeating is not the same as annihilating. Although some have brought up the notion that counter-terrorism is 'all about winning the struggle of ideas, destroying the legitimacy of a competing ideology' (Carafano and Rosenzweig 2005: 174), thus far the United States and its partners have done too little to confront the ideology and narrative of al Qaeda and its like (Ryan 2013: 2–4, 255; Geltzer 2011: 136–139; Reed 2006a: 36; Jenkins and Godges 2011: 5; Rabasa 2011: 65–66; *The Economist* 2013c; Hoffman 2009: 360).

Conclusion

Al Qaeda may be expected to remain able to scale up its levels from the local to the global by creating operational bases and train terrorists for global operations, just like it may decide to scale down (Jenkins 2012: 3; Kulish and Gettleman 2013; Express 2013). Any counter-terrorism strategy would have to function at several levels at once: supranational, regional, national and subnational (cf. Crelinsten 2009: 232, 236), tactical, operational and strategic. Meanwhile there will remain uncertainty as to who exactly the opponent is, a continuous lack of means, an abundance of impotent partners and a lot of debate over what the overall effectiveness of counter-terrorist and counterinsurgency actions is. Emphasising prevention, pre-emptiveness or preclusion will run the risk of provoking the peril it would like to prevent, while emphasising containment or quarantining may cause blazing fires that can not be timely extinguished. There is no grand strategy thinkable that can organise this type of choreography.

Given this outcome one would do well to take into consideration the axiom given by the American professor for war and peace studies Richard K. Betts: 'Whatever the costs of refraining from war may be, they can seldom be greater than those from killing without strategy.' (Betts 2004: 47) It may be true that al Qaeda and its affilates possess the capacity to deny the West military victory (Bacevich 2006). But at least the West should not allow them to deliver defeat, meanwhile trying to gain victory itself by non-military approaches, primarily by a war of ideas. If it looks like muddling through, it is. There is no alternative.

Notes

1 President Bush quoted in Thissen, 'Core al-Qaeda'.
2 The definition of 'insurgency' used in this article is 'an organized movement that aims at overthrowing the political order within given territory, using a combination of subversion, terrorism, guerrilla warfare and propaganda', in which the 'given territory' in the case of al Qaeda constitutes the whole world and the 'political order' is the political order within the entire Muslim world and the relationship between the world's Muslim community, *ummah*, and the rest of the world society (Kilcullen 2009: 12–13).

References

Ackerman, S. (2013a) 'Spy Chiefs Point to a Much, Much Weaker Al-Qaeda', *Wired*, 12 March.
Ackerman, S. (2013b) 'What's Next in National Security Shadow Wars', *Danger Room*, 16 May.
Adamu, L.D. (2013) 'Hezbollah behind Kano weapons cache', *Daily Trust*, 31 May.
Adoyl, A. (2013) 'Military will never solve Boko Haram insurgency – Former CDS, Agwai', *Daily Post*, 29 September.
Africa Report (2013), 'Niger: Another Weak Link in the Sahel?', *Africa Report*, 208, 19 September.
Ahmed, A. (2013) 'The Drone War Is Far From Over', *New York Times*, 30 May.
Aid, M.M. (2012) *Intel Wars. The Secret History of the Fight Against Terror*, New York etc.: Bloomsbury Press.
Akwagiram, A. (2013) 'Islamist radicalism: Why doe sit lure some Africans?', *BBC News*, 30 May.
Alexander, Y. (2012) *Special update report: terrorism in North, West and Central Africa: from 9/11 to the Arab Spring*, Arlington, VA: Potomac Institute for Policy Studies – International Center for Terrorism Studies.
Ali, T. (2002) *The Clash of Fundamentalisms. Crusades, Jihads and Modernity*, London/ New York: Verso.
Allam, H. and Baron, A. (2013) 'New vision of al Qaida rises from U.S. Embassy closings', McClatchy, 8 August. Available at: www.mcclatchydc.com/2013/08/08/198898/new-vision-of-al-qaida-rises-from.html#.UiB7GBYmuCo (last accessed 8 October 2013).
Allen, Ch. (2006) *God's Terrorists. The Wahhabi Cult and the Hidden Roots of Modern Jihad*, Cambridge, MA: Da Capo Press.
Al-Shishani, M.B. (2013a) 'Terrorists without a cause. Boston to the Caucaus, the same jihad?', *Le Monde Diplomatique*, June.
Al-Shishani, M.B. (2013b) 'Al Qaeda grows as its leaders focus on the "near enemy"', *The National*, 30 August.
AP (2012), 'U.K. spy chief: Arab Spring creates "permissive environment" for al Qaeada in Middle East', *AP*, 26 June.
AP (2013) 'Local, foreign Islamic militants turn Egypt's Sinai a new front for jihad', *AP*, 3 September.
Aslan, R. (2009) *How to Win a Cosmic War. God, Globalization, and the End of the War on Terror*, New York: Random House.
Atassi, B. (2013) 'Qaeda chief annuls Syrian-Iraqi jihad merger', *Aljazeera*, 9 June.
Augstein, J. (2013) 'Europe Must Protect Itself from America', *SpiegelOnline*, 17 June.
Awadh Asseri, A.S. (2009) *Combating Terrorism: Saudi Arabia's Role in the War on Terror*, Oxford etc.: OUP Pakistan.
Bacevich, A.J. (2006) 'The Islamic Way of War', *The American Conservative*, 11 September.
Bamford, J. (2004) *A Pretext for War. 9/11, Iraq, and the Abuse of America's Intelligence Agencies*, New York etc.: Doubleday.
Barfi B. (2013) 'How U.S. Strikes on Syria Help al Qaeda', *The Daily Beast*, 28 August.
Barnard, A. and Schmitt, E. (2013) 'As Foreign Fighters Flood Syria, Fears of a New Extremist Haven', *New York Times*, 8 August.
Barnett, D. (2013) 'Jihadi ideologue calls on Egyptian Muslims to prepare for "the coming war"', *The Long War Journal*, 19 August.

Baroud, R. (2012) 'The Afghanistan of Africa', *Counterpunch*, 2 August.
Barrett, D. and Ibrahim, A.M. (2013) 'On Terror's New Front Line, Mistrust Blunts U.S. Strategy', *Wall Street Journal*, 27 February.
Barry, E. (2013) 'Dagestan's Shadow War, Fought by "Many Tsarnaevs"', *New York Times*, 19 May.
Bennoune, K. (2013) 'The Taliban of Timbuktu', *New York Times*, 23 January.
Betts, R.K. (2000) 'Is Strategy an Illusion?', *International Security*, 25 (2), pp. 5–50.
Betz, D. (2008) 'The virtual dimension of contemporary insurgency and counterinsurgency', *Small Wars & Insurgencies*, 19 (4), pp. 510–540.
Bezhan, F. (2013) 'The Rise of Al-Qaeda 2.0', *The Atlantic*, 24 July.
Biddle, S.D. (2013) American Grand Strategy after 9/11: an Assessment, April 2005. Available at: www.strategicstudiesinstitute.army.mil/pdffiles/pub603.pdf (last accessed 28 September 2013).
Bilmes, L.J. (2013) *The Financial Legacy of Iraq and Afghanistan: How Wartime Spending Decisions Will Constrain Future National Security Budgets*, Cambridge, MA: HKS Faculty Research Working Paper Series RWP13–006.
Blair, E. (2013) 'Kenya's intelligence work hurt by corruption, rivalries', *Reuters*, 4 October.
Bobbitt, P. (2008), *Terror and Consent. The Wars for the Twenty-First Century*, London: Allen Lane.
Bowden, M. (2012) *The Finish. The Killing of Osama bin Laden*, New York: Atlantic Monthly Press.
Brinkbäumer, K. (2013) 'The War on Terror Is America's Mania', *SpiegelOnline*, 16 July.
Brinkman, P.D. (2013) 'Terrorism More About "Bloods and Crips" than "Korajn and Hadith"', *US News and World Report*, 26 February.
Bullough, O. (2013) 'Beslan Meets Columbine', *New York Times*, 19 April.
Brunker, M. (2013) 'New al-Qaida terror guidebook urges young extremists to think small', *NBC News*, 3 March.
Burke, J. (2011) *The 9/11 Wars*, London: Allen Lane.
Burke, J. (2013) 'Al-Qaida: how great is the terrorism threat to the west now?', *Guardian*, 29 January.
Buruma, I. (2013) 'Tsarnaev Brothers and America's Enemy Within', *Moscow Times*, 20 May.
Carafano, J.J. and Rosenzweig, P. (2005) *Winning the Long War. Lessons from the Cold War for Defeating Terrorism and Preserving Freedom*, Lanham, MD: Heritage Books.
Carafano, J.J., Bucci, S. and Zuckerman, J. (2012) 'Fifty Terror Plots Foiled Since 9/11: The Homegrown Threat and the Long War on Terrorism', *Backgrounder*, 2682, (25 April).
Carafano, J.J., Bucci, S. and Zuckerman, J. (2013) '60 Terrorist Plots Since 9/11: Continued Lessons in Domestic Counterterrorism', The *Heritage Foundation Special Report*, 137 (22 July).
Cardash, S., Cilluffo, F.J. and Marret, J.-L. (2013) 'Foreign Fighters in Syria: Still Doing Battle, Still a Multidimensional Danger', *Fondation pour la Recherche Stratégique*, 24 (August).
Celso, A.N. (2012) 'Al Qaeda's Post-9/11 Organizational Structure and Strategy: The Role of Islamist Regional Affiliates', *Mediterranean Quarterly*, 23 (2), pp. 30–41.
Chouet, A. (2013) *Au coeur des services spéciaux. La menace Islamiste: fausses pistes et vrais dangers*, Paris: Éditions la Découverte.

The Clarion Project (2013) 'Online Jihadi Publications Luring Teens', *The Clarion Project*, 20 May.
Cloherty, J. (2012) 'Virtual Terrorism: Al Qaeda Video Calls for "Electronic Jihad"', *ABC News*, 22 May.
CNBC (2013) 'Al-Qaeda leader calls to bleed US economy', *CNBC*, 13 September.
Colebatch, H.G.P. (2009) 'Domino theory for the age of terror', *The Australian*, 19 March.
Connable, B. (2012) *Embracing the Fog of War. Assessment and Metrics in Counterinsurgency*, Santa Monica, CA: Rand.
Copenhagen Post (2013) '40 Danes trained by al-Shabaab', *Copenhagen Post*, 24 September.
Coren, C. and Walter, K. (2012) 'Mid-East Expert Phares: Al-Qaeda Is Growing', *Newsmax*, 9 August.
Corum, J.S. (2007) *Fighting the War on Terror. A Counterinsurgency Strategy*, St. Paul, MN: Zenith Press.
Courrier international (2013), 'Égypte. Une nouvelle loi élargit la notion de terrorisme', *Courrier international*, 4 September.
Cragin, K. (2011) 'The Strategic Dilemma of Terrorist Havens Calls for Their Isolation, Not Elimination', in B.M. Jenkins and J.P. Godges (eds), *The Long Shadow of 9/11. America's Response to Terrorism*, Santa Barbara, CA: Rand, pp. 113–120.
Crelinsten, R. (2009) *Counterterrorism*, Cambridge/Malden, MA: Polity Press.
Crumpton, H.A. (2012) *The Art of Intelligence. Lessons from a Life in the CIA's Clandestine Service*, New York: The Penguin Press.
CTV News (2013) 'Al Qaeda claims responsibilty for Iraq bombings', *CTV News*, 30 August.
Daalder, I.H. and Lindsay, J.M. (2003) *America Unbound. The Bush Revolution in Foreign Policy*, Washington DC: Brookings Institution Press.
Danner, M. (2005) 'Taking Stock of the Forever War', *New York Times*, 11 September.
Defence IQ (2013) 'U.S. Policy on Boko Haram', *Defence IQ*, 28 March.
Derrick, J.C. (2013) 'Nigerian terrorists target the U.S.', *World Magazine*, 16 August.
Deutsche Welle (2013a) 'German Islamists increasingly going to Syria', *Deutsche Welle*, 8 September.
Deutsche Welle (2013b) 'Al Qaeda's Turkish base?', *Deutsche Welle*, 18 September.
Dilanian, K. (2013) 'With Al Qaeda shattered, U.S. counter-terrorism's future unclear', *Los Angeles Times*, 15 April.
Dowd, C. and Raleigh, C. (2013) 'The myth of global Islamic terrorism and local conflict in Mali and the Sahel', *African Affairs*, 29 May.
Dreyfuss, B. (2013) 'Al Qaeda and the Iraq-Syria Civil War', *The Nation*, 30 July.
Drezner, D.W. (2006) 'The Grandest Strategy Of Them All', *Washington Post*, 17 December.
Economist, The (2013a), 'What is Boko Haram?', *The Economist*, 1 May.
Economist, The (2013b) 'Rivalry among jihadists', *The Economist*, 26 June.
Economist, The (2013c) 'Al-Qaeda returns. The new face of terror' and 'The unquenchable fire. The state of al-Qaeda', *The Economist*, 28 September.
Ehrenfeld, R. and Jensen, K. (2013) 'Saudi Arabia's Efforts to Expand Radical Islam and Support Terrorism', *American Center for Democracy* blog, 2 February.
Erlanger, S. (2013a) 'French Intervention in Mali Raises Threat of Domestic Terrorism, Judge Says', *New York Times*, 23 February.
Erlanger, S. (2013b) 'Outrage in Europe Grows Over Spying Disclosures', *New York Times*, 1 July.

Europol (2013), TE-SAT 2013. *EU Terrorism* Situationand Trend Report.
Express (2013) 'MI5 fears over 60 Somali jihad plotters in UK', *Express*, 29 September.
Farrall, L. (2011) 'How al Qaeda Works. What the Organization's Subsidiaries Say About Its Strength', *Foreign Affairs*, 90 (2), pp. 128–138.
Farrell, Th. and Giustozzi, A. (2013), 'The Taliban at war: inside the Helmand insurgency, 2004–2012', *International Affairs*, 89 (4), pp. 845–871.
Foley, F. (2013) *Countering Terrorism in Britain and France. Institutions, Norms and the Shadow of the Past*, Cambridge etc.: Cambridge University Press.
Frantz, D. (2002) 'Defining Al Qaeda. They're coming after us, but who are they now?', *New York Times*, 20 October.
Gallup (2013) 'Americans Say Preventing Terrorism Top Foreign Policy Goal', *Gallup*, 20 February.
Gambrell, J. (2013) 'US: Islamic extremists move between Nigeria, Mali', *AP*, 14 March.
Ganor, B. (2005) *The Counter-Terrorism Puzzle. A Guide for Decision Makers*, New Brunswick/London: Transaction Publishers.
Garfield, A. and Boyd, A. (2013) 'Understanding Afghan Insurgents: Motivations, Goals, and the Reconciliation and Reintegration Process', *Foreign Policy Research Institute E-Notes*, April.
Gartenstein-Ross, D. (2011) *Bin Laden's Legacy. Why We're Still Losing the War on Terror*, Hoboken, NJ: Wiley.
Gartenstein-Ross, D. (2013) 'Al Qaeda in the Islamic Maghreb and Al Qaeda's Senior Leadership', *Gunpowder & Lead*, 19 January.
Geltzer, J.A. (2011) *U.S. Counter-Terrorism Strategy and al-Qaeda. Signalling and the terrorist world-view*, London/New York.
Gerges, F.A. (2011) *The Rise and Fall of Al-Qaeda*, Oxford etc.: OUP USA.
Gertz, B. (2013) 'American, European Jihadists in Syria Raise New Domestic Terror Fears', *The Washington Free Beacon*, 20 August.
Ghosh, P.R. (2013) 'Algeria's Brutal DRS Intelligence Agency: The Nation's Real Power?', *International Business Times*, 21 January.
Gill, P. and Wilson, L. (2013) 'Intelligence and Security-Sector Reform in Indonesia', in Ph.H.J. Davies and K.C. Gustafson (eds), *Intelligence Elsewhere. Spies and Espionage Outside the Anglosphere*, Washington DC: Georgetown University Press.
Gold, D. (2004) *Hatred's Kingdom: How Saudi Arabia Supports the New Global Terrorism*, Washington DC: Regnery Publishing.
Goldman, R. (2013) 'Fort Hood Judge Bans Evidence of Shooter's "Jihadi" motives', *ABC News*, 19 August.
Gorman, R. (2013) 'Terrorist group al-Qaeda has launched its first twitter account', *MailOnline*, 28 September.
Graaff, B. de (2013) 'Why Kant Is Wrong: The World on its Way to Eternal War', in H. Amersfoort, R. Moelker, J. Soeters and D. Verweij (eds), *Moral Responsibility & Military Effectiveness*, NL ARMS, Netherlands Annual Review of Military Studies, 2013, The Hague: T.M.C. Asser Press, pp. 279–299.
Graaff, B. de and Graaf B. de (2010), 'Bringing politics back in: the introduction of the "performative power" of counterterrorism', *Critical Studies on Terrorism*, 3 (2), pp. 261–275.
Graham, B. (2004) *Intelligence Matters. The CIA, the FBI, Saudi Arabia, and the Failure of America's War on Terror*, New York/Toronto: Random House.
Guardian (2013a) 'David Cameron's statement on the Algerian hostage crisis', *Guardian*, 20 January.

Guardian (2013b) 'Al-Qaida in Syria is most serious threat to UK, says report', *Guardian*, 11 July.

Guardian (2013c) 'Kenya mall attack: Somalia's al-Shabaab group claims responsibility', *Guardian*, 21 September.

Habeck, M. (2012) 'Can we declare the war on al-Qaeda over?' *Foreign Policy – Shadow Government*, 27 June.

Hackensberger, A. (2012) 'Gottesstaat Azawad, das Islamisten-Paradies in Mali', *Die Welt*, 25 October.

Haddick, R. (2009) 'This Week at War: The Domino Theory returns', *Foreign Policy*, 24 July.

Hall, M. (2013) 'Tony Blair: military intervention in Syria vital to prevent "breeding ground for extremism"', *The Telegraph*, 27 August.

Hansen, S.J. (2013) *Al-Shabaab in Somalia. The History and Ideology of a Militant Islamist Group, 2005–2012*, London: C. Hurst & Co.

Hayden (2013) 'Michael V. Hayden on the Future of the CIA', 18 April 2013. Available at: http://matthewaid.tumblr.com/post/48302084261/michael-v-hayden-on-the-future-of-the-cia, (last accessed 8 October 2013).

Hegghammer, T. (2013a) 'Should I Stay or Should I Go? Explaining Variation in Western Jihadists' Choice between Domestic and Foreign Fighting', *American Political Science Review*, 107 (1), pp. 1–15.

Hegghammer, T. (2013b) 'Jihadi foreign fighters: How dangerous?', *The Monkey Cage*, 31 May.

Herridge, C. (2013) 'Exclusive Documents: Was Anwar al-Awlaki government asset?', *FoxNews*, 2 July.

Herridge, C. and Browne, P. (2013) 'Hasan sends writings to Fox News ahead of Fort Hood shooting trial', *FoxNews*, 1 August.

Herszenhorn, D.M. (2013) 'Delegates Visit Moscow for Insight on Boston Attack', *New York Times*, 2 June.

Hinnant, L. (2013) 'Intel dilemma in Boston, London, Paris attacks', *AP*, 31 May.

Hironaka, A. (2005) *Neverending Wars. The International Community, Weak States, and the Perpetuation of Civil War*, Cambridge, MA/London: Harvard University Press.

Hoffman, B. (2009) 'A Counterterrorist Strategy for the Obama Administration', *Terrorism and Political Violence*, 21 (3), pp. 359–377.

Hoffman, B. (2013) 'Al Qaida's Uncertain Future', *Studies in Conflict & Terrorism*, 36 (8), pp. 635–653.

Homeland Security News Wire (2013a) 'AQAP now central pillar of a decentralized al Qaeda', *Homeland Security News Wire*, 19 August.

Homeland Security News Wire (2013b) 'Terrorism threat at home: shift from radicalized groups to radicalized individuals', *Homeland Security News Wire*, 12 September.

Homeland Security News Wire (2013c) 'Powerful groups abandon rebel coalition, join Jihadist al Nusra Front', *Homeland Security News Wire*, 27 September.

Homeland Security News Wire (2013d) 'African terrorist groups driven by local issues', *Homeland Security News Wire*, 2 October.

Hubbard, B. (2013) 'Qaeda Branch in Syria Pursues Its Own Agenda', *New York Times*, 1 October.

Hustad, K. (2013) 'Terrorists' best weapons: guns, bombs, Twitter', *The Christian Science Monitor*, 24 September.

Ilias, P. (2013) 'The Al Qaeda Presence in Africa', defensegreece.com, 19 February, Available at: www.defencegreece.com/index.php/2013/02/the-al-qaeda-presence-in-africa/ (last accessed 2 October 2013).

Jacinto, L. (2013) 'France, US top al Qaeda's list of Western targets', *France24*, 5 August.

Jenkins, B.M. and Godges, J.P. (2011) 'Introduction: The Shadow of 9/11 Across America', idem (eds), *The Long Shadow of 9/11. America's Response to Terrorism*, Santa Barbara, CA: Rand, pp. 1–8.

Jenkins, B.M. (2012) *New Challenges to U.S. Counterterrorism Efforts. An Assessment of the Current Terrorist Threat*, Santa Monica, CA: Rand.

The Jihad and Terrorism Threat Monitor (2013) 'Al-Qaeda Cleric Praises Tsarnaev Brothers As Models for Muslim Children', *The Jihad and Terrorism Threat Monitor*, 5436, 6 September.

Johnsen, G.D. (2013) 'How We Lost Yemen. The United States used the Pakistan playbook on Yemen's terrorists. It didn't work', *Foreign Policy*, 6 August.

Johnston, R. (2013) 'Pakistan's Inter-Services Intelligence', P.H.J. Davies and K.C. Gustafson (eds), *Intelligence Elsewhere. Spies and Espionage Outside the Anglosphere*, Washington DC: Georgetown University Press, pp. 115–139.

Jones, S.G. (2011) 'Lessons from the Tribal Areas', in B.M. Jenkins and J.P. Godges (eds), *The Long Shadow of 9/11. America's Response to Terrorism*, Santa Barbara, CA: Rand, pp. 37–46.

Jones, S.G. (2013) *Re-Examining the Al Qa'ida Threat to the United States*, Santa Monica, CA: Rand.

Jordans, F. (2013) 'The Big Story. Germany ends Cold War spying pact with US, Britain, *AP*, 2 August.

Joscelyn, Th. (2013a) 'Al Qaeda central tightened control over hostage operations', *The Long War Journal*, 17 January.

Joscelyn, Th. (2013b) 'Global al Qaeda: Affiliates, Objectives, and Future Challenges', testimony for the U.S. House Committee on Foreign Affairs, Subcommittee on Terrorism, Nonproliferation, and Trade, 18 July 2013: Foundation for Defense of Democracies.

Joscelyn, Th. (2013c) 'Al Qaeda and the threat in Syria', *The Long War Journal*, 10 September.

Joscelyn, Th. and Roggio, B. (2013) 'AQAP's emir also serves as al Qaeda's general manager', *The Long War Journal*, 6 August.

Kagan, F.W. (2013) 'Testimony: The Continued Expansion of Al Qaeda Affiliates and their Capabilities', *Critical Threats*, 18 July.

Karouny, M. (2013) 'Syria's Nusra Front Eclipsed by Iraq's Al-Qaeda', *Daily Star*, 18 May.

Keating, M. (2013) 'How Hezbollah is Winning in West Africa', *World Policy*, 30 September.

Keenan, J. (2009) *The Dark Sahara. America's War on Terror in Africa*, New York: Pluto Press.

Keenan, J. (2010) 'General Toufik: "God of Algeria"', *Al Jazeera*, 29 September.

Keenan, J. (2012) 'How Washington helped foster the Islamist uprising in Mali', *New Internationalist*, December.

Keenan, J. (2013) *The Dying Sahara. US Imperialism and Terror in Africa*, London: Pluto Press.

Kelly, M. (2013) 'CIA Analyst Details The Fundamental Paradox Of The "War on Terror"', *Business Insider*, 1 October.

Kilcullen, D. (2009) *The Accidental Guerrilla. Fighting Small Wars in the Midst of a Big One*, London: Hurst & Co.

Killough, A. and Cruikshank, P. (2013) 'Al Qaeda magazine encourages Boston-style bombings', *CNN*, 31 May.

Kitfield, J. (2013) 'Why Terrorism Is the New Big African Issue for Obama', *The Atlantic*, 27 June.

Kofas, J. (2013) 'Does the generic use of "terrorism" have any meaning?', 21 January. Available at: http://jonkofas.blogspot.be/2013/01/does-generic-use-of-terrorism-have-any.html (last accessed 15 September 2013).

Kolko, G. (2002) *Another Century of War?*, New York: The New Press.

Kulish, N. and Gettleman, J. (2013) 'U.S. Sees Direct Threat in Attack at Kenya Mall', *New York Times*, 25 September.

Kulish, N., Mazzetti, M. and Schmitt, E. (2013) 'Kenya Mall Carnage Shows Shabaab Resilience', *New York Times*, 22 September.

Kurzman, Ch. (2011) *The Missing Martyrs. Why There Are So Few Muslim Terrorists*, Oxford etc.: OUP USA.

Levitt, M. (2013) *Hezbollah. The Global Footprint of Lebanon's Party of God*, London: C. Hurst & Co.

Lewis, D. (2013) 'Insight: U.S. and allies target Hezbollah financing, ties in Africa', *Reuters*, 20 September.

Lewis, J.D. (2013) *Al-Qaeda in Iraq Resurgent, Part I and II*, Washington DC: Institute for the Study of War.

Liddell Hart, B.H. (1967), *Strategy*, London: Meridian.

The Long War Journal (2013) 'Free Syrian Army units ally with al Qaeda, reject Syrian National Coalition, and call for sharia', *The Long War Journal*, 26 September.

Lum, C., Kennedy, L.W. and Sherley, A.J. (2006) *The Effectiveness of Counter-Terrorism Strategies. A Campbell Systematic Review*, The Campbell Collaboration.

Lynch, C. (2013) 'Is the U.S. Ramping Up a Secret War in Somalia?', *Foreign Policy*, 22 July.

MacDonald, H. (2010) 'Sensibly Selective Screening', *National Review Online*, 6 January.

McDougall, W.A. (2010) 'Can the US do Grand Strategy?', *Foreign Policy Research Institute*, April.

McGregor, A. (2013a) 'Niger: New Battleground for North Africa's Islamist Militants?', *The Jamestown Foundation*, 29 May.

McGregor, A. (2013b) 'Westgate Mall Attack Demonstrates al-Shabaab's Desperation Not Strength', *The Jamestown Foundation*, 24 September.

McLaughlin, J. (2013) 'Terrorism at a moment of transition', *CNN*, 12 July.

Maher, S. and Neumann, P.R. (2012) *Al-Qaeda at the Crossroads: How the terror group is responding to the loss of its leaders & the Arab Spring*, London: The International Centre for the Study of Radicalisation.

Manea, O. (2013) 'The Fallacies of Big Expeditionary Counterinsurgency: Interview with T.X. Hammes', *Small Wars Journal*, 6 September.

Masters, J. (2013) 'Al-Qaeda in the Islamic Maghreb (AQIM)', *Council on Foreign Relations*, 24 January.

Megenta, A.T. (2011) 'The journalist as terrorist: an Ethiopian story', *OpenDemocracy*, 7 December.

Meijer, R. (ed.) (2012) *Counter-Terrorism Strategies in Indonesia, Algeria and Saudi Arabia*, The Hague: Wetenschappelijk Onderzoek- en Documentatiecentrum van het Ministerie van Veiligheid en Justitie.

Meleagrou-Hitchens, A. (2011) *As American as Apple Pie: How Anwar al-Awlaki Became the Face of Western Jihad*, London: The International Centre for the Study of Radicalisation.

Michaels, M. (2013) 'Surveillance of Student Group Raises Spectre of Police Overreach', *Mint Press News*, 24 August.

Miller, G., Whitlock, C. and Gellman, B. (2013) 'Top-secret U.S. intelligence files show new levels of distrust of Pakistan', *Washington Post*, 3 September.

Mishal, S. and Rosenthal, M. (2005) 'Al Qaeda as a Dune Organization: Toward a Typology of Islamic Terrorist Organizations', *Studies in Conflict & Terrorism*, 28 (4), pp. 275–293.

Mohamedou, M.M.O. (2013) 'AQIM: Maghreb to Mali, and back', *OpenDemocracy*, 19 April.

Mond, Y. (2013) 'Fulfilling Bin Laden's Will: al-Qaeda & the Arab Spring', *The Times of Israel*, 17 September.

Morgenstein, J. (2013) 'Speak Softly and Let Others Carry the Big Stick', *Foreign Policy*, 6 March.

Mueller (2013) 'Director Mueller on the Future of Cyber Security', 8 August. Available at: www.fbi.gov/news/news_blog/director-mueller-on-the-future-of-cyber-security (last accessed 8 September 2013).

Muñoz, A. (2011) 'A Long-Overdue Adaptation to the Afghan Environment', in B.M. Jenkins and J.P. Godges (eds), *The Long Shadow of 9/11. America's Response to Terrorism*, Santa Barbara, CA: Rand, pp. 23–36.

The National Security Strategy of the United States (2002), Washington DC.

National Strategy for Combating Terrorism (2003), Washington DC.

Nelson, R. and Sanderson, Th.M. (2011) *A Threat Transformed. Al Qaeda and Associated Mevements in 2011*, Washington DC: Center for Stategic & International Studies.

Nevin, J.A. (2003) 'Retaliating Against Terrorists', *Behavior and Social Sciences*, 12/2 pp. 109–128.

Nielsen, N. (2013) 'US defends spy programme to sceptical EU', *EUobserver*, 14 June.

Nimmo, K. (2013) 'Tsarnaev Narrative Change: Instead of a Radical Muslim, Tamerlan a Rightwing Extremist', *Infowars.com*, 6 August.

Noriega, R.F. (2013) 'Hezbollah's strategic shift: A global terrorist threat', *Foreign and Defense Policy*, 20 March.

Omand, D. (2005) 'Countering international terrorism: The use of strategy', *Survival: Global Politics and Strategy*, 47 (4), pp. 107–116.

Pape, R.A. and Feldman, J.K. (2010) *Cutting the Fuse: The Explosion of Global Suicide Terrorism and How to Stop it*, Chicago: University of Chicago Press.

Parker, G. (2013a) 'Africa desert helps breed radicals, from Al Shabaab to Boko Haram to Mr. Marlboro', *The Christian Science Monitor*, 29 September.

Parker, G. (2013b) 'Is barbaric Boko Haram winning in Nigeria's north country?', *Christian Science Monitor*, 1 October.

Patton, K. (2010) *Sociocultural Intelligence. A New Discipline in Intelligence Studies*, London/New York: Continuum.

Pearlstein, R.M. (2004) *Fatal Future. Transnational Terrorism and the New Global Disorder*, Austin, TX: University of Texas Press.

Pellerin, Ch. (2013) 'Intelligence Agency Director Discusses Roadmap for Future', *American Forces Press Service*, 16 September.

Perry, W.L. and Gordon IV, J. (2008), *Analytic Support to Intelligence in Counterinsurgencies*, Santa Monica, CA: Rand.

Polgreen, L. (2013) 'Mali Army, Riding U.S. Hopes, Is Proving No Match for Militants', *New York Times*, 14 January.

Pratt, D. (2012) 'Boko Haram's threat to Nigeria ... and beyond', *The Herald (Scotland)*, 21 December.

The Quilliam Foundation (2013), *A New Index to Assess the Effectiveness of Al Qaeda*, London.

Quitta, O. (2013) 'Rising satjes for the US in Mali', *Washington Examiner*, 5 August.

Rabasa, A. (2011) 'Where Are We in the "War of Ideas?"', in B.M. Jenkins and J.P. Godges (eds), *The Long Shadow of 9/11. America's Response to Terrorism*, Santa Barbara, CA: Rand, pp. 61–70.

Raghavan, S. (2013) 'Al-Shabaab leader's ambitions appear to be as complex as his personality', *Washington Post*, 26 September.

Reed, D.J. (2006a) *On Strategy: The War on Terror in Context*, Monterey, CA: Naval Postgraduate School.

Reed, D. (2006b) 'Why Strategy Matters in the War on Terror', *Homeland Security Affairs*, 2/3.

Rees, W. (2006) *Transatlantic Counter-Terrorism Cooperation. The new imperative*, London/New York: Routledge.

Reuter, Chr. (2013) 'How Dangerous Are Syria's Foreign Fighters?', *SpiegelOnline*, 27 September.

Reuters (2012) 'Al-Qaeda leader backs Syrian revolt against Assad', *Reuters*, 12 February.

Reuters (2013a) 'Al Qaeda calls for new recruits to fight France', *Reuters*, 17 March 2013.

Reuters (2013b) 'Hundreds of Syria rebels pledge loyalty to Qaeda groups – activists', *Reuters*, 20 September 2013.

Reveron, D.S. (2013) 'When Foreign Policy Goals Exceed Military Capacity, Call the Pentagon', February. Available at: www.fpri.org/articles/2013/02/when-foreign-policy-goals-exceed-military-capacity-call-pentagon (last accessed 8 October 2013).

Rich, P. (2003) 'Al Qaeda and the Radical Islamic Challenge to Western Strategy', in T.R. Mockaitis and P.B. Rich (eds), *Grand Strategy in the War against Terrorism*, London/Portland, OR: Taylor & Francis, pp. 39–54.

Riedel, B. (2013a) 'The Al Qaeda Menace in Africa', *Brookings*, 21 January.

Riedel, B. (2013b) 'New Al-Qaeda Generation May Be Deadliest One', *Al Monitor*, 24 January.

Riedel, B. (2013c) 'Algeria a Complex Ally in War Against al Qaeda', *Brookings*, 3 February.

Riedel, B. (2013d) 'Al Qaeda Is Back', *The Daily Beast*, 26 July.

Riedel, B. (2013e) 'Kenya Terror Strike Was Part Of Al-Qaeda's Latest Global Jihad', *Al-Monitor*, 28 September.

Robb, J. (2007) *Brave New War. The Next Stage of Terrorism and the End of Globalization*, Hoboken, NJ: John Wiley & Sons.

Rogers, P. (2013) 'Al-Qaida and the wider jihadist phenomenon', *Oxford Research Group Monthly Global Security Briefing*, March.

Roggio, B. (2013a) '4 Threat Matrix: Pakistani Taliban "has a global agenda", commander says', *The Long War Journal*, 16 July.

Roggio, B. (2013b) '4 Threat Matrix: So, is al Qaeda still defeated?', *The Long War Journal*, 5 August.

Rosner, Y., Mendelbaum, A. and Schweitzer, Y (2013) 'Backdoor Polts: The Darknet as a Field for Terrorism', INSS Insight 464/10 September. Available at: www.inss.org.il/publications.php?cat=21&incat=&read=12031 (last accessed 11 September 2013).

RT (2013a) 'Mali crisis: French withdraw troops amid fears of prolonged war', *RT*, 10 April.

RT (2013b) '"Far from defeated": Al-Qaeda is expanding and its "most significant foreign enemy" is France', *RT*, 24 July.

Rubin, A.J. (2013) 'Departing French Envoy Has Frank Words on Afghanistan', *New York Times*, 27 April.

Ryan, M.W.S. (2013) *Decoding Al-Qaeda's Strategy. The Deep Battle Against America*, New York: Columbia University Press.

Sanger, D.E. (2013) *Confront and Conceal. Obama's Secret Wars and Surprising Use of American Power*, New York: Broadway Paperbacks.

Satter, D. (2013) 'Russia and the Boston Bombings: the mystery deepens', May. Available at: www.fpri.org/articles/2013/05/russia-and-boston-bombings-mystery-deepens (last accessed 8 October 2013).

Scahill, J. (2013) *Dirty Wars. The World Is A Battlefield*, New York: Nation Books.

Schindler, J. (2012) 'The ugly truth about Algeria', *The National Interest*, 10 July.

Schmidt, M.S. and Moynihan, C. (2012) 'F.B.I. Counterterrorism Agents Monitored Occupy Movement, Records Show', *New York Times*, 24 December.

Schmitt, E. (2013a) 'Militant Threats Test Role of a Pentagon Command in Africa', *New York Times*, 11 February.

Schmitt, E. (2013b) 'Drones in Niger Reflect New U.S. Tack on Terrorism', *New York Times*, 10 July.

Schmitz, G.P. (2013) 'American Psycho. Do Tsarnaev Brothers Represent New Breed of Terrorist?', *SpiegelOnline*, 22 April.

Schneider, B. (2013) 'Mission Creep: When Everything Is Terrorism', *The Atlantic*, 17 July.

Schwarz, S. (2004) *The Two Faces of Islam: Saudi Fundamentalism and Its Role in Terrorism*, New York: Anchor Books.

Scoop (2013) 'Former CIA terrorism expert questions need for GCSB changes', *Scoop*, 6 August.

Secrecy News (2013) 'Insider threat policy equates leakers, spies, terrorists', *Secrecy News*, 65 (16 June).

Selected Wisdom (2013a) 'From AQIM in the Sahel to Shabaab in the Horn, al Qaeda Affiliates Squabble & Fracture', *Selected Wisdom*, 29 May.

Selected Wisdom (2013b) 'Shabaab in Somalia Getting Left Out of Al Qaeada's Party', *Selected Wisdom*, 28 August.

Semple, M. (2013) 'Soldierless Jihad', *Foreign Affairs*, 26 July.

Sen, A.K. (2013) 'Al Qaeda drives Iraq towards chaos; U.S. withdrawal left door open to sectarian battle for power', *Washington Times*, 8 August.

Shane, S. (2013a) 'Suspects With Foot in 2 Worlds, Perhaps Echoing Plots of Past', *New York Times*, 20 April.

Shane, S. (2013b) 'A Homemade Style of Terror: Jihadists Push New Tactics', *New York Times*, 5 May.

Simcox, R. (2013) *Al-Qaeda's Global Footprint. An Assessment of Al-Qaeda's Strength Today*, London: The Henry Jackson Society.

Simcox, R. and Dyer, E. (2013a), *Al Qaeda in the United States. A Complete Analysis of Terrorist Offenses*, London: The Henry Jackson Society.

Simcox, R. and Dyer, E. (2013b) 'Terror Data: US vs. UK', *World Affairs Journal*, July/August.

Simpson, J. (2013) 'The long war against al-Qaeda isn't over', *The Globe and Mail*, 17 August.

Sklarz, E. (2013) 'Hezbollah threatens Latin America'. Available at: http://infosurhoy.com/en_GB/articles/saii/features/main/2013/09/06/feature-01 (last accessed 10 September 2013).

Smith, P.J. (2008) *The Terrorism Ahead. Confronting Transnational Violence in the Twenty-first Century*, Armonk, NY/London: M.E. Sharpe.

Somalia (2013) 'Somalia – Al Shabaab "Infiltrates" Intelligence Services in Mogadishu: UN', 21 July. Available at: http://allafrica.com/stories/201307210335.html (last accessed 10 September 2013).

SpiegelOnline (2012) 'Interview with Ahmed Rashid. The West Should "Change Its Approach to Failing States"', *SpiegelOnline*, 31 December.

SpiegelOnline (2013) 'US Rejects Criticism of Intelligence Practices', *SpiegelOnline*, 19 June.

Starr, B., Yan, H. and Carter, Ch.J. (2013), 'Analyst: Al Qaeda affiliate in Syria now best-equipped of the group', *CNN*, 18 June.

Stern, S.N. (2012) *Saudi Arabia and the Global Islamic Terrorist Network: America and the Fatal Embrace*, London: Palgrave Macmillan.

Stivachtis, Y.A. (2009) 'Searching for Justice and Salvation: Islamic Fundamentalism as a challenge to Western-Centric international order: the case of al Qaeda', *RIEAS Research Paper*, 136 (October): Research Institute for European and American Studies.

Stoffer, H. (2013) 'The Need for a Global Counter-Terrorism Coordinator', *ICCT Policy Brief*, August.

Sullivan, J.P. (2006) 'Terrorism Early Warning and Co-Production of Counterterrorism Intelligence', *Marine Corps Intelligence Association*, Spring.

Susskind, J. (2013) 'Cyber Security, Not Terrorism, Number One Threat to National Security', 15 March. Available at: http://ivn.us/2013/03/15/cyber-security-not-terrorism-number-one-threat-to-national-security/ (last accessed 8 September 2013).

Tawil, C. (2013) 'Al-Qaeda in the Islamic Maghreb Calls on North African Jihadists to Fight in Sahel, Not Syria', *Terrorism Monitor*, 11/6 (20 March).

Taylor, G. (2013) 'Election-year shock: Obama boasts of "decimated" al Qaeda undermined by intel briefs', *Washington Times*, 9 September.

Tertrais, B. (2004) *War Without End. The View from Abroad*, New York/London: The New Press.

Thiessen, M.A. (2013) '"Core al-Qaeda" is not defeated', *Washington Post*, 8 August.

Today's Zaman (2013) 'Turkey not planning to designate Hezbollah terrorist group', *Today's Zaman*, 1 August.

Tope, E.M. (2013) 'The Benefits and Costs of Taking on Al Qaeda in Mali', *International Security Observer*, 25 March.

Travis, A., Osborne, L. and Davis, L. (2013) 'World leaders seek answers on US collection of communication data', *Guardian*, 10 June.

US Department of Defense (2006), *National Military Strategic Plan for the War on Terrorism*, Washington DC.

US Senate Permanent Subcommittee on Investigations (2012) *Federal Support for and Involvement in State and Local Fusion Centers*, Washington DC.

Valenta, J. (2013) 'Al Shabaab's Operation Nairobi: From an ethnic base to a global arena', *Institute of Terrorism Research and Response*, 26 September.

Voice of America (2013) 'Obama: Al-Qaida Core "On Its Way to Defeat"', *Voice of America*, 7 August.

Wall Street Journal (2013) 'The al Qaeda Franchise Threat', *The Wall Street Journal*, 30 April.

Ward, C.A. (2013) 'U.S. Policy on Boko Haram', *Defence iQ*, 28 March.
Warrick, J. (2011) *The Triple Agent. The al-Qaeda Mole Who Infiltrated the CIA*, New York etc.: Doubleday.
Washington Post (2013a) 'French surprise intervention in Mali aims to stop terrorists, but will it trap Paris, too?', *Washington Post*, 14 January.
Washington Post (2013b) 'Text of President Obama's May 23 Speech on national security (full transcript)', *Washington Post*, 23 May.
Watts, C. (2012) 'Radicalization in the U.S. Beyond al Qaeda. Treating the disease of the disconnection'. Available at: www.fpri.org (last accessed 27 August 2013).
Watts, C. (2013) 'Al Qaeda in Iraq publicly rebuts al Qaeda's leader Ayman al-Zawahiri', 17 June. Available at: www.fpri.org/geopoliticus/2013/06/al-qaeda-iraq-publicly-rebuts-al-qaedas-leader-ayman-al-zawahiri (last accessed 8 September 2013).
Watts, D.W. (2009) *How We Can Win the Long War: A New Interagency Approach to the GWOT*, Alabama: Air Command and Staff College.
Webb, B. (2013) 'Navy SEAL: US Special Ops Are Starting To Look A Lot Less Special', *The Business Insider*, 25 September.
The Weekly Number (2013) 'Weekend of terror highlights high and rising hostilities in Kenya and Pakistan', *The Weekly Number*, 24 September.
Wege, C.A. (2012) 'Hizballah in Africa', *Perspectives on Terrorism*, 6/3 (August).
White House (2013). Available at: www.whitehouse.gov/the-press-office/2013/05/23/remarks-president-national-defense-university (last accessed 8 September 2013).
Whittington, K. (2013) 'Terrorism is Gray', *Fair Observer*, 3 July.
Wolton, T. (2005) *4e Guerre Mondiale*, Paris: Bernard Grasset.
Woolsey, J.R. (2002) 'World War IV, speech, 16 November 2002. Available at: www.globalsecurity.org/military/library/report/2002/021116-ww4.htm (last accessed 27 August 2013).
Youssef, M. (2013) 'Al-Qaida leader urges Muslims to unite in struggle', *AP*, 7 April.
Zelin, A.Y., Lebovich, A. and Gartenstein-Ross, D. (2013) 'Al-Qa'ida in the Islamic Maghreb's Tunisia Strategy', *CTC Sentinel*, 23 July.
Zenn, J. (2013) 'Boko Haram's international connections', *CTC Sentinel*, 14 January.
Zimmerman, K. (2013) *The Al Qaeda Network. A new framework for defining the enemy*, Washington DC: American Enterprise Institute Critical Threats Project.

2 Counter-terrorism

The ends of a secular ministry

Charlotte Heath-Kelly

Introduction

It can reasonably be said that political systems require a continued belief from their subjects in order to exist. The collapse of political authority during revolutionary turmoil, where states lose their ability to convince and command, provides a pertinent example of this. Using insights from Lacan and Zizek this paper argues that political authority is produced within a multi-directional relationship between people and state, where the maintenance of belief contributes to the illusion of a foundation beneath law and governance. This symbolic order requires a continuous ideological labour. For example, just as the conception of God disappears without constant efforts by ministers and followers, political authority requires constant ideological reinforcement to maintain its performance. The chapter argues that the practice of counter-terrorism speaks clearly of this 'secular ministry'. Where terrorism challenges the foundations of political authority by destroying aspects of the symbolic order, counter-terrorism attempts to reinstitute the sanctity of the order by silencing the challenge. Across history the secular ministry of counter-terrorism has usually silenced the heretic with force, but the recent emergence of the radicalisation discourse (and its precursors in 1970s dissociation programmes) has focused the unmaking of political challenges upon mindsets. The production of 'radicalisation knowledge' about the vulnerabilities of certain subjects to ideological manipulation has led the secular ministry of counter-terrorism towards the pre-emption and governance of those subjects who deviate from the prescribed symbolic order. In essence, the paper argues that the ends of counter-terrorism are concerned with the continued performance of political authority.

To begin this discussion of secular ministry, it is perhaps best to acknowledge that it is not easy to define sovereignty. How can we quantify the mysterious ability to command with authority? How should we consider the sovereign foundation which underwrites law? There is a wealth of literature in political science which attempts to grapple with this question, but this chapter sides with the philosophical trajectories of figures such as Derrida, Walter Benjamin, Lacan and Žižek and starts from the claim that sovereignty is foundationless. It is instead performed, reproduced and invented. I suggest, following these scholars, that the concept somehow eludes the grasp of easy representation and it requires a sideways glance to capture any of its meaning. We cannot adequately look directly at sovereignty and frame it descriptive terms. Instead it is shrouded in ritual and ceremony. For example, as Shirin Rai (2010) has argued, parliamentary democracy is purposely performed through majestic rituals in grand buildings – and dry analyses of law and political procedure miss the reproduction of political authority through ceremony. These performances and rituals work to constitute the meaning of political authority: the chimera of the sovereign foundation upon which politics rests. And language struggles to approximate this powerful signification work.

In this chapter I will argue that there is a continuous ideological labour undertaken to reproduce the political authority which underwrites state functionality, with a particular focus on practices of counter-terrorism. I will suggest that these processes are the performance of a secular ministry, where foundations are performed in order to underwrite the performance of governance. I will make analogies to the performance of Judeo-Christian religion, which avoids the solid definition of God and, importantly, is founded upon the prohibition of saying his revealed name. This – as with sovereignty – is a tradition which deploys a range of practices to constitute meaning through 'sideways glances' of ritual. The production of centrally important meanings and concepts like sovereignty and God, which cannot otherwise be directly accessed through language, through symbolic performances speaks to psychoanalytic readings of language – where central concepts have a spectre-like existence, and are inaccessible despite (and because of) their importance. In the appropriations of psychoanalytic theory used in international politics, the symbolic order is conceived as the mass of signs, symbols and practices, which make up structures of understanding.

The coherence of the symbolic order (that which connects the linguistic signifier with its signified referent) rests upon a lynchpin called the 'master signifier'. The master signifier itself resists signification – it occupies the place of key concepts such as 'God' or 'sovereignty' which cannot be explained without tautology. They are radically absent from language, and as a result they can hold the symbolic order together. In Zizek's analogy, the symbolic order enables language and politics to function but is itself requiring of ideological labour. Using a reference to the 'point de capiton' (meaning 'upholstery button' or 'anchoring point') he suggests that systems of meaning are held together like upholstery, where buttons pin down stuffing inside a quilt and stop it sliding around. 'Point de capiton' arrest the sliding around between words and their objects in the world. They are anchoring points that temporarily stop the constant shifting of language (Zizek 1989: 102–103). For example, the word 'freedom' does not mean the same thing to all people. Zizek points to how there are varying understandings of the concept, from bourgeois to Marxist. Given all possible interpretations, the meaning of the word freedom could float around endlessly. So how do we ever follow someone's speech when they use the word 'freedom'? Zizek argues, following Lacan, that in every instance the floating of the signifier is arrested retroactively by the 'point de capiton' which locates the word within either left-wing or right-wing constellations (ibid.). There is no inherent meaning to the word, but its usage is fixed for us within constellations of other words.

How does this relate to the performance of political authority? In the same way that monetary value and economic systems require continuous faith in order to exist (the loss of 'market confidence' being so evidently devastating), so political authority disintegrates if people lose faith in it. Authority, like the notion of the 'state' itself, requires belief. Of course, should its salience become questioned, the state resorts to force in an attempt to reinstate itself, but the importance of the intact symbolic order is clear. Systems which arrest the slippage of signifiers must be kept in place – otherwise the performance of authority becomes meaningless. In the following section I link the practice of terrorism to the exposure of this ideological labour and the exploitation of gaps within the symbolic order. Counter-terrorism then emerges as a practice which aims to plug the gaps in the performance of order and security, and to reinstate the symbolic order.

How does terrorism disrupt the symbolic order?

While psychoanalytic theory is often abstract and difficult to read, the explosion of bombs and the collapse of buildings are undeniably visceral. But I am going to argue that there is an interesting connection between the tenets of psychoanalysis and the practice of political violence. The purpose of political violence is to damage the links in the symbolic order that hold political authority in place, thereby (it is imagined) bringing people to the revolutionary cause through this revelation, or via the equally visceral state response. Violence and meaning are intimately connected, even if the literature within International Relations does not often address this. Targets, such as symbolically significant buildings or bodies, are selected because of their place in the symbolic order and deliberately remade through the experience of violence and pain. One need only speak to militants about the selection of targets and the utilisation of violence to reveal the connection between violence and the remaking of meaning (Heath-Kelly 2013a). Political violence functions to remakes its target – erasing its previous constitution through discursive processes and remaking it to symbolise something else. Key examples include the targeting of the Oslo government quarter and Utoya island by Anders Breivik, or the devastating unmaking of the New York World Trade Center and the Pentagon on 9/11. If the practice of political violence was not about the destruction of important nodes in the symbolic order, then symbolically important targets would not have been chosen by the perpetrators.

'Terrorist' violence, then, is not a breakdown of politics – it is political action with meaning. It acts upon meaning, trying to break down the hegemonic symbolic order by exploding certain key locations which hold it together. And state reactions confirm this. Political violence produces a hyperbolic response. Legal and political prohibitions of such violence suggest that terrorism is a terribly destructive force, a particularly awful kind of violence and threat. But all rational argument shows that it poses a statistically insignificant threat to life. For example, John Mueller has shown that the likelihood of dying in a terrorist event, if you are American, is the same as being hit by lightning, killed by 'accident-causing-deer', or though severe peanut allergy (Mueller 2006: 13). We do not see many campaigns against lightning, deer or peanuts – and there would be public outrage if any such campaign were allocated the amount of funds dedicated to counter-terrorism! This apparent imbalance suggests, however, that political authority finds terrorism particularly dangerous *even if human bodies do not*. This chapter argues that states locate this extreme level of threat in the damage terrorism can inflict upon the symbolic order. But how does it do this?

In Jenny Edkins' description of the reactions to the 9/11 attacks, the interruption of meaning and language was placed centrally. She highlighted how people stood with mouths gaping, unable to process the horror or to put it into words:

> One of the most striking images of September 11 was that of people on the sidewalks in New York, their hands clasped over their mouths, transfixed in horror as they watched the impossible turning into the real in front of their eyes. This gesture was repeated, endlessly, on our television screens, along with the repetitions of the planes slamming into the buildings, and it testified to the unspeakable [...]. Newspapers the following day printed nothing but pictures. And, in all the television coverage, time and time again, not a voiceover, but an image behind all the reports and discussions, as if to show, again and again, to anyone who hadn't seen it yet, that this was real. People sat in silence, absorbed, thinking yet unable to think, overwhelmed.
>
> (Edkins 2002: 243)

The visceral horror of the attacks temporarily overwhelmed the capacity of language and the attribution of meaning. In studies of trauma these arguments are common place – trauma is understood as a reaction to violence which disrupts expression, and disrupts meaning. It is beyond the politics of everyday language where signifiers are 'quilted', by point de capiton, so that they refer to commonplace objects. Spectacular violence disrupts language and this symbolic order. The myths of security and the sovereign state then temporarily cease to exist. The performance of politics is disrupted. To refer again to the selection of targets in political violence: the symbols of a regime are used, and grotesquely remade, against it. With the jolt of a bombing at a key node in the performance of political authority, the quilting of signifier-to-signified is disrupted and meaning is (temporarily) up for grabs.

This is something that the CIA and the US government understand very well, as they have played important roles in the development of torture techniques and 'shock and awe' campaigns which exploit the psychological (linguistic, and symbolic) shock of violence. The US National Defense Strategy (1996) document 'Shock and Awe: Achieving Rapid Dominance' traces the doctrine of shock and awe back to the era of the Chinese military strategist Sun Tzu, who observed around 500 BC that disarming an enemy before battle through violent intimidation was the most effective tactic a commander could employ (Ullman and Wade 1996: 19). Recent military thought has developed this focus on the coercive visual and affective power of the spectacular violent act – attributing to violence a force which can cognitively disarm its witnesses, creating a temporary blank canvass upon which an outside will can be inscribed. The 'glazed expressions' noted of the survivors of great bombardments have been interpreted as symptoms of a software crash – one which presents an opportunity to reboot the disoriented subject with a new political programme:

> The basis for Rapid Dominance rests in the ability to affect the will, perception and understanding of an adversary through imposing sufficient Shock and Awe [...]. One recalls from old photographs and movie or television screens, the comatose and glazed expressions of survivors of the great bombardments of World War I and the attendant horrors and death of trench warfare. These images and expressions of shock transcend race, culture, and history. Indeed, TV coverage of Desert Storm vividly portrayed Iraqi soldiers registering these effects of battlefield Shock and Awe. In our excursion, we seek to determine whether and how Shock and Awe can become sufficiently intimidating and compelling factors to force or otherwise convince an adversary to accept our will.
>
> (Ullman and Wade 1996: 19–20)

Naomi Klein has provided a detailed analysis of successive US administrations' uses of violence as shock treatment – developing from the discovery, in the 1950s at McGill University, that electroshock therapy can radically reorganise the political subject into a more malleable state (Klein 2007). The 'shock' that war, terror attacks, *coup d'état* and natural disasters produce has been repeatedly harnessed within political projects to extend hegemony and to rollback social democratic systems. Klein has traced the inducement and manipulation of shock by US agencies and their partners through the removal of President Salvador Allende from government in Chile on 11 September 1973, the mass disappearances in Argentina and Uruguay, the Thatcher years in Britain, the 9/11 attacks in New York and Washington, and the US mission in Iraq. All these examples (and more) share a crucial feature – the use of violence to unmake political worlds and to found new ones. Indeed, paralleling Elaine Scarry's thesis (1985) on the potential of pain to unmake language, two CIA manuals were declassified in the 1990s which detail the understandings behind interrogation – such that violence is not used to coerce, but rather to *unmake* the victim before they are politically reconstructed:

> There is an interval – which may be extremely brief – of suspended animation, a kind of psychological shock or paralysis. It is caused by a traumatic or subtraumatic experience that explodes, as it were, the world that is familiar to the subject as well as his image of himself within that world. Experienced interrogators recognise this effect when it appears and know that at this moment the source is far more open to suggestion, far likelier to comply.
>
> (CIA 1963: 66, see also 82–100)

The connection between violence and meaning becomes very clear when we contrast the levels of political attention, and funds, directed towards counter-terrorism and other phenomena which could be considered threatening. As stated earlier, 'accident-causing deer' cause more fatalities than terrorism, but they are not made the subject of security practice. Similarly, security practice does not often address events and structures that produce, or have the potential to produce, large scale levels of death and disruption – like climate change, or poverty. So, security must be doing something else, other than preventing death.

If we look the central themes of security practice – dangerous external others, terrorists – then it becomes possible to argue that its function is the maintenance of ontological security. As David Campbell has persuasively argued, the construction of threats provides an 'other' against which the self can be defined (Campbell 1998). Security is about the performance of national self rather than the prevention of death, the performance of secular ministry – if you will. And to adapt Campbell's argument for the resilience and counter-terrorism era, where the external other can be hidden within the home territory, security functions to quash challenges to the symbolic order. Where efforts are made to disrupt the production of meaning and reality, the state responds with huge resources to reassert its performance of authority and identity.

This performance of political authority and identity can be understood as the 'name' which situates the performance of sovereignty and politics. As Zizek describes, politics appeared for the first time in ancient Greece when the members of the demos presented themselves as stand-ins for the whole of society (Zizek 1998: 988). This movement involved a 'short-circuit' between the universal and the particular, where the singular presented itself as the embodiment of society by taking and performing 'in its name' (Ibid: 989). Politics, then, can be understood as the functioning of the 'in the name' operation. Zizek describes the function of politics as the attempt to foreclose the emergence of political challenge – where another salient identification of the singular 'in the name' of a universal might threaten its terms. Here the relevance of terrorism and counter-terrorism should become clear: political violence offers a challenge to established systems of meaning. It contests. And because the performance of political authority requires an intact symbolic order, the function of security and counter-terrorism is to quash these challenges to the 'name' in which politics is performed.

While this suppression has often been performed through violence and extraordinary police powers such as assassinations or internments, a particularly interesting recent development in the protection of the 'name' is the radicalisation discourse. This discourse permeates contemporary counter-terrorism architectures and explicitly identifies the existence of another 'name' for political performance – the 'radicalised' name – as threatening.

Practices of counter-terrorism as secular ministry

In the past, counter-terrorism has smashed and imprisoned those who use violence to contest the sovereignty of the political and legal order. It still does; but since the

1980s it has also taken an interest in remaking radicals. Counter-terrorism now explicitly needs you to believe in the legitimacy of the existing order. Those who do not often find themselves subjected to disciplinary practices of counter-terrorism, despite having never handled a weapon. I will trace these developments in this section, while arguing that they reveal a consistent orientation of counter-terrorism towards the maintenance of the symbolic order. Counter-terrorism functions to eliminate and remake those challenges to the reproduction of sovereignty. And in the contemporary era, you need not undertake actions to be framed as a threat to the symbolic order. If your views are identified as threatening and destabilising to the discourse which legitimates power, then practices of secular ministry (specifically counter-radicalisation) will likely target you.

The history of counter-terrorism and colonial policing (as they are often practised as one and the same – the marshalling and subjection of a racialised other) is replete with examples of extraordinary force. This force operates beyond the normal bounds of the law to render, detain, beat, maim and kill. Often it is of no importance if the recipient has committed any particular crime, only that their body is representative of an antagonistic discourse or way of life. For example, the mass internment of 1.5 million Kikuyu in Kenya by British forces during the Mau-Mau 'emergency' of 1952–1960 (Elkins 2005); the mass internment of Greek-Cypriots during the EOKA 'emergency' of 1955–1960 (Heath-Kelly 2013a); the mass internment practiced in Northern Ireland (Feldman 1991: 86–89); the brutal (and often lethal) 'policing' of autonomist and workerist demonstrations in Italy during the 1970s (Hajek 2013; Heath-Kelly 2013a); and, of course, the extraordinary rendition and detention of suspect bodies during the War on Terror (Gregory 2004; Steyn 2004; Williams 2012). This selection of diverse examples indicates something about the variety of cases where force beyond the normal extent of the law is utilised to suppress bodies deemed representative of a threatening political challenge – threatening and political because their existence could point to the arbitrariness of the existing symbolic order, from which meaning and the reproduction of power are obtained.

These movements and bodies are interpreted as posing a challenge to the reproduction of the sovereign order and massive force is deployed against them. But it is interesting to highlight the discrepancy between the relative strength of these 'terrorists' and the states which subjugate them. None of these movements or groupings could have conceivably overturned the imperial formations they opposed, with armed force or democratic momentum. These pathways were closed to them, precisely because of that same power differential. Bands of EOKA fighters in Cyprus would never have been able to militarily defeat the British Empire, in the same way that Italian demonstrators would never have come to power in their own country (especially in the Cold War climate where the United States had a habit of covertly removing elected socialist governments). And yet rather than ignore these movements, and rest easy in their power, states and international forces have dedicated huge resources to crushing small groups of rebels. Why? And why would movements and individuals accept these huge risks to their success?

The ex-militants I have spoken to were cognisant of this power differential and its ramifications. They even used it to their advantage on several occasions. For example, Thassos Sophocleous (a district commander in the Cypriot EOKA group) stated that:

> It was very fun to believe that we could beat the English Empire! We are only a small village without ammunition, without any weapons, – we didn't believe such a thing. We didn't believe we could beat the English, but we could trouble them. And we could do it forever, as the IRA did. Even one fighter in Cyprus could cause trouble to the English. Even one fighter. You go into Kyrenia with a weapon, you shoot one today, the other day we will go to battle – even one fighter could keep them. But we didn't believe, never believe, even Grivas said that. We make our revolution so as to give all over the world to the people, their countries, that we want our freedom. To send a sign to the other people, to send a sign all over the world that here there is a small island under the English, the colonial – to let them know all over the world that we want our freedom. That was really the fighting. We never believed that we could beat the English Empire.
>
> (Sophocleous quoted in Heath-Kelly 2013a: 70)

It did not really seem to matter to Sophocleous that a group of militants could not 'win' over the British Empire. Instead their immediate goal was to break the media blackout and British symbolic order by committing acts of violence that would 'send a sign all over the world'. Similarly, the huge power differential between the imperial force and band of rebels with archaic rifles did not matter for the British constitution of those rebels as a 'significant threat'. This paradox is very interesting as it suggests that the function of political violence, and its suppression, is a struggle over the unchallenged performance of political discourse and the symbolic order. It does not matter that the rebels cannot win, because their mere existence destabilises the performance of sovereignty – that mythical, invented foundation which underwrites law. The existence of another possible interpretation of nation or authority is enough to unleash the full-force of counter-terrorism, because it affects the temporary fixing of meaning in the symbolic order. While master-signifiers consolidate the order by arresting the slippage of signifiers and signified, the existence of alternate readings of legitimacy begin to unravel the fabric which has been held together by Zizek's 'point de capiton'. The secular ministry then deploys extraordinary force upon groups which have no real chance of militarily or democratically overturning existing relations of power (as these doors have already been forced closed upon them).

Italian ex-militants also described their experiences of revolutionary struggle in similar terms. Sergio Segio, a leading figure in the autonomist-leftist group *Prima Linea*, described the differences between his group and the more Marxist *Brigate Rosse* to highlight the strategy of obtaining small spaces of counter-power where subjects could be remade:

I'm mentioning these to make you understand the difference between us and *Brigate Rosse*. *Brigate Rosse* thought, their theory was that they had to attack the heart of the state – like in Russia, they had to attack the Winter Palace – and we thought this vision was old and not for us. We had a different concept of power, a sort of distributed power; we referred more to Foucault. The vision was of creating a counter-power, not a power that was replacing the old one. A different society. It was not a struggle towards taking power or being powerful, but against power. This was a small revolution in terms of theory. *Brigate Rosse* thought of struggle to get the power, and this is the main difference.

(Segio quoted in Heath-Kelly 2013a: 94)

Given the mighty power of the Italian state and its US protector, *Prima Linea* aimed to open small spaces of autonomy through protest and occupation – where normal relations of power no longer existed. And while *Prima Linea* developed over time towards the use of assassination to open these new spaces of politics, their autonomist colleagues who only utilised strategies of housing occupation and demonstration also felt the brunt of state repression. Offering an alternative conception of politics undermines the secular ministry and provokes a security response, even if the 'threat' has no potential to seriously undermine or overturn the existing order. This is due to the destabilisation of the symbolic order, mentioned earlier.

However in the contemporary era, the practice of hard counter-terrorism has become supplemented with counter-radicalisation policy – a softer, disciplinary type of intervention. This strategy also speaks clearly to the suppression of alternative 'names' of authority and the consolidation of the symbolic order through counter-terrorism. Incidentally, the roots of counter-radicalisation can be traced to the discoveries of the Italian judiciary and prison system that imprisoned militants were much more likely to renounce their challenges to authority when given inducements, rather than beaten or tortured. The dissociation process in Italy is not widely written upon, but a trend of footnoting the experiment as an early 'deradicalisation process', or within literature on disengagement from terrorism or effective counter-terrorism, is beginning to appear (Bjorgo and Horgan 2009; Bovenkerk 2011: 272; Horgan 2008; Muro 2010).

During their incarceration, Italian militants organically organised discussion groups to 'rethink' their struggle. The dissociation process emerged from these discussions, although that term is controversial because it is often interpreted as relating to the legal inducements offered by the Italian government for militants to renounce the name of their struggle (such as reductions in sentences). These discussions and inducements worked in tandem during the 1980s and produced remarkable phenomena. While it is not surprising that militants serving life sentences would want to collectively reflect on the choices that led them to jail, the reaction of the state was astonishing. By 1986, when it became clear that the 'terrorist organisations' had been defeated, Italy passed the dissociation laws – which reduced sentences for those who had abandoned the armed struggle *without the need for collaboration or confession.* Only a renunciation of the armed struggle was required. These laws also engendered the 'rehabilitation' of militants through programmes of professional training and day release to work outside prison.

If a militant renounced the struggle, they would no longer be considered an enemy of society. If they renounced the alternative 'name' of authority which so challenged the state's secular ministry, their sentences were reduced and they would find themselves moving towards the work-release programme – in preparation for eventual freedom. This from the same state that killed demonstrators, tortured leftists suspects and conspired with neofascist proxies to bomb public places on multiple occasions during the 1960s, 1970s and 1980s (Cento Bull 2007). This remarkable example highlights the central importance of contesting/defending the symbolic order to the terrorism/counter-terrorism dynamic. Once the 'name' of the struggle was renounced by militants, they did not need to share information with the Italian state or cooperate in any other way to lose their identification as a threat (Heath-Kelly 2013a). Their renunciation of alternate forms of legitimacy and sovereignty ended their perceived danger to the state. They began their path to freedom by renouncing the 'name' of their struggle.

This remarkable era in Italian counter-terrorism has interesting parallels for the contemporary era of radicalisation discourse. This paradigm also centralises adherence to a counter-hegemonic 'name' or discourse as the central facet of terrorism and counter-terrorism. This discourse of radicalisation has come to underwrite community counter-terrorism policies across Europe, the United States and Australia and is featured within the deradicalisation programmes which exist in Indonesia, Saudi Arabia, the Philippines and Pakistan. It takes the most salient and arresting components of terrorist attacks (their performance in the name of an ideology) and reads this backwards to assert the causality of ideology in the process of becoming-terrorist. It does not seem to matter that such processes of 'becoming-terrorist' through radicalisation have been resoundingly rejected by the academic literature (Githens-Mazer and Lambert 2010; Heath-Kelly 2013b; Thomas 2010), nor that counter-radicalisation strategies result in the creation of suspected communities and perpetuate unhelpful notions of improper citizenship on which extremist right-wing groups feed. These facts are ignored by the political sponsors of radicalisation policy. All that really matters about radicalisation policy is that it functions to perform interventions in an invented trajectory towards militancy, enabling counter-terrorism to pre-emptively target, suppress and remake subjects who articulate alternative visions of politics.

Importantly, for our discussion of counter-terrorism as 'secular ministry', it is the performance of an alternate 'name' that provokes the attention of the security services. One need no longer actively take up arms to become a subject of counter-terrorism. Instead, counter-radicalisation policies target those who espouse alternate theories of political legitimacy. The ideas behind potential violence are made problematic through the radicalisation discourse and counter-radicalisation policy dedicates itself to intervening in lives made 'dangerous' by, and 'vulnerable' to, those beliefs. In the framing of the UK's Prevent strategy, for example, 'the ideology of violent extremism' is centralised as the threatening kernel of contemporary terrorism, and security practice dedicates itself to 'isolate apologists for terrorism and provide support to vulnerable individuals' (Home Office 2009: 84).

How have ideas become so threatening in a supposedly liberal state? How can the context of counter-terrorism affect the deployment of liberal tolerance so profoundly? Much interesting work has been published on the contemporary fate of liberal tolerance vis-à-vis the articulation of an Islamist threat (Croft 2012; Dobbernack and Modood 2013). Limitations of space prevent a full engagement with these issues here, except to highlight the paradoxical situation whereby liberal states wholeheartedly espouse convictions that certain ideas are risky and can turn citizens into bloodthirsty terrorists. These dangerous ideas are thus prohibited, lest they work their evil witchcraft upon vulnerable minds (Heath-Kelly 2012). After a brief description of ways in which dangerous ideas are prohibited and the interventions made by counter-radicalisation policy in lives understood as vulnerable, I will return to connect the securitisation of radical ideas to the practice of secular ministry.

In its various formulations, Prevent has acted upon spheres and persons that supposedly propagate dangerous extremist ideas which hijack vulnerable minds. This has included a focus on university campuses, Internet forums, prisons, schools and the monitoring of 'Muslim communities' (themselves produced through demographic statistics). In a review (published by the Department of Communities and Local Government) of how local authorities spent the original £6 million Prevent budget between 2007 and 2008, funded projects were divided into seven types of governmental intervention within 'Muslim communities' — aimed at conducting the conduct of those deemed vulnerable to 'extremist ideology'. These involved training activities, education, debate/discussion, leadership and management activities, sports and/or recreation, arts/cultural and 'other' (DCLG 2008: 19). The most common activities (54 per cent) funded by local authorities involved fostering discussion and debate among Muslims about violent extremism, with arts and cultural activities (such as a local theatre production on extremism in communities) making up 19 per cent of the total, and sports and recreation activities (such as the funding of a boxing club as a diversion for young Muslims) making up 13 per cent (DCLG 2008: 18–23). Such interventions attempt to instil responsibility for the self-management of one's conduct, a central feature of 'liberal' assumptions about the self (Rose 2000), while simultaneously deploying conceptions about the potential riskiness of Muslim communities. Local authorities have reached the apparently bizarre conclusion, given the discourses of 'radicalisation' and security risk, that terrorism can and should be prevented through funding young Muslims to play cricket and football (as Wakefield council have done with their DCLG grant, among other things: Kundnani 2009: 18).

To express the importance of this shift in counter-terrorism bluntly, the activities of PREVENT suggest that cricket and football will somehow make you appropriately British and unthreatening. According to the deployment of counter-radicalisation policy, an immersion in an inclusive British society with British pastimes will increase the resilience of the vulnerable racialised subject to radical ideas. Counter-radicalisation policy frames lives as vulnerable and then attempts to inoculate them against counter-hegemonic ideologies by integrating them into a particular symbolic order of beliefs – often through very banal activities like cricket or 'discussion groups'. On other occasions, these interventions are less banal. The Channel Programme, for instance, responds to information from teachers and social workers to make tailored and individualised interventions in young lives. By 2009, 200 children (some as young as 13) had been subject to 'interventions' vis-à-vis the Channel Programme, according to the Association of Chief Police Officers' spokesman on terrorism, Norman Bettison (Kundnani 2009: 33). By June 2011, this figure had exceeded 1,000 young people (Bettison 2011). Should you express 'risky' views, you will draw the attention of counter-terrorism policy – regardless of your intentions to commit violent acts. The subject of counter-radicalisation policy might not pose a risk to society, but they may be 'vulnerable' to becoming risky. Which, paradoxically, renders them as a threat.

The paradoxical unification of riskiness and vulnerability has been formalised by government in advice given to schools (who can refer pupils for Channel interventions). In the document *Learning Together to be Safe: A Toolkit to Help Schools Contribute to the Prevention of Violent Extremism*, the Department for Children, Schools and Families merged the categories of 'at risk' and 'riskiness' to form a new subjectivity of 'young people [who need to be protected] from harm or causing harm' (DCSF 2008, 13). Indeed, in advice from government to teachers, indicators that flag a child who needs to be 'protected from becoming risky' include 'expressions of political ideology such as support for the Islamic political system', 'a focus on scripture as an exclusive moral source', 'a conspiratorial mindset' and 'seeing the West as a source of evil' (Heath-Kelly 2013b).

This subjectivity of 'at-risk of becoming risky' is prescient for our discussion of secular ministry, because even the state admits that these young people are not dangerous. Instead they are targeted for intervention under counter-terrorism policy because they might believe in a different formulation of political authority, one which destabilises the articulation and reproduction of hegemonic power through the symbolic order and its associated rituals. Here we find the mirror image of the Italian revolutionary subjects serving jail terms for their participation in subversion. Where their renunciation of an alternate 'name' was perceived to end their constitution as 'threatening', the radicalised subject of the contemporary era is rendered as dangerous through their supposed articulation of, and subscription to, a different 'name'.

Counter-terrorism, then, can be interpreted as ideological labour which serves to perpetuate and consolidate a particular symbolic order. Where challenges emerge to the constitution of authority, counter-terrorism (in its many forms) acts to suppress the articulation of dissent. Dissent is identified through security technologies as the propagation of threatening actions and views – threatening because they impinge upon the constitution of the symbolic order. Counter-terrorism does not simply target actors within armed networks, but those bodies who are identified as representative of challenges to the reproduction of political authority. It creates its own threat-subjects from racialised bodies, vulnerable subjects and dangerous ideas. Authority must continually evoke its own foundations to justify the use of power and to elide the indeterminacy which plagues the practice of politics and sovereignty. The ends of counter-terrorism, then, are connected to a secular ministry which protects the 'name' of the sovereign or the divine from those bodies and views that might supposedly expose this indeterminacy.

Conclusion

It can reasonably be said that political systems require a continued belief from their subjects in order to exist. In this chapter I have highlighted the perverse tendency of counter-terrorism strategies to target bodies and groups that lack any material ability to overturn political systems, and I have argued that their perceived (and discursively constructed) threat emerges from their disruption of processes of ideological labour which reproduce sovereignty. As Thassos Sophocleous of the Cypriot anti-colonial group EOKA so clearly stated, the mission of the group was to continually disrupt the operation of imperial power and send a message. They knew that a band of lightly armed rebels could never overturn the British Empire, but they understood that they could demonstrably contest and disrupt the discourses of power which framed Cyprus as the rightful property of that empire. This disruption of the ideological labour required to continually reproduce authoritative foundations for the imperial concept was interpreted, as they intended, as extremely threatening by the British regime – who dedicated huge efforts and resources to crushing the struggle and demonising the fighters as terrorists.

This, I contend, is how the terrorism/counter-terrorism dynamic works. It is bound up within wider political practices of maintaining and performing political authority. One is identified as a terrorist, or a potential terrorist, subject if one contests and disrupts the ideological work undertaken to consolidate sovereignty and to produce illusory foundations for its political existence. The performance of an alternative 'name' disrupts the processes of ritual and discourse which secure authority. It damages the imposition of 'point de capiton', which arrest the sliding of meaning. Persons are identified as security threats not because they pose a material challenge to the state, but because they disrupt discursive processes of legitimation and the imagining of foundations for sovereignty. Here the mass imprisonment of (often non-militant) bodies in Kenya, Cyprus, Italy, Northern Ireland and Guantanamo Bay becomes conceivable. These persons are not detained and punished for anything they have done – otherwise judicial systems would have to prove their guilt (something avoided, in the contemporary era, by the United States judicial system relative to the Guantanamo detainees). Instead they are interpreted to represent a discursive threat to the rendering of authority. As such, counter-terrorism must plug up the gaps in the symbolic order that these subjects pose. Counter-radicalisation pre-emptively practices this project by identifying and intervening upon these subjects-rendered-as-dangerous, and by providing a narrative of their inherent pathology which silences any political content of their beliefs. By rendering the alternative 'radicalised' discourse as 'extremist' and pathological, counter-terrorism policy attempts to invalidate and neutralise its relevance – thereby neutralising its potential disruption of the rituals and discursive processes that legitimate authority.

The 'name' of the sovereign must be protected at all costs. Welcome to the secular ministry and its performance through practices of counter-terrorism.

References

Bettison, N. (2011) 'Sir Norman Bettison: Prevent Review, 7 June 2011', Association of Chief Police Officers. Available at: www.acpo.police.uk/ThePoliceChiefsBlog/SirNormanBettisonPreventReview7June2011.aspx. (last accessed 11 June 2013).

Bjorgo, Tore and Horgan, John (eds) (2009) *Leaving Terrorism Behind: Individual and Collective Disengagement* (Abingdon: Routledge).

Bovenkerk, Frank (2011) 'On Leaving Criminal Organisations', *Crime, Law and Social Change*, 55 (4), pp. 261–276.

Campbell, David (1998) *Writing Security: United States Foreign Policy and the Politics of Identity* (Minneapolis: University of Minnesota Press).

Cento Bull, Anna (2007) *Italian Neofascism: The Strategy of Tension and the Politics of Nonreconciliation* (Oxford: Berghahn).

CIA (1963) *Kubark Counterintelligence Interrogation* in 'Torturing Democracy: The Torture Archive', http://torturingdemocracy.org/ (last accessed 28 September 2011).

Croft, Stuart (2012) *Securitizing Islam: Identity and the Search for Security* (Cambridge: Cambridge University Press).

DCLG (Department for Communities and Local Government) (2008) *Preventing Violent Extremism Pathfinder Fund: Mapping of Project Activities 2007/2008* (London: HM Government).

DCSF (Department for Children, Schools and Families) (2008) *Learning Together to be Safe: A Toolkit to Help Schools Contribute to the Prevention of Violent Extremism* (London: Department for Education).

Dobbernack, Jan and Tariq Modood (2013) *Tolerance, Intolerance and Respect: Hard to Accept?* (Basingstoke: Palgrave Macmillan).

Edkins, Jenny (2002) 'Forget Trauma? Responses to September 11', *International Relations*, 16 (2), pp. 243–256.

Elkins, Caroline (2005) *Britain's Gulag: The Brutal End of Empire in Kenya* (London: Jonathan Cape).

Feldman, Allen (1991) *Formations of Violence: The Narrative of the Body and Political Terror in Northern Ireland* (Chicago: The University of Chicago Press).

Githens-Mazer, Jonathan and Robert Lambert (2010) 'Why Conventional Wisdom on Radicalization Fails: The Persistence of a Failed Discourse', *International Affairs*, 86 (4), pp. 889–901.

Gregory, Frank (2004) *The Colonial Present: Afghanistan, Palestine, Iraq* (Oxford: Blackwell).

Hajek, Andrea (2013) *Negotiating Memories of Protest in Western Europe: The Case of Italy* (Basingstoke: Palgrave Macmillan).

Heath-Kelly, Charlotte (2012) 'Can we Laugh Yet? Reading Post-9/11 Counter-Terrorism Policy as Magical Realism and Opening a Third Space of Resistance', *European Journal on Criminal Policy and Research*, 18 (4), pp. 343–360.

Heath-Kelly, Charlotte (2013a) *Politics of Violence: Militancy, International Politics, Killing in the Name* (Abingdon: Routledge).

Heath-Kelly, Charlotte (2013b) 'Counter-Terrorism and the Counterfactual: Producing the "Radicalisation" Discourse and the UK Prevent Strategy', *British Journal of Politics and International Relations*, 15 (3), pp. 394–415.

Home Office (2009) *Pursue Prevent Protect Prepare: The United Kingdom's Strategy for Countering International Terrorism* (London: HM Government).

Horgan, John (2008) 'Deradicalization or Disengagement? A Process in Need of Clarity and a Counterterrorism Initiative in Need of Evaluation', *Perspectives on Terrorism* 2/4. Available at: http://terrorismanalysts.com/pt/index.php/pot/article/view/32/html (last accessed 9 October 2013).

Klein, Naomi (2007) *The Shock Doctrine* (London: Penguin).

Kundnani, A. (2009) *Spooked: How Not to Prevent Violent Extremism* (London: Institute of Race Relations).

Mueller, John (2006) *Overblown: How Politicians and the Terrorism Industry Inflate National Security Threats, and Why We Believe Them* (New York: Free Press).

Muro, Diego (2010) 'Counter-Terrorist Strategies in Western Europe: A Comparative Analysis of Germany, Italy, Spain and the UK', *EUI Working Papers* MWP 2010/06.

Rai, Shirin M. (2010) Analysing Ceremony and Ritual in Parliament, *The Journal of Legislative Studies*, 16 (3), pp. 284–297.

Rose, N. (2000) 'Government and control', *The British Journal of Criminology*, 40 (2), pp. 321–339.

Scarry, Elaine (1985) *The Body in Pain: The Making and Unmaking of the World* (Oxford: Oxford University Press).

Steyn, Johan (2004) 'Guantanamo Bay: The Legal Black Hole', *International and Comparative Law Quarterly*, 53 (1), pp. 1–15.

Thomas, Paul (2012) 'Failed and Friendless: The UK's 'Preventing Violent Extremism' Program, *British Journal of Politics and International Relations*, 12 (3), pp. 442–458.

Ullman, Harlan and Wade Jr., James (1996) *Shock and Awe: Achieving Rapid Dominance* (Washington DC: National Defense University).

Williams, Andrew T. (2012) *A Very British Killing: The Death of Baha Mousa* (London: Jonathan Cape).

Zizek, Slavoj (1989) *The Sublime Object of Ideology* (London: Verso).

Zizek, Slavoj (1998) 'A Leftist Plea for "Eurocentrism"', *Critical Inquiry*, 24 (4), pp. 988–1009.

3 Spatial and temporal imaginaries in the securitisation of terrorism[1]

Kathryn Marie Fisher

> At the time a senior Western intelligence officer was quoted as saying that a "very senior Egyptian was killed" in the raid, along with three Kenyans and a Somali. That was technically true – but in reality the Egyptian had not even been born in the country for which he held a passport. It would have been more accurate to describe him as a British terror suspect who once ran a car valeting business in London.
>
> (Woods *et al.* 2013)

> Indeed, contemporary neoimperialism resides in part on the dominance of a spatial story that inhibits the recognition of alternatives. A geopolitical imaginary, the map of nation-states, dominates ethical discourse at a global level.
>
> (Shapiro 1997: 175)

> Not civilization but civility (civilitas) was the word coined to justify a new code of social behavior and, at the same time, to distinguish between those who used or were aware of it from those who were out of the game.
>
> (Mignolo 2010: 34)

Introduction

On 28 February 2013, an article appeared in the British newspaper the *Independent* that was titled 'British terror suspects quietly stripped of citizenship ... then killed by drones: Exclusive: Secret war on enemy within'. The spatial and temporal tones of the article's title permeate its discussion on United Kingdom (UK) and United States (US) security practice. Stemming from a 2002 measure to strip citizenship from dual passport holders if they had done anything 'seriously prejudicial' towards the UK, the authors describe how British citizenship was removed from suspected terrorists. A similar phenomenon of citizenship removal was recently discussed in an article on the US 'Disposition Matrix'. With respect to four men recently killed in US drone strikes it is explained how 'they were all Muslims, all accused of terrorism offences, and all British (or they *were* British: curiously, all of them unexpectedly lost their British citizenship just as they were about to become unstuck)' [emphasis added] (Cobain 2013: 2).

Even though these individuals had been born in the UK or had lived there for decades, once they were accused of terrorism offences and targeted through counter-terrorism practice, their identities were reconfigured to erase any presence of Britishness. With this erasure externalising the threat they posed as one from a foreign other, there was no longer a fear of 'civilizational erosion' (Persaud 2004: 77) from within.[2] Their Britishness was replaced by their past connections to other geographic spaces; their identities reconfigured as terrorist outsiders with no binding association to the self.[3] These spatial imaginaries of identification, what I would consider geographic assumptions of belonging, were significant in this context because they informed intersubjective understandings of risk as largely 'foreign' in nature: as external to the self. Such disconnection between threat and referent, between them and us, enabled exceptional security practices such as drone strikes to be legitimised even if such strikes could result in situations of insecurity or be counterproductive in the fight against terror. These imaginaries are important, more broadly, because they demonstrate the significance that assertions about history and geography – about time and space – have in constructions of self and other, and the consequences that follow these.

Terrorist threat construction is a forever-unfinished practice of othering. Pre-emptive counter-terrorism practices that go beyond what may be considered normal politics are legitimised through processes of securitisation that frame the threat and referent in particular ways at particular times.[4] 'International terrorism' as a threat identifier has had a distinctive consequence in terms of collective meaning and material practice by positioning the threat in terms of inside/outside borders of inclusion and exclusion. This chapter focuses on the significance of temporal and spatial imaginaries to these processes by exploring the role of discourses of distance, danger and otherness in the securitisation of terrorism during the late twentieth century, and the centrality of the 'international' in constructions of threat in this context.

The chapter begins with an introduction to some postcolonial themes, helping us to conceptualise the 'international' commonplace of counter-terrorism with a more critical eye in terms of racial and geographic assumptions. The next section provides an empirical illustration of how some official British discourse in the 1980s and 1990s securitised terrorism by spatially differentiating the international other from the referent 'self', as well as from 'other' terrorist others through patterns of externalisation. Discourses of legitimation for counter-terrorism increasingly drew upon international framings, with the core of twenty-first century British counter-terrorism strategy known as CONTEST (until 2011) itself called 'The United Kingdom's Strategy for Countering *International* Terrorism' [emphasis added].[5] But collective meanings of 'international terrorism' and its possible implications have yet to be sufficiently investigated. It is not especially innovative to claim here that knowledge associated with terrorism depends upon inside/outside boundary construction, or that threatening others are personified in opposition to a presumably uncontroversial self. However, focusing on the way that the 'international' is articulated in these securitisations of terrorism will hopefully provoke some new thoughts in terms of how identity, discourse, security and insecurity can interrelate over time.

Situate yourself: landscapes of identity

To understand the influence of identity on understanding and practice is to investigate processes and implications of bordering.[6] Whether physical or ideational, material or subjective, boundaries are an unavoidable component of discourse and action. Borders imply a sense of order and control, a seemingly bounded means to harness the complexity of human relations. With the national level still a dominant (and often dominating) source of power in areas of counter-terrorism, processes of identity construction tied to national senses of inclusion and exclusion call for continued inquiry. As explained by Michael J. Shapiro, 'The nation-state and its related world of Others persists in policy discourses because of ontological impulses that are dissimulated in strategic policy talk, articulations in which spatial predicates are unproblematic' (1997: 30). Shapiro goes on to state, 'the emphasis must be on the practices, discursive and otherwise, for constructing space and identity, on the ways that the self-alterity relationships are historically framed and played out' (1997: 31). Frequently positioned alongside these framings of space are deployments of temporal identity tropes.[7] The international terrorist for example was often framed in terms of a future unknown, a constantly evolving threat. But the relational configurations[8] deployed to stabilise this particular other often draw upon notions of barbarism and incivility linked with historically entrenched notions of the Orientalised other.[9] 'Relational configurations' can be understood as particular patterns of identity construction observed across discourses. Such patterns temporarily stabilise certain intersubjective understandings of identity over others. It is not that discourse *determines* meanings of identity. Rather, that the way relational configurations are positioned frame the terms of debate in particular ways to shape what parameters of collective meaning are most prominent. This framing is of consequence for what security practices then become more 'politically possible' than others (Jackson 2006: 132), influencing outcomes in particular ways.

Postcolonial literature is an important reference point to better conceptualise the way that embedded and consequential notions of space and place play out in processes of securitisation: How the way that an issue is securitised through relational configurations of threat/referent construction can enable certain types of counter-terrorism knowledge and security practices to be justified over others. To say postcolonial here does not imply an end to the colonial period. Rather, it underscores the persistence of colonial patterns of meaning making and power relations for contemporary identity perceptions, international relations, and security practice in terms of east/west, north/south, and white/non-white boundary markers. Insights built through such perspectives help analysis better understand, 'the ways in which the imperial juncture is implicated in the construction of contemporary relations of power, hierarchy, and domination'

(Chowdhry and Nair 2004: 11–12). Whether through work by Michael J. Shapiro on 'violent cartographies' (1997) or Walter D. Mignolo on the 'darker side of the renaissance' (2010), historical studies and perspectives on the role of spatial processes of othering provide key insights into how inequality and insecurity persist over time through misplaced associations of race and place. As explained by Persaud, 'the relationality of identities is dependent upon a field of racialized discourses and has to be historicized' (2004: 66). Spatial and temporal us/them notions of separation have a significant history whereby 'imperialism constitutes a critical historical juncture in which postcolonial national identities are constructed in opposition to European ones, and come to be understood as Europe's "others"' (Chowdhry and Nair 2004: 2).

Different commonplaces of inside and outside signal different assumptions of the other depending on historical and contemporary contexts. In Britain, for example, the category 'immigrant' is historically associated with 'black'; in the US, 'terrorist' and 'Arab' are similarly connected (Biswas 2004: 199). Such perceptions and assumptions link to temporal myths of development whereby a 'universal history of humanity' represented, 'the peoples of the West as the most advanced, [implying] that those who remained behind the West were also less advanced in their moral and intellectual capacities' (Hindess 2007: 336). Counter-terrorism was framed as a preventive strategy against future risks that are defined in terms of an underdeveloped historical other from another place. As explained by Shampa Biswas,

> the Western secularism/Eastern fundamentalism binary, and the progressivist teleology that undergirds it, masks and indeed reproduces a racialized and gendered construction of the Third World that has real material effects for people of color in the First and the Third World.
>
> (2004: 200)

Explicit articulations such as 'the West' played a key part in twentieth-century official British discourses securitising terrorism, with the international other then associated with a kind of 'moral and intellectual failure' (Hindess 2007: 328). Notions of temporality, east, and west are frequently associated with religious assumptions, with 'orientalist constructions' of the other treating 'religion as an atemporal, essential, static realm of backward patriarchy' (Biswas 2004: 200). Not only can temporal static associations form a kind of presumed historical continuity of identity, but they can also 'mark out new exclusions, and are deployed in new exclusionary ways – exclusions with clear racial and gendered implications' (Biswas 2004: 200). The terrorist threat could have been framed as a single category constructed along understandings of terrorism as a method of violence irrespective of geographic positioning. But instead, the threat was securitised along presumed spatial boundaries of inclusion and exclusion. By reinforcing certain colonial themes of us/them identity, terror*ists* were identified along perceived degrees of distance and danger separating different types of others from the referent in need of protection.

Assumptions of spatial belonging and patterns of inclusion/exclusion are not new to twenty-first century security practice but link to historically embedded notions of temporal development (e.g. secular versus nonsecular society) and spatial places of belonging (e.g. east vs. west). As discussed by Tarak Barkawi and Mark Laffey (2006) with respect to security studies more broadly, self/other understandings have a long history of spatial differentiation in distinguishing a Eurocentric core from the 'rest'. With respect to counter-terrorism more specifically, literature on suspect communities (see Hillyard 1993; also, McGovern and Tobin 2009; Hickman et al. 2012; Heath-Kelly 2012) highlights how security processes and discourse can further marginalise already excluded individuals and communities by positioning certain racial and religious characteristics as (mis)identifying a higher likelihood of risk. In this context the nation remains a key source of knowledge production for discourses on security. National identity is 'premised on the co-production and reproduction of race and nation' (Chowdhry and Nair 2004), and though resulting racial hierarchies are not fixed, they 'tend to be long-term in nature, and are at once structural and emotive' (Persaud 2004: 79).

By focusing on the spatial and temporal imaginaries of terrorist threat construction, we can analyse how assumptions of race, religion, and geography are not just an effect of discourses and practices, but inform their substance, legitimation, and direction. The diffusion of knowledge around terrorism is a mutually reinforcing feedback loop constructing the threat and legitimising counter-terrorism practice. Historically embedded assumptions of the other can play a key part in the way that discourse and practice are formed, albeit in different ways in different contexts. In terms of British counter-terrorism law specifically, spatial and temporal demarcations of belonging go back to the first counter-terrorism laws from the early 1970s. Exclusion orders differentiated 'sides of the water' between Ireland and the 'mainland', further alienating already marginalised individuals and communities, as demonstrated by Parliamentary debates years later:

> 1993, Kevin McNamara (Lab): one in 10 Irish males living in Britain have been detained under or affected by the prevention of terrorism [sic] Act. This harassment only adds to the sense of **alienation** felt by the Irish community in Britain ... 80 per cent of the Irish in Britain **doubted that they would receive a fair trial** for a terrorist-related offence.[10]

> 1996, Dennis Canavan (Lab, SP): **the prevention of terrorism** [sic] **Act has succeeded in alienating many innocent people**, their families and their communities. It has caused hostility between communities and the police, particularly among young people, who are often arrested and detained—their only crime being their Irish accent, Irish name or Irish family connections.[11]

Conceptions of the Irish as a colonised and dangerous other are rooted in many years of exceptional security practices and tense social and political relationships. As stated by D.G. Boyce with relation to the early twentieth century, 'As far as Liberal and Labour men were concerned Unionist Ulster had been, still was, and undoubtedly always would be the bête noire of Irish politics – bigoted, self-assertive, and, above all, aggressive.' (1972: 107). In 1422 in Oxford, the English legislated against 'wild Irishmen' (Moody and Martin: 2001: 131), and in the late 1400s, laws were made against Gaelic 'style' and fashion (Moody and Martin: 2001: 134–135). During parliamentary debate around the *British Nationality Act 1948*, Irish was explicitly categorised as 'alien'[12] even as it was also stated that 'the people of Eire and the people of Britain should not be foreign to one another'.[13] Perceptions of difference separating Irish from British (and English) have slowly minimised over time even as Irish related threats were always constructed as an external other. But by the late twentieth century, reference to 'international terrorism' provided a new threat image that was perceived as more foreign, and more dangerous.[14]

The Peace Process in Northern Ireland occurred as Irish-related threats were positioned along different boundaries and perceptions of danger than in previous years. Negotiations and shifting discourses yoked[15] (some) Irish-related others to legitimate politics, reallocating the boundary patterns of threat/referent construction and increasing the perceived danger from international others. The way that terrorism was securitised altered the parameters of debate, with framings such as 'dissident republicanism' differentiating political violence in Northern Ireland from the political violence of international or domestic terrorism, in particular when linked to Islam. The space between Northern Irish and British was reduced, while the 'international' commonplace came to signify a foreign other defined through greater perceived degrees of distance and danger.[16] Processes of externalisation associated with international terrorism distinguished possible future risks through assumptions of foreignness, non-belonging, race and religion. Perceptions of non-Western geographic belonging with ambiguous assessments of future risk from international terrorist others influenced particular processes and consequences of securitisation into the twenty-first century.

With a conceptual framework guided by postcolonial themes, and an empirical illustration from the British case, this chapter aims to help us better understand how constructions of threat around the 'international' were of causal significance for discourses and practices of counter-terrorism. It is not that patterns of identity construction determined or 'caused' outcomes in a linear sense, but that discourse was causally consequential for outcomes. Processes of us/them construction influenced intersubjective understanding while also constituting the language and substance of counter-terrorism policy, with resultant collective meanings establishing the conditions of possibility for what security practices were then legitimised. Through the construction of 'international terrorism', assumptions of inside/outside belonging were stabilised through differentiated patterns of externalisation that positioned perceived degrees of danger alongside perceived degrees of distance separating threat(s) and the referent. Increasingly normalised politics of exception (Huysmans and Buonfino 2008) and the establishment of terrorism as a risk beyond a risk (Aradau and Van

Munster 2007, 2008, 2009) justified exceptional security practice in the name of combating an 'international' terrorist other.

Degrees of distance and danger: 'international terrorists' and British counter-terrorism

In the context of securitisation, discourse, terrorism and counter-terrorism, the word 'international' is not an inconsequential or purely objective signifier, but a label allocated to possible sources of insecurity through political and social practice (Jackson *et al.* 2011). It is a term without any inherent meaning, the understanding of which frequently depends upon spatial and temporal notions of identification through assumed inside/outside degrees of difference. From the mid-1980s onward, particular relational configurations around 'international' terrorism were linked to notions of foreign eastern others. These configurations were positioned as distinct from Irish-related terrorism, domestic terrorism, the British self, and the (Western) democratic referent, even as the boundaries between such groupings overlapped.

A kind of 'foreignisation' reinforced certain us/them understandings over others, further alienating members of the referent 'self' who were already positioned on the borders of society. This can be seen in how commonplaces of immigration were intertextually linked to international terrorism through securitisation, with consequential patterns of externalisation:

> 1985, David Waddington (Con): The enforcement of the provisions of the Prevention of Terrorism (Temporary Provisions) Act 1984 is principally for the police. As part of their training **Immigration Officers** (and customs officers employed as immigration officers under the Immigration Act 1971) are made **aware of their powers of examination** under the 1984 Act have have [*sic*] instructions to bring to the attention of the police any matter which might involve **international terrorism**.[17]

> 1987, Clare Short (Lab): Will the right hon. Gentleman confirm that the extension of the Prevention of Terrorism Act to include **international terrorism** is new? Secondly, will he explain exactly on what grounds those people were detained, so that we may judge whether they could have been detained under **other powers in the criminal law or in immigration legislation**? My belief is that the Government have extended the Act to international terrorism to justify legislation that does not stand up in its own right.[18]

> 1987, Minister of State Home Office (Earl of Caithness, Con): It has been suggested by those who believe the Prevention of Terrorism Act is unnecessary in the fight against terrorism that the **Immigration Act 1971 provides sufficient powers for the authorities to proceed against international terrorists**.[19]

From its nascent references in official British discourse, international terrorism was linked with concerns over 'a greater flow of international terrorists *into* Britain' [emphasis added].[20] While all terrorism was positioned as in need of exceptional counter-terrorism responses, international terrorism was also positioned alongside discussions that pointed to powers such as deportation. Assumptions of what it meant to be an 'international terrorist' blurred identity boundaries for members of the self who were not a security threat but were already marginalised through 'foreignising' inequalities based on divisive notions of difference. By associating these characteristics with terrorism, the ultimate threat to democratic order and values, perceptions of inside/outside belonging reinforced the formation of Muslim and Irish suspect communities. From some perspectives it may seem that for the 'contemporary nation-state cartography is wholly absent' (Shapiro 1997: 73). But the way that terrorism was securitised through British discourse and practice along Irish, domestic and international labels relied upon a type of spatial mapping of identity.

The international terrorist was distinguished from 'other' others such as 'Irish-related terrorists' that were increasingly criminalised through the 1980s. As noted above, the Irish other has also been colonised in terms of spatial and temporal differentiations, and focusing on the international commonplace is not to silence the Northern Irish context. With respect to Northern Ireland, over time processes of securitisation framed the Irish terrorist not only as a terrorist from the other side of the water, but also as a thuggish gangster defined by callous brutality:

> 1991, Kenneth Baker (Secretary of State for the Home Department, Con): Members of those organisations [IRA and INLA] are **criminals, murderers and thugs** who callously use violence in all its forms—death, brutality and destruction.[21]
>
> 1993, David Alton (LD): We know that many of them are involved in **thuggery and gangsterism** of the worst sort —not unlike that of the **Mafia**.[22]
>
> 1997, Baroness Blatch (Minister of State Home Office, Con): Within our midst, a **callous, murderous** minority remains determined to use violence to achieve its ends.[23]

Criminal framings were amplified through the 1990s at the same time as the non-Irish international terrorist was constructed as non-Western, more foreign, and more dangerous. These constructions aligned with a broader move in policy and research to identify a 'new terrorism' positioned as essentially different from previous acts and actors.[24] Both types of terrorism were positioned outside the core British referent, but along different perceived degrees of spatial distance and risk. This enabled different types of security practices to be legitimised. The international terrorist was not just a serious criminal, but also a growing threat to democracy and civilisation. Insecurity related to Ulster was also positioned as an evil contrary to the civilised British self. But processes of criminalisation in the

Northern Irish context and eventual political negotiations helped to further differentiate types of terrorism identified by different geographic labels of identification. Investigating the 'international' can help us analyse how different articulations of the threat led to different counter-terrorism outcomes.

Framings of identity were brokered across different actors and discourses, with this brokerage reasserting certain forms of knowledge over others by uniting previously unconnected actors and discursive sites.[25] The self was positioned in opposition to terrorist through discourses that emphasised the rule of law and law-abiding citizens. Through relational configurations such as 'democratic society', processes of securitisation raised the stakes of the terrorist risk. It was increasingly difficult[26] to move beyond certain identity framings as us/them constructions formed a type of rhetorical skeleton constraining what security practices were considered legitimate:

> 1990, David Waddington (Sec State Home Dept, Con): Whether it strikes at military or civilian targets, barracks or private homes, it is **attacking democracy itself**...[27]

> 1992, Michael Mates (Con): Terrorist organisations are criminal conspiracies, representing perhaps the **most dangerous threat to the fabric of any democratic society**.[28]

> 1994, David Winnick (Lab): the terrorists—**the enemies of democracy and of Britain**.[29]

> 1997, Jack Straw (Lab): terrorist crime is seen as an **attack on society as a whole, and our democratic institutions**. It is akin to an act of war. Those are powerful words, but they accurately define **the nature of terrorism and the threat that it poses to our society**.[30]

In 1990, Secretary of State for Northern Ireland (Con) Peter Brooke said 'terrorism, by its very nature, represents a *relapse* into **barbarism** and **savagery** that unites the entire **civilised world** in determined and unquenchable opposition' [emphasis added].[31] Signifiers such as 'relapse', and evaluative judgments such as 'civilised', associated terrorism with distinctive spatial and temporal imaginaries of belonging. Discourses around 'civil' reinforced intersubjective rules that limited possibilities for alternative knowledge and practice, with those that challenged counter-terrorism themselves labelled as 'uncivil':

> 1991, Lord Belstead (Con): The actions of the terrorist have no place in a **civilised society**.[32]

> 1992, Alex Carlile (LD): I share the right hon. Gentleman's aspiration to achieve convictions in terrorist cases where guilt can be established by proper and **civilised standards**.[33]

1992, Ivor Stanbrook (Con): It is appalling that the Labour party has made no sensible, **civilised** contribution to the argument.[34]

1995, Mo Mowlam (Lab): In a **civilised society**, Governments cannot ignore the rule of law; otherwise, by their very actions, they destroy what they are trying to protect and defend.[35]

The spatial and temporal imaginaries that temporarily stabilised international terrorism as a particular category of incivility were causally consequential for how terrorism was securitised, influencing what outcomes were considered politically reasonable.

By associating degrees of danger with degrees of distance, international terrorism was constructed through assertions of an Eastern other that was presumed to be essentially different from Irish and domestic terrorists. Identity tropes formed along east/west assumptions of belonging around race and geography as discussed in postcolonial literature can be observed as fostering a problematic separation of the terrorist within from the terrorist without in official discourse and practice. These perceptions exacerbated inclusive/exclusive boundaries, removed any possibility that members of the collective self could be terrorists, and implied a particular savagery of outsiders coming 'in' to the referent:

1990, Keith Speed (Con): The **security of our nation and, indeed, of the west** demands substantial resources to safeguard it ... It is important to consider the threat out of areas, notably in the **middle east** [sic].[36]

1990, Stuart Bell (Lab): Yasser Arafat during the last few days has said that in the event of a war the **PLO would unleash upon the west** a terrorist campaign the likes of which we had never seen before[37]

1999, Ken Maginnis (UUP): For the next 20 or 30 years, terrorism will mean the nuclear device that is loaded on to a ship and sailed up the Thames and into London docks, or into Boston, or the nuclear device that is placed in the back of a container lorry and driven **from eastern Europe** to this country, or somewhere else.[38]

Such framings hardened perceptions of 'Eastern others' (cf. Neumann 1999) that played a part in us/them constructions in a variety of earlier contexts by brokering different political parties and contexts. The durability of such identity structures emboldened patterns of inequality associated with constructed geographies and colonial self/other imaginaries. Irish-related violence continued, but official discourse increasingly securitised terrorism in terms of an international threat based upon Middle Eastern and Islamic articulations of spatial identification (see Jackson 2007):

1988, James Molyneaux (UUP): My second point is brief. As the order is based on a Bill that extends mainly to Great Britain, which originated only in Great Britain and which now refers to **international terrorism** and not solely to Irish terrorism, I wonder whether someone in authority could tell us whether the **Libyan** or **Iranian Government** have had the same facility for consultation as the Irish Government.[39]

1988, Douglas Hurd (Secretary of State Home Department, Con): There is still a threat of terrorism hanging over the citizens of this country, including Northern Ireland. That arises not just out of the affairs of Northern Ireland but, as the right hon. Gentleman said, from the **middle east and the subcontinent**...[40]

1988, Kenneth Hind (Con): We are dealing not only with international terrorism, or only with domestic terrorism, but with a mixture: the **IRA**, the **Libyans**, the **Iranians**—all kinds of **terrorists who come to this country** bearing its people no good will. Those are the people whom we must exclude, and this Bill will exclude them.[41]

1999, John Taylor (UUP): What is the potential for **extreme Islamist terrorism** within the United Kingdom? There are links with the United Kingdom in the case in **Yemen**. Is there a growing threat within our own territory?[42]

1999, Jack Straw (Lab): The problem is **middle eastern terrorism** based on territorial challenges and on tribalism, which seeks to justify itself by reference to Islam ... I make that point at some length because it is a real issue of sensitivity for the **British Muslim community**, which is entirely lawful.[43]

The international commonplace broadened securitisation to include threats coming *in* to the UK from beyond Ireland and would set a consequential precedent for 'knowledges' of terrorism and terrorists throughout the twenty-first century. Even though '88 percent of the time, terrorist attacks occur in the perpetrators' country of origin', and thus 'most international terrorism is in fact local', even violence that could have been interpreted as local and domestic in the Middle East was positioned as 'international terrorism' (Krueger 2007: 71):

1996, Ivan Lawrence (Con): "Terrorism is being used at the moment to undermine the peace in the middle east, with the most horrific acts of violence in Jerusalem and in Tel Aviv and other parts of Israel. We have to play our part in helping to defeat international terrorism."[44]

By the late 1990s, intersubjective understandings of the externalised other and associations of 'evil international terrorist' with 'Eastern' otherness increased insecurity for Muslim communities in ways not dissimilar to consequences from counter-terrorism for Irish communities (McGovern and Tobin 2009; Hickman *et al.* 2012). The durability of colonial processes of othering facilitated a securitisation of terrorism that continued to draw upon spatial assumptions of belonging, even as domestic/international and inside/outside means of identification were unreliable and inconsistent.

While the 1998 East African bombings were officially referenced as an early example of 'international' terrorism, according to the US Federal Bureau of Investigation, these attacks were also linked to British citizens (Bamford 2004: 743). Irish actors carrying out attacks in the Netherlands and Germany were referred to as 'Irish' rather than 'international', domestic actors were reconfigured as outsiders when it came to the international threat, and 'domestic terrorism' was largely associated with concerns such as animal rights extremists. Importantly, Irish terrorism was in many ways an international threat comprising international actions, ideological ties and financial networks. Whether by reference to arms shipments linking Libya, the Czech Republic and Northern Ireland (Townshend 2002: 28), South Africa-Northern Ireland connections,[45] American financial and moral support of Northern Irish terror groups,[46] or two Australians killed in the Netherlands by Northern Irish actors because they were driving a car with British plates,[47] Irish-related threats could have been securitised as 'international', but were not:

> 1990, Lord Harris of Greenwich (LD): It is deplorable that after attacks on innocent citizens in this country a **fund-raising organisation remains in existence in the United States** and is generously supported by many American citizens. Is the Leader of the House aware of our strong approval of the words of the United States ambassador in describing as contemptible the acts of the Mayor of New York who has seen fit to **name a street in New York after a convicted IRA terrorist**?[48]

> 1990, John Butcher (Con): When he gives them [Dutch counterparts] our thanks for helping to preserve the lives of British service men abroad, will he also offer his full support to the necessity for proper co-ordination, functional and organisational, in attacking **terrorism in mainland Europe, whether it comes from Northern Ireland or elsewhere**?[49]

> 1990, Stuart Randall (Lab): It is important to recognise that the **problems of terrorism, particularly the IRA, extend to other member states**, rather than being associated only with the United Kingdom.[50]

This failure to classify Irish-related terrorism as international could have been viewed as inconsistent. Instead, observable patterns of externalisation along civilisational and east/west assumptions supported an intersubjective separation of threat and referent by distancing Irish from international, and both threats from the British referent.

The type of 'foreignisation' that differentiated Irish from international terrorism enabled a particular set of counter-terrorism policy options. While counter-terrorism has in many ways always been dominated by law enforcement, separating foreign outsider from domestic insider through the 'international' commonplace legitimised an intensification of measures in terms of foreign and national security policy. The further a terrorist other was positioned from the self, the easier it seemed to be to justify a suspension of 'their' liberties for 'ours'. Irish-related threats were always viewed as external to the British mainland. But these 'others' were closer to the referent than non-Western foreigners who were further in temporal perceptions of development and spatial assumptions of belonging. Over time, the international other was constructed as a space east and south of the UK, spatially distinct from other types of terrorism. Identity oppositions corresponded to historically embedded civilized-barbarian polarisations, with the Irish-related sphere of risk presented as more manageable than, and distinct from, the dangerous international other.

Framings such as 'Islamic radicalism' in discussions of the international threat were positioned alongside an explicit articulation of 'overseas' and a perceived disconnect between UK territory (and British 'selves') and terrorist violence:

> 1995, Michael Howard (Con): with the growth of Islamic radicalism, we need to remain vigilant against the possibility that **Britain will be used as a base** for plotting acts of violence overseas and raising money for terrorist purposes.[51]

> 1998, Jack Straw (Secretary of State for the Home Department, Lab): We have to send the clearest message to **international terrorist groups** that we in **the United Kingdom will not allow this country to be used as a base** for plotting and supporting terrorist operations abroad.[52]

International terrorism was understood as *foreign* and external to the British referent as well as being external to 'other' others. This intensified pre-existing issues of alienation and insecurity by reinforcing the perception of certain groups and individuals as both 'risky' and 'at risk' (Heath-Kelly 2012). Such spatial assumptions of belonging were frequently misguided, with international terrorism committed by domestic actors who were part of the self as much as by foreign others.

Rather than being a value-neutral means of identification, the construction and allocation of Irish, international, and domestic threat labels depended upon (re)configurations of us/them identity constructions drawing upon unquestioned generalisations of inside/outside belonging. Even if actors used similar methods (strategic bombing) or had similar philosophies of self-legitimation (anti-colonial liberation), processes of securitisation distinguished degrees of physical and cultural distance between terrorist others and the referent in need of protection. Stuart Croft is right in stating that 'Over time, discourses decay under the weight of internal contradictions and external alternative narratives' (2006: 12), but threat/referent assumptions in the case of British counter-terrorism seemed to overpower historical inconsistency and definitional overlap. Implicit attention to this inconsistency can perhaps be inferred in observing the recent removal of 'international' from the title of CONTEST. But explicit attention to the 'international' as a (mis)signifier remains under-investigated. Innocent individuals and communities who happened to share perceived characteristics such as race or religion with perceptions of the international other through explicit articulations of identity were increasingly excluded from full participation and access to society, with us/them boundaries of identification associated with spatial assumptions of belonging aggravated and aggravating.[53]

Spatial demarcations, degrees of foreignisation

> British citizens are being banished from their own country, being stripped of a core part of their identity yet without a single word of explanation of why they have been singled out and dubbed a risk.
> (Gareth Peirce, cited in Woods *et al.* 2013)

By the turn of the century, the construction of terrorist others along differentiated physical and symbolic distances helped to constitute and legitimise a shift in British counter-terrorism. The danger of Irish related terrorism was a reduced category of intensity, even as violence in Northern Ireland continued, with commonplaces such as 'dissident' rather than 'terrorist' growing in frequency. At the same time, international terrorism was aligned with articulations of non-Western others, such as 'Arab terrorism',[54] with significant consequences considering assumptions of terrorist entity-others as those who 'by their **nature**, do not obey the law'[emphasis added].[55] Indeterminate spatial boundaries around forms of terrorism were presented as a value-neutral means with which to bound possible future risk by identifying who was and who was not 'a terrorist'.

The international commonplace in discourses of securitisation and counter-terrorism has in many ways been a consequential (mis)signaller: an ineffective attempt at threat identification that will forever be both always and never in definitive existence. This ambiguity of identification can lead to negative effects in terms of identity related both to essentialisation and 'derealisation', whereby 'increasingly abstract and distancing modes of symbolic representation mediate the relationships through which persons and places acquire meanings' (Shapiro 1997: 88). From the mid-1980s on, 'international' did not indicate actors from multiple citizenships or transnational operations, but assumed 'foreign' racial and religious characteristics. Framings demarcated enemies 'within' from enemies 'without' even as the distinction between international and domestic terrorism remained unclear (Sanchez-Cuenca and de la Calle 2009: 132).

The argument of this chapter is not that a threat did/does not exist from groups categorised as international terrorists, such as al Qaeda. Nor is it that the formation of security measures against non-traditional uses of terrorist violence was a surprise. However, *the way* that these measures were formed along particular labels of identification was not predetermined and incurred a variety of consequences. Certain relational configurations in official discourse enabled a political legitimation of new legal precedents and higher thresholds of state power with implications for situations of insecurity. As of 13 July 2013, since the first British law with terrorism placed explicitly in its title (the Prevention of Terrorism Act (PTA) 1974), there have been 179 UK legal measures with terrorism in their title. This included 158 statutory instruments, 13 public general acts, six Scottish statutory instruments and two Northern Ireland statutory rules.[56] During this period legal moves with terrorism in their title increased at an average rate of approximately 4.5 measures per year, with twenty-first century initiatives such as CONTEST further broadening the institutionalisation of counter-terrorism more generally. The perspective is not that rising and falling threats necessarily correspond with rising and falling levels of counter-terrorism. Rather, that patterns of identity construction based on spatial and temporal imaginaries of belonging were of particular significance considering what kinds of counter-terrorism measures and security/insecurity outcomes were politically possible.

The construction of international terrorists as external to the British referent was linked to historically-entrenched perceptions of belonging and difference that distinguished types of terrorist others along inside/outside boundaries of danger and distance. These spatial and temporal processes of identification became an unquestioned contributor to and consequence of how terrorism was securitised in the context of counter-terrorism discourse and practice. Us/them relational configurations securitised terrorism in particular ways to stabilise certain meanings of threat over others. The durability of such meanings is of continued consequence for intersubjective understanding, counter-terrorism practice, security and insecurity. The 'international' is not merely a rhetorical signpost pointing to a level of analysis. Rather, it has constituted a presumed signifier of distance that is defined by embedded assumptions of danger and belonging. If we are to minimise the insecurity of terror today such processes of identification and their consequences must not be passed by but questioned through continued critical inquiry.

Notes

1 With thanks to Meera Sabaratnam and Paul Kirby for guidance on postcolonial literature, and to Charlotte Heath-Kelly, Lee Jarvis and Michael Lister for very helpful comments on earlier drafts.
2 On the Self's erasing of the Other in the context of globalisation see Agathangelou and Ling (2009: 15, 31).
3 The recent killing of US citizen(s) in US drone attacks may challenge this. However, such individuals are still largely identified in terms of their association with spaces physically separate from the self (e.g. Yemen).
4 See Waever (1995) and Buzan *et al.* (1998) for introductions into securitisation theory.
5 CONTEST was formed in 2003 and published in 2006, 2009 and 2011.
6 See Salter (2003, 2008), Albert *et al.* (2001), and Tilly (1998) on bordering practices.
7 On the War on Terror and temporality see Jarvis (2009).
8 'Relational configurations' being a term drawn from Lawson (forthcoming).

9 See Croft (2012) on the 'orientalised' securitisation of Islam in Britain.
10 Prevention of Terrorism, 10 March 1993, *Parliamentary Debates*, Commons, 6th ser., vol. 220, col. 993.
11 Prevention and Suppression of Terrorism, 14 March 1996, *Parliamentary Debates*, Commons, 6th ser., vol. 273, col. 1163.
12 Clement Attlee (PM, Lab): 11 March 1949, *Parliamentary Debates*, Commons, col.1855 (Cited in 'Northern Ireland: political developments since 1972,' 11 May 1998, HC Research Paper 98/57, p. 20).
13 Ibid.
14 On the 'making foreign' of the threat with respect to the 7 July 2005 London bombings see Bulley (2008).
15 See Abbott (1995) on yoking.
16 On 'degrees of Otherness' see Hansen (2006).
17 Prevention of Terrorism, 21 October 1985, Parliamentary Debates, Commons, 6th ser., vol. 84, col. 35.
18 Prevention of Terrorism, 10 February 1987, *Parliamentary Debates*, Commons, 6th ser., vol. 110, col. 265.
19 Parl. Deb, H.L., 19 February 1987, 5th ser., vol. 484, col. 1236.
20 Andrew Hunter (Con): Parl. Deb, H.C., 6 December 1988, 6th ser., vol. 143, col. 248.
21 Parl. Deb, H.C., 4 March 1991, 6th ser., vol. 187, col. 22.
22 Parl. Deb, H.C., 8 June 1993, 6th ser., vol. 226, col. 191.
23 Prevention of Terrorism (Temporary Provisions) Act 1989 (Continuance) Order 1997, 10 March 1997, Parliamentary Debates, Lords, 5th ser., vol. 579, col. 10.
24 On the debate of a 'new terrorism' see Bolanos (2012) and Duyvesteyn and Malkki (2012).
25 On brokerage see McAdam *et al.* (2001), Goddard (2009) and Fisher (2013).
26 'Difficulty' should not be interpreted as *impossible*, agency is not dissolved.
27 Parl. Deb, H.C., 26 June 1990, 5th ser., vol. 520, col. 185.
28 Parl. Deb, H.C., 10 June 1992, 6th ser., vol. 209, col. 414.
29 Prevention and Suppression of Terrorism, 9 March 1994, *Parliamentary Debates*, Commons, 6th ser., vol. 239, col. 293.
30 Prevention of Terrorism, 5 March 1997, *Parliamentary Debates*, Commons, 6th ser., vol. 291, col. 927.
31 Parl. Deb, H.C., 19 November 1990, 6th ser., vol. 181, col. 24.
32 Parl. Deb, H.L., 19 April 1991, 5th ser., vol. 527, col. 1662.
33 Parl. Deb, H.C., 24 February 1992, 6th ser., vol. 204, col. 698.
34 Ibid., col. 718.
35 Parl. Deb, H.C., 8 March 1995, 6th ser., vol. 256, col. 390.
36 Ibid., col. 833.
37 The Gulf, 6 September 1990, Parliamentary Debates, Commons, 6th ser., vol. 177, col. 811.
38 Parl. Deb, H.C., 16 March 1999, 6th ser., vol. 327, col. 1013.
39 Parl. Deb, H.C., 16 February 1988, 6th ser., vol. 127, col. 925.
40 Ibid., col., 925.
41 Ibid., col. 940.
42 Parl. Deb, H.C., 16 March 1999, 6th ser., vol. 327, col. 1001.
43 Ibid.
44 Parl. Deb, H.C., 14 March 1996, 6th ser., vol. 273, col. 1153.
45 Kevin McNamara (Lab): Northern Ireland (Prevention of Terrorism), 10 June 1992, Parliamentary Debates, Commons, 6th ser., vol. 209, col. 382.
46 Lord Harris (LD): Carlton Club: Bomb Incident, 26 June 1990, Parliamentary Debates, Lords, 5th ser., vol. 520, col. 1459.
47 Lord Lyell (Con): The Defence Estimates 1990, 17 July 1990, Parliamentary Debates, Lords, 5th ser., vol. 521, col. 823.

48 Parl. Deb, H.L., 26 June 1990, 5th ser., vol. 520, col. 1459.
49 Dutch Defence Minister, 19 June 1990, Parliamentary Debates, Commons, 6th ser., vol. 174, col. 792.
50 Weapons, 29 November 1990, Parliamentary Debates, Commons, 6th ser., vol. 181, col. 1076.
51 Prevention and Suppression of Terrorism, 8 March 1995, Parliamentary Debates, Commons, 6th ser., vol. 256, col. 352.
52 Criminal Justice (Terrorism and Conspiracy) Bill, 2 September 1998, Parliamentary Debates, Commons, 6th ser., vol. 317, col. 736.
53 See also Croft (2012) on spatial imaginaries and the securitisation of Islam in Britain through different temporal snapshots of discourse and practice in the UK.
54 'Conclusions,' 1974, CAB/128/53/25.
55 Lord Brain: Border Control of People, ECC Report, 5 April 1990, *Parliamentary Debates*, Lords, 5th ser., vol. 517, col. 1572.
56 www.legislation.gov.uk/all?title=terrorism (Search performed 20 September 2012).

References

Abbott, A. (1995) 'Things of boundaries', *Social Research*, 62 (4), pp. 857–882.
Albert, M., D. Jacobson and Y. Lapid (2001) *Identities, Borders, Orders: Rethinking IR Theory*, Minneapolis: University of Minnesota.
Agathangelou, A.M. and L.H.M. Ling (2009) *Transforming World Politics: From empire to multiple worlds*, London: Routledge.
Aradau, C. and R. Van Munster (2007) 'Governing Terrorism Through Risk: Taking Precautions, (un)Knowing the Future', *European Journal of International Relations*, 12 (1), pp. 89–115.
Aradau, C. and Van Munster, R. (2008) 'Taming the Future: the dispositive of risk in the war on terror', in L. Amoore and M. de Goede (eds) *Risk and the War on Terror*, Abingdon: Routledge, pp. 23–40.
Aradau, C. and Van Munster, R. (2009) 'Exceptionalism and the 'War on Terror': Criminology Meets International Relations', *British Journal of Criminology*, 49 (5), pp. 686–701.
Bamford, B.W.C. (2004) 'The United Kingdom's "War Against Terrorism"', *Terrorism and Political Violence*, 16 (4), pp. 737–756.
Barkawi, T. and M. Laffey, (2006) 'The postcolonial moment in security studies', *Review of International Studies*, 32, pp. 329–352.
Biswas, S. (2004) 'The "New Cold War": Secularism, orientalism, and postcoloniality', in G. Chowdhry and S. Nair (eds) *Power, Postcolonialism and International Relations: Reading race, gender and class*, London: Routledge. pp. 184–208.
Bolanos, A. (2012) 'YES: The 'new terrorism' or the 'newness' of context and change', in R. Jackson and S.J. Sinclair (eds) *Contemporary Debates on Terrorism*. Routledge: London. pp. 29–34.
Boyce, D.G. (1972) *Englishmen and Irish Troubles: British Public Opinion and the Making of Irish Policy, 1918–1922*, Cambridge: MIT Press.
Bulley, Dan. (2008) "'Foreign' Terror? London Bombings, Resistance and the Failing State."' *British Journal of Politics and International Relations*, 10, pp. 379–394.
Buzan, B., O. Waever and J. de Wilde (1998) *Security: A New Framework for Analysis*, Boulder: Lynn Rienner Publishers.
Chowdhry, G. and S. Nair (2004) 'Introduction: Power in a postcolonial world: race, gender, and class in international relations', in G. Chowdhry and S. Nair (eds) *Power,*

Postcolonialism and International Relations: Reading race, gender and class, London: Routledge, pp. 1–32.

Cobain, I. (14 July 2013) 'Obama's secret kill list – the disposition matrix', *Guardian*. Online. Available at: www.guardian.co.uk/world/2013/jul/14/obama-secret-kill-list-disposition-matrix (accessed 20 July 2013).

CONTEST: The United Kingdom's Strategy for Countering International Terrorism, 2006. (Cm. 6888).

CONTEST: The United Kingdom's Strategy for Countering International Terrorism, 2009, (ISBN: 9780101754729).

CONTEST: The United Kingdom's Strategy for Countering Terrorism, 2011. (Cm. 8123).

Croft, S. (2006) *Culture, Crisis and America's War on Terror*, Cambridge: Cambridge University Press.

Croft, S. (2012) *Securitising Islam*, Cambridge: Cambridge University Press.

Donohue, L. (2008) *The Costs of Counterterrorism: Power, politics, and liberty*, Cambridge: Cambridge University Press.

Duyvesteyn, I. and L. Malkki. (2012) 'A 'new terrorism' in existence today?', 'NO: The fallacy of the new terrorism thesis', in R. Jackson and S.J. Sinclair (eds) *Contemporary Debates on Terrorism*, Routledge: London, pp. 35–42.

Fisher, K.M. (2013) 'From 20th Century Troubles to 21st Century International Terrorism: Identity, Securitization, and British Counterterrorism from 1968 to 2011', unpublished thesis, London School of Economics and Political Science.

Goddard, S. (2009) 'Brokering change: networks and entrepreneurs in international politics', *International Theory*, 1 (2), pp. 249–281.

Hansen, L. (2006) *Security as Practice: Discourse Analysis and the Bosnian War*, London: Routledge.

Heath-Kelly, C. (2012) 'Counter-Terrorism and the Counterfactual: Producing the 'Radicalization' Discourse and the UK PREVENT Strategy', *British Journal of Politics and International Relations*, 1–22.

Hickman, M.J., L. Thomas, H. Nickels and S. Silvestri (2012) 'Social cohesion and the notion of 'suspect communities': a study of the experiences and impacts of being "suspect" for Irish communities and Muslim communities in Britain', *Critical Studies on Terrorism*, 5 (1), pp. 89–106.

Hogan, G. and C. Walker (1989) *Political Violence and the Law in Ireland*, Manchester: Manchester University Press.

Hindess, B. (2007) 'The Past Is Another Culture', *International Political Sociology*, 1, pp. 325–338.

Hillyard, P. (1993) 'Suspect community: people's experience of the prevention of terrorism acts in Britain', London: Pluto Press.

Huysmans, J. and A. Buonfino (2008) 'Politics of Exception and Unease: Immigration, Asylum and Terrorism in Parliamentary Debates in the UK', *Political Studies*, 56 (4), pp. 766–788.

Jackson, P.T. (2006) *Civilizing the Enemy: German Reconstruction and the invention of the West*, Ann Arbor: University of Michigan Press.

Jackson, R. (2007) 'Constructing Enemies: 'Islamic Terrorism' in Political and Academic Discourse', *Government and Opposition*, 42 (3), pp. 394–426.

Jackson, R., L. Jarvis, J. Gunning, and M. Breen-Smyth (eds) (2011) *Terrorism: A Critical Introduction*, Basingstoke: Palgrave Macmillan.

Jarvis, L. (2009) *Times of Terror*, London: Palgrave Macmillan.

Krueger, A.B. (2007) *What makes a terrorist: Economics and the Roots of Terrorism*, Princeton: Princeton University Press.
Lawson, G. *Anatomies of Revolution*. Forthcoming.
McAdam, D., S. Tarrow and C. Tilly (2001) *Dynamics of Contention*, New York: Cambridge University Press.
McGovern, M. and A. Tobin (2009) 'Countering Terror or Counter-Productive? Comparing Irish and British Muslim Experiences of Counter-insurgency Law and Policy Report', Lancashire: Edge Hill University.
Mignolo, W. (2010) *The Darker Side of the Renaissance: Literacy, territoriality, and colonization*, Ann Arbor: University of Michigan Press.
Moody, T.W. and F.X. Martin (2001) *The Course of Irish History. 4th edn*, Lanham: Roberts Rinehart Publishers.
Neumann, I. (1999) *Uses of the Other: The East in European Identity Formation*, Manchester: Manchester University Press.
Persaud, R.B. (2004) 'Situating Race in International Relations: The dialectics of civilizational security in American immigration', in G. Chowdhry and S. Nair (eds) *Power, Postcolonialism and International Relations: Reading race, gender and class*, London: Routledge. pp. 56–81.
Said, E. (1979) *Orientalism*, 25th Ed., New York: Vintage Books Random House.
Salter, M.B. (2003) *Rights of passage: the passport in international relations*, London: Lynn Rienner Publishers.
Salter, M.B. (2008) 'When the exception becomes the rule: borders, sovereignty, and citizenship', *Citizenship Studies*, 12 (4), pp. 365–380.
Sanchez-Cuenca, I. and L. de la Calle (2009) 'Domestic Terrorism: The Hidden Side of Political Violence', *Annual Review of Political Science*, 12, pp. 31–49.
Shapiro, M.J. (1997) *Violent Cartographies*, Minneapolis: University of Minnesota Press.
Tilly, C. (1998) *Durable Inequality*, Berkeley: University of California Press.
Townshend, C. (2002) *Terrorism: A Very Short Introduction*, Oxford: Oxford University Press.
Waever, O. (1995) 'Securitization and desecuritization', in R.D. Lipschutz (ed.) *On Security*, New York: Columbia University Press. pp. 46–86.
Woods, C., A.K. Ross and O. Wright (28 February 2013) 'British terror suspects quietly stripped of citizenship ... then killed by drones: Exclusive: Secret war on enemy within', *Independent*. Online. Available at: www.independent.co.uk/news/uk/crime/british-terror-suspects-quietly-stripped-of-citizenship-then-killed-by-drones-8513858.html (accessed 2 March 2013).

Primary sources (chronological)

Conclusions, 1974, CAB/128/53/25.
Amnesty International activity in Northern Ireland, 1 January 1978–31, December 1978, FCO/87/821.
10 February 1987, *Parliamentary Debates*, Commons, 6th ser., vol. 110, col. 265 (Prevention of Terrorism).
19 February 1987, *Parliamentary Debates*, Lords, 5th ser., vol. 484, col. 1243 (Prevention of Terrorism (Temporary Provisions) Act 1984 (Continuance) Order 1987).
16 February 1988, *Parliamentary Debates*, Commons, 6th ser., vol. 127, col. 942 (Prevention of Terrorism).

6 December 1988, *Parliamentary Debates*, Commons, 6th ser., vol. 143, col. 208 (Prevention of Terrorism (Temporary Provisions) Bill).

6 March 1990, *Parliamentary Debates*, Commons, 6th ser., vol. 168, col. 822 (Prevention of Terrorism).

12 March 1990, *Parliamentary Debates*, Commons, 6th ser., vol. 169, col. 66 (Northern Ireland (Terrorism)).

5 April 1990, *Parliamentary Debates*, Lords, 5th ser., vol. 517, col. 1572 (Border Control of People, ECC Report; Aviation and Maritime Security Bill).

19 June 1990, *Parliamentary Debates*, Commons, 6th ser., vol. 174, col. 792 (Dutch Defence Minister; Defence Estimates).

26 June 1990, *Parliamentary Debates*, Lords, 5th ser., vol. 520, col. 1459 (Carlton Club: Bomb Incident).

17 July 1990, *Parliamentary Debates*, Lords, 5th ser., vol. 521, col. 823 (The Defence Estimates 1990).

6 September 1990, *Parliamentary Debates*, Commons, 6th ser., vol. 177, col. 811 (The Gulf).

19 November 1990, *Parliamentary Debates*, Commons, 6th ser., vol. 181, col. 24 (Northern Ireland (Emergency Provisions) Bill).

29 November 1990, *Parliamentary Debates*, Commons, 6th ser., vol. 181, col. 1076 (Weapons).

4 March 1991, *Parliamentary Debates*, Commons, 6th ser., vol. 187, col. 32 (Prevention of Terrorism).

19 April 1991, *Parliamentary Debates*, Lords, 5th ser., vol. 527, col. 1662 (Northern Ireland (Emergency Provisions) Bill).

24 February 1992, *Parliamentary Debates*, Commons, 6th ser., vol. 204, col. 696 (Terrorism).

10 June 1992, *Parliamentary Debates*, Commons, 6th ser., vol. 209, col. 382 (Northern Ireland (Prevention of Terrorism)).

10 March 1993, *Parliamentary Debates*, Commons, 6th ser., vol. 220, col. 992 (Prevention of Terrorism).

9 March 1994, *Parliamentary Debates*, Commons, 6th ser., vol. 239, col. 293 (Prevention and Suppression of Terrorism).

8 March 1995, *Parliamentary Debates*, Commons, 6th ser., vol. 256, col. 352 (Prevention and Suppression of Terrorism).

14 March 1996, *Parliamentary Debates*, Commons, 6th ser., vol. 273, col. 1163 (Prevention and Suppression of Terrorism).

19 March 1996, *Parliamentary Debates*, Lords, 5th ser., vol. 570, col. 1240 (Prevention of Terrorism (Temporary Provisions) Act 1989 (Continuance) Order 1996).

19 June 1996, *Parliamentary Debates*, Commons, 6th ser., vol. 279, col. 959 (Northern Ireland).

5 March 1997, *Parliamentary Debates*, Commons, 6th ser., vol. 291, col. 927 (Prevention of Terrorism).

30 October 1997, *Parliamentary Debates*, Commons, col. 1027 (Counter-terrorism Legislation).

10 March 1997, *Parliamentary Debates*, Lords, 5th ser., vol. 579, col. 10 (Prevention of Terrorism (Temporary Provisions) Act 1989 (Continuance) Order 1997).

12 January 1998, *Parliamentary Debates*, Lords, 5th ser., vol. 584, col. 905 (Northern Ireland (Emergency Provisions) Bill).

10 March 1998, *Parliamentary Debates*, Lords, 5th ser., vol. 587, col. 201 (Prevention of Terrorism (Temporary Provisions) Act 1989 (Partial Continuance) Order 1998).

Northern Ireland: political developments since 1972. 11 May 1998, HC Research Paper 98/57.

2 September 1998, *Parliamentary Debates*, Commons, 6th ser., vol. 317, col. 736 (Criminal Justice (Terrorism and Conspiracy) Bill).

The Criminal Justice (Terrorism and Conspiracy) Bill, Bill 244 of 1997–98, Research Paper 98/87, 2 September 1998.

16 March 1999, *Parliamentary Debates*, Commons, 6th ser., vol. 327, col. 999 (Prevention of Terrorism).

Terrorism Bill, Research Paper 99/101, 13 December 1999.

Abbreviations

Con – Conservative Party
DUP – Democratic Unionist Party
HC – House of Commons, UK Parliament
HL – House of Lords, UK Parliament
Lab – Labour Party
LD – Liberal Democrats Party
SDLP – Social Democratic and Labour Party
UUP – Ulster Unionist Party

4 Counter-terrorism as conflict transformation

*Laura Zahra McDonald, Basia Spalek,
Phillip Daniel Silk, Raquel Da Silva and
Zubeda Limbada*

Introduction

The unprecedented transnationality, intensity and sustained activity of terror and counter-terror in the post-9/11 era has defined the political, social and strategic direction of contemporary nations worldwide. From wars, drone attacks, insurgencies, revolutions and coups, state foreign policies and internal security strategies, to community tensions, decreased human security and damaged state-citizen engagement (Spalek *et al.* 2008, 2010, 2013): relations between and within nations have been shaped by and experienced through a lens of security and violence, both actual and threatened. The framework is one in which a cycle of violence has been perpetuated and sustained, legitimised by oppositional narratives of justice. From a state perspective, there are two main counter-terrorism goals: responding to current threats and preventing new atrocities. These goals may be pursued through wide-ranging strategies, including the use of force, the use of repressive measures, the use of legalistic measures and/or the use of conciliatory measures.

This chapter looks at the validity and efficacy of the frequently used and varying forms of 'hard' strategy, including the use of stop and search, detention without charge and forms of repression. 'Hard' approaches consist of those that are explicitly linked to counter-terrorism strategies that involve surveillance and the implementation of anti-terror laws and policies (Spalek and Imtoual 2007: 185–202).

Such approaches may be effective (Ashour 2010) but also counterproductive (Weeks 2013): the question that this chapter therefore seeks to raise and explore is whether an alternative framework of conflict transformation is possible, looking at current and future trends in which more conciliatory measures are utilised in changing relationships between terrorists and the state. The balance of power in such models is markedly different and based on notions of mutual recognition, cooperation and need. Those involved in terrorist movements are expected to desist from violence, whilst states are expected to comply with the agreements and concessions made, alongside the maintenance of human rights and law. This chapter, based upon empirical data gathered by the ConnectJustice[1] team since 2007, places a particular emphasis upon exploring conciliatory measures that might be adopted by drawing on the experiences and perspectives of state and non-state actors in relation to counter-terrorism.

Philosophies, laws and aims of counter-terrorism

According to scholars associated with the field of critical terrorism studies, it is important to be sensitive to the politics and ideological interests involved in the 'labelling' of individuals or groups as 'terrorist' (Jackson 2008). This is because labels usually result from external interests, are political in nature, and often lack the crucial underpinning of in-depth analysis or research (Sluka 2002; Gunning 2007). Furthermore, labelling allows different forms of terrorism and other forms of political violence to be categorised under the same umbrella and thus managed in the same way, contributing to gross mistakes within domestic and/or international criminal justice systems (Jackson 2008). As a result, analysts such as Wilkinson (2006: 2) consider that terrorism should not be understood in terms of its 'label', but as a relative concept and tool of analysis, and it is this concept of terrorism whose definition shapes research in the field, informs public opinions and perceptions and sets in motion more holistic counter-terrorism strategies and practices (Stern 1999; Schmid 2006; Jackson 2008). By approaching terrorism as a concept, it becomes possible to understand that there are many state and non-state actors and agencies, including policing bodies, government institutions, international bodies, researchers, and community members, who define terrorism and counter-terrorism differently.

Yet the issue of definition remains: while highly contested and subject to ongoing ontological criticisms, broad academic definition generated from the analysis of a number of already existing definitions suggest that terrorism may be understood as:

> a politically motivated tactic involving the threat or use of force or violence in which the pursuit of publicity plays a significant role.
> (Weinberg *et al.* 2004: 786)

and

> an anxiety-inspiring method of repeated violent actions employed by (semi-) clandestine individual, group, or state actors, for idiosyncratic, criminal or political reasons, whereby – in contrast to assassination – the direct targets of violence are not the main targets. The immediate human victims of violence are generally chosen randomly (targets of opportunity) or selectively (representative or symbolic targets) from a target population, and serve as message generators. Threat- and violence-based communication processes between terrorist (organization), (imperiled) victims, and main targets are used to manipulate the main target (audience(s)), turning it into a target of terror, a target of demands, or a target of attention, depending on whether intimidation, coercion, or propaganda is primarily sought.
> (Schmid and Jongman 2005: 28)

Many policy definitions – such as that used by the EU – are complementary, suggesting that terrorism is,

> not an ideology but is a set of criminal tactics that deny the fundamental principles of democratic societies. Terrorist acts are those which aim to intimidate populations, compel states to comply with the perpetrators' demands, and/or destabilise or destroy the fundamental political, constitutional, economic or social structures of a country or an international organisation.
>
> (Europol TeSat 2010: 5)

All three definitions focus on terrorism as a means of violent communication (Schmid 2004). However, both Schmid and Jongman's and the EU's definitions broadens the spectrum of terrorist motivations, considering not only *political* factors, but also *idiosyncratic* and *criminal* ones. Crucially, Schmid and Jongman's definition also includes the *state* as a possible perpetrator, something that is often ignored by mainstream definitions of terrorism (Banks 2008; Blakeley 2007; Martin 2013). Authors such as Jenkins (1980) and Stern (1999) reinforce this idea, affirming that 'governments, their armies, their secret police may also be terrorists' (Jenkins 1980: 3) and that 'states and their leaders can and do unleash terrorist violence against their own civilians' (Stern 1999: 14). According to Jackson (2008: 27), however, many established scholars in the field of terrorism studies do not write about those atrocities committed by states as 'terrorism', but rather view these as alternative forms of political violence such as *repression*. In this sense, terrorism must be seen as 'a social fact rather than a brute fact', which is created and recreated by and within forms of 'social and political discourse' (Jackson 2008: 28). Therefore, historical and contextual analysis sheds light on the dynamics between the state and individuals, between the state and violent organisations, between individuals and violent organisations, and between violent organisations and other social movements.

This analysis has the epistemic power to change an actor's place in the terrorist scenario, possibly placing some states' actions at the origin of terrorism (Gunning 2007). It is in this frame that the line between acts of terrorism and counter-terrorism can be seen as tenuous (Jackson 2008) with state-led approaches to combat terrorism refusing to acknowledge the individual and community dynamics impacted by their measures (Breen Smyth 2007; Jackson 2007; Spalek 2008). The fundamental discourse which maintains state justification of 'hard' counter-terrorism measures is one of dehumanisation: where repressive measures are supported by the majority of a population, 'terrorists' as defined by the state, are presented as irrational, obsessed and morally condemnable (Banks 2013). An example of this type of reaction is shown in a survey from 2009, when 58 per cent of US voters considered that 'waterboarding and other aggressive interrogation techniques should be used to gain information from the terrorist who attempted to bomb an airliner on Christmas Day' (Rasmussen Reports 2009 cit. in Guiora 2012: 164). This is illustrative of a broad trend, in which populations, when targeted or threatened by terrorist attacks generally agree with a range of restrictions on individual rights and freedoms (Guiora 2012; Banks 2013). It is also worth noting that in this scenario state actions that might have contributed to terrorism are simply ignored despite the utilisation of counter-terrorism measures that blur the lines with non-state terrorism (Banks 2013). Additionally, the use of violence within counter-terrorism is notable for encouraging the reactive escalation of non-state terrorism, the hindering of possible negotiations, and for posing moral and ethical questions to which a state by definition is accountable (Banks 2003). The paradox here is that actions taken by the state to counter-terrorism potentially increase levels of non-state terrorism and the related grievances felt by target communities, at the same time as they appear as the state's ethical responsibility towards all its citizens.

In this sense, the 'War on Terror' is a literal rather than 'metaphorical war', (Banks 2003: 262): it targets individuals and groups, and injures civilians. Thus, a government engaged in a literal war on terror must also be ready to follow the existing rules and conventions that frame any war, including the Geneva Conventions. In this case, democratic and humanitarian principles, values of liberty, justice and equality apply (Wilkinson 2006). In such a context, counter-terrorism approaches must address moral issues at all levels, from individual liberties restrictions to its aims and must, above all, not kill, sanction or arrest indiscriminately (Banks 2013).

Understanding traditional approaches to countering terrorism

As illustrated by the diverse and far reaching impacts of post-9/11 security policies and practice, the range of potential counter-terrorism (CT) measures is immense, and future tactics – both good and bad – are limited only by the imagination of those with the authority, funding and support to implement them. One of the key challenges for all involved, however, is to strive to build current and future CT efforts on activities that 'work', while simultaneously also striving to ensure government efforts do not make the situation worse. Effective policy, planning, and operations in this area are hampered because terrorism research is itself difficult, and not surprisingly, the evidence for truly effective CT measures is weak or questionable (LaFree and Ackerman 2009; Lum *et al.* 2006, 2009).

Firstly, then, when we investigate the effectiveness of CT, we are obligated to consider a question of scale. Is the inquiry one that looks at strategic goals, or is the appropriate concern more correctly focused on smaller, tactical outcomes? For example, when we discuss 'effectiveness', do we seek to understand how terrorist groups and their campaigns come to their demise in a grand sense, in a manner similar to the viewpoint taken by Cronin (2006, 2011; see also Crenshaw 1991)? Or is the priority to more specifically delve into the most effective manner in which terrorist plans and the involved individuals or cells and are intercepted, arrested, and convicted? Alternatively, from a research standpoint, is the most solid foundation perhaps to look at the question from a 'thematic perspective' that collectively considers the tactical *and* strategic implications (Lum *et al.* 2009, referring in particular to the study of CT policing)? And, if we do this, do we run the risk of trying to look at two potentially distinct though related phenomena simultaneously through the same microscope? Or, again in the context of CT policing, are the effects of individual officer contacts and the role of procedural justice a more appropriate and acute emphasis (such as in Tyler 2012; Tyler *et al.* 2010)?

If we look at the question through a strategic, long-term lens, we can refer to Cronin's thorough study of 'how terrorism ends' (Cronin 2006; 2011). This is a pragmatic starting point, as few politicians, law enforcement, military, or intelligence leaders, or members of the public would argue that the overall or ultimate goal must indeed be anything other than the end of terrorist groups – not just an endless litany of interventions against localised actors. It is additionally useful because Cronin has illustrated that 'ending' terrorism is a complex consideration, relying on a variety of factors that are not easily – if ever –completely controllable by government. This suggestion is not new (Crenshaw 1991), but seems to have failed to take root in the popular mindset. The interaction of a numerous potential variables, to potentially include leadership removal, negotiations, the implosion of terrorist organisations, state repression, and movement into the strategic mainstream have all played a role in the conclusion of some terrorist campaigns (Cronin 2011: 206).

Important to note in this strategic view is the inclusion of the role of effective policing measures and the arrest of terrorist leaders ('decapitation', a term which Cronin uses to refer to killing *or* capturing a leader), especially in comparison to other potential government interventions. The imprisonment of a terrorist leader can indeed affect the decline of a movement (Cronin 2006, 2011), which therefore reinforces the sense that quality investigative work is valuable, and 'hard' CT activities have their place. It would therefore appear that law enforcement can work to assist in the strategic demise of terrorist movements, but of course we must then ask what are the appropriate tactics for police, or governments more widely. Hard approaches, while perhaps attractive, are limited, and as Cronin straightforwardly acknowledges, 'the long term effects of decapitation are inconsistent' (2011: 14). Clearly, thoughtful approaches to counter-terrorism, blending the 'hard' and 'soft' sides of police, military, intelligence, and diplomatic interventions are required. However, these 'blended' approaches (see also Kilcullen 2009), while offering some hope, also lack a sufficiently solid research base. As LaFree and Ackerman observe:

> ...early assumptions that rapid military interventions are the only viable response to terrorism have given way to more nuanced approaches that seek to reduce the benefits of joining a terrorist movement by non-military approaches such as addressing grievances or engaging in negotiations. *Although there is some evidence that strategies like this might work, without systematic evaluations strong conclusions cannot be drawn.*
> (LaFree and Ackerman 2009: 366, emphasis added)

What makes these considerations even more difficult is that at this level there is general agreement that a true dearth of 'scientific' research exists to support the effectiveness of any specific police CT measures (LaFree and Ackerman 2009; Lum et al. 2006, 2009). As Lum et al. note, 'there is more uncertainty than certainty about the effectiveness of counter-terrorism programs' (2006: 508). Indeed, Lum et al. were only able to find *seven studies out of more than 20,000* that sought through sufficiently sound means to measure the effectiveness of CT efforts, observing that 'the scarcity of evaluation research leaves us with limited ability to draw strong conclusions about the effectiveness of counter-terrorism strategies' (2006: 508; see also Legrand, this volume). Those authors considered a wide variety of actions that potentially fall within the realms of both 'hard' and 'soft' CT, to include investigations, arrests, education, religious interventions, situational crime prevention and imprisonment. In the end, they were only able to substantiate one proven CT response: that research supports the positive effect of metal detectors at airports in preventing hijackings – leaving all other types of CT interventions as unproven or worse yet, counter-productive. This, of course, provides little guidance to CT personnel, other than to say 'we just don't know'.

Unfortunately, a persistent, wide variety of criticisms regarding law enforcement counter-terrorism measures have been voiced since 9/11 (e.g. Choudhury and Fenwick 2011; Thomas 2010, this volume; Vertigans 2010; Pantazis and Pemberton 2009), reflecting fears, doubts and concerns, and underlining the need to identify what objectively works. While these criticisms may not meet the standards of rigor set forth by Lum et al., (2006, 2009) they –like other evidence of the effectiveness of police CT efforts – are certainly worthy of note. Indeed, these concerns cannot be minimised, especially when one considers the potential effect of 'hard' CT measures such as stop and search. In this case, after 10 years and more than 500,000 uses in the UK under the Terrorism Act, these powers 'have not led to any convictions in relation to terrorism' (Choudhury and Fenwick 2011: viii). Thus, while street level stops may play a role in countering terrorism, how can they be utilised in a manner that prevents feeding into terrorist narratives? Indeed, there are concerns that poor counter-terrorism practices may actually *increase* the likelihood of terrorism (Tyler 2012; LaFree et al. 2009; Donohue 2008).

These concerns point to the space available for an alternative view of policing in broad terms, and counter-terrorism policing more specifically, in which procedural justice may more appropriately and accurately describe the ways in which police should frame their crime-fighting role and relationship with communities (see, for example, Sunshine and Tyler 2003; Tyler 2012, 2011, 2009; Tyler et al. 2010; Huq et al. 2011), reorienting what has traditionally been seen as 'effective'. 'The procedural justice perspective argues that the legitimacy of the police is linked to public judgments about the fairness of the processes through which the police make decisions and exercise authority' (Sunshine and Tyler 2003: 514), and in particular gives attention to the way in which police treat members of the public. This lens does not seek to dismiss the role of 'hard' tactics such as street level stops, for example, but instead underlines the way in which quality decisions and positive interactions during these stops have the potential for positively affecting police-community cooperation and compliance with the law. Future discussions of 'hard' and 'soft' CT measures should perhaps more usefully be understood in terms of procedural justice concerns as opposed to instrumental models used to explain the veracity of specific tactics and strategies. As Tyler notes, while 'it may be a natural and instinctive response to project force in response to threat ... police and other authorities need to engage in the potentially less emotionally satisfying but more useful approach of building support among those populations' in which terrorists may seek support (2012: 361).

Even on the side of the spectrum that prioritises community input and relationships we must carefully question how we define 'success' within counter-terrorism policing (O'Rawe *et al.* 2013). Additionally, it may be helpful to remember that success is perhaps best understood as government offering a more compelling argument for 'the fairness of their policies' (LaFree and Ackerman 2009: 357; see also Tyler 2012), while reflecting that 'success may be less about local legitimacy and more about the ability to energise and mobilise support, and to deny energy and mobility to the [terrorist] support base' (Kilcullen 2006–2007: 121). At the risk of objectifying the populace, effectiveness and success must be linked to the understanding that 'the people remain the prize' (Kilcullen 2006–2007: 117).

From counter-terrorism to conflict transformation: Lessons, challenges and the future

As discussed above, terrorism remains a contested notion. Different actors and institutions have different understandings, definitions, and viewpoints about how terrorism should be prevented – thus, there will be points of divergence and contestation, alongside points of convergence. Counter-terrorism can also involve conflict – struggle, incompatibility, collision, or disagreement – between different actors, institutions and nation states, for if terrorism is a contested notion then doing counter-terrorism will mirror and generate further loci of contestation. Ideas about what works, what approaches should be developed, who should be included, what the causes of terrorism are, these are all unresolved questions. Different political, organisational and emotional cultures will impact upon counter-terrorism practices and so there are likely to be disagreements and incompatibilities over approaches. By exploring counter-terrorism as conflict transformation, this enables a shift of focus and frame: towards dialogue, engagement, partnership and change.

A pertinent case study in the development of more open, community focused and driven forms of counter-terrorism – arguably a step towards more clearly defined notions of conflict transformation, remains the British Government's CONTEST strategy, in which Prevent measures have accompanied more traditional covert operational tactics under the Pursue strand.

The British Government has relied heavily on the legitimacy and communication gained from the policy and practice of 'community consultation', 'partnerships', 'collaboration' and 'community capacity building'. Such language is part of the frontline tools of its counter-terrorism strategy (Home Office 2011), and is used to indicate that communities are the frontline in fighting terrorism and violent extremism. Yet this discourse within policy and academia can create a false hope around the existence of neat solutions to the problems of counter-terrorism while camouflaging the messy realities of partnership-led solutions. The attractive, simple policy notion of engagement and partnership belies the level of skill and length of time necessary for counter-terrorism practitioners and community members alike to develop trust, take risks and align mutual needs and goals, in the highly sensitive, politicised and stigmatising contexts in which they must all not just operate in a professional sense, but live their lives.

For too long, counter-terrorism practice has involved 'hard' approaches that involve infiltrating and spying on communities, and stigmatising and securitising them. Counter-terrorism policy and practice has been severely criticised, particularly as this may in reality often be similar to the actions carried out by terrorists (Jackson 2008). For this reason, the call for future counter-terrorism policy and practice to be reframed as a form of conflict transformation has both practical and ethical grounding. Perhaps most profoundly, reframing counter-terrorism as conflict transformation helps state and non-state actors to work through their differences, to value each others' differing perspectives and experiences, and to work together in order to reduce the potential for extreme forms of violence.

Yet the path is neither linear nor general. For counter-terrorism to be effectively undertaken as conflict transformation it is important to draw upon the perspectives and experiences and work of state and non-state actors who are credible in this field, in the multitude of contexts in which security – in its complete sense – is an issue. This is the humanity of the work, the experiential and the emotional. Our research highlights that credibility is more than experience or learning, but about a person's positionality, about how a person draws upon their multiple identities in order to build trust and relationships with their key audiences and potential partners (Hewitt *et al.* 2012). Credibility can be challenging, for this is about being prepared to challenge dominant power structures in order to try and secure social justice, in a world characterised by social, economic and political injustice. Often those state and non-state actors who might be understood as credible are those who subvert the power relations that create social harms, and enable marginalised individuals and communities to work towards securing a better environment for themselves. It may be that individuals and communities are grappling with wide-ranging issues such as drug addiction, gang violence, domestic violence, anti-social behaviour: for counter-terrorism to be a form of conflict transformation it is important for this to include credible state and non-state actors beyond the traditional security paradigm, who see themselves as striving towards a society where there is less social harm and more social justice. This can involve state and non-state actors not only working to prevent terrorism and counter violent extremism, but also to prevent a broad range of intersecting social problems, whose measurement of harm may be more deeply and frequently felt at the grassroots. Indeed, communities are more likely to be accepting of terrorism prevention work if this includes creating solutions to other social issues facing communities (Spalek 2013), including the community tensions and suspicions generated and sustained by counter-terrorism in the first instance.

The empirical data that we have gathered since 2007 also highlights the importance of community policing models within a counter-terrorism context. There is a danger that community policing is co-opted into state-driven agendas that almost exclusively focus on Muslim communities when responding to terrorism, and more recently the white working-class pathologised by and through far-right activities and discourse. However, when carried out effectively, and when involving credible state and non-state actors, community policing can be an important tool in approaching counter-terrorism as conflict transformation. Especially effective have been those initiatives in which communities have developed and led initiatives, from youth work and mentoring to the disruption of unwanted extremist elements using state institutions and actors for support where needed and when asked for. The power dynamic is thus switched, and the role of state as a service to citizens is reasserted.

The following definition of community policing within a counter-terrorism context highlights the importance of community consent and trust in relation to any policing initiatives that are implemented:

> community policing comprises community-oriented goals and objectives. It relies upon community consent in relation to policing initiatives and operations within communities. Trust between community members and police officers is an essential component of community policing.
>
> (Spalek 2010: 793)

Therefore, the future of counter-terrorism as conflict transformation should include community policing models that are based on trust and consent. This is because community policing can be an important mechanism through which information and intelligence is shared between police officers and community members. Community policing can help prevent terrorism, even though it is difficult to provide conclusive evidence as to a non-event! Community policing is an important tool for the future of counter-terrorism as conflict transformation for it involves relationship-building and even partnerships between state and non-state actors, and therefore can be an important mechanism through which to avoid the stigmatisation and securitisation of communities (Spalek 2010; Lambert 2011). Any future initiatives involving community policing models should not exploit trust for intelligence gathering purposes, but rather, should build trust for intelligence sharing. This is an important distinction because there have been numerous accusations of community policing models being used as intelligence-gathering exercises (Kundnani 2009). It is also important to note that there is a danger for policing generally to overlook the role that social and political factors that underpin any community support for terrorism or other forms of extreme violence. Therefore, community policing offers an important way through which police officers and community members can regularly engage with each other, outside of any crisis event or terrorist act, serving to humanise police and community relations.

Future developments within counter-terrorism must also carefully consider the question of citizenship. It may be that individuals living within Western democratic societies experience differentiated citizenship, in that wider social and political factors influence the relationship between different citizens and the State (Spalek 2013). Indeed, the identities and loyalties of minority Muslim communities in the West have in particular been scrutinised by states due to state-led approaches to counter al Qaeda linked terrorism in particular. In a report by the Equality and Human Rights Commission in the UK, into the impact of counter-terrorism legislation on Muslim communities, it was highlighted that:

> When it comes to experiences of counter-terrorism, Muslims and non-Muslims from the same local areas who participated in this research appear to live 'parallel lives'. Counter-terrorism measures are contributing to a wider sense among Muslims that they are being treated as a 'suspect community' and targeted by authorities simply because of their religion. Many participants, while not referring to specific laws or policies, felt that counter-terrorism law and policy generally was contributing towards hostility to Muslims by treating Muslims as a 'suspect group', and creating a climate of fear and suspicion towards them.
>
> (Choudhury and Fenwick 2001: v)

A key issue for future counter-terrorism policy and practice is how states may encourage their citizens to work within state-driven agendas? This is particularly pertinent within a context of differentiated citizenship, with competing 'loyalties' associated with a diverse citizenry that experiences forms of belongingness at a global, as well as national and local level, In this context, how is it possible or desirable for states to encourage their citizens to work within state-driven agendas? Do individual citizens have a duty to actively question counter-terrorism policies and practices that are unethical? Can citizens create their own approaches to counter-terrorism that reflect the needs of local contexts and communities and gain the support of state actors and agendas? These are key questions for future policy, practice and research.

Engagement and partnership are also key issues for the future of counter-terrorism. Our research has highlighted a number of key issues in relation to engagement and partnerships. For example, our work has indicated the significance of general engagement with wide-ranging community members; the importance and challenges of engaging and partnering non-violent radicals; and, how engagement and partnership can involve several different meanings and approaches relating to enhancing the quality of life for communities, building inclusivity, developing connections with women, building relationships, engaging with wider political issues, moving at the community's pace, respect and understanding (McDonald 2011; Spalek 2013). Engagement and partnership therefore require further scrutiny and analysis.

Our research has also highlighted the importance of the role of emotions in counter-terrorism practice (Spalek *et al.* 2009; Spalek and McDonald 2011; Spalek 2013). Terrorists can exploit and even generate destructive emotions in individuals who are susceptible to their messages and this in turn can lead to further violent action. This is the personal, group, social and political power of emotion: Wallace and Flanagan (2002: 53) explain 'destructive emotions are those emotions that are harmful to oneself or others'. For Goleman (2003: 119), destructive emotions might be viewed as those that are 'byproducts of something useful in human behaviour that in themselves serve no survival function and, in fact, at times have negative survival value'. These include craving, anger, fear, sadness, envy and jealousy (Spalek 2013: 129).

From this perspective 'hard' counter-terrorism measures can also help to perpetuate destructive emotions, potentially leading to individuals engaging in violent rather than non-violent political action within target communities, but also amongst counter-terrorism and security practitioners, for example the dehumanising and othering of suspect individuals and groups, and the normalisation of power imbalance and forms of violence within and outside of state law. Through this analysis, we would argue that future counter-terrorism practice must consider emotions much more centrally. We would suggest that effective counter-terrorism as conflict transformation should involve state and non-state actors in working towards transforming destructive emotions into constructive emotions, thereby potentially transforming violent political action into non-violent political action. Whilst policing organisations may value detached rationality, this can create tensions for police officers because not only is police work itself often emotional, but also because policing cultures and rules are effect-laden. At the same time, communities themselves have complex emotional landscapes with inter- and intra-group dynamics and tensions further adding to the complexities. Tensions can be created between state and non-state actors when state actors attempt to be emotionally distant within highly emotionally charged contexts (Spalek 2013). Therefore, in the future counter-terrorism practitioners need to engage much more centrally with emotion, their own and that of the emotional landscapes of the communities within which they work. Emotions must lie at the core of counter-terrorism as conflict transformation, for this is an area ripe with emotional as well as psychological and political conflict.

Conclusions

The shifting and complex layers of social and political, group and individual circumstances constantly shape and reshape the contexts in which the discourse and acts of terror and counter-terror operate, which are themselves conceptually contested by multiple perspectives. At the heart of the terrorism-counter-terrorism binary lies the binarisation of state-community/citizen, greatly magnified by the 'hard' tactics and strategies of state security and its traditional exclusion or lack of understanding towards human and community security. In the face of this framework in which cycles of violence are perpetuated and even escalated, we have argued for the reassertion of the humanity of all actors not only as an assertion of ethics but in better understanding the human dynamic as key to resolving conflict – the mutual interests, the role of emotions, the location and alignment of common frameworks and goals. In this we envision a shift – conceptual and practical – from the terrorism-counter-terrorism nexus, to one of partnership across traditional boundaries of 'state' and 'citizen', with an intention and strategic approach to conflict transformation.

Note

1 **ConnectJustice** is a social enterprise: we research, evaluate, train and facilitate on issues of social justice including terrorism, extremism, sexual exploitation and diversity. We work closely with communities, practitioners, government and non-government agencies to bridge divides, transform conflict and make lasting positive change. Further information is available at:www.connectjustice.org.

References

Banks, C. (2008) *Criminal justice ethics: theory and practice*. Second Edition. Thousand Oaks: Sage.

Blakeley, R. (2007) 'Bringing the state back into terrorism studies', *European Political Science*, 6, pp. 228–235.

Breen Smyth, M. 2007. 'A Critical Research Agenda for the Study of Political Terror', *European Political Science*, 6 (3), pp. 260–267.

Choudhury, T. and Fenwick, H. (2011) *The Impact of Counter-Terrorism Measures on Muslim Communities* London: Equality & Human Rights Commission.

Crenshaw, M. (1991) 'How terrorism declines', *Terrorism and Political Violence*, 3 (1), pp. 69–87.

Cronin, A.K. (2006) 'How al-Qaida ends: The decline and demise of terrorist groups', *International Security*, 31 (1), pp. 7–48.

Cronin, A.K. (2011) *How Terrorism Ends: Understanding the Decline and Demise of Terrorist Campaigns*, Princeton, New Jersey: Princeton University Press.

Donohue, L. (2008) *The Cost of Counter-terrorism: Power, Politics, and Liberty*, New York: Cambridge University Press.

Dudouet, V. (2011) 'Anti-terrorism legislation: impediments to conflict transformation', *Berghof Policy Bried*, 02, pp. 1–16.

Europol TeSat (2010) EU terrorism situation and trend report.

Ewald, U. and Turkovic, K. (eds) (2006) *Large-scale victimisation as a potential source of terrorist activities: importance of regaining security in post-conflict societies*, Amsterdam: IOS Press. (NATO Security through Science Series).

Guiora, A. (2012) 'Due process and counter-terrorism', *Emory International Law Review*, 26, pp. 163–188.

Gunning, J. (2007) 'A case for critical terrorism studies', *Government and Opposition*, 42 (3), pp. 363–393.

Hewitt, S., Spalek, B. and McDonald, L.Z. (2012) 'Dissent, Protest and Conflict within and between Communities' *Summary Report* AHRC Connected Communities Programme.

Huq, A.Z., Tyler, T.R. and Schulhofer, S.J. (2011) 'Mechanisms for eliciting cooperation in counter-terrorism policing: Evidence from the United Kingdom', *Journal of Empirical Legal Studies*, 8 (4), pp. 728–761.

Jackson, R. (2007) 'The core commitments of critical terrorism studies', *European Political Science*, 6, 244–251.

Jackson, R. (2008) An argument for terrorism, *Perspectives on Terrorism*, II (2), pp. 25–32.

Jenkins, B. (1980) *The study of terrorism: definitional problems*. Santa Monica, CA: RAND.

Kilcullen, D. (2006–2007) 'Counter-insurgency redux', *Survival*, 48 (4), pp. 111–130.

Kilcullen, D. (2009) *The Accidental Guerilla: Fighting Small Wars in the Midst of a Big One*, New York: Oxford University Press.

Kundnani, A. (2009) *Spooked: How Not to Prevent Violent Extremism*, London: Institute of Race Relations.

LaFree, G., and Ackerman, G. (2009) 'The empirical study of terrorism: Social and legal research', *Annual Review of Law and Social Science*, 5, pp. 347–374.

LaFree, G., Dugan, L. and Korte, R. (2009) 'The impact of British counterterrorist strategies on political violence in Northern Ireland: Comparing deterrence and backlash models', *Criminology*, 47 (1), pp. 17–45.

Lambert, R. (2011) *Countering Al-Qaeda in London: police and Muslims in partnership* London: Hurst.

Lum, C., Kennedy, L.W. and Sherley, A. (2006) 'Are counter-terrorism strategies effective? The results of the Campbell systematic review on counter-terrorism evaluation research', *Journal of Experimental Criminology* 2 (4), pp. 489–516.

Lum, C., Haberfeld, M., Fachner, G. and Lieberman, C. (2009) 'Police activities to counter terrorism: What we know and what we need to know', in D. Weisburd, T.E. Feucht, I. Hakimi, L.F. Mock and S. Perry (eds), *To Protect and To Serve: Policing in an Age of Terrorism*, New York: Springer, pp. 101–142

Martin, G. (2013) *Understanding terrorism*. Fourth Edition. Thousand Oaks, CA: Sage.

McDonald, L.Z. (2011) 'Securing Identities, Resisting Terror: Muslim Youth Work in the UK and its Implications for Security', *Religion, State and Society*, 39 (2/3), pp. 177–190.

O'Rawe, M., Silk, P.D. and Spalek, B. (2013) 'Introduction', in P.D. Silk, B. Spalek and M. O'Rawe (eds), *Preventing Ideological Violence: Communities, Police and Case Studies of "Success"*, New York: Palgrave Macmillan.

Pantazis, C. and Pemberton, S. (2009) 'From the "old" to the "new" suspect community: Examining the impacts of recent UK counter-terrorism legislation', *British Journal of Criminology*, 49, pp. 646–666.

Schmid, A. and Jongman, A. (2005) *Political terrorism*. Piscataway, NJ: Transaction Publishers.

Schmid, A. (2004) Terrorism: the definitional problem, *Case Western Reserve Journal of International Law*, 36, pp. 375–420.

Schmid, A. (2006) 'Magnitudes and focus of terrorist victimization', in U. Ewald, A. Schmid and A. Jongman (eds) (1988), *Political terrorism: a new guide to actors, authors, concepts, data bases, theories and literature*. Amsterdam: North Holland Publishers Company.

Sluka, J. (2002) 'What anthropologists should know about the concept of terrorism', *Anthropology Today*, 18 (2), pp. 22–23.

Smyth, M. (2007) 'A critical research agenda for the study of political terror', *European Political Science*, 6, pp. 260–267.

Spalek, B and Imtoual, A. (2007) 'Muslim Communities and Counter-Terror Responses: "Hard" Approaches to Community Engagement in the UK and Australia' *Journal of Muslim Minority Affairs*, 27 (2), pp. 185–202.

Spalek, B. (2008) *Communities, identities and crime*. The Policy Press, University of Bristol.

Spalek, B. (2010) 'Community Policing, Trust and Muslim Communities in relation to "new terrorism"', *Politics & Policy*, 38 (4), pp. 789–815.

Spalek, B. (2013) *Governing Terror: trust, community and counter-terrorism*, Bloomsbury Academic Press.

Spalek, B., El-Awa, S. and McDonald, L.Z. (2009) 'Engagement and Partnership Work in a Counter-Terrorism Context' University of Birmingham.

Spalek, B. and McDonald, L.Z. (2011) 'Preventing Religio-Political Violent Extremism Amongst Muslim Youth: a study exploring police-community partnership' University of Birmingham.

Stern, J. (1999) *The ultimate terrorists*, Cambridge: Harvard University Press.

Sunshine, J., and Tyler, T.R. (2003) 'The role of procedural justice and legitimacy in shaping public support for policing', *Law & Society Review*, 37 (3), pp. 513–548.

Tyler, T.R. (2011) 'Trust and legitimacy: Policing in the USA and Europe.' *European Journal of Criminology*, 8 (4), pp. 254–266.

Tyler, T.R. (2012) 'Toughness v. fairness: Police policies and practices for managing the risk of terrorism', in C. Lum and L.W. Kennedy (eds), *Evidence-Based Counter-terrorism Policy*, New York: Springer.

Tyler, T.R., and Huo, Y.J. (2003) *Trust in the Law: Encouraging Public Cooperation with the Police and Courts.* New York: Russell Sage Foundation.

Tyler, T.R., Schulhofer, S.J. and Huq, A.Z. (2010) 'Legitimacy and deterrence effects in counter-terrorism policing: A study of Muslim Americans.' *Law & Society Review*, 44 (2), pp. 365–402.

Vertigans, S. (2010) 'British Muslims and the UK government's "war on terror" within: Evidence of a clash of civilizations or emergent de-civilizing process?', *The British Journal of Sociology*, 61 (1), pp. 26–44.

Weinberg, Pedahzur and Hirsch-Hoefler (2004) 'The challenges of conceptualizing terrorism', *Terrorism and Political Violence*, 16 (4), pp. 777–794.

Wilkinson, P. (2006). *Terrorism versus democracy: the liberal state response*. Second Edition. Oxon: Routledge.

5 Contemporary Spanish anti-terrorist policies
Ancient myths, new approaches[1]

Agata Serranò

Introduction

This chapter aims to study three core issues: *which players* are entitled to operate in the end of terrorism, *what* the end of terrorism means, and *with what kind* of anti-terrorist policies can the end of terrorism be reached. These three issues will be analysed, keeping in mind the Spanish experience in the fight against ETA's terrorism.[2]

Regarding the players entitled to operate in the end of terrorism we will argue if the State is the only player that should take part in the fight against terrorism or, as the Spanish experience shows, if civilian society and victims are also entitled to play an active social role against this crime.

Vis-à-vis the meaning of the end of terrorism, some key points of ETA and Basque nationalist rhetoric will be examined. According to this narrative, the end of terrorism is presented as a status of 'peace' that would be automatically achieved when the players involved in the 'conflict' stop carrying out violence. We will contrast this view, highlighting that the end of terrorism cannot be considered as only a mere absence of violence.

In the conclusion, taking into consideration the Spanish context, we will propose some guidelines to follow for the drafting of anti-terrorist policies, whose objective is an *ideal* end of terrorism where respect for the rights to truth, memory and justice is guaranteed.

To outline these guidelines, we will put forward a theoretical assumption: there are two 'false myths' regarding *the players* entitled to fight against terrorism, and *what* the end of terrorism means. Refuting these two 'false myths' will allow drafting anti-terrorist policies that, to the most possible extent, strive for the attainment of an *ideal* end of terrorism.

To achieve this, we will adopt the *type method* which is a cognitive procedure that will allow us to build *conceptual archetypes* from which to deliberate and explain the three above-mentioned issues regarding the end of terrorism. The type method is an instrument that can 'render the study fruitful' as it will help us to design a methodology to use in our area of research (Jellinek 1981: 20–30).

The *type method* uses the construction of *type-concepts* as a base to formulate generalisations. As shown by Del Real (2007: 309–318), typological generalisations offer a more extensive level of conceptual analysis of the mental representation of reality compared to other methods such as that of universal generalisations (Natural Law) which build upon universal generic concepts, causal generalisation methods which use law concepts (Natural science) or historical individualisation methods which use individual historical concepts (Historical science). Given that the application of type-methods allows for a greater level of abstraction and generality, the use of this method to refute 'false myths' means that some of their historical characteristics will be disregarded (Jellinek 1981: 20–30).

Jellinek, the first theoretician of this method, speculated that *empirical types* are the mechanism with which we classify and understand most of our social life. According to this method, *thinking in types* induces the creation of *fundamental concepts* which group together in a dual mode like *dichotomies of opposite types*. Among the dichotomous types created – usually bipolar – the researcher will solve the tension between the two parts of the conceptual pair. These are doctrinally the opposite of each other so choosing one implies rejecting the validity of the one not chosen.

According to Weber, *ideal types* are abstract constructions of concepts by which reality is measured and compared for it to be studied in depth. The comparison between *ideal type-concepts* which are pure and ideal and *empirical type-concepts* aims to show the clear and evident conceptual distance between them. Thus, according to Weber, given that a pure ideal type is far from reality, it contributes to its understanding by classifying historical phenomena via the indication of proximity of them to a number of said theoretical concepts (Weber 1964).

In order to be able to draft the guidelines for anti-terrorist policies that aim to attain an end of terrorism that would guarantee respect for the rights of truth, memory and justice, this study first classifies two false myths believed to exist in Western democracies, above all in Spain. Secondly, two ideal principles (ideal type-concepts) are compared with these two false myths (empirical type-concepts) which allow the latter to be refuted. According to Weber's method, these ideal principles would form the guidelines for the anti-terrorist policies which would aim to achieve an ideal end of terrorism.

Firstly, we theorise the 'myth of the exclusivity of the State' which is based on the belief that the only players who should take part in the fight against terrorism are the State and all the institutions that constitute it. Consequently, according to this belief, civilian society and victims are not entitled to play an active role against terrorism. This study counters this false myth with 'the ideal principle of the socialisation of the fight against terrorism', which considers society and victims to be important players in the fight against terrorism.

The second false myth we address in this study is 'the myth of peace as the end of violence', based on the belief that the solution to terrorism corresponds to the mere end of the violence perpetrated by the terrorist group/s involved. Peace, according to this belief, would be a status that would be automatically attained, in the context of the conflict, when the terrorists stop carrying out fatal attacks. This vision is therefore very similar to that which emerges from the terrorists' narrative and does not take into consideration that to achieve an end to terrorism, along with a cessation of violence, it is necessary to respect individual and collective rights (Alonso 2009). This false myth is countered with 'the ideal principle for peace as a synonym for justice'.

In the conclusion, and bringing together the ideal principles created, we will attempt to identify the fundamental points of the anti-terrorist policies that could, in practice, and to all extents possible, attain an *ideal* end of terrorism.

The myth of the exclusivity of the state vs. the ideal principle of socialisation in the fight against terrorism

In this section, after defining 'the myth of the exclusivity of the State', we will discuss the role of civilian society in the fight against terrorism. Studying the Spanish experience affords us an example of how civilian society, and in particular victims of terrorism, can become players in the social fight against this crime.

When the bibliography of a number of European States regarding terrorism engendered throughout the twentieth century is examined, it can be seen that academic interest focuses on what has led terrorists to carry out such inhuman acts. From some of the research, and by means of qualitative interviews with terrorists, it has been possible to study their personal motivations and opinions regarding the 'conflict' they took part in (Reinares 2001; Alonso 2003; Catanzaro 1990). However, it should be stressed that research that has addressed the issue of the experiences of victims of terrorism is much more recent and less common (Alonso et al. 2010; McKittrick et al. 2006; Presidenza della Repubblica 2008). More specifically, the analysis of Spanish literature in this field reveals that the testimonies of victims of terrorism appear in very few publications written by researchers and/or by relatives of those affected (Pagazaurtundua 2004; Baglietto 1999; Villa 2004; Cuesta 2000).

The lack of attention given to victims of terrorism in academic studies perhaps reflects a *traditional view* which had an influence on many of the anti-terrorist policies adopted by Western democracies in the twentieth century. In our opinion, this view is probably based on a false myth that we will call the 'myth of the exclusivity of the State', linked to the players in a democratic society who are entitled to fight against terrorism. We believe the roots of this myth lie in the following conviction: given that terrorism is a problem that affects the State, the responsibility of operating against this criminal phenomenon falls exclusively to the State and all of the bodies established for its defence. Therefore, according to this traditional view, civilian society is not considered to be a player entitled to fight against terrorism, and so terrorism is understood as a 'conflict' solely between the State and the terrorists. In our view, this traditional perspective does not take into account two key issues: firstly, those affected by terrorist violence are not only democratic powers, State bodies, its territory and/or political-economic interests, but also – and above all – individuals, citizens, civilian society. Secondly, civilian society is not only an affected part of such violence but can also be considered a player in the fight against terrorism in democratic States (Serranò 2012).

It should be highlighted that following the attacks of September 11, 2001, a number of measures adopted in the United States and the United Kingdom have re-evaluated the active role of citizens in the fight against terrorism.[3] By giving citizens the responsibility of alerting police forces of suspicious behaviour, these measures directly implicate citizens in the fight against crime and, in a specific way, against terrorism. However, a number of scholars criticise these initiatives as they see many disadvantages in them for both individuals as well as for society as a whole. Among these problems, Vaughan-Williams (2008: 72) highlights that the emergence of the figure of the 'citizen–detective' – a vigilante constantly on the look-out for suspicious behaviour – could create a climate of 'mutual suspicion' within society. Furthermore, this author believes that 'the promotion of this form of surveillance could constitute a form of generalised borderwork whereby the borders of sovereign communities are (re) reproduced not only at the edge of territories but throughout society at large' (2008: 77). Likewise, Jarvis and Lister (2010: 182) stress that this participation in counter-terrorism mechanisms is viewed increasingly as a social commitment. Thus, citizens are obligated – not merely expected – to contribute to the national security project in specific ways. This obligation to participate in the provision of security is becoming, in some instances, the key responsibility of citizenship. In conclusion, according to Jarvis and Lister (2010: 174), these new mechanisms for combating terrorism 'from below' 'lead to the ever more precarious positioning of individuals within Western states as simultaneously they become suppliers of, beneficiaries from, and challengers to the successful provision of security'.

It is important to note that, via these measures the United States and the United Kingdom have tried to promote the active participation of citizens, in particular in the *police* fight against terrorism. By contrast, in Spain, the spontaneous participation of civilian society, thanks to the impulse of victims of terrorism, has been instrumental in the *social* fight against terrorism. In fact, in the twentieth century, from the 1980s and 1990s onwards, victims' associations and civic movements have organised very significant collective actions of public condemnation against the crime of terrorism and, primarily, against ETA's violence. The acts of protest carried out by these associations and movements show how Spanish civilian society in general, and Basque civilian society in particular, comprise an important delegitimising force regarding ETA's terrorism (Uriarte 2003).

Examining the half-yearly surveys carried out by the Euskobarómetro Research Team from the University of the Basque Country,[4] attitudes of Basque citizens to ETA show a trend for less support for the terrorist group and more rejection of its violence. More specifically, among those interviewed:

- 'Total support' for the terrorist group decreased from 8 per cent in 1981 to 3 per cent in 1989, to 2 per cent in 1999 and to 1 per cent in 2013.

- The percentage of those who support ETA's goals, but does not accept violence went from 3 per cent in 1981 to 9 per cent in 1989, to 15 per cent in 1999 and to 12 per cent in 2013.
- 'Total rejection' of ETA's terrorism increased from 23 per cent in 1981 to 45 per cent in 1989; went down to 25 per cent in 1999 and is at 59 per cent in 2013.

The massive and peaceful demonstrations that took place throughout the 1980s and 1990s in the Basque Country reached their peak in 1997 with the kidnapping and subsequent assassination by ETA of Miguel Ángel Blanco,[5] a Popular Party town councillor in the Basque municipality of Ermua. According to Funes (1998: 13), that peak of demonstrations constituted 'the express, exceptional and decisive manifestation of a long and complex transformation of Basque society'. Citizen involvement in the condemnation of terrorism was key in creating awareness for part of society and politicians, giving rise to new political agreements in the fight against this crime and to the development of laws regarding compensation and help for victims.

One of the steps carried through by the main political parties was, for example, the *Pact in favour of freedoms and against terrorism*. In this anti-terrorist pact – which will be outlined further on – signed in 2000 by the Popular Party (PP) and the Spanish Socialist Workers' Party (PSOE), both parties committed themselves to work jointly in the fight against ETA's terrorism and, more specifically, in the areas of prison policies, international cooperation and the recognition and care of victims of terrorism (Alonso 2004).

Likewise, another significant measure – which will be dealt with in more depth later on – was the Political Parties Law of 2002 which established the banning by judicial channels of any political party or movement that did not condemn terrorism or that maintained links with terrorist organisations. After this law was passed, *Batasuna* – ETA's political wing – and many other organisations that form part of this terrorist group's network were banned, considerably weakening its political and social support[6] (Alonso 2010).

In particular from the 1990s until today, Spanish legislators have built a legal framework that publicly recognises victims of terrorism and guarantees them compensation and personalised care regarding medical and psychological help including for the socio-family sphere. For this help to be appropriately provided, various central and local bodies such as the General Directorate for Support to Victims of Terrorism and the Directorate of the Basque Government for Service to Victims of Terrorism were, on the one hand, created to offer victims care and attention (Pulgar 2004). On the other, innovative Laws regarding compensation and care were passed, with the 1999 Law of Solidarity (Pérez 2003) and the 2011 Law for the Recognition and Comprehensive Protection for Victims of Terrorism being among the most significant.

Although these mobilisations against terrorism in Spain can be categorised mainly as being in opposition to ETA's violent acts, they have also taken place after other fatal attacks, again with extraordinary levels of public participation.

In the face of the massacre in Madrid perpetrated by Jihadist terrorism on the 11 March 2004, over two million people took part in demonstrations in defence of democracy. This constituted possibly one of the most peaceful responses ever seen in Europe against this crime. These responses show how civilian society can be 'a rational weapon against terrorism', as citizens did not use the irrational outrage of the violence to oppose terrorism, but resorted to the *ratio* of a State where rule of law is correctly applied: the defence of human rights and democracy, using peaceful means and within the Law (Serranò 2009).

Despite the injustices suffered, victims of terrorism in Spain have never reacted to terrorism with violence but have complied with the Law and respected the constitutional values of a democratic State. They can, therefore, be considered 'moral beacons' (Brewer and Hayes 2011) that must be present and visible within society. However, what we understand as visibility is a far cry from the attainment of power or privileges that they could obtain from their participation in public life. Visibility as we understand it is identified with the opportunity of making their experiences known given that, as Mate (2008: 17–43) states, victims see things that the rest of us do not see, they are able to read what is not written, that which is missing, that which was lost along the way. Victims add to the knowledge of reality the viewpoint of what was hidden or concealed, silenced, deprived of its meaning.

Victims, therefore, must be present in society – must not be marginalised or silenced – because their victimhood also has an undeniably public dimension. In fact, given that the terrorist act that made them victims was committed with the political intention of subverting constitutional order and democracy, at the moment of being assassinated they took on a public value and political significance (Arregi 2008). They therefore deserve recognition by society and the constitutional State for having defended the *res publica*, democracy, fundamental freedoms, and constitutional values that endure, in exchange for their loss of life (Alonso et al. 2010). Likewise, the visibility of victims could be an obstacle in the manipulation of what happened and for the making of political decisions that could intentionally, or not, legitimise terrorist crimes. Denying victims visibility and respect for their political significance would mean permitting the 'dehumanisation of the enemy', one of the goals terrorist groups usually seek (Sabucedo et al. 2001).

As the narrative of victims is, in good part, based on the defence of pluralism, of fundamental freedoms and the constitutional values of a democratic State, it could be considered a counter-narrative with which to contrast the terrorists' narrative. It could also be a useful means for deradicalising violent extremist collectives, with a particular focus on youngsters. The narrative of victim can therefore constitute an educational and cultural legacy that should be transmitted to younger generations so that the events of many decades of terrorism do not become history in line with the version promoted by terrorist propaganda.

According to Del Real (2013), at this point in the evolution of Western constitutional States, the aim of this era must consist in converting the respect for the dignity and the public recognition of victims of terrorism into a moral value within the public ethic of democracy. To achieve this goal it will, most likely, be necessary to leave the traditional viewpoint regarding the phenomenon of terrorism behind, and thus consider civilian society and victims to be relevant players in the *social* fight against terrorism (Serranò 2012). So, in light of the 'myth of the exclusivity of the State', which has characterised some of the anti-terrorist policies of Western democracies in the twentieth century, it would be timely to direct future policies towards a 'socialisation in the fight against terrorism'. Not excluding victims of terrorism from the players entitled to operate against terrorism would be the first step in paying a collective debt that society as a whole owes to them (Del Real in Garrido [ed.] 2011).

The myth of peace as the end of violence vs. the ideal principle for peace as a synonym for justice

In this section, we will introduce 'the myth of peace as the end of violence', deduced from the study of a number of fundamental points of ETA's rhetoric and Basque nationalist ideology. Bearing in mind the complex nature of terrorism and the indirect effects it can have on the societies where it manifests itself, we will contrast this myth by putting forward an end of terrorism where respect for the rights to truth, memory and justice is guaranteed.

In both moderate and radical nationalist discourses, the Basque question has historical roots whose cause is attributed to the permanent oppression – that goes back to the nineteenth century – that the Basques suffered under Spain when the *Fueros* were abolished.[7] On the one hand, in the moderate discourse of the Basque Nationalist Party (PNV), the use of violence is not accepted nor are its means condoned, but it does state – in the same way as ETA and Basque radical nationalism's discourses do – that the 'Basque conflict' can only be resolved by attacking its root causes, in other words, *Spanish colonisation*, via the concession of self-determination by the Spanish Government.[8] Only with a political solution – the self-determination of the Basque people – to a political problem – the Basque conflict – can peace and the end of violence be attained (Montero 2006: 57–63).

On the other hand, the terrorist organisation ETA justifies 858 assassinations and other crimes such as extortion, threats and kidnapping with the aim of achieving independence for the territories it considers the 'Basque homeland': the so-called 'Euskal Herria'. These territories are the current provinces of Álava, Biscay and Guipuzcoa (Autonomous Community of the Basque Country) and the *Foral* Community of Navarre in Spain; the current region of Lower Navarre, and the municipalities of Labord and Soule (Pyrenean Atlantic Department) in France.

Following the dichotomous and totalitarian logic of 'friend-enemy' (Schmitt 1975), whoever opposes the attainment of this goal is an enemy of ETA and the Basque people. According to ETA's rhetoric, the Basque people are dominated by the Spanish government's imperialism which takes advantage of its economic and industrial resources (Aulestia 1993; Domínguez 1998). Therefore, according to ETA, its 'armed struggle' is necessary and fair, and is in line with its logic; a reaction to said moral injustice it feels it has received on an individual level, on a group level and towards the political community they imagine they represent (Waldmann 1989). The terrorists, in fact, feel they are, and describe themselves as being, victims of the violation of the right to self-determination both individually and as members of this imaginary community. Their goal is to do justice with their 'armed struggle', with their 'revolution', to create a society where they can feel they are among equals (Giddens 1994: 22). The following declaration made in one of ETA's communiqués in 2009 confirms this:

> [...] while the national rights of Euskal Herria are being violated and oppressed, while the imposition of States [here ETA refers specifically to Spain and France] against their own people is going on with the use of arms and violence, ETA reasserts its commitment to continue to strike out at Euskal Herria's enemies and their interests.[9]

However, in line with our point of view, said rhetoric is based on a false myth we will call 'the myth of peace as the end of violence', according to which peace is a status that would be achieved automatically in the context of the conflict when fatal attacks are no longer carried out. We thus believe that to consider the concept of peace as a cessation of deaths, of injuries to people and physical violence against individuals is too superficial, simplistic and misleading an approach and does not encompass the true nature of terrorism. Although terrorism manifests itself in a specific context via *direct violence* whose most evident consequences are fatalities or bodily/psychological injuries to innocent people, the coexistence of an *indirect and structural violence* that affects civilian society as a whole cannot be overlooked.

While the use of direct violence mainly violates the right to life and the physical integrity of human beings, the presence of indirect violence hinders the growth of democratic culture and the full enjoyment of fundamental freedoms by citizens, leaving room for the predominance of an extremist/totalitarian political ideology which leads to radicalism (Bonanate 1983). This can be seen in the words of Fernando Buesa,[10] spokesperson for the Socialist Party of Euskadi in the Basque Parliament, killed by ETA along with his bodyguard Jorge Diez, on 22 February 2000, who stated that: 'there is a kind of violence that kills and another kind of violence that does not allow you to live' (Alonso in Cuesta and Alonso 2007: 177). This violence that does not allow one to live is embodied by the social pressure that terrorism exerts through the use of various criminal practices which, over time, can lead to serious trauma on the social and political conscience of the society that suffers them. These criminal practices range from kidnapping (Pérez 2008), extortion carried out to affect businessmen and women, and denigration of victims, to death threats aimed at people working in the sphere of democratic politics, the legal system, the media and any other sphere where the terrorists' totalitarian ends are opposed. Symbols and rituals such as graffiti, flags, and demonstrations organised by the terrorists and their followers can be added to the above criminal practices inflicted by terrorism on society. These are different in each conflictive context and their goal is to flaunt the terrorist group's dominance in the territory where they are exhibited as a reminder of its constant presence, to defend its ideology and legitimise its practices, trying to neutralise, as a consequence, any divergent view. This symbolism comes under the umbrella of what Galtung defined as *cultural violence*, in other words 'those aspects of culture, the symbolic sphere of our existence – exemplified by religion and ideology, language and art, empirical and formal sciences – which can be used to justify or legitimise direct violence or structural violence' (cited in Harto de Vera 2004: 241).

Thus, when the violence exerted on the population is direct, *tangible and immediate* consequences can be felt: the victimisation of innocent people. When in addition to direct violence, indirect violence is exerted, as in the case of terrorism, besides victimisation, there are other *intangible and deferred* consequences: the malfunctioning of democracy and the negation of fundamental rights. In light of these reflections, the end of violence can be understood as a first and essential step towards the end of terrorism, and which must go hand in hand with what Galtung described as 'positive peace'. For Galtung, 'negative peace' merely corresponds to an 'absence of war and systematic, organised and direct violence', in other words, the absence of the kind of physical violence committed directly by individuals; 'positive peace', on the other hand is understood to be 'the absence of direct as well as structural or indirect violence' (Galtung 1969: 167–191). This last kind is, for Galtung, a sort of violence that hinges on the structure of society and manifests itself in the inequality of powers and, consequently, in inequality regarding life opportunities. While a state of 'negative peace' is compatible with situations where a deeply authoritarian status quo is in force, a state of 'positive peace', in contrast, coincides with respect for desired values such as justice, freedom and human rights. Consequently, according to Galtung, 'positive peace' would mean achieving 'negative peace' – in other words the absence of direct violence – together with the presence of social justice (Galtung 1971: 81–117).

When it comes to drawing up anti-terrorist policies to work towards the end of terrorism, they should not be based on the myth of 'peace as the end of violence' but on the ideal principle of 'peace as a synonym of justice'. 'Peace as a synonym of justice' is understood to be a status where respect for the right to truth, memory and justice are guaranteed: all vital elements for building a healthy society that can gradually return to normality after having suffered terrorism over a long period of time. A society based on lies, on the oblivion of what happened and the impunity of culprits cannot enjoy a totally democratic coexistence (Alonso 2013).

Truth is an individual right, but also a collective right of society as a whole. In fact, the knowledge of events by society of violations suffered is part of its legacy and should be preserved as such. Likewise, the right to the truth comprises a 'collective duty of remembrance' whose respect could prevent future terrorist crimes from being repeated. As Joinet asserts, it can therefore be affirmed that the right to the truth involves, on the one hand, the *right to know* what happened, individually as well as collectively, and on the other, the *right to remember* known events while preserving their truthfulness throughout time.[11]

The right to justice confers on the State a series of obligations: that of investigating violations, pursuing the perpetrators and, if found guilty, ensuring their sanction.[12] By not fulfilling these obligations, the effects of impunity – be they legal, political or moral – would result in highly detrimental consequences for citizens as a whole, but in particular for victims: exposure to continuous re-victimisations thus making it impossible for them to have closure and rebuild their lives. Maite Pagazaurtundúa, ex-president of the Victims of Terrorism Foundation – sister of Joseba Pagazaurtundúa,[13] a sergeant in the municipal police force in the Basque municipality of Andoain who was murdered by ETA on 8 February 2003 – stated:

> Days without fatalities are spoken of in a frivolous way. They are not days without fatalities but days without attacks because murder is irreversible, and each day that passes following the murder of a human being is, for their loved ones, another day with death because closure from terrorism is not attained while justice is not done. Specific [justice] is when those responsible face up to their responsibility to society, and general [justice] consists in defeating them, and not in us adapting to those who did not respect the life and dignity of others and do not feel responsible for anything.
> (cited in Alonso 2008)

Conclusion

Based on the theoretical assumption that two 'false myths' exist in Western democracies – and especially in Spain – related to the players who are entitled to fight against terrorism and to what the end of terrorism means, this chapter has set out to refute them. Resorting to Jellinek's method of *empirical types* and Weber's method of *ideal types*, this study counters each *false myth* with an *ideal principle* with which to overturn it. Thus, the 'myth of the exclusivity of the State', which considers the State to be the sole player entitled to fight against terrorism is countered by 'the ideal principle of the socialisation of the fight against terrorism', which, conversely, considers society and victims to be important players in this fight. Secondly, 'the myth of peace as the end of violence', based on the belief that peace could be a status that would be automatically achieved when the terrorists stop carrying out fatal attacks, is countered by 'the ideal principle for peace as a synonym for justice'.

In this closing section some of the possible characteristics of anti-terrorist policies will be evaluated, which could, to some degree, adopt and put into practice these ideal principles. If an end to terrorism with no impunity and the active participation of society and victims were possible, with which policies could it be achieved? In order to answer this question, we will take the Spanish experience as an example, and to be specific we will examine the *Pact in favour of freedoms and against terrorism*, approved by the main political parties in Spain in 2000.

If an anti-terrorist policy wanted to put into practice, to some degree, the above-mentioned ideal principles, it would firstly consider that the players entitled to fight against terrorism are the State as well as society as a whole, the latter being a peaceful weapon that delegitimises terrorism. Secondly, this policy would be based on the premise that the end of terrorism cannot be reduced to the mere cessation of violence but that it seeks the creation of a democratic context based on respect for fundamental rights, among which are those of truth, memory and justice. Thirdly, since terrorism is a multifaceted phenomenon that affects the deepest political and social spheres of society, it should be tackled simultaneously on various fronts such as the police, judicial, political, social and cultural ones (Alonso 2007).

The policies that would tackle terrorism simultaneously on various spheres should ensure constant police actions and carry them out within the legal and democratic framework of the constitutional State (Alonso and Reinares 2005). On the judicial front, among other issues, they should judge and sanction those guilty of the crimes committed, ensure equality before the Law and respect the laws of the constitutional legal system (Jiménez 2002). On the cultural and educational front, among other actions, one of their objectives should be to foster activities whose main goal is the respect for democratic principles, the delegitimisation of terrorism, the social rejection of violence, and the encouragement of tolerance and respect towards other cultures, identities, religions and races. On the political front, among other concerns, democratic political forces should come together in the decision and adoption of anti-terrorist measures, while a lack of political unity would weaken the fight against anti-terrorism and contribute to the ideological disarming of democracy in the face of terrorism (Reinares 1998).

If the case of Spain is taken into consideration, one of the anti-terrorist measures undertaken against ETA that most puts into practice the ideal principles previously outlined coincides with that set out by the *Pact in favour of freedoms and against terrorism*. This pact, signed in 2000 by the Popular Party (PP) and the Spanish Socialist Workers' Party (PSOE) was established in order to 'strengthen unity [between the two parties] to make freedoms fully effective and to end terrorism'.[14] The pact stresses that political unity in the fight against ETA's terrorism must be carried out observing the legal framework of the Spanish Constitution and the Statute of the Autonomous Community of the Basque Country:

> For over two decades of democracy, the Basque people have exercised their capacity for self-government within the framework of the Constitution and the Statute of Guernica.[15] This framework has ensured the political, cultural and social pluralism that is present within Basque society. Any existing political discrepancy between Basques can and must be addressed within

> this institutional framework. Any political project, even those that aim to review the institutional framework itself, must respect the rules and the procedures set out therein.[16]

The pact also established that,

> terrorism is a problem of the State [and that] it is up to the Spanish Government to lead the fight against terrorism, but combating terrorism is a task that is the responsibility of all democratic political parties, whether in Government or in the opposition.[17]

Conscious of the fact that,

> the definitive eradication of terrorist violence in Spain is not an exclusive task for democratic political parties [but that] it requires the active commitment of everyone, governmental institutions and citizens in the constant affirmation of civic and democratic values, [...] the PP and PSOE reaffirm their determination to foster and support mobilisations by citizens against terrorist violence and in rejection of the assassins.

Within the framework of this agreement, the two parties agreed to carry out legislative reforms and establish measures inherent to penitentiary policies, international cooperation, the delegitimisation of terrorism, and compensation for victims of terrorism. The strong consensus in support of the Pact enabled the State to apply pressure on ETA simultaneously on political, social and judicial fronts together with the one on law enforcement to obtain very effective results.[18]

In conclusion, this pact demonstrates that, in addition to the appropriate anti-terrorist policies established by the Government to counter the terrorist phenomenon on various fronts, it is important that society as a whole, with the participation of victims, play an active role in the *social* fight against terrorism. However, for this ambitious social project to be gradually carried out by all citizens, they must, *in primis*, accept a number of responsibilities such as the delegitimisation of terrorist violence, the recognition of victims, and the active participation in the peaceful rejection of terrorism in every sphere of daily life. Therefore, given that the end of terrorism is an objective that would be attained for society as a whole, it is important not only to respect the fundamental rights of individuals, but also the collective rights of truth, memory and justice.

In this chapter, taking into consideration the Spanish experience and especially the case of ETA, a number of guidelines to follow for the drafting of anti-terrorist policies have been proposed. It must be stressed that the long and violent path of this terrorist group – ETA carried out attacks in Spain for five decades – makes the Spanish case *sui generis* with regard to other European cases. Likewise, Spanish society's massive and peaceful reaction to some of the actions committed by ETA demonstrates that the Spanish case is probably *unique* with respect to the *social* fight against terrorism. Therefore, although these guidelines are general enough to be applied to other situations, we believe that it would be more appropriate to apply them to the Spanish case rather than to other contexts.

Notes

1 This chapter has been translated into English by Monique Fuller.
2 *Euskadi Ta Askatasuna* (ETA) – Basque Homeland and Freedom in the Basque language – is the most long-lived and bloodiest terrorist group in Spain. From 1960 to 2010 it was responsible for 858 deaths – 784 since 1978 when the democratic Constitution was approved – and thousands of injuries (Alonso *et al*. 2010). For five decades ETA has maintained a campaign of coercion and pressure on the Basque citizens who did not share their nationalist political project. It has been calculated that, due to this coercion, at least 200,000 Basques have gone into exile, leaving their native land, their jobs and their homes in the face of death threats (Eskerra 2009; Calleja 1996). This coercion, which has been defined as 'violence of persecution' (Martin-Peña *et al*. 2011) has been manifested by aggressions, threats, kidnapping, harassment, and the physical and psychological persecution against thousands of citizens. Of these aggressions those called 'kale borroka' or street violence stand out (Van den Broek 2004; Llera *et al*. 2010), being a 'low intensity terrorism' (Pizarro 2001).
3 As Jarvis and Lister recall (2010: 177–180), among the many measures undertaken in the USA after the 9/11, the 'Terrorism Information and Prevention Service' (Operation TIPS) stands out. Operation TIPS, which emerged under the US Freedom Corps and Citizen Corps programmes (Homeland Security and Defense Act 2002), encouraged Americans to report suspicious activities directly to the FBI. Among many other initiatives along the same lines, the American 'Ready Campaign', launched in February 2003, is a national public service advertising campaign designed to educate and empower Americans to prepare for and respond to emergencies including natural disasters and potential terrorist attacks. In the context of the UK, citizens were provided with access to national intelligence architecture via the introduction of a confidential Anti-Terrorist Hotline. Among many other initiatives, the British CONTEST 2 Strategy, launched in 2009, called for anti-terrorism training for 'ordinary' citizens: recognising, preparing for, and reporting on potential and emergent threats.
4 The Euskobarómetro with the aid of half-yearly surveys – 'the half-yearly waves of the opinion barometer' – analytically gathers the opinions and attitudes of Basque society with regard to current political topics, nationalist and pro-independence feelings, violence and terrorism, etc. Consulting its data bank is particularly interesting for studying the evolution of Basque society on the difficult path to the political delegitimisation of ETA's terrorism. In addition to a valuable series of data compiled via the half-yearly waves, also included in this data bank are five national surveys called *Percepción ciudadana sobre el terrorismo y sus víctimas* [Citizens' perception of terrorism and its victims] that the Euskobarómetro Research Team carried out with the collaboration of the *Fundación Víctimas del Terrorismo* [FVT – Victims of Terrorism Foundation] and the *Centro de Investigaciones Sociológicas* (CIS – Centre for Sociological Studies) from 2004 to 2008.
5 For the biography and the circumstances of the kidnapping and subsequent murder of Miguel Ángel Blanco, see Alonso *et al*. (2010: 1013–1016).
6 ETA's network was also weakened thanks to the banning of the *Jarrai, Haika*, and *Segi* youth movements. Following the 'order of suspension' by Judge Baltasar Garzón of Jarrai-Haika's activities, on 10 May 2001, the Spanish National Court ruled on the illegality of said organisations in judgment 27/2005, stating them to be 'unlawful

associations'. Later, the Spanish Supreme Court ruling 50/2007 established that these organisations constitute an offshoot of ETA and are therefore 'terrorist organisations' having 'the same goal and operating in sync by using street violence for the organisation'. See Ruling n° 27/2005 of the National Court – Criminal Division, 20 June 2005 and Ruling n° 50/2007 of the Supreme Court, Division 2 of the Criminal Division, 19 January 2007.

7 The *Fueros*, communities of chartered regime, definitively abolished in 1876, was a legal system dating back to the High Middle Ages that ruled life in the Basque provinces via laws, rights and privileges (Fusi 1990).

8 Basque nationalist ideology was consolidated at the end of the nineteenth century with the definitive abolition of the *Fueros* and the rapid industrialisation process that the Basque Country underwent from that year onwards. This ideology was drawn up by Sabino Arana (1805–1903), who defined Basque identity and its differentiating features as constitutive elements of a separate, different and distinctive nationality. According to Arana, it was clear that the Basque people were a separate nationality given that they satisfied the five elements, which in his opinion, constituted it: race, language, government and laws, historical personality. For Arana therefore, Euskera was not simply an autochthonous language unrelated to Latin, but represented the national language of the Basques; the communities of chartered regime were not simply a secular administrative regime of the Basque provinces, but they constituted the national codes of sovereignty (Fusi 1990). Using Llera's (2003) categorisation, the origin of Arana's Basque nationalism can be summarised by three principles. The first refers to the ethnic definition of what is Basque; what makes Basque nationality, sacred and ancestral, incompatible with Spanish nationality. The second principle is linked to the character of what is Basque and its quintessence, Euskera, believed to be a discrete and exclusive language that, in order to survive, must displace Spanish. The third principle is based on the idea that the Spanish State is the equivalent of a foreign State that is militarily occupying Basque soil and which must be rebelled against in order to establish a true Basque State. According to Llera, these principles, commonly found both in moderate and constitutional Basque nationalist narrative as well as in the radical and violent Basque nationalist narrative, lean towards totalitarianism and within them lies the seed of violence and anti-democratic imposition. In fact, if they are taken to the extreme, as radical nationalism does in general and the terrorist network does in particular, they are incompatible with democracy. Similarly, the moderate nationalism and radical nationalism pursue a main goal: the attainment of the self-determination of the Basque people and the creation of an independent Basque Nation, called Euskal Herria. However, if moderate nationalism's approach is limited to democratic political actions, violent nationalism focuses both on political actions as well as terrorist ones.

9 ETA communiqué of 12 April 2009.

10 For the biography and circumstances of the Fernando Buesa Blanco and Jorge Diez Elorza murder see Alonso *et al.* (2010: 1044–1050).

11 For the rights to memory, truth and justice as individual and collective rights, see Louis Joinet, *Final report by the special rapporteur on impunity and the set of principles for human rights via the fight against impunity*, in application for UN decision 1996/119 of the Subcommission for Prevention of Discrimination and Protection of Minorities.

12 As set out in the European Convention on Human Rights, Instrument for the Ratification of the Convention for the Protection of Human Rights and Fundamental Freedoms approved in Rome on 4 November 1950, and amended by additional Protocols n° 3 and 6 May 1963 and 20 January 1966 respectively. See BOE (Official Gazette) n° 243 of 10 October 1979, p. 23564 to 235702.

13 For the biography and circumstances of the murder of Joseba Pagazaurtundúa see Alonso *et al.* (2010: 1152–1158).

14 The *Pact in favour of freedoms and against terrorism* between the Popular Party (PP) and the Spanish Socialist Workers' Party (PSOE), of 8 December 2000, preamble.
15 After the Francoist dictatorship (1936–1975), the Autonomous Region of the Basque Country was established in 1979 and its Statute was approved by referendum. Thanks to this Statute, also known as the Statute of Guernica, the Basque Country not only enjoys fiscal autonomy and very broad powers in areas such as the economy, the justice system, education, and culture, but a Basque police force – the Ertzaintza – was also created, and the Basque vernacular – Euskera – was recognised as an official language. See Alonso (2004: 213–254).
16 The *Pact in favour of freedoms and against terrorism* between the Popular Party (PP) and the Spanish Socialist Workers' Party (PSOE), of 8 December 2000, item n° 2.
17 The *Pact in favour of freedoms and against terrorism* between the Popular Party (PP) and the Spanish Socialist Workers' Party (PSOE), of 8 December 2000, item n° 1.
18 On the one hand, from 2000 onwards, there was a strengthening and improvement in cross-border cooperation between Spain and France. This was reinforced during the last decade and resulted in the dismantling of many terrorist cells, followed by successful prosecutions of ETA members in both countries. On the other, another significant measure was the banning of ETA's political wing, known as *Batasuna* (*Unity* in the Basque language). In 2002 the Spanish Parliament approved new legislation – Organic Law 6/2002 on Political Parties – that allowed the executive to demand judicial procedures to outlaw political groups that were unwilling to condemn terrorism or that maintained links with a terrorist group. As Alonso reminds us (2004: 223), this initiative was widely criticised by nationalist politicians in the Basque Country which accused the Spanish State of violating fundamental rights and the liberties of Basque citizens. The Basque government decided on September 2003 to formally accuse the Spanish State of violating articles 6, 7 and 11 of the European Convention on Human Rights (ECHR). In February 2004, however, the European Court of Human Rights (ECtHR) unanimously agreed to reject the Basque government's claim. Another judgment which confirmed the banning of *Batasuna* was that of June 2009, when the ECtHR confirmed the ruling by the Spanish Supreme and Constitutional Courts that had banned *Batasuna*. The banning of *Batasuna* deprived the political party of generous public funding from different institutions on both national and European levels and resulted in the party's expulsion from municipal institutions and local government throughout the Basque Country. Consequently, ETA's ability to exert social and political control over the population eroded and this terrorist group lost popular support over the years. In 2011 a new political party called *Sortu* (*to be born* in the Basque language) was created in order to present itself at autonomous and municipal elections in May 2011. In its statute it claimed that it was not linked to any terrorist organisation and that it believed exclusively in democratic and political means. It also rejected the use of violence and the threat of using it, including any future possible ETA violence in any shape or form. It did not, however, condemn any of ETA's 858 murders, nor did it face up to the past, which other non-nationalist democratic parties, victims and most of society expected it to do. The Supreme Court banned *Sortu* because it deemed it a clear continuation of *Batasuna*. As a result of that, a number of *Sortu* leaders decided to run for said elections in a coalition with two other parties, Eusko Alkartasuna (EA, *Basque Solidarity* in the Basque language) and Alternatiba (*Alternative* in the Basque language) thus creating the coalition *Bildu*. Bildu (*to join together* in the Basque language) was legalised by the Constitutional Court and it was therefore able to run in the May 2011 elections, winning enough votes to govern 89 town halls in the Basque Country and Navarre and the 'Diputación *Foral*' of Guipúzcoa (Llera 2011).

References

Alonso, R. (2003) *Matar por Irlanda, el IRA y la lucha armada*. Madrid: Alianza. [English edition: Alonso, R. (2007) *The IRA and armed struggle*. Routledge, London– New York].

Alonso, R. (2004) 'Pathways out of terrorism in Northern Ireland and the Basque Country: the misrepresentation of the Irish model', *Terrorism and Political Violence*, 16 (4), pp. 695–713.

Alonso, R. (2007) 'Políticas antiterroristas y 'procesos de paz': ¿Qué papel y qué consecuencias para las víctimas del terrorismo?', in C. Cuesta and Alonso R. (coords.), *Las víctimas del terrorismo en el discurso político*. Madrid: Dilex.

Alonso, R. (2007) 'Los frentes de ETA y del Estado', ABC, 28 September 2007. Available at: www.abc.es/hemeroteca/historico-28–09–2007/abc/Opinion/losfrentes-de-eta-y-del-estado_164997576189.html (last accessed 18 September 2013).

Alonso, R. (2008) 'Irlanda del Norte: 'paz' sin justicia', ABC, 30 April 2008. Available at: www.abc.es/hemeroteca/historico-10–04–2008/abc/Opinion/irlanda-del-norte-paz-sin-justicia_1641783896184.html (last accessed 20 November 2013).

Alonso, R. (2009) 'Justicia, reconciliación y 'procesos de paz' ante fenómenos de violencia política', Yolanda Gamarra (coord.), *Lecciones sobre justicia internacional*. Saragossa: Fundación Fernando el Católico.

Alonso, R. (2010) 'The challenges for democracy and legitimacy while confronting terrorism in Northern Ireland and the Basque Country', in Martha Crenshaw (ed.), *The Consequences of Counterterrorist Policies in Democracies*. New York: Russell Sage Foundation, pp. 213–254.

Alonso, R. (2013) 'The Madrid Bombings and Negotiations with ETA: a Case Study of the Impact of Terrorism on Spanish Politics', *Terrorism and Political Violence*, 25 (1), pp. 113–136.

Alonso, R., Domínguez, F. and García, M. (2010) *Vidas rotas: historias de los hombres, mujeres y niños víctimas de ETA*. Madrid: Espasa.

Alonso, R. and Reinares, F. (2005) 'Terrorism, Human Right and Law Enforcement', *Terrorism and Political Violence*, 17 (1–2), pp. 265–278.

Apter, D. (1997) *The legitimization of violence*. New York: New York University Press.

Arregi, J. (2008) 'El significado político de las víctimas', paper presented at "III Jornadas Internacionales sobre Terrorismo: Terrorismo y antiterrorismo" organised by the Giménez Abad Foundation, held on 24 and 25 November 2008 at the Aljafería Palace, seat of Aragon's Regional Parliament, Saragossa.

Aulestia, K. (1993) *Días de viento sur: La violencia en Euskadi*. Barcelona: Editorial Antártida/Empuries.

Baglietto, P. (1999) *Un grito de paz: Autobiografía póstuma de una víctima de ETA*. Madrid: Espasa-Calpe.

Bonanate, L. (1983) 'Terrorismo e governabilità', *Rivista italiana di Scienza Politica*, XIII (1), pp. 37–64.

Brewer, J. and Hayes, B.C. (2011) 'Victims as Moral Beacons: Victims and Perpetrators in Northern Ireland', *Contemporary Social Science*, 6 (1), pp. 73–88.

Calleja, J.M. (1999) *La diáspora vasca*, Madrid: El País Aguilar.

Catanzaro, R. (1990) *Ideologie, movimenti, terrorismi*, Ricerche e Studi dell'Istituto Cattaneo. Bologna: Il Mulino.

Cuesta, C. (2000) *Contra el olvido: Testimonios de víctimas del terrorismo*. Madrid: Temas de Hoy.

Del Real, Alcalá J.A. (2007) *Nacionalismo e identidades colectivas: la disputa de los intelectuales (1762–1936)*. Madrid: Dykinson.
Del Real, Alcalá J.A. (2011) 'El derecho a la paz frente a la nación obligatoria', in Garrido, I. (ed.), *El derecho a la paz como un derecho emergente*. Barcelona: Atelier, pp. 87–104.
Del Real, Alcalá J.A. (2013) 'El derecho a la identidad cultural: criterios de fundamentación', *Derechos y Libertades*, 29 (II), pp. 183–216.
Domínguez, F. (1998) *De la negociación a la tregua: el final de ETA?* Madrid: Taurus.
Eskerra, I., (2009) *Exiliados en democracia*. Madrid: Ediciones B.
Funes, M.J. (1998) *La salida del silencio, movilizaciones por la paz en Euskadi, 1986–1998*. Madrid: Akal ediciones.
Fusi, J.P. (1990) *El País Vasco, pluralismo y nacionalidad*. Madrid: Alianza Editorial.
Giddens, A. (1994) *Más allá de la izquierda y la derecha: el futuro de las políticas radicales*. Madrid: Cátedra Teorema.
Harto De Vera, F. (2004) *Investigación para la paz y resolución de conflictos*. Valencia: Tirant Lo Blanch.
Jarvis, L. and Lister, M. (2010) 'Stakeholder security: the new western way of counterterrorism?', *Contemporary Politics*, 16 (2), pp. 173–188.
Jellinek, G. (1981) *Teoría General del Estado* [1900 and 1905]. Buenos Aires: Albatros.
Jiménez, O.J. (2002) *Policía, terrorismo y cambio político en España, 1976–1996*. Valencia: Tirant Lo Blanch.
Joinet L. (1997) Final report by the special rapporteur on impunity and the set of principles for human rights via the fight against impunity, in application for UN decision 1996/119 of the Subcommission for Prevention of Discrimination and Protection of Minorities.
Llera, F.J. (2003) 'La red terrorista: subcultura de la violencia y nacionalismo en Euskadi', en Antonio Robles (ed.), *La sangre de las naciones. Identidades nacionales y violencia política*. Granada: Universidad de Granada.
Llera, F.J. (2011) 'Sortu: ¿El fin de ETA?', *Claves de Razón Práctica*, 210, pp. 32–44.
Llera, F.J., Leonisio, R. and y Retortillo, A., (2010) 'Las elecciones locales y forales vascas de 2007: ¿El inicio del cambio?' in Arenilla Sáez, M. (coord.), *La administración pública entre dos siglos. Homenaje a Mariano Baena del Alcázar*. Madrid: INAP, pp. 113–140.
Martin-Peña, J., Opotow and Rodríguez-Carballeira, A. (2011) 'Amenazados y víctimas del entramado de ETA en Euskadi: un estudio desde la teoría de la exclusión moral', *Revista de Psicología Social*, 26 (2), pp. 177–190.
Mate, R.M. (2008) *Justicia de las víctimas, terrorismo, memoria, reconciliación*. Barcelona: Anthropos.
McKittrick, D., Kelters, S., Feeney, B. and Thornton, C. (2007) *Lost lives: The stories of the men, women and children as a result of the Northern Ireland Troubles*, 6th ed., Edinburgh: Mainstream Publishing Company Ltd.
Montero, M. (2006) 'El 'nacionalismo vasco moderado' y la violencia terrorista, 1976–2006', *Cuadernos de Alzate: revista vasca de la cultura y las ideas*, pp. 51–70.
Pagazaurtundua, M. (2004) *Los Pagaza. Historia de una familia vasca*. Madrid: Temas de hoy.
Pérez, K. (2008) *Secuestrados, símbolos de libertad: Crónica de todos los secuestros de ETA*. Bilbao: Asociación para la Defensa de la Dignidad Humana.
Pizarro, P.A. (2001) 'Terrorismo de baja intensidad: la Kale-Borroka', Cuadernos de la Guardia Civil, Revista de Seguridad Pública, 24, pp. 99–104.

Presidenza della Repubblica (2008) *Per le Vittime del Terrorismo nell'Italia Repubblicana, Istituto Poligrafico e Zecca dello Stato*. Roma: Libreria dello Stato.
Pulgar, M.B. (2004) *Víctimas del Terrorismo, 1968–2004*. Madrid: Dykinson.
Reinares, F. (2001) *Patriotas de la muerte: quiénes han militado en ETA y por qué*. Madrid: Taurus. [latest edition: Reinares F. (2011), *Patriota de la muerte: quiénes han militado en ETA y cuándo abandonan*. Madrid: Taurus].
Reinares, F. (1998) *Terrorismo y Antiterrorismo*. Barcelona: Ediciones Paidós.
Sabucedo, J.M., Blanco, A. and De la Corte, L. (2003) 'Beliefs which legitimize political violence against the innocent', *Psicothema*, 15 (4), pp. 550–555.
Sabucedo, J.M., Rodríguez, M. and Fernández, C. (2001) 'Construcción del discurso legitimador del terrorismo', *Psicothema*, 14 (supl.), pp. 72–77.
Schmitt, C. (1975) *La dittatura: Dalle origini dell'idea moderna di sovranità alla lotta di classe proletaria*, Roma, Bari: Editori Laterza.
Serranò, A., (2009) *Le armi razionali contro il terrorismo contemporaneo, la sfida delle democrazie di fronte alla violenza terroristica*. Prologue written by Silvio Gambino and Alberto Del Real Alcalá. Milan: Giuffré editore.
Serranò, A. (2012) 'La lucha social contra el terrorismo: testimonios de algunas víctimas de ETA', *Eguzkilore. Cuaderno del Instituto Vasco de Criminología*, n° 26, pp. 253–279.
Uriarte, E. (2003) *Cobardes y Rebeldes, por qué pervive el terrorismo*. Madrid: Temas de Hoy.
Van den Broek, H. (2004) 'Borroka – The legitimation of street violence in the political discourse of radical Basque nationalists', *Terrorism and Political Violence*, 16 (4), pp. 714–736.
Vaughan-Williams, N. (2008) 'Borderwork beyond Inside/Outside? Frontex, the Citizen-Detective and the War on Terror', *Space and Polity*, 12 (1), pp. 63–79.
Villa, I. (2004) *Saber que se puede: Recuerdos y reflexiones de una víctima del terrorismo*. Madrid: Martínez Roca.
Waldmann, P. (1989) *Radicalismo étnico, análisis comparado de las causas y efectos en conflictos étnicos violentos*. Madrid: Ediciones Akal.
Weber, M. (1964) *Economía e sociedad, Esbozo de sociología comprensiva* [1922]. Mexico: FCE.
Wilkinson, P. (2006) *Terrorism versus democracy: the liberal state response*. London and New York: Routledge.

6 'I read it in the FT'

'Everyday' knowledge of counter-terrorism and its articulation

Lee Jarvis and Michael Lister[1]

Introduction

In the years that have now passed since the 9/11 attacks, numerous states around the world have adapted and upgraded their menu of counter-terrorism programmes and initiatives (for overviews, see Banks *et al.* 2008; Cole 2003; Haubrich 2003; Jackson *et al.* 2011: 222–248; Roach 2011; Walker 2009). In the UK, these changes included alterations to the scope of pre-charge detention powers; the introduction of a control orders regime, now replaced with Terrorism Prevention and Investigation Measures or TPIMs; and, a range of initiatives attempting to 'Prevent' terrorism and violent extremism (Baker-Beall *et al.* forthcoming). Much critical commentary on measures such as these has focused on their impact on civil liberties in general, as well as their particular consequences for specific minority populations widely deemed 'suspect' or risky (for example, Choudhury and Fenwick 2011; Gearty 2007; Kundnani 2014; Said, 2004; Sivanandan 2006). What has been largely missing from this debate until recently, however, is any form of sustained engagement with the voices of 'ordinary' citizens themselves and their views about these developments and their impacts (Gillespie and O'Loughlin 2009; Johnson and Gearty 2007).

More recent interventions have attempted to correct this imbalance (see Jarvis and Lister 2013a, 2013b, 2013c; forthcoming; Gillespie and O'Loughlin 2009; Mythen 2012; Mythen *et al.* 2013; O'Loughlin and Gillespie 2013). Such research has brought to prominence the ways in which citizens think about terrorism and (more frequently) counter-terrorism measures, as well as offering insights into how such developments have affected citizens' attitudes, behaviour and perceptions. Our previous research has, for example, noted the ways in which many citizens, and particularly those within minority ethnic groups, feel that their citizenship has been directly compromised by counter-terrorism measures since 9/11 (Jarvis and Lister 2013a). Yet this research – and the associated interest in the politics of the 'vernacular' and the 'everyday' (see Jackson and Stanley, forthcoming) has opened a series of subsequent questions around how citizens know what they know (or think they know) about (counter-) terrorism. Jackson and Hall (2012), for example, have noted that whilst there is a great deal of attention paid to terrorism discourse emanating from politicians, the media and security professionals, rather less is afforded to what 'ordinary' people think about (counter-)terrorism, and how their views thereof are formed and articulated.

This chapter seeks to address these questions and, in so doing, to contribute further to contemporary 'vernacular' security research (Jarvis and Lister 2013b). To do so, we draw on a UK-based research project that made use of a focus group methodology to explore the relationships between the lived experiences of citizenship, security and counter-terrorism powers. Four key sources of knowledge upon which individuals drew in these discussions are explored below. These are: (i) personal experiences, whether direct or vicarious; (ii) media sources, including the news media and popular entertainment; (iii) exemplary events and especially high profile government errors; and, paradoxically, (iv) a perceived lack of reliable or accurate information from which to assess the necessity, effectiveness or legitimacy of counter-terrorism powers.

Our analysis of how and from where citizens form their views of counter-terrorism offers, we suggest, scope for optimism and pessimism alike for critical scholars concerned with the impact of such policies on specific communities, citizenship and politics more broadly (with some methodological caveats noted below). Optimism resides in that we encountered a prevalence of sceptical readings of media and governmental narratives around terrorism and the threat that it poses. We find, amongst participants in our research at least, very little evidence either of a hegemonic discourse on (counter-) terrorism, or indeed, of uncritical acceptance of potentially hegemonic sources. Pessimism, however, might be found in that the absence of authoritative sources, and the reliance upon personal experience for knowledge in this context, perhaps precludes large-scale oppositional discourses to contemporary counter-terrorism logics, measures and frameworks. Indeed, echoing Jackson and Hall's (2012) findings, the lack of authoritative, trustworthy, sources of information about counter-terrorism led some of our participants to describe a form of powerlessness and acquiescence to government decisions in this context. An inability to 'know' about (counter-) terrorism, in other words, led some participants to defer to government, trusting that political elites knew best (or at least better than the average citizen).

On the sources and contexts of political knowledge

Whilst Jackson and Hall note a certain lack of engagement within terrorism research around what people do or do not know about (counter-) terrorism, there does exist a much more developed literature on political knowledge more generally. Aspects of this literature typically employ survey-based methods in an attempt to understand awareness of political institutions and processes, as well as to explore the impact of factors such as class and education thereupon (see, for example, Delli Carpini and Keeter 1996). Other strands of this work seek to assess the impact of the overall 'information environment' on political awareness (Jerit *et al.* 2006), although this is often approached in fairly narrow terms relating to print and television news. A broader approach to these questions might be found in research emphasising the extent to which media consumption alone fails to fully explain political knowledge. Gamson (1992), for example, argues that personal experiences are important in shaping people's awareness of political issues. He states that whilst the mass media is an important source for citizens' political knowledge and information it is not the only one, in that personal experiences, 'subcultural knowledge and popular wisdom' are also important (Gamson 1992: 4).

A key debate which stems from these discussions is that around audiences. Stuart Hall's (2009 [1980]) seminal work on coding/decoding is perhaps exemplary of a range of studies seeking to emphasise that individuals are not passive 'dupes' when it comes to media texts and images. Audiences – readers, viewers, listeners and so on – engage in active processes of decoding and/or interpretation which may lead to understandings quite different from any 'original' meaning encoded in the media text (see also Livingstone 2010 for an overview and defence of audience research). Silverstone terms this process of communication and meaning construction 'mediation', noting the role of audience interpretation as well as the interrelationship between lived and mediated experiences, such that 'one cannot inquire into one without simultaneously inquiring into the other' (Silverstone 2002: 763). This suggests both that media texts play a crucial role in the framing of everyday experiences, but also that everyday experiences play a critical role in the reading and understanding of media (and other) texts.

The dialogical relationship that exists between a text, its producer and audience, has been explored in research examining the security/terrorism/media nexus, most notably within the *Shifting Securities* project. This was a multi-strand project examining the interactions between media, government and citizens around key security challenges in the post-9/11 period. Using a mixed method approach which included audience interviews, textual analysis of media, and interviews with security and media elites, the project sought to analyse the security politics mediascape (see Gillespie 2007). This research emphasises the ways in which information about security politics is derived from the media, but that this is read and understood through other lenses. For example, Hoskins and O'Loughlin (2009), also part of the project team, emphasise the importance of political and religious beliefs as well as local experiences in the framing and interpreting of media texts.

Thus, as much of this (and related) literature recognises, the media represents an important source of political knowledge yet other factors (such as personal experiences or partialities) contribute directly and indirectly to the ways in which an information environment is accessed and negotiated. This suggests that individual knowledge about terrorism and counter-terrorism is likely to be highly differentiated. An era of multiple media outlets – themselves understood and consumed differently – suggests a situation of plurality rather than uniformity. Indeed, Jackson and Hall (2012) tentatively conclude along these lines, suggesting that there may not be a dominant discourse on terrorism amongst the public at all, given that public understandings of terrorism may be lacking in stability, concurrence and even coherence. They also note that citizens frequently profess an ignorance about the area, and that this may lead to a sense of inability to assess policy initiatives.

A final point to emphasise is that recent strands of literature on media and public knowledge have stressed that we should not look only to news media as sources of public information. A range of scholars have pointed to the importance of entertainment media (van Zoonen 2005), music and video games (Inthorn et al. 2012; Street et al. 2012) as potential sources of political learning and knowledge. Street et al. (2012), in research with young people found that, whilst recognised as fictional, entertainment media prompted speculation and reflection on political themes. Discussing sci-fi television, for instance, they note: 'In other words, the fact that popular culture involved an entirely imaginary, fictional world did not preclude it from being seen as how the world is, and indeed how politics operates within it' (Street et al. 2012: 348). The suggestion is that fictional entertainment is subjected to critical appraisal in relation to its realism, which in turn leads to reflection about the 'real' world (ibid.: 349).

This brief overview of several large literatures suggests a number of important arguments. The first is that there may be multiple sources of citizen knowledge about counter-terrorism. Whilst the news media is likely to be prominent among these, we should expect that it is not unique. Other entertainment media, for instance, may play important roles in influencing what and how people think in this context. Second, 'ordinary' people are likely also to be influenced by their own experiences and those of their peers or acquaintances in their understandings of counter-terrorism. Indeed, although this may exert a secondary influence, in terms of shaping how media texts are understood, the relationship may be more complex in that media texts may also shape perceptions of personal experience (Silverman 2002).

The chapter now turns to sources of knowledge of counter-terrorism discussed by respondents in a recent ESRC project, *Anti-Terrorism, Citizenship and Security* (RES-000-22-3765).[2] Following the aforementioned literature, our findings suggest that the media does indeed represent an important source of public knowledge about counter-terrorism, but that it is read critically, often in the shadow of personal experiences. Importantly, however, while mainstream news media was often invoked in critical, sceptical terms by our participants, entertainment media was fairly frequently invoked as an authoritative and reliable source of knowledge. A third source of knowledge we explore is the importance of key or exemplar events seen as emblematic of wider trends and processes. Finally, and slightly paradoxically, we also encountered the absence of information as an important source of citizens' views in this policy area. Here, a perceived lack of knowledge about counter-terrorism powers, their legitimacy or effectiveness was frequently invoked as a reason for accepting government policy in this area (see also Jackson and Hall 2012).

Research methodology

The findings contained in this chapter draw on a series of 14 focus groups conducted in 2010 with a range of communities in the UK. The groups concentrated on issues around British counter-terrorism policy, and its impact on everyday life, citizenship and security. Participating in the research were 81 individuals: 48 women and 33 men; 31 Asian participants, 28 White and 22 Black. Participants were selected via a purposive sampling strategy and recruited through a combination of enumeration, snowballing and organisation sampling techniques. Our groups were organised around two primary factors: geographical residence (metropolitan/non-metropolitan) and ethnicity (Black/White/Asian). They took place in London and Birmingham (as metropolitan sites), and Oldham, Swansea, Llanelli and Oxfordshire (as non-metropolitan sites). This research design was selected to enable an exploration of differences in perceptions and experiences amongst UK populations. In particular, we were interested in assessing the existence and relevance of differential perceptions of vulnerability to terrorist attacks (metropolitan or non-metropolitan), and the significance of ethnic identity in perceptions of exposure to (coercive dimensions of) anti-terrorism measures. Despite its obvious simplifications, our use of ethnicity (with Asian referring to individuals from a South Asian background) was introduced to add context to relevant recent research on religious identity and counter-terrorism policy, much of which has focused on Muslim communities (see Said 2004; Gillespie 2007; Choudhury and Fenwick 2011).

The focus groups employed a range of deliberately open-ended questions (see Morgan 1996; also Kitzinger and Barbour 1999), in which individuals were invited to discuss the impact of contemporary counter-terrorism powers at different levels of analysis: individual, family, community and nation. In addition, participants were asked to evaluate the legitimacy of particular measures such as stop and search and pre-trial detention periods, to outline alternative responses to combat terrorism that they would institute if in a position to do so, and (at the start of the focus group) to explore the concept of security. Follow-up questions varied according to the development of the conversation within the group. We did not ask specific questions about the media, nor about the grounds upon which participants were basing their views. Such information emerged spontaneously in the course of discussion.

A point was made above concerning methodological caveats. There are a number which should be made explicit. As a piece of qualitative research, we can make no claims here to representativeness, and there are, of course, issues of researcher bias that may impact our findings. A particular caveat concerns selection bias. It may be that those willing to participate in academic research about counter-terrorism measures are those who already think critically in a political, normative sense; those, in other words, who are interested in political issues and who consider themselves politically literate or 'worldly-wise'. Whether our research has captured the voices of those who are less overtly interested in politics and who have different views and sources of knowledge is unclear.

Selection bias is a perennial issue with research of this nature but it should engender a certain circumspection about generalising from our participants in the analysis that follows.

Knowing and not knowing about (counter-)terrorism

The following discusses the four main sources of knowledge around counter-terrorism powers we encountered: personal experience, media consumption, inductive reasoning from events deemed exemplary, and a lack of knowledge or ability to evaluate government actions. In the following, we examine each in turn.

Personal experience

As indicated above, our research questions focused on counter-terrorism measures and their operation within the UK. This meant that a number of our participants reported direct experience of contact with anti-terrorism measures (or measures perceived as such, or otherwise relevant), including stop and search by police or border security. Perhaps the most prevalent example was that of airport security, in which experiences of Schedule 7 of the 2000 Terrorism Act, concerning powers of stop, search and temporary detention were described by several of our participants (importantly, the distinction between 'ordinary' security measures and Schedule 7 stops were not always clear in respondent's statements).

A number of participants from ethnic minority communities had direct experience of being stopped by security personnel. Of particular interest in the recounting of these experiences, however, is that they are seen not (only) as isolated incidents which are personally troubling (although they certainly are seen frequently as such). Rather, that they are also seen, in some cases, as experiences offering insights into the operation of broader political processes; as lessons about how the world works in the present and future. The following extract taken from an Asian female in Oldham illustrates this:

> I remember coming home; we went from Pakistan [...] I'd just come back from my dad's funeral and I was stopped. I had a British passport and I was stopped by this lady, antiterrorist officer she was or Scotland Yard or something, and even after I ... and her initial comment was, yeah, why did you go. And I said, I went for my father's funeral. Her comment was, oh, I'm sorry, how long were you there. And it just carried on and I'd just been on a ten-hour flight, physically and emotionally exhausted and she insisted on interrogating me, not in a small office quietly somewhere, you know, discreetly, but in front of a whole airport of people. And it was like you're only picking on me because I look a bit different from ... and because of all these perceptions and this idea that you've built up of what I am and who I am without actually engaging me in any sort of manner at all. That's one intrinsic fear I have that, you know, that this 12-year-old, eight-year-old nephews

and kids are growing up and having some sense of, you know, reservation when they go out, of being, you know, picked on or stereotyped in a certain way, and not being able to do anything about it either.

(Oldham, Asian Female)

A similar experience was recounted by another participant in the same focus group:

[W]hen I went to Pakistan because my mother-in-law died in February and at the airport there were so many people, and the way they searched me was so humiliating, honestly. I really felt like I was hated and not wanted and everything and maybe I shouldn't have come back or something. They made me stand up, take my jumper and everything off, my shoes off as well, and the way I was made to stand and everybody … it was really humiliating, I tell you […]. They wouldn't do that to somebody who's white but they would do it to me […] it was so humiliating.

(Oldham, Asian Female)

In other instances, experience of UK counter-terrorism practice was vicarious rather than direct. In the following, for example, a participant draws upon the experiences of their friends and their relatives:

I've got friends who have got relatives who actually were detained for up to 28 days without charge, and they've got children, and they are just as educated as me. Just because I don't wear a headscarf, I may not practice a lot of the religious parts that our religion promotes, but they have a degree, they were a British citizen, why the hell are they actually being interrogated; it will be me next. That is what I see it as.

(London, Asian Female)

As this indicates, for a number of people in our research, one's own response to these experiences (of being 'interrogated', 'picked on', 'humiliated' and feeling 'hated') leads to a fear that they or others will encounter the same, along with a similar powerlessness to oppose such treatment, in the future. Thus there is a process of learning here in which wider inferences are drawn from personal experience.

An interesting qualification to this, and one which speaks to the above points above the interweaving of personal experience and media constructs, is that the experience of being stopped does not produce a singular 'lesson'. Rather, experiences such as stop and search are related to broader discourses (of Islamophobia, for example) which work to place them within specific interpretive frameworks (being singled out, for example) rather than others (as an inconvenience, for example). This is illustrated in the following, where another Asian participant (who self-identified as a non-Muslim) recounts being stopped at a travel hub:

A: I mean I travelled a lot to Paris back and forth, and I used to ... and it's happened much, much less in the last few years, but I used to always get stopped by the ... what's now the border agency, but was previously the Home Office guy asking me all kinds of questions about where I'm from; what I'm doing, this and that. And yes, obviously that's ... it's not obviously, but it's probably due to the way I look.

MODERATOR: How did that make you feel?

A: I don't really ... I don't really mind, because I really have nothing to hide, and I can tell someone exactly what my background is and what I'm doing here there and everywhere. So I don't really mind, I just, sort of ... it is what it is. But...

B: At some levels, don't you resent it?

A: Yes, I do. A little bit.

(London, Asian, Male (A) and Female (B))

After prompting by another person in the group, this participant states that they do resent the, seemingly repeated, incidents. But their initial response is that they 'don't mind' and 'it is what it is'. Thus we can see the potential for very similar experiences to be understood quite differently. Where the non-Muslim participant expresses a degree of resentment, this response is some distance from the above expressions of 'humiliation' described by those in our research identifying as Muslim. Similarly, white participants who recount being stopped at airports referred to the 'ridiculousness' (Oxford, White, Female) rather than injustice of being stopped and having to surrender their safety pin and sewing kit.[3]

As this suggests, the 'lessons' that are inferred from personal experiences with counter-terrorism professionals are not given or determined by the nature and quality of the experience. Rather, they are interpreted through other discursive lenses. In these instances, discourses, found in the media and elsewhere, of Islamaphobia and the targeting of Muslims, leads to one set of participants interpreting their experiences as emblematic of discriminatory practices likely to be perpetrated on other Muslims (clearly the experience of *being* Muslim also plays a significant role in this). Other participants do not register their experiences as part of a singling out or systematic targeting in the same way. Personal experiences, therefore, are important sources of information for our participants, in terms of how they think about counter-terrorism measures, but the significance and wider meaning of the experiences is, of course, mediated (Silverman 2002).

Before turning to the importance of media consumption within these processes, one further point is worth noting. Those, mainly white, participants who reported no direct experience of counter-terrorism and/or security measures in our focus groups, sometimes expressed a form of empathy for others, such as Muslims, they perceived to be likely targets of counter-terrorism measures:

Yes, one of their parents being stopped because of these laws, you know, and those kids they're from good families, you know, they're trying hard, working hard and so on, and you know, as a result of these laws they've just been stopped like that. And they'll probably feel quite alienated and you know, why are you stopping me, because of the way I look and so on, you know.

(London, White Female)

But just in terms of the community, if it, you know, if all of a sudden, somebody, you know, five doors down from us, had what's the … had a Control Order […] if [Participant C] had a control order, as a foreign national, and was subjected to house arrest, and you weren't allowed to move and associate and communicate […] if people saw your house under house arrest, they will start to view you differently, even if you're what, entirely innocent, and it starts to make people feel suspicious of their community and of the people that they're around. And I'm just … and so that's a quite a negative consequence of these powers.

(Oxford, White Female)

These individuals empathise with the stigmatisation and subsequent alienation potentially felt by those with direct experience of counter-terrorism measures. In the latter example, this exercise in empathy leads to a questioning of the counter-terrorism measures themselves given the negative consequences called forth by this effort to imagine oneself into the position of another. We would not want to make too much of this point, but it is worth noting for two reasons. First, we have described elsewhere the role and importance of empathy in 'vernacular' discussions and constructions of security, which is perhaps unexpected in terms of traditional and 'critical' IR approaches in which the negative consequences of security speech are typically emphasised (Jarvis and Lister 2013b). Second, exercises in empathy such as this suggest, or hint, that Islamaphobia and attempts to stigmatise and 'other' Muslims are not complete or uncontested discursive frameworks. Whilst there is wider survey evidence that many people associate Islam with certain characteristics, such as support for terrorism and extremism, our research (with the above caveats about (self) selection bias and lack of representativeness in mind) suggests that such associations are not universally held, and that individuals can, and do, positively and sympathetically empathise with those who might be more subject to counter-terrorism measures.[4]

Media

As noted above, the media may play an indirect role in shaping knowledge about counter-terrorism by providing one (but perhaps not the only or most powerful) frame through which individuals make sense of specific personal experiences. It also plays a more direct role in our participants' knowledge about counter-terrorism, albeit in multiple ways. In the following, we identify three different relationships between our participants and the media that emerged in our focus groups. The first is descriptions of the mainstream news media as untrustworthy and unreliable, with certain formats, especially tabloid newspapers, being singled out. The second is invocations of the media as a reliable and trustworthy source of knowledge by some of our participants. The third is where non-news media, and particularly film was identified as a source of authentic and 'true' information about counter-terrorism.

That media institutions were unreliable, inaccurate, self-interested, or, for some, downright deceitful was a common attitude amongst our participants, irrespective of ethnicity, gender or location. The following extracts are illustrative of these views:

> is the media portraying a mirror, an image of what is happening, or is the media portraying an image to sell their papers?
>
> (London, Black Female)

> they [the media] can kind of have a say in what you should think about it and certainly some media outlets kind of like to glorify the threats to our country a lot more than some others.
>
> (London, White Female)

> A: I'm so ... so kind of clouded now, by the media that actually I really take it, a lot of it, with a pinch of salt.
> B: I think, that's partly why I don't read the newspapers, or...
> A: Yes, I don't buy newspapers.
>
> (Oxford, White Female (A) and Female (B))

> The media plays a role in overemphasising terrorism and threat and fear. And it's all over the news, and when I say the media, I don't just mean the news per se. I mean, the films. And the social media ... the Internet. Everywhere you go it's terrorism. Every time you switch your telly on, it's terrorism, terrorism.
>
> (London Black, Female)

Whilst tabloid newspapers were frequently singled out as unreliable, other, more reputable, news media outlets did not escape portayal as problematic. The BBC, for example, was seen as possessing of its own (here unspecified) agenda:

> I think maybe something like the BBC which is meant to be like a public broadcasting company, I think some people view that as in, this is telling us the truth, this is really what's happening and of course it also has an ideology and is showing us certain things.
>
> (London, White Female)

Newsnight was likewise criticised for its selection of interviewees on subjects around Islam and extremism:

> A: The problem is the mainstream are being marginalized, and the radicals are being given the media limelight. This is the problem.

B: The best example is Newsnight when they had Anjam Choudry. It was a complete opposite spectrum to Islam. [...]

A: On the other spectrum, Anjam Chowdy of Islam for UK, the idiot, these are the people they bring into the media, and this is the problem. The people who base their perspective of Islam, base it on these fringe minorities, on both ends; but we never see that they actually go out and actually find somebody from the east London mosque or the Imam of let's say Regents Park mosque. How many times have you ever seen two of the main mosques in the UK, the Regents Park mosque or the east London mosque, how many times have you seen representatives from these organisations representing the views? I can't remember a single incidence when they have been asked to give an opinion on a matter pertaining to Muslims in the country.

(London, Asian Male (A) and Male (B))

And, a Channel 4 documentary by Andrew Gilligan, entitled *Britain's Islamic Republic*, was singled out for especial criticism, and seen as 'demonising' and contributing to a 'them and us situation' (London, Asian, Male). Broadsheet newspapers such as the *Daily Telegraph* were also mentioned as unreliable and distorting (Oldham, Asian, Female). These findings are perhaps unsurprising, echoing Hoskins and O'Loughlin's (2009: 13) analysis of a contemporary 'crisis of news discourse', in which, 'news fails to deliver on its promise to provide credible, reliable information about security events (in particular)'.

Slightly paradoxically, some of these participants also spoke of news media as authoritative and reliable sources of information about counter-terrorism, perhaps echoing Jackson and Hall's (2012) account of the cognitive inconsistency individuals display when talking about terrorism. Thus, individuals who were critical of news media and their manipulations later cited similar sources as credible and authoritative. The participant cited above who criticised *Newsnight* for its selection of voices to speak on Muslim issues, for example, later discussed putative state surveillance in British universities:

Again there was an article recently where basically MI5 officers were approaching people, especially after the Abdul Talib ... Omar Faruk incident, December 25th incident. There was a sort of report that MI5 agents were approaching people to spy on fellow students; obviously what was going on at our university. And there were issues in terms of people.... The thing was the techniques and the tactics, the scare tactics that are being used by the secret services more than anything.

(London, Asian Male)

What is interesting in this discussion is that the content of the article (from an undisclosed source) is taken to be truthful and accurate. Or, put otherwise, that the news media is resorted to as a way of establishing the credibility of the story he is narrating to others in the group. Rather than problematising the source, or considering its partialities, this participant accepts and recounts this story as factual *because* it has been reported in a newspaper. In the same group, similarly, another participant stated: 'I think an anti-terrorism law was used against an Icelandic bank, wasn't it? Freezing assets. I read it in the FT' (London, Asian, Male). In the discussion which followed this, there was little of the critical analysis seen around the *Newsnight* or *Dispatches* reporting noted above. This suggests that at least some participants in our research filter their critical faculties, as we might expect, such that when media sources confirm or support existing political or other beliefs, critical readings are less evident (see also Hoskins and O'Loughlin 2009). Thus, while the media appears an important source of lay knowledge in relation to counter-terrorism, its reception is complicated. In some instances, critical interpretation comes to the fore, perhaps akin to Hall's (2009: 38) 'oppositional code'. In others, a less critical reading is in evidence, perhaps mirroring Hall's (2009: 36) 'dominant code'. Which comes to the fore rather depends on other interpretive frames and factors which may include personal experiences.

Perhaps in relation to the 'crisis' of news discourse mentioned above, we also found, amongst some of our participants, a willingness to accept non-news media as authoritative in relation to the working of counter-terrorism agencies and powers. Entertainment media, and particularly film, was cited on a number of occasions as reliable and informative. This is not to suggest that participants were confused between 'real life' and fictional entertainment. Rather, that fictional media was turned to for its 'realistic' representation of wider processes. Of particular note, one Bollywood film, *New York* (Khan 2009), was cited in three separate focus groups, with its 'realism' noted on each occasion:

> A: A few of the terrorist plots, movies that they has been, jokes apart, I know that Bollywood can be a bit of a joke, but seriously, there has been a couple. Don't ask me to name any but I have seen them honestly, and they have shown the amount of stress that recently has happened because of the 9/11.
> [Overtalking]
> B: Well there that was that recent one, what was it, My Name is Khan?
> C: Yeah – and New York was the other one.
> D: I've not seen it.
> E: All these movies are very anti Islamic and anti Muslim, rather than you know, showing both sides of the argument.
> F: New York wasn't. That was quite realistic, the way they got treated in the prison and...
> E: I'm sure they were still the villains.
> G: Yes, but they showed the reason behind why they became that, you know in that movie, so...
> (Birmingham, Asian male (B & D) and Female (A, C, E, F, & G))

While received with scepticism by others in the group, this film is valued by this particular individual (G) for its depiction of terrorism's root causes. In another focus group, the same film was discussed for its depiction of wrongful detention at immigration – so, the consequences of counter-terrorism powers, rather than the causes of terrorism – of which a number of these discussants were wary due to personal experiences (Oxford Asian Female and Male).

In other places, participants discussed what was initially referred to as 'a documentary', the Channel 4 drama *Britz* (Kosminsky 2007). This British show set around two Muslim siblings was, interestingly, seen by some as 'lifting the veil' on the media and their manipulative impact in processes of radicalisation:

> There was a documentary, I think a year ago, it was an actual drama for two days, I don't know the name of it, but it was basically an Asian Muslim girl [...] Britz ... who was seen as a terrorist, I think. And what it had shown is a lot of the indoctrinations of the media actually expressed in that programme. So, I think it's a very good example to show you, or show society, about the government use initiatives, how they approach people and who they take to their organisation to be used against their own community.
>
> (London, Asian Female)

Despite the programme being a fictional drama, it is seen here as an authoritative exposition of media distortions and government policies and their impact upon local communities. Our findings, therefore, echo the work of Street *et al.* (2012) with the apparent 'realism' of entertainment media a seemingly important criteria in its evaluation and an important source of political consideration. For some of our participants, too, it seems that entertainment media can be seen as realistic, and in some instances, perhaps even more complete than conventional news media (which is often viewed with suspicion).

Exemplary events

A third source of knowledge upon which our participants drew was that of exemplary events. Specifically, this was the citing of specific, discrete events from which wider lessons were (or could be) inferred. Thus individuals, across the groups, without moderator prompting, brought up specific counter-terrorism incidents, and frequently did so to suggest that these were far from isolated 'one offs'.[5] In this discussion, we focus on two: the Forest Gate Incident and the Jean Charles de Menezes shooting.

The Jean Charles de Menezes shooting refers to an event in 2005 when the Brazilian national was shot dead by armed police at Stockwell Tube station in London. The police had been given information that he was part of a terrorist cell, wanted for a failed bombing attempt. The incident and the tragic case of mistaken identity at its heart received widespread media coverage and was the subject of subsequent enquiries. This episode was mentioned by a number of participants in our focus groups, frequently because it had made them feel more fearful and less secure. In a discussion about anti-terrorism legislation (specifically, the now repealed detention without charge for foreign nationals suspected of terrorism, from the 2001 Anti-Terrorism, Crime and Security Act), a connection was made to the Menezes shooting, in terms of whether the state/government was always right in its actions and deliberations:

> A: Without trial, there must be some proof, right? There's no way they're going to hold you if they didn't have something against you.
> B: Yes, they may do, but then that might be completely ... Jean Charles de Menezes – they shot the guy.
> C: It's really scary.
>
> (London, Asian male (B) and Female (A & C))

What is of note here is the way one event (the shooting dead of an unarmed man in error) is invoked in relation to an entirely separate debate (on whether the state/government would detain someone on counter-terrorism charges without evidence). That a mistake was made in one case suggests to these participants the possibility of mistakes in others, leading them to be fearful of counter-terrorism measures more generally.

The Forest Gate incident refers to an anti-terrorism operation that took place in East London in June 2006, in which armed police raided two properties believing there to be a chemical bomb at the premises. Two men were arrested, one of whom was shot during the operation, but both were later released without charge. This incident was mentioned in a number of different groups in Birmingham and London in particular. One participant from London, unprompted, raised the incident, expressing a fear that something similar might befall them:

> Coming back to this idea that they [anti-terrorism measures] stoke fear. Especially when we saw the two lads in the Forest Gate, the two Bengali lads that got shot, I don't want to be walking at 5am in the morning with a CO19 outside my house with, you know, M16s or whatever they use these days, and then get shot in the leg for no.... Because they got released without charge eventually. But this is a precedence this is setting. I have a genuine fear, because of what I speak or what I believe in, that tomorrow or the day after, you know, I might have the same sort of ending, you never know. Next time they could potentially be fatal.
>
> (London, Asian Male)

The comment is interesting for a number of reasons. First, it is noteworthy that it is mentioned at all. The focus groups were conducted in 2010, and the Forest Gate incident was not, at the time, current. This was not something that had 'just' happened, and whilst it did receive media attention, it was not (unlike the de Menezes shooting) something that received regular and recurrent public scrutiny. Thus, the event, and its reporting had sufficient resonance with certain individuals for it to be mentioned four years after its occurrence and three years after the Independent Police Complaints Commission's enquiry into it. The second noteworthy element is that unlike in the above discussion of the de

Menezes shooting, the 'lesson' here is not analogous (that if something happens in one sphere of government, it could happen in others) but direct. This participant expresses a fear that *exactly the same thing* may happen to him. Therefore it seems that certain decisions or events can cast very long shadows and be generalised either as potential futures, or, as above, as reflective of wider state agendas. Thus a single 'mistake' can be taken not as a one-off error, but as revealing the larger and broader way counter-terrorism functions.

This suggests that the errors and mistakes of government and security services can have long and significant legacies. Whilst all events are open to multiple interpretations,[6] this polysemy means that individuals can draw upon incidents as evidence and as illustrations of broader issues, pointing once more to the conjunctural, dialectical nature of knowledge formation in this area. These 'emblematic events' were not, as far as we could tell, directly experienced by any of our participants. They are thus, mediated, but the meaning and significance which individuals draw thereof (as well as the selection of 'events' in these discussions) seems influenced by other considerations and frames.

Absence of knowledge

A fourth source of public understandings of counter-terrorism policy that emerged in our research, rather perversely, was a professed lack of knowledge. A number of our participants suggested that they lacked sufficient awareness about the working of counter-terrorism powers, or of the threat posed by terrorism, to come to any kind of definitive view on the legitimacy or effectiveness of government activities. The following are some indicative examples of this stance:

> I wouldn't have a clue, it's nothing to do with me not having the kind of right attitude towards terrorists, I don't know how to deal with it and you ... I do rely on the fact that there are security services and I suspect that despite the kind of downside, they actually do a remarkable job in making us kind of feel that terrorism isn't a threat.
>
> (London, White Male)

> From the outside, they [anti-terrorism measures] all look like kind of huge infringements of civil liberty and invitations to prejudice. But I kind of ... the big problem with it is that you don't know enough about the threat to actually kind of judge for yourself and that's kind of a ... that's a problem. But ... and it may be that there isn't any ... that they don't deal with any kind of threat in any kind of way, but I don't ... I'm not in a position to judge that.
>
> (London, White Male)

> The problem that I have with these is ... I don't really know how big the threat of terrorism is. I couldn't tell you if there is one attempted attack every ten

> years, if there's attempted attacks every week that are foiled. The only information I get is from newspapers, and if I see this, this [Metropolitan Police posters] is stirring up some sort of paranoia in me, but for what threat? For what, what is the threat to me? […] I think that's one of the main problems with these kind of things, is I don't really know how much threat I'm under.
>
> (Swansea, White Male)

Each of these respondents describes their own lack of sufficient information about (counter-) terrorism that would allow them to clearly and reliably judge the appropriateness of government responses. There is a perception in two of the comments that this absence of knowledge may stand in place of an overblown and exaggerated threat, but that one cannot be sure. Thus outright opposition to government security practices is qualified here because things may be sufficiently grave that such measures are warranted and necessary. In this we echo Hall and Jackson's (2012) findings that in the (perceived) absence of full knowledge, some citizens seem, albeit at times reluctantly, content to defer to the government. And, in so doing, to grant, if not outright support, then a degree of acceptance thereto. It has been argued that the precautionary principle (in which where knowledge is uncertain but the risk is grave, action is to be preferred over inaction) has animated politicians in terms of counter-terrorism policing. In the words of the former UK Prime Minister Tony Blair, for example:

> Sit in my seat. Here is the intelligence. Here is the advice. Do you ignore it? But of course, intelligence is precisely that: intelligence. It is not hard fact. It has its limitations. On each occasion, the most careful judgement has to be made taking account of everything we know and advice available. But in making that judgement, would you prefer us to act, even if it turns out to be wrong? Or not to act and hope it's ok? And suppose we don't act and the intelligence turns out to be right, how forgiving will people be?
>
> (Blair, cited in Aradau and Van Munster 2007, p. 105)

It seems that something akin to this principle can be seen in the views of some of our participants. This in turn, leads to a level of trust of government and so is, in many ways, a source of lay opinions and views.

This precautionary logic that is arguably at work in some of the above statements connects to Hoskins and O'Loughlin's (2009) argument that individuals will be selective in terms of how much risk and insecurity they are willing to permit. They argue that a decision about how much ontological insecurity to allow into everyday existence leads to a decision about how much media (and of what kind) to engage with. It may be, therefore, that the absence of knowledge claims are an exercise in the preservation of ontological security. It is, in this sense, interesting to note that nearly all of the participants who expressed the view that they lacked sufficient information about (counter-)terrorism, were white and removed, in personal terms, from any direct contact with many counter-terrorism measures.

As a final note on this point, allow us to speculate as to whether there is something specific about the counter-terrorism policy area and a perceived lack of lay knowledge. Empirical studies of public opinion such as those discussed at the article's outset have revealed large gaps in public knowledge of political events, issues and institutions. Gamson (1992: 5), for example, states 'The mystery [for such studies] ... is how people manage to have opinions about so many matters about which they lack the most elementary understanding'. The public, therefore, consistently seem to lack knowledge about many political issues, but do express opinions thereof. Is there something, then – and here the leading candidate must be the prominence (secret) intelligence plays in government and media discourse on counter-terrorism – that is distinctive about counter-terrorism that leads to public uncertainty? Our focus group data does not provide clear evidence on this, but it remains an intriguing question.

Conclusion

Although long-marginalised in academic and political discourse, public attitudes, understandings and opinions about alterations to post-9/11 counter-terrorism practices have begun to receive increasing attention (although far short of that which is, in our view, merited). Yet what remains unclear is how citizens themselves form such opinions. In this chapter we have sought to shed some light on this, through analysis of focus group data gathered in our own empirical research. Our findings cannot claim any representativeness, but they do point to a range of intriguing postulates with which we conclude.

In the first instance, we found no evidence of hegemonic sources of knowledge at work in this context. The media is treated selectively and whilst it clearly does shape and inform public opinion about (counter-)terrorism, different participants interpreted media sources in different ways. In this, our findings echo much cultural and media studies research concerning the importance of textual negotiation by audiences (for an overview see Livingstone 2010). Silverman's (2002) arguments that media and experience are dialectically understood by individuals also seems to be borne out in our data. Traditional elements of the news media are viewed with suspicion by some, whilst others appeal to the veracity and authenticity of films and television dramas. Our participants seem to engage in selective critical readings with media texts which both confirm and challenge existing discursive frames and are capable of being 'read' in quite different ways. Important within this is the role of prior personal experience, which was invoked by a number of our participants in their discussion of the wider counter-terrorism field.

Our findings resonate with those of related literature in this area (Hall and Jackson 2012; Hoskins and O'Loughlin 2009) as well as broader contributions to cultural and media studies (Silverman 2002; Livingstone 2010; Hall 2009). At the same time, they have specific significance, we suggest, in terms of counter-terrorism for government, media and public debate. There is something slightly paradoxical about this area. Despite the presence of widespread, coherent and powerful narratives about the threat of terrorism, which in turn spill over into discourses such as Islamaphobia (Kundnani 2014), in our work we find not only an absence of any hegemonic narrative, but also a highly individuated ensemble of experiences, narratives and interpretive frameworks. Whilst we have identified four main sources of lay counter-terrorism knowledge, these are constructed and negotiated in quite diverse ways, with similar experiences and texts being understood and arranged in different ways, and similar events leading to different 'lessons'. Similarly, how much knowledge people seek, and what significance they attach to any gaps also varies.

Events and the lessons drawn thereof seem to play a significant role in 'vernacular' understandings of counter-terrorism. High profile errors cast long shadows. This might be conjoined with the relative absence of knowledge and information in the area. The government and security services frequently make claims about the threat from terrorism but without giving the public access to information (BBC News 2013). This may either contribute to the lack of knowledge/acceptance nexus explored above, on the one hand. Or, on the other, lead to greater significance being attributed to highly visible events (de Menezes; Forest Gate) precisely because of this information vacuum. In an information-starved environment, put otherwise, the public may fasten on to whatever source of knowledge they can access, with mistakes and errors perhaps looming disproportionately large in a policy field so frequently conducted in the shadows. Thus the positive effects (of tacit support) that may be derived from an absence of knowledge may be offset by the negative effects of that which is visible (often, but not always, high profile errors).

As stated above, there are potential methodological constraints to the above analysis beyond a simple lack of representativeness. There include concerns that those who volunteer for research of this sort are atypically informed (feeling that they have something to say) and thus offer a sample bias (yet many of our findings are in broad concurrence with other research in this and related fields). Our findings suggest that citizens access a range of sources to inform their views about counter-terrorism, including non-news entertainment media, experiences and key events. Yet these are combined in heterogeneous and individuated ways. Specific aspects of the policy area, including the prominence of (secret) intelligence and gaps in information and knowledge may exacerbate this trend, with citizens either filling these gaps with narratives from diverse sources, or averting their gaze entirely. For critical scholars, these findings might be suggestive of both optimism and pessimism. Optimism can be drawn from the seeming lack of a hegemonic narrative, and certainly the lack of hegemonic sources. Pessimism, and here again, we echo Hall and Jackson's (2012) conclusions, can be seen in the difficulty, in such an individuated milieu, of mounting a sustained challenge to such measures. Whilst lay knowledge may be compiled in a differentiated fashion, from differentiated sources, this does not easily lead to challenge and opposition. As one of our participants memorably put it:

A: It's a very scary thing, and what's most scary is possibly that we don't really give a shit. We should be doing something about this.

B: We're going to think about this for the next half an hour, and after that, slip back. Eastenders is on ...

(Birmingham, Asian Male and Female)

Notes

1 The authors would like to thank Barrie Axford, Victoria Brown, Tamsin Barber, Abbey Halcli, Tina Miller, Math Noortmann and Christina Steenkamp for comments and suggestions on an earlier version of this paper. We would also like to acknowledge and thank the ESRC for funding the research on which this article draws (RES 000-22-3765) as well as all of those who helped to organise and/or participated in the focus groups.
2 For more information please see the project website, available at: www.esrc.ac.uk/my-esrc/grants/RES-000-22-3765/read.
3 None of this, of course, reflects on the 'reality' of Islamophobia or the intentions of the security personnel discussed by our participants.
4 This might be contrasted to an area such as the welfare state, where stigmatisation of those receiving welfare benefits has increased (Taylor-Gooby 2013).
5 There is an interesting parallel here with official counter-terrorism discourse which is saturated with worst-case scenarios and extrapolation from peculiar, one-off events (Mueller 2009).
6 Indeed, in another focus group, the perceived 'lesson' of the de Menezes shooting was that this one-off mistake demonstrates the typical proficiency of the UK's security services.

References

Baker-Beall, C., Heath-Kelly, C. and Jarvis, L. (forthcoming) *Counter-Radicalisation: Critical Perspectives*. Abingdon: Routledge.

Banks, W., De Nevers, R. and Wallerstein, M. (2008) *Combating Terrorism: Strategies and Approaches*. Washington, DC: CQ Press.

BBC News (2013) 'UK intelligence work defends freedom, say spy chiefs' (7/11/13). Available at: www.bbc.co.uk/news/uk-politics-24847399 (last accessed 14 March 2014).

Choudhury, T. and Fenwick, H. (2011) The Impact of Counter-Terrorism Measures on Muslim Communities. *Equality and Human Rights Commission Research Report 72*. Available at: www.equalityhumanrights.com/uploaded_files/research/counter-terrorism_research_report_72.pdf (last accessed 28 February 2014).

Cole, D. (2003) 'The New McCarthyism: Repeating History in the War on Terrorism', *Harvard Civil Rights-Civil Liberties Law Review*, 38 (1), pp. 1–30.

Delli Carpini, M.X. and Keeter, S. (1996) *What Americans Know About Politics and Why It Matters*. Yale University Press, New Haven.

Gamson, W. (1992) *Talking Politics*, Cambridge University Press, Cambridge.

Gillespie, M. and O'Loughlin, B. (2009) 'Multilingual News Cultures and Cosmopolitan Citizenship', in P. Noxolo and J. Huysmans (eds), *Community, Citizenship and the War on Terror: Security and Insecurity*. Basingstoke: Palgrave, pp. 89–112.

Gillespie, M. (2007) 'Security, media and multicultural citizenship: A collaborative ethnography', *European Journal of Cultural Studies*, 10 (3), pp. 275–293.

Hall, S. (2009 [1980]) 'Encoding/Decoding' in S. Thornham, C. Bassett and P. Marris (eds) *Media Studies: A Reader*, Edinburgh University Press, Edinburgh, pp. 28–38.

Haubrich, D. (2003) 'September 11, Anti-terror Laws and Civil Liberties: Britain, France and Germany Compared', *Government and Opposition*, 38 (1), pp. 3–28.

Hoskins, A. and O'Loughlin, B. (2009) *Television and Terror: Conflicting Times and the Crisis of News Discourse*, Palgrave, Basingtoke.

Inthorn, S., Street, J. and Scott, M. (2012) 'Popular Culture as a Resource for Political Engagement' *Cultural Sociology*, 7 (3), pp. 336–351.

Jackson, R. and Stanley, L. (forthcoming) *Everyday Narratives in World Politics* special issue, *Politics*.

Jackson, R. and Hall, G. (2012) 'Knowing Terrorism: A Study on Lay Knowledge of Terrorism and Counter-terrorism', Paper prepared for the 5th biennial Oceanic Conference on International Studies (OCIS), 18–20 July 2012, University of Sydney, Australia.

Jackson, R., Jarvis, L., Gunning, J. and Breen Smyth, M. (2011) *Terrorism: A Critical Introduction*. Basingstoke: Palgrave.

Jarvis, L. and Lister, M. (2013a) 'Disconnected Citizenship? The Impacts of Anti-Terrorism Policy on Citizenship in the UK', *Political Studies*, 61 (3), pp. 656–675.

Jarvis, L. and Lister, M. (2013b) 'Vernacular Securities and their Study: A Qualitative Analysis and Research Agenda', *International Relations*, 27 (2), pp. 158–179.

Jarvis, L. and Lister, M. (2013c) 'Disconnection and Resistance: Anti-Terrorism and Citizenship in the UK', *Citizenship Studies*, 17 (6–7), 756–769.

Jarvis, L. and Lister, M. (forthcoming) *Anti-Terrorism, Citizenship and Security in the UK*. Manchester, Manchester University Press.

Jerit, J., Barabas, J. and Bolsen, T. (2006) 'Citizens, Knowledge, and the Information Environment' *American Journal of Political Science*, 50 (2), pp. 266–282.

Johnson, M. and Gearty, C. (2007) 'Civil Liberties and the Challenge of Terrorism', in A. Park, J. Curtice, K. Thomson, M. Phillips and M. Johnson (eds), *British Social Attitudes: The 23rd Report: Perspectives on a Changing Society*. London: Sage, pp. 143–182.

Khan, K. (2009) *New York*. Yash Raj Films.

Kitzinger, J. and Barbour, R. (1999) 'Introduction: the challenge and promise of focus groups', in R. Barbour and J. Kitzinger, (eds), *Developing focus group research*, Sage, London, pp. 1–20.

Kosminsky, P. (2007) *Britz*. Channel 4.

Livingstone, S. (2010) 'Giving people a voice: On the critical role of the interview in the history of audience research', *Communication, Culture & Critique*, 3 (4), pp. 566–571.

Morgan, D. (1996) 'Focus groups', *Annual Review of Sociology*, 22 (1), pp. 129–152.

Mueller, J. (2009) *Overblown: How Politicians and the Terrorism Industry Inflate National Security Threats and Why We Believe Them*. New York, NY: The Free Press.

Mythen, G. (2012) '"No one speaks for us": security policy, suspected communities and the problem of voice', *Critical Studies on Terrorism*, 5 (3), pp. 409–424.

Mythen, G., Walklate, S. and Khan, F. (2013) 'Why Should We Have to Prove We're Alright? Counter-Terrorism, Risk and Partial Securities', *Sociology*, 47 (2), pp. 383–398.

O'Loughlin, B. and Gillespie, M. (2013) 'Dissenting Citizenship? Young People and Political Participation in the Media-security Nexus', *Parliamentary Affairs*, 65 (1), pp. 115–137.

Roach, K. (2011) *The 9/11 Effect: Comparative Counter-Terrorism*. Cambridge: Cambridge University Press.

Said, T. (2004) 'The Impact of Anti Terrorism Powers on the British Muslim Population', Liberty. Available at: www.liberty-human-rights.org.uk/policy/reports/impact-of-anti-terror-measures-on-british-muslims-june-2004.pdf (last accessed: 27 February 2014].

Sivanandan, A. (2006) 'Race, Terror and Civil Society', *Race and Class*, 47 (3), pp. 1–8.

Street, J., Inthorn, S. and Scott, M. (2012) 'Playing at Politics? Popular Culture as Political Engagement', *Parliamentary Affairs*, 65 (2), pp. 338–358.

Taylor-Gooby, P. (2013) 'Why Do People Stigmatise the Poor at a Time of Rapidly Increasing Inequality, and What Can Be Done About It?', *Parliamentary Affairs*, 84 (1), pp. 31–42.

Walker, C. (2009) *Blackstone's Guide to the Anti-terrorism Legislation*. Oxford: Blackwell.

van Zoonen, L. (2005) *Entertaining the Citizen: When Politics and Popular Culture Converge*, Rowman & Littlefield, Oxford.

7 Prosecuting suspected terrorists
Precursor crimes, intercept evidence and the priority of security

Stuart Macdonald

Introduction

The UK's counter-terrorism strategy – CONTEST – is divided into four strands: Pursue, Prevent, Protect and Prepare. This chapter focuses on the pursue strand in particular, which aims to reduce the terrorist threat to this country by disrupting terrorists and their operations. A number of methods of disruption are available, including: prosecution; deportation; proscription; seizing and freezing assets; and, Terrorism Prevention and Investigation Measures (TPIMs). Of these, the CONTEST strategy states that the preferred method is prosecution (Home Office 2011a). This chapter examines this so-called 'priority of prosecution' (Home Office 2011b: 40) and argues that, in fact, the emphasis placed on prosecution is equivocal and better understood as a manifestation of the priority that contemporary counter-terrorism policies attach to national security.

The chapter examines two key issues that lie at the heart of the UK's efforts to prosecute suspected terrorists in order to illustrate this 'priority of security'. First, it examines the existing raft of terrorism precursor offences. There are important rule of law reasons for prosecuting suspected terrorists whenever possible. Requiring the state to prove its case against the suspect in open court beyond reasonable doubt and affording the suspect the opportunity to respond to the case against him mean that prosecution has a moral authority other forms of disruption may lack. But, the chapter argues, these considerations have not been the primary driving force behind the expanding scope of the criminal law. Indeed, many of the precursor offences pay insufficient regard to human rights and the rule of law. Instead, it is security-based considerations that have proven the most influential. The imposition of long prison terms is more protective of national security than alternative measures such as deportation and TPIMs, which has 'an obvious appeal to security-minded politicians and an anxious public' (Zedner 2012: 10). There is also the politically persuasive retributive argument that conviction for a terrorism offence results in the public ascription of the label 'terrorist' and a commensurate prison sentence. It will be argued that the danger with this approach is that it threatens to undermine the very qualities that give the criminal law its moral authority in the first place.

The second half of the chapter examines the UK's ban on the use of intercept as evidence. Here, the chapter argues that prosecution has not been prioritised at all. For, whilst the previous and current governments have supported lifting the ban in principle, a precautious, security-based approach has prevailed which has prevented the development of a workable legal regime. This also has the potential to undermine the moral authority of the criminal law, by necessitating greater reliance on exceptional measures like TPIMs.

Precursor offences

There are many criminal offences of general application that might be used in cases involving terrorism. For cases involving fatalities there are the offences of murder and being an accessory to murder. If there were no fatalities there are the non-fatal offences against the person, including causing grievous bodily harm with intent.[1] There are offences of hostage-taking[2] and kidnap.[3] There are numerous explosives offences.[4] And there are offences of hijacking aircraft and ships.[5] In keeping with the criminal law's focus on harmful wrongdoing, for one of these 'full' offences to apply the harm in question must have occurred. The victims must have suffered death or injury, or been kidnapped or taken hostage. The substance must have exploded. Or the vehicle must have been hijacked.

The punishment of those who have caused harm is not the criminal law's only concern, however (Horder 2012). It also has a preventive role. As Ashworth and Zedner have observed, 'If a certain form of harmful wrongdoing is judged serious enough to criminalize, it follows that the state should assume responsibility for taking steps to protect people from it' (Ashworth and Zedner 2012: 543). Indeed, 'a law that condemned and punished actually harm-causing conduct as wrong, but was utterly silent on attempts to cause such harms, and on reckless risk-taking with respect to such harms, would speak with a strange moral voice' (Duff 1996: 134). For this reason, the criminal law also contains offences of attempt, conspiracy and encouraging crime. These 'inchoate' offences have a preventive rationale, allowing authorities to intervene before any harm is actually caused.

In the context of terrorism offences, there are two difficulties with the inchoate offences. The first is that the offences of conspiracy and encouraging crime are notoriously difficult to prove. Obtaining admissible evidence of an agreement or words of encouragement within secretive organisations is difficult, particularly given the UK's ban on the use of intercept as evidence (discussed further below). Even if admissible evidence is obtained, it may lack evidential value (many members of terrorist organisations observe good communications security and disguise the content of their communications) or there may be public interest reasons for not disclosing it (perhaps because it would expose other ongoing investigations or reveal sensitive techniques or capabilities) (Privy Council Review of Intercept as Evidence 2008).

Second, the law governing criminal attempts has a limited scope. A person only commits the offence of attempt once he has performed an act that is 'more than merely preparatory' to the commission of the full offence.[6] So in the case of *R v. Campbell*,[7] the Court of Appeal quashed the defendant's conviction for attempted robbery – notwithstanding the fact that he was stopped by police outside a post office wearing sunglasses and in possession of an imitation firearm and threatening note – because he had not yet embarked on the crime. Similarly, in *R v. Geddes*[8] the Court of Appeal quashed the defendant's conviction for attempted false imprisonment. The defendant was found in the boys' toilets in a school (which he had entered without permission), in possession of rope, masking tape and a knife. The Court explained that the defendant would only have gone beyond mere preparation once he actually came into contact with a pupil. Views differ on whether these decisions are unduly restrictive (Clarkson 2009; cf. Simester *et al.* 2013: 339–359). But in the specific context of terrorism, the level of risk and severity of the potential harm provide strong reasons to penalise conduct at an earlier stage. In the words of the Independent Reviewer of Terrorism Legislation, it is necessary to 'defend further up the field' (Anderson 2013b: 237). This is the function of precursor – or pre-inchoate – offences. Whilst the law of attempts criminalises acts that are more than merely preparatory, precursor crimes focus on various forms of preparatory conduct.

There are a large number of terrorism precursor offences in the UK, found predominantly in the 2000 and 2006 Terrorism Acts (similar offences are found in other jurisdictions: see McSherry (2009)). Examples include:

- Membership of a proscribed organisation (Terrorism Act 2000, section 11).
- Support for a proscribed organisation (Terrorism Act 2000, section 12).
- Fundraising for terrorist purposes (Terrorism Act 2000, section 15).
- Use or possession of money or other property for terrorist purposes (Terrorism Act 2000, section 16).
- Failure to disclose information that might assist in preventing an act of terrorism (Terrorism Act 2000, section 38B).
- Possession of an article for terrorist purposes (Terrorism Act 2000, section 57).
- Collecting information or possessing a document likely to be useful to a terrorist (Terrorism Act 2000, section 58).
- Inciting terrorism overseas (Terrorism Act 2000, section 59).
- Encouragement of terrorism (Terrorism Act 2006, section 1).
- Dissemination of terrorist publications (Terrorism Act 2006, section 2).
- Preparation of terrorist acts (Terrorism Act 2006, section 5).
- Training for terrorism (Terrorism Act 2006, section 6).
- Attendance at a place used for terrorist training (Terrorism Act 2006, section 8).

As this list illustrates, precursor offences encompass a wide range of preparatory activities. An individual who receives training in any 'method or technique' with an intention to use these skills to commit an act of terrorism commits an offence.[9] An individual who, without reasonable excuse, collects information that is likely to be useful in the commission of an act of terrorism commits an offence.[10] This may include taking photographs of a target or downloading information from the Internet.[11] An individual found in possession of any 'article' in circumstances which give rise to a reasonable suspicion that he has a terrorist purpose commits an offence.[12] And, most sweepingly of all, a person commits an offence if he engages in 'any conduct' with an intention to commit an act of terrorism.[13]

The precursor offences not only extend the temporal reach of the criminal law. As well as enabling intervention at an earlier point in time they also encompass a broader range of individuals, penalising those with an associative or facilitative role as well as potential perpetrators and accessories (Zedner 2012). So, for example, it is an offence to be an active member of a proscribed organisation[14] and to arrange a meeting that furthers the activities of a proscribed organisation.[15] It is an offence to disseminate terrorist publications either with an intention to (directly or indirectly) encourage or assist the commission of acts of terrorism, or being reckless as to whether such encouragement or assistance is provided.[16] And it is an offence to provide or receive money or other property where there is reasonable cause to suspect that it may be used for terrorist purposes.[17]

Moreover, there are two further features of the precursor offences which mean that their reach extends still further. First, many of the offences focus not only on the facilitation of terrorist attacks, but also the facilitation of acts which may assist or encourage a terrorist attack. So it is not only an offence for an individual (D1) to provide training to someone (D2) with an intention that D2 will use the skills to commit a terrorist act. It is also an offence for D1 to provide training to D2 with an intention that D2 will use the skills to assist someone else (D3) to commit a terrorist act.[18] By the same token, it is an offence for an individual (D1) to fail to disclose information that might be of material assistance in apprehending another person (D2) who is involved in instigating an act of terrorism by someone else (D3).[19] Second, just as it is possible to commit full offences like murder in inchoate form (e.g. attempted murder, conspiracy to murder), so too is it possible to commit many of the precursor offences in inchoate form. Simple examples would be where two people conspire to engage in conduct that is preparatory to an act of terrorism[20] and where an individual intentionally encourages someone else to provide money for use for a terrorist purpose.[21]

When these two features are combined, the full extent and complexity of the precursor offences becomes clear. Together, they mean that it is an offence for an individual (D1) to intentionally encourage someone else (D2) to engage in any preparatory conduct that is intended to assist another (D3) to commit a terrorist act.[22] Even more strikingly, it is an offence for an individual (D1) to intentionally encourage someone else (D2) to cause someone else (D3) to publish a statement which indirectly encourages someone else (D4) to instigate someone else (D5) to commit an act of terrorism.[23] And it does not end there! In certain circumstances, the law governing inchoate offences allows one layer of inchoate liability to be piled upon another (so-called double inchoate liability). So, it is an offence for an individual (D1) to intentionally encourage someone else (D2) to intentionally encourage someone else (D3) to cause someone else (D4) to publish a statement that indirectly encourages someone else (D5) to instigate someone else (D6) to commit an act of terrorism.[24] What is more, D1 is guilty of this offence even if his initial encouragement never reached D2, as long as his act was capable of providing encouragement. These 'parasitic extensions of liability to ever more remote preparations for crime' (Leader-Elliott 2011: 82) not only raise questions about the justifiability of penalising individuals several steps removed from the feared eventual harm. They also raise rule of law concerns such as whether the law is sufficiently clear and comprehensible and whether citizens have received fair warning of the precursor offences' extended reach.

The justifiability of precursor offences

Whilst emphasising the need to defend further up the field, the Independent Reviewer of Terrorism Legislation also stresses the dangers associated with precursor offences:

> [T]he *potential* for abuse is rarely absent.... By seeking to extend the reach of the criminal law to people who are more and more on the margins, and to activities taking place earlier and earlier in the story, their shadow begins to loom over all manner of previously innocent interactions. The effects can, at worst, be horrifying for individuals and demoralising to communities.
>
> (Anderson 2013b: 240, emphasis in original)

In recent years criminal law theorists have grappled with the expanding use of the criminal law (see, for example, Duff *et al.* 2010; Simester and von Hirsch 2011; Ashworth and Zedner 2012; Sullivan and Dennis 2012). Whilst recognising that there may be both retributive and consequentialist reasons for using the criminal sanction pre-emptively, their work also raises some fundamental concerns. Ashworth and Zedner (2012: 556) explain:

> It is one thing to hold someone to account for a harm that she has done or risked herself or has induced another to commit or risk. It is another thing to hold an individual responsible for the possible future acts of herself or of a third party.

To hold a person responsible now for her possible future actions is to undermine her autonomy and to treat her as one 'who lack[s] the insight or self-control to resist the later temptation ... [S]uch treatment fails to respect her as a moral agent, capable of deliberation and self-control' (Simester and von Hirsh 2011: 81). To hold a person responsible now for the possible future actions of another is to judge her not according to her own actions but according to the conduct of others. This is contrary to the 'fundamental right to be treated as separate individuals, as autonomous moral agents who are distinctively responsible for the consequences of their *own* actions' (Simester and von Hirsch 2011: 80–81, emphasis in original). This is not to say that the criminal law does not have a preventive role. Rather, it is to urge the importance of principles that guide and constrain the preventive use of the criminal sanction.

Taking up this challenge, Ashworth and Zedner have advanced a framework of 11 principles. Particularly relevant for present purposes are the following two:

> In principle, a person may be held liable for acts he or she has done, simply on the basis of what he or she may do at some time in the future, only if the person has declared an intent to do those acts in a form that satisfies the requirements of an attempt, conspiracy, or solicitation.
>
> In principle, a person may be held liable for the future acts of others only if that person has a sufficient normative involvement in those acts (e.g., that he or she has encouraged, assisted, or facilitated), or where the acts of the other were foreseeable, with respect to which the person has an obligation to prevent a harm that might be caused by the other.
>
> (Ashworth and Zedner 2012: 557)

The second of these principles draws on the earlier work of Simester and von Hirsch. Explaining the notion of normative involvement, they state that when an individual 'in some sense affirms or underwrites' the other person's subsequent choice it is fair to say that she has endorsed the possible future actions of that other person; responsibility for the feared eventual harm may therefore be imputed to her (Simester and von Hirsch 2011: 81).

Applying these two principles to the existing raft of terrorism precursor offences, the first point to note is the possibility of an individual being convicted of a terrorism offence notwithstanding the absence of any normative involvement in a terrorist plot. An example is *R* v. *G*.[25] The defendant in this case was a paranoid schizophrenic who had been detained for non-terrorism offences. While in custody he collected information on explosives and bomb-making, and also drew a map of the Territorial Army centre in Chesterfield and wrote down plans to attack the centre. The prosecution accepted expert evidence that he had collected the information as a direct consequence of his illness (he said he wanted to 'wind up' the prison staff because he believed they had been whispering about him). G was charged with an offence under section 58 of the Terrorism Act 2000. This simply says that a person commits an offence if, without reasonable excuse, he collects information of a kind likely to be useful to a person committing or preparing an act of terrorism. On the face of it, this offence is enormously broad. There is a vast array of information that might be useful to a terrorist, such as a train timetable, telephone directory and street map. The House of Lords narrowed the scope of the offence by stating that, whilst the information need not only be useful to a terrorist, it must by its very nature call for an explanation. So information on explosives would qualify (even though it might also be useful to a bank robber), but a train timetable would not. Therefore, the key question in

G's case was whether or not he had a reasonable excuse. The House of Lords held that it is not reasonable to antagonise prison guards, and G's illness could not render his actions *objectively* reasonable. So G was guilty of a serious terrorism offence, carrying a maximum sentence of 10 years' imprisonment, even though no terrorist connections had been established. The effect was to 'make a terrorist out of nothing' (Hodgson and Tadros 2009).

The second point is that there may be cogent reasons not to create an offence even if it *does* require proof that the individual either intended to commit, or had normative involvement in, future terrorist acts. An example that has generated much comment is the offence of preparation of terrorist acts, created by section 5 of the Terrorism Act 2006. In order to establish liability for this offence it is sufficient for the prosecution to prove that the defendant engaged in 'any conduct' with an intention to commit or assist acts of terrorism. The legislation's accompanying explanatory notes explain that this was designed to complement the inchoate offences of attempt and conspiracy in two respects: first, by encompassing cases where the individual's conduct is merely preparatory and there is no evidence of any agreement with others; and, second, by only requiring proof of a general intention to carry out some terrorist act, rather than proof of intention to commit a specific offence (as in conspiracy and attempt). What the notes fail to mention is that there are already numerous other precursor offences which target specific preparatory acts, such as training, fundraising and collecting and disseminating information. Section 5 seems to serve a catch-all purpose, which raises the question whether there are in fact gaps in the wide range of other precursor offences that need to be plugged. In addition, in *R* v. *Iqbal*[26] the Court of Appeal confirmed that section 5 overlaps with the other precursor crimes; so, in that particular case, the fact that the defendant's conduct might also have fallen under the section 6 offence (training for terrorism) did not preclude him from being convicted of the section 5 offence. The significance of this is that section 5's sentencing powers are more severe than for many of the more specific preparatory offences. Its maximum sentence of life imprisonment thus gives the state access to more severe sentencing powers than might otherwise be available.

As well as these questions about the necessity of section 5 and its sentencing powers, there are also concerns about its expansive reach. For, if carried out with the requisite intention, any form of conduct could potentially be penalised. Giving the example of an individual eating muesli for breakfast as part of a fitness programme in preparation for a terrorist act, Simester concludes 'Morally speaking, the section probably overreaches, extending the criminal law beyond its legitimate bounds. On balance, the prohibition seems too invasive of privacy and autonomy' (Simester 2012: 71). Where the conduct charged is something innocuous, like eating muesli, the authorities will need to find some other evidence of the individual's intention to commit terrorist acts. This could result in intrusive methods of policing. There is also the danger that the offence will be enforced in a discriminatory manner with certain groups feeling compelled to forgo some innocent behaviour for fear it may be misconstrued.

The third point is that, in a number of the precursor offences, there is a discrepancy between the wrong that the offence targets and what it actually encompasses. So while the offence might be targeted at individuals with an intention to commit, or normative involvement in, future terrorist acts, a far wider range of people fall within its scope. An example is the encouragement of terrorism, found in section one of the Terrorism Act 2006. The Government explained that this offence targets those who encourage violent extremism:

> Unfortunately, there are young and impressionable people in our society who can all too easily be manipulated by people preaching or advocating a message of hate. Such people can create the climate of hate in which terrorism can more easily flourish. That is what we are trying to tackle with the offence.
> (Hazel Blears HC Hansard vol. 439 col. 430 9 November 2005)

Yet the combination of the wording of this offence and the broad statutory definition of terrorism mean that the offence is not limited to those who nurture a culture of hate. Someone publishing a statement celebrating the actions of Nelson Mandela in the early 1960s could fall within the offence, if: first, it is likely that some of the members of the public to whom the statement was published could reasonably have been expected to infer that Mandela's actions were being glorified as conduct that should be emulated; and, second, the person either (i) intended that those members of the public would be (directly or indirectly) encouraged to commit, prepare or instigate acts of terrorism, or (ii) was reckless as to whether the statement would have this effect and failed to make it clear that the statement neither expressed his views nor had his endorsement. Edwards accordingly describes the offence as 'breathtakingly wide. It arguably catches everyone from outspoken Islamic clerics, to North Korean exiles who criticise their native regime, to those, like Cherie Blair, who express their ability to understand the actions of Palestinian suicide-bombers' (Edwards 2010: 730). It would also catch many of those who have commented on the events of recent years in countries like Libya, Egypt, Tunisia and Syria.

When there is such a discrepancy between what an offence targets and what it actually encompasses, the conclusion must be that the offence was not created to produce non-offending responses from all who would otherwise commit it (Edwards 2011). In the case of the encouragement of terrorism offence, this is confirmed by the Government's stressing the importance of the requirement that the Director of Public Prosecutions consent to any prosecution (Edwards 2010). For terrorism precursor offences, it seems fair to assume that a primary consideration in decisions to prosecute will be whether the individual poses a risk to national security. But, at trial, the question will be whether the requirements set out in the offence definition are satisfied. The national security considerations that led to the decision to prosecute will sit in the background. So 'Even though the pursuit of security is central to the justification for the law itself, it is not open to challenge by the defendant with respect to his particular case' (Tadros

2007: 688). Edwards has accordingly labelled such offences 'ouster offences', for they deprive the courts of the opportunity to adjudicate on the actions that the offence is targeting (Edwards 2010). Ouster offences are created, he argues, to facilitate the conviction of those targeted by the offence by lightening the prosecutorial burden. However expedient this may be, denying individuals the opportunity to address the reasons they have been selected for prosecution undermines the courts' ability to deliver procedural justice. This poses a significant challenge to the moral authority of the criminal law, especially given that social psychological research has found that people's views on authority are strongly connected to their judgments of the fairness of the procedures through which those authorities make decisions (Tyler 1990).

The use of intercept as evidence

Under the UK's Regulation of Investigatory Powers Act 2000 (RIPA), specified intelligence and law enforcement agencies may apply to the Secretary of State for a warrant to intercept any form of communication – including telephone calls, emails, text messages, Voice over Internet Protocol (VoIP), ordinary post and faxes – in order to protect national security, prevent or detect serious crime and safeguard the UK's economic wellbeing. In 2012 a total of 3,372 lawful intercept warrants were issued; a 16 per cent increase on the total of 2,911 in 2011 (Kennedy 2013). Warranted interception of communications is 'a critical tool in protecting the public from terrorists and other serious criminals' (Home Office 2010: 10). It provides both tactical information on the plans and actions of individual terrorists, and strategic information from which a broad understanding of the terrorist threat can be derived and preventative strategies developed (Privy Council Review of Intercept as Evidence 2008). But whilst intercept is used for intelligence and investigative purposes, section 17 of RIPA states that, save in certain limited circumstances, it is inadmissible in legal proceedings. There have been repeated claims that if this self-imposed ban were lifted, allowing intercept to be used as evidence in criminal trials, the UK would be able to successfully prosecute a greater number of suspected terrorists.

The issue has been examined on a number of occasions: since 1993 there have been no fewer than eight investigations (Anderson 2013a). Both Lord Lloyd's review of counter-terrorism legislation (Lloyd 1996) and the Newton Committee's report (Privy Counsellor Review Committee 2003) recommended that the ban be lifted, as did a major report by the prominent law reform and human rights organisation JUSTICE in 2006. In contrast, a Government review commissioned by then Prime Minister Tony Blair in 2004 concluded that the ban should not be lifted since it had not been clearly established that the potential benefits outweighed the risks.[27] After becoming Prime Minister in 2007, Gordon Brown announced that the issue would be revisited. The subsequent review, which was headed by Sir John Chilcot, concluded that in principle the use of intercept as evidence should be introduced (Privy Council Review of Intercept as Evidence 2008). However, it stated that any legal regime for the use of intercept as evidence would only be operationally workable if it complied with a total of nine conditions. According to these: intercepting agencies should have the final say over the use of intercept material in legal proceedings in order to protect sensitive techniques and capabilities (conditions one to three); agencies should have continued discretion over the retention, examination and transcription of intercept material (conditions four to five); agencies should be able to maintain their real-time tactical and long-term strategic capabilities, with day-to-day cooperation between law enforcement and intelligence agencies unaffected (conditions six to eight); and, at trials the defence should not be able to conduct speculative fishing expeditions (condition nine). These nine conditions reflect the Chilcot review's insistence that '*any* material risk to the strategic capability of the UK's intelligence agencies would be unacceptable' (Privy Council Review of Intercept as Evidence 2008: 23, emphasis added). This unyielding position was criticised by proponents of lifting the ban:

> A reading of the Chilcot report leaves the impression that the authorities want to have their cake and eat it – to use intercept as evidence where it might bring an advantage but at no 'risk'. This is unrealistic. Some risk that terrorists gain fractionally more information about surveillance techniques or 'trade-craft' or that overseas agencies chafe at disclosure, may have to be tolerated; just as some compromise will be necessary on the principles of open justice and adversarial trial in any such regime.
>
> (Leigh 2009: 945)

Following the publication of the Chilcot report, a cross-party Advisory Group of Privy Counsellors commenced work on devising a legal regime that not only complied with the nine Chilcot conditions, but also with the requirements of Article 6 of the European Convention on Human Rights (ECHR). The Group's work focused on an approach known as Public Interest Immunity Plus. Under this model, all material from intercepted communications is potentially admissible as evidence. In order to protect sensitive material, agencies would have the final say over the use of their intercept as evidence. If the defence were to challenge the use of intercept in circumstances where there could be a risk of disclosing sensitive material, techniques or relationships, closed admissibility hearings – similar to existing Public Interest Immunity sessions – would be held. Importantly, intercepting agencies would also have discretion over monitoring, retention and transcription practices. Any material assessed as potentially exculpatory by the agencies at the time of examination would be retained.

When the Group reported in December 2009, its conclusion was that the Public Interest Immunity Plus model would not be legally viable (Home Office 2009). The report explained that the proposed arrangements for retention of intercept materials would violate the Article 6 ECHR right to a fair trial. The decision of the European Court of Human Rights in *Natunen* v. *Finland*[28] was cited to support this. Natunen had been convicted of drugs offences. He claimed that he had intended to buy weapons, not drugs, and that this could be verified by recordings of his telephone conversations. At his appeal against conviction the prosecutor explained that, whilst some telephone conversations had been included in the pre-trial case file, others that did not concern the purchase of drugs had been destroyed in accordance with Finnish law. The European Court held that this violated Article 6 ECHR, explaining that the principle of equality of arms requires that the defence be given the opportunity to participate in the process of deciding which materials should be destroyed, and that the process is subject to judicial oversight. Applying this ruling, the Advisory Group concluded that the Public Interest Immunity Plus model is incompatible with Article 6 since it 'does not give judicial control over the intercepting agencies' retention, examination and review processes' (Home Office 2009: 7). It proposed that further work be conducted to: examine in greater detail the operational, legal and public policy issues surrounding a full retention store; assess whether advances in technology might make full retention and review more manageable; and, consider other approaches which are predicated on full retention (Horne 2011). At the time of writing (September 2013), this work is still ongoing.

The Chilcot review's starting point that national security should be treated as an 'overriding imperative' (Privy Council Review of Intercept as Evidence 2008: 23) may be contrasted with the increasing 'judicialisation of intelligence' (Walker 2011). In recent years the courts have developed a particular expertise and knowledge in the area of national security, such that the small and experienced body of judges who hear these cases may now be regarded as experts in this particular field.[29] Whilst the courts may have traditionally deferred to the executive in matters of national security, today they subject decisions to intense scrutiny in order to ensure compliance with Article 6 ECHR (Tomkins 2010). Given this, and the work of the Advisory Group to date, it follows that for the ban on intercept as evidence to be lifted, the fourth and fifth Chilcot conditions (no intelligence or law enforcement agency should be required to retain raw intercepted material for significantly more or less time than needed for operational purposes or to examine, transcribe or make notes of intercepted material to a substantially higher standard than it believes is required to meet its objectives) need to be revisited. The Joint Committee on Human Rights has commented that, whilst it understands 'the agencies' anxieties about ceding their discretion in favour of judicial control,... this is an inevitable consequence of the agencies engaging with legal processes' (JCHR 2010: 33). Without this, the Advisory Group's ongoing efforts are 'already doomed to failure' (JCHR 2010: 32).

Lifting the ban: the risks

At the heart of the debate on the use of intercept as evidence lie two sets of issues that, broadly speaking, concern the possible risks and potential benefits of lifting the ban. First are the possible implications of disclosure. The Chilcot review stated:

Any disclosure of interception capabilities could have a profound impact on national security, by encouraging a wide range of targets (not only criminals but also terrorists and other individuals of intelligence value) to change their behaviour in ways that would make them more difficult to investigate in the future.

(Privy Council Review of Intercept as Evidence 2008: 18)

The report went on to explain that, whilst targets are aware of the authorities' capability to intercept communications and attempt to obfuscate their communications or avoid interception altogether, at present they cannot know which of their efforts are successful and which are not. These concerns about disclosure were reiterated in the Advisory Group's 2009 report, which warned that 'If terrorists and other criminals develop a more accurate understanding of the techniques and capabilities deployed against them, the task of protecting the public and national security will be considerably harder' (Home Office 2009: 5).

The Chilcot report claimed that disclosure would also have a number of other harmful effects. At present intelligence agencies use their techniques and capabilities in support of law enforcement, to prevent serious crime and terrorist acts through disruption operations and generate leads that result in prosecutions. If the ban on intercept as evidence were lifted, continuing this level of support might place sensitive techniques and capabilities at risk of exposure and so no longer be feasible (Privy Council Review of Intercept as Evidence 2008). Lifting the ban could also impact on relationships with Communication Service Providers (CSPs). According to a former Interception of Communications Commissioner, CSPs 'are totally opposed to the concept of intercept being admissible in Court' (Thomas 2007: 11). This is due: firstly, to the commercial consideration that CSPs do not want to be seen by their customers intercepting their communications and providing them to Government agencies; and, secondly, to their employees' concerns about the possible consequences for themselves and their families of having to go to court and testify about what they do (JCHR 2007: 44). Lastly, there are the potential resource implications of lifting the ban. Agencies would need to: retain more intercepted material and for longer than is necessary for intelligence purposes; transcribe and translate more of the material, and in greater detail, than they would otherwise need to; and, provide an effective guide to the content of the intercept in order to enable exculpatory material to be identified. Trials could also become more complex and last for longer. If extra resources were not made available to meet these costs, there would be a reduction in agencies' capacity – meaning that it may not be possible to cover some targets (Privy Council Review of Intercept as Evidence 2008).

Having identified these risks, it is important to assess their magnitude. To begin, it should be noted that intercepted material is already admissible in some legal proceedings, including proceedings before the Special Immigration Appeals Commission, the Proscribed Organisations Appeal Commission and under the Terrorism Prevention and Investigation Measures Act 2011 (TPIMs Act). If there is concern in any of these proceedings that disclosure of the intercept to the individual could harm national security, closed sessions may be held in which the individual and his lawyer are not present and the individual's interests are represented by a Special Advocate. Importantly, however, in proceedings under the TPIMs Act there will be a breach of the individual's right to a fair trial if the case against him is based solely or to a decisive degree on closed materials: Article 6 ECHR requires that the individual is given sufficient information about the allegations to have an effective opportunity to challenge the case against him (the *AF (No 3)* principle[30]). The fact that it has been possible to lift the ban on intercept evidence in these proceedings, in spite of the obligation imposed on the prosecution by the *AF (No 3)* principle, demonstrates that it may also be possible to admit intercept as evidence in criminal trials under specially protective rules. Moreover, even if a judge were to order the disclosure of material that would reveal methods used by intelligence agencies, in practice the authorities would be able to discontinue the trial. The former Director of Public Prosecutions, Lord Macdonald, has explained:

> If the worst came to the worst and in a criminal trial we were, for some bizarre reason, ordered by a judge to disclose some secret to the defence, we would not have to do it. There is always the option to stop the prosecution. We do that all the time in informer cases, where judges will occasionally, no doubt for good reasons, say that if you want to continue with the case you are going to have to tell the defence who the informer is. Invariably, we would offer no evidence.
>
> (JCHR 2011: 11)

The ban on the use of intercept as evidence is also out of sync with the approach taken to other technologies. No equivalent prohibition applies to the evidential use of material obtained through surveillance, including bugging, covert closed-circuit television, observations made by covert surveillance officers or telephone conversations recorded by a hidden microphone not connected to the telephone (Horne 2011). If the concerns about intercept evidence revealing sensitive techniques and capabilities were insurmountable, one would expect to find a similar prohibition on the use of evidence from these other sources (JUSTICE 2006). It is also striking that Ireland is the only other comparable legal jurisdiction to prohibit the use of intercept as evidence (Anderson 2013a). This anomaly has led to calls that the Government end 'the absurd pretence that the United Kingdom, uniquely, cannot use intercept evidence in criminal trials without doing serious damage to its national security or public safety' (Fenwick and Phillipson 2011: 914). Also anomalous is the fact that the UK's prohibition on intercept evidence does not extend to the use of UK intercept in foreign courts (if the intelligence agencies are prepared to provide it), nor to the use of foreign intercept in UK courts (JUSTICE 2006). It has been claimed that the latter of these has in the past resulted in the embarrassing situation where UK agencies have had to go to other countries to ask for evidence that they already have in their files.[31] The fact that other countries do not have an equivalent prohibition also diminishes the force of the argument that the UK's ban prevents individuals from gaining an understanding of intelligence agencies' techniques and capabilities. It seems safe to assume that the methods used by UK intelligence agencies do not differ significantly from comparable countries. Individuals who wish to do so may therefore draw reasonable inferences about UK intelligence agencies' capabilities by studying cases from other countries in which intercept evidence has been used (and then complement this with the wealth of information on interception techniques that is readily available on the Internet).

There are also cogent reasons to believe that the other possible risks have been overstated. The experience of other countries has been that employees of CSPs are rarely called to give evidence and, in the rare event where it is necessary to testify, various witness protection measures are available (JCHR 2007). It is important to note, therefore, that when Lord Lloyd introduced an amendment to the Serious Crime Bill (now Act 2007) which would have lifted the ban on intercept evidence, he received a letter from the Mobile Broadband Group (comprising all the main network operators in the UK) that explained that, provided their staff were protected, they had no objection in principle to intercept evidence being admitted.[32] The experience of other countries also suggests that lifting the ban need not have an adverse impact on the relationship between intelligence and law enforcement agencies. In Australia, for example, investigations into terrorism offences are generally conducted by a number of different intelligence and law enforcement agencies working cooperatively (Blackbourn and McGarrity 2012). Moreover, as explained above, the risk of sensitive techniques and capabilities being exposed in court is remote. As Lord Macdonald stated:

> The idea that a Director of Public Prosecutions would reveal a piece of information to the defence in defiance of the wishes of the Director General of MI5, the head of GCHQ and chief of SIS is preposterous. It would never happen.
> (JCHR 2011: 11)

Lastly, the Home Affairs Committee has disputed the argument that lifting the ban would lead to vastly increased costs, pointing out that there would not be 'a fundamental shift in agency activity' since information that is currently collected as intelligence could be used for evidential purposes (Home Affairs Committee 2010: 17). Allowing the use of intercept evidence could also result in significant savings as more defendants could be persuaded to plead guilty and the availability of intercept evidence would sometimes obviate the need for other, more costly, investigative techniques such as surveillance. The conclusion of the Chilcot report was that it is 'very hard' to predict whether these savings will be outweighed by any additional costs (Privy Council Review of Intercept as Evidence 2008: 26). What is clear, however, is that even if the costs do outweigh the savings, lessons may be learned from the practices developed in other countries to alleviate the burden on intercepting agencies (Blackbourn and McGarrity 2012).

Lifting the ban: the potential benefits

The second set of issues concern the potential benefits of lifting the ban. The Chilcot report explained that intercept can provide 'extremely powerful evidence' (Privy Council Review of Intercept as Evidence 2008: 15). Playing a recording of the defendant's own words gives the jury an insight into his intentions and state of mind. This can be particularly valuable in terrorism cases since the UK's statutory definition of terrorism requires proof of a political, religious, racial or ideological motive.[33] Moreover, the availability of intercept as evidence makes it easier to establish liability for inchoate offences like conspiracy (which requires proof of an agreement between the parties and an intention to carry the agreement out) and terrorism precursor offences (where the key issue will often be the defendant's state of mind since his conduct may at worst have been morally ambiguous). As well as increased convictions for terrorism offences, the Crown Prosecution Service expects that lifting the ban will result in more early guilty pleas and fewer abortive trials (Privy Council Review of Intercept as Evidence 2008). Not only will this lead to savings in time and money, but defendants who realise that their case is hopeless may also agree to provide assistance to the prosecution. It was by using intercept evidence in this way that the US authorities were able, for the first time, to secure convictions of the heads of all five New York mafia families (Privy Council Review of Intercept as Evidence 2008).

As with the possible risks, the key issue here is the scale of these potential benefits. Lord Macdonald has remarked 'I am absolutely confident that our experience would mirror the experience of other jurisdictions where [intercept] is used frequently to great effect and results in the saving of considerable expense' (Home Affairs Committee 2010: 16). By contrast, although the former Independent Reviewer of Terrorism Legislation, Lord Carlile, supported the use of intercept as evidence, he warned that it would not be 'the quick and easy solution that some have assumed and asserted' (Carlile 2011: 25). In a similar vein, the current Independent Reviewer, David Anderson, has indicated that he would support lifting the ban in principle but also warned that 'the admissibility of intercept is no "*silver bullet*"' (Anderson 2013a: 64, emphasis in original).

Two sets of empirical findings also suggest that any increase in the number of successful prosecutions might not be as great as hoped. The first piece of work was carried out as part of the 2004 review commissioned by Tony Blair. It took a number of real cases in which interception had been used, examined whether the actual intercept obtained would have been of evidential value, and then estimated the effect on the outcome. The conclusion was that lifting the ban would result in 25 to 30 additional convictions each year across the UK. Importantly, however, these would mainly be of second and third tier organised criminals. The review concluded that there would be few additional convictions of first tier organised criminals or suspected terrorists since they generally observe good communications security (Privy Council Review of Intercept as Evidence 2008). The second piece of work was conducted by independent senior criminal Counsel for the Home Office. It reviewed a total of nine Control Order cases and assessed whether the availability of intercept as evidence would have enabled a criminal prosecution to be brought in any of the cases. The conclusion was that it would not. In four cases, Counsel concluded that the intercepted material would not have been of any evidential value. In the other five cases the intercepted material would have had evidential value, but the damage that using the material would have caused to national security meant that no prosecution would in fact have been brought (Privy Council Review of Intercept as Evidence 2008). To similar effect are the Independent Reviewers' statements that 'It is unlikely that the admissibility before the jury of intercept would have led to the prosecution of any controlees since control orders were introduced in 2005' (Carlile 2011: 29) and 'the admissibility of intercept evidence would not have enabled the prosecution of those subjected to TPIMs in 2012' (Anderson 2013a: 64).

There are, however, two reasons to believe that the impact of lifting the ban on intercept evidence would not be as limited as this empirical data suggests. The first is that the studies appear to have assumed that intercept evidence would be used under the current adversarial rules in a criminal trial and not a specially adapted procedure. Yet, as noted above, intercept evidence is already admissible in proceedings under the TPIMs Act (and was admissible in the earlier control order proceedings). It is unclear why, in five of the nine control order cases in the second study, national security would have precluded the use of intercepted material with evidential value in a criminal trial, when presumably that same material had already been deployed in the application for a control order. As Leigh has observed:

> The decision had already been taken in the five cases mentioned to apply for a control order – evidently national security concerns had not outweighed *that* decision. It is unclear why a prosecution under specially protective rules should be seen so very differently.
>
> (Leigh 2009: 946, emphasis in original)

A further difficulty with both sets of data is that the studies examined material which had been intercepted for intelligence, not evidential, purposes. Lord Macdonald has explained that this difference in approach is critical:

> If you look at material which is acquired for intelligence purposes, it is acquired on a different basis, with a different motive and with a different expected outcome than material which is targeted and acquired for evidential purposes. The whole point about intercept obtained for evidential purposes is that you target people who you think may be involved in crime and you look to intercept them talking about crimes which they are committing with prosecutions in mind.
>
> (JCHR 2007: 35)

He added that intercepted material 'will be of enormous benefit to us in bringing prosecutions against serious criminals, including terrorists' (JCHR 2007:

35). This view has been echoed by the current Director of Public Prosecutions, Keir Starmer (Home Affairs Committee 2010), the former Attorney General, Lord Goldsmith (JCHR 2007), and the Association of Chief Police Officers (Horne 2011). So there is a widely held view among law enforcement agencies that lifting the ban could significantly increase the number of successful prosecutions. In the words of the Joint Committee on Human Rights, 'It would require exceptionally good reasons and clear evidence to disagree with their judgment on a question so central to their experience and expertise' (JCHR 2007: 37).

Conclusion

This chapter has argued that the priority of prosecution maxim is misleading, and that it would be more accurate to speak of the priority of security. Notwithstanding the CONTEST strategy's stated commitment to prosecuting suspected terrorists, the ban on the use of intercept as evidence remains in place. National security considerations have taken precedence, even though there are cogent reasons to believe that these have been overstated and that lifting the ban would result in a greater number of successful prosecutions. At the same time, the priority of security has resulted in the creation of numerous terrorism precursor offences which have expanded the scope of the criminal law. Whilst this may facilitate a greater number of prosecutions, many of these offences potentially diminish the moral authority and legitimacy of the criminal law by paying insufficient regard to human rights and rule of law values.

To conclude, it is important to note the one-dimensional nature of the priority of security. This is in keeping with the failure of much contemporary counter-terrorism policy to recognise that some measures that are designed to enhance security also have incidental security-diminishing effects (Macdonald 2008; Waldron 2010). Convicting individuals of broadly drafted precursor offences which result in severe sentences and lighten the prosecutorial burden by denying defendants the opportunity to challenge the reasons they have been selected for prosecution risks generating resentment and a sense of grievance that contributes to the spread of violent extremist ideology. The same is true of the use of executive measures like TPIMs – and whilst lifting the ban on intercept as evidence may not eliminate the need for TPIMs altogether (Anderson 2013a), there are strong grounds for believing it will reduce their use. It is therefore time to re-evaluate our efforts to prosecute suspected terrorists and recognise that there are both security and liberty-based reasons for the procedural protections and safeguards of the criminal law.

Notes

1 Offences Against the Person Act 1861, section 18.
2 Taking of Hostages Act 1982, section 1.
3 R v D [1984] AC 778.

4   See, e.g. the Explosive Substances Act 1883.
5   Aviation Security Act 1982, section 1; Aviation and Maritime Security Act 1990, section 9.
6   Criminal Attempts Act 1981, section 1. A different test is used in the USA (whether the person has taken a substantial step towards commission of the crime), but the point still applies.
7   (1990) 93 Cr App R 350.
8   [1996] Crim LR 894.
9   Terrorism Act 2006, section 6(2).
10 Terrorism Act 2000, section 58(1).
11 Terrorism Act 2000, section 58(2).
12 Terrorism Act 2000, section 57(1).
13 Terrorism Act 2006, section 5(1).
14 Terrorism Act 2000, section 11(1). Although the offence penalises membership, the individual has a defence if he has not taken part in any of the group's activities since it was proscribed (section 11(2)(b)).
15 Terrorism Act, section 12(2).
16 Terrorism Act 2006, section 2(1).
17 Terrorism Act 2000, section 15(2)–(3).
18 Terrorism Act 2006, section 6(1)(b)(ii).
19 Terrorism Act 2000, section 38B(1)(b).
20 Criminal Law Act 1977, section 1(1); Terrorism Act 2006, section 5(1).
21 Serious Crime Act 2007, section 44(1); Terrorism Act 2000, section 15(3).
22 Serious Crime Act 2007, section 44(1); Terrorism Act 2006, section 5(1).
23 Serious Crime Act 2007, section 44(1); Terrorism Act 2006, section 1(2).
24 Sections 44–46 of the Serious Crime Act 2007 create three separate offences. The form of double inchoate liability described in the text is only available in respect of the section 44 offence of intentional encouragement or assistance (see section 49 and Schedule 3).
25 [2009] UKHL 13.
26 [2010] EWCA Crim 3215.
27 HC Hansard vol. 430 col. 19WS 26 January 2005.
28 Application number 21022/04.
29 See, e.g. the comments of Lord Brown in *Secretary of State for the Home Department* v. *AP* [2010] UKSC 24.
30 *Secretary of State for the Home Department* v. *AF* [2009] UKHL 28.
31 See the speech by David Davis MP in the House of Commons debate on intercept evidence HC Hansard vol. 551 col. 574 18 October 2012.
32 HC Hansard vol. 690 col. 302 7 March 2007.
33 Terrorism Act 2000, section 1(1)(c).

References

Anderson, D. (2013a) *Terrorism Prevention and Investigation Measures in 2012: First Report of the Independent Reviewer on the Operation of the Terrorism Prevention and Investigation Measures Act 2011*, London: The Stationery Office.

Anderson, D. (2013b) 'Shielding the compass: how to fight terrorism without defeating the law', *European Human Rights Law Review*, pp. 233–246.

Ashworth, A. and Zedner, L. (2012) 'Prevention and Criminalization: Justifications and Limits', *New Criminal Law Review*, 15, pp. 542–571.

Blackbourn, J. and McGarrity, N. (2012) 'Listening and Hearings: Intercept Evidence in the Courtroom', *Journal of Commonwealth Criminal Law*, November, pp. 257–282.

Carlile, A. (2011) *Sixth Report of the Independent Reviewer Pursuant to Section 14(3) of the Prevention of Terrorism Act 2005*, London: The Stationery Office.

Clarkson, C. (2009) 'Attempt: The Conduct Requirement', *Oxford Journal of Legal Studies*, 29, pp. 25–41.

Duff, A. (1996) *Criminal Attempts*, Oxford: Clarendon Press.

Duff, A.R., Farmer, L., Marshall, S.E., Renzo, M. and Tadros, V. (eds) (2010) *The Boundaries of the Criminal Law*, Oxford: Oxford University Press.

Edwards, J. (2010) 'Justice Denied: The Criminal Law and the Ouster of the Courts', *Oxford Journal of Legal Studies*, 30, pp. 725–748.

Edwards, J. (2011) 'Coming Clean About the Criminal Law', *Criminal Law and Philosophy*, 5, pp. 315–332.

Fenwick, F. and Phillipson, G. (2011) 'Covert Derogations and Judicial Deference: Redefining Liberty and Due Process Rights in Counterterrorism Law and Beyond', *McGill Law Journal*, 56, pp. 863–918.

Hodgson, J. and Tadros, V. (2009) 'How to Make a Terrorist Out of Nothing', *Modern Law Review*, 72, pp. 984–998.

Home Affairs Committee. (2010) *The Home Office's Response to Terrorist Attacks*, Sixth Report of Session 2009–10, HC 117, London: The Stationery Office.

Home Office. (2009) *Intercept as Evidence: A Report*, Cm 7760, London: The Stationery Office.

Home Office. (2010) *The Government Reply to the Sixth Report from the Home Affairs Committee Session 2009–10 HC 117 The Home Office's Response to Terrorist Attacks*, Cm 7788, London: The Stationery Office.

Home Office. (2011a) *CONTEST: The United Kingdom's Strategy for Countering Terrorism*, Cm 8123, London: The Stationery Office.

Home Office. (2011b) *Review of Counter-Terrorism and Security Powers: Review Findings and Recommendations*, Cm 8004, London: The Stationery Office.

Horder, J. (2012) 'Harmless Wrongdoing and the Anticipatory Perspective on Criminalisation', in G.R. Sullivan and I. Dennis (eds) *Seeking Security: Pre-Empting the Commission of Criminal Harms*, Oxford: Hart Publishing.

Horne, A. (2011) *The Use of Intercept Evidence in Terrorism Cases*, House of Commons Standard Note SN/HA/5249.

Joint Committee on Human Rights. (2007) *Counter-Terrorism Policy and Human Rights: 28 days, intercept and post-charge questioning*, Nineteenth Report of Session 2006–07, HC 394, London: The Stationery Office.

Joint Committee on Human Rights. (2010) *Counter-Terrorism Policy and Human Rights (Seventeenth Report): Bringing Human Rights Back In*, Sixteenth Report of Session 2009–10, HC 111, London: The Stationery Office.

Joint Committee on Human Rights. (2011) *Counter-Terrorism Review – Oral Evidence*, HC 797, London: The Stationery Office.

JUSTICE. (2006) *Intercept Evidence: Lifting the Ban*, London: JUSTICE.

Kennedy, P. (2013) *2012 Annual Report of the Interception of Communications Commissioner*, HC 571, London: The Stationery Office.

Leader-Elliott, I. (2011) 'Framing Preparatory Inchoate Offences in the Criminal Code: The Identity Crime Debacle', *Criminal Law Journal*, 35, pp. 80–97.

Leigh, I. (2009) 'Changing the rules of the game: some necessary legal reforms to United Kingdom intelligence', *Review of International Studies*, 35, pp. 943–955.

Lloyd, A. (1996) *Inquiry into Legislation Against Terrorism*, Cm 3420, London: The Stationery Office.

Macdonald, S. (2008) 'Why We Should Abandon the Balance Metaphor: A New Approach to Counterterrorism Policy', *ILSA Journal of International and Comparative Law*, 15, pp. 95–146.

McSherry, B. (2009) 'Expanding the Boundaries of Inchoate Crimes: The Growing Reliance on Preparatory Offences', B. McSherry, A. Norrie and S. Bronitt (eds) *Regulating Deviance: The Redirection of Criminalisation and the Futures of Criminal Law*, Oxford: Hart Publishing.

Privy Council Review of Intercept as Evidence. (2008) *Report to the Prime Minister and the Home Secretary*, Cm 7324, London: The Stationery Office.

Privy Counsellor Review Committee. (2003) *Anti-Terrorism, Crime and Security Act 2001 Review: Report*, HC 100, London: The Stationery Office.

Simester, A.P. (2012) 'Prophylactic Crimes', in G.R. Sullivan and I. Dennis (eds) *Seeking Security: Pre-Empting the Commission of Criminal Harms*, Oxford: Hart Publishing.

Simester, A.P., Spencer, J.R., Sullivan, G.R. and Virgo, G.J. (2013) *Simester and Sullivan's Criminal Law: Theory and Doctrine*, 5th edn, Oxford: Hart Publishing.

Simester, A.P. and von Hirsch, A. (2011) *Crimes, Harms, and Wrongs: On the Principles of Criminalisation*, Oxford: Hart Publishing.

Sullivan, G.R. and Dennis, I. (eds) (2012) *Seeking Security: Pre-Empting the Commission of Criminal Harms*, Oxford: Hart Publishing.

Tadros, V. (2007) 'Justice and Terrorism', *New Criminal Law Review*, 10, pp. 658–689.

Thomas, S. (2007) *Report of the Interception of Communications Commissioner for 2005-2006*, HC 315, London: The Stationery Office.

Tomkins, A. (2010) 'National Security and the Role of the Court: a Changed Landscape?', *Law Quarterly Review*, 126, pp. 543–567.

Tyler, T.R. (1990) *Why People Obey the Law*, New Haven: Yale University Press.

Waldron, J. (2010) *Torture, Terror and Trade-Offs: Philosophy for the White House*, New York: Oxford University Press.

Walker, C. (2011) 'The Judicialisation of Intelligence in Legal Process', *Public Law*, April, pp. 235–237.

Zedner, L. (2012) 'Terrorizing Criminal Law', *Criminal Law & Philosophy*. Online. Available at: http://link.springer.com/article/10.1007/s11572-012-9166-9 (last accessed 13 September 2013).

8 Banishing the enemies of all mankind

The effectiveness of proscribing terrorist organisations in Australia, Canada, the UK and US

Timothy Legrand

Introduction

Designating and outlawing enemies of the state – the act of proscription – has a long and ignoble political history that stretches back to the industrious empire-building of pre-Christendom Rome. In 82 BC Lucius Cornelius Sulla published lists of those he considered enemies of the state, stripping them of their Roman citizenship, confiscating their wealth, and sanctioning their extrajudicial killing. Cicero, the classical philosopher and statesman was killed under such an order at Sulla's command. Similar proscriptions, under the rubric of 'outlawry', were apparent in Britain a millennium later. Before the Magna Carta was signed by King John in 1215, the British sovereign could outlaw foes with the declaration of *caput lupinum*: literally, 'May his be a wolf's head'. As with Sulla's proscriptions, a declaration of *caput lupinum* withdrew state protections from the unfortunate subject, placing him or her on an equal footing with wild animals and thus likewise be killed as such. These are more than interesting historical footnotes. Today, variations of Sulla's proscription have been used energetically in pursuit of today's class of (those designated) terrorist.

The powers to outlaw organisations and target extremists employed in Australia, Canada, the UK, US and elsewhere bear a striking resemblance to Sulla's proscriptions. Powers to strip citizenship are already partly in place; the confiscation of wealth is lawful in all Anglosphere states; and extrajudicial killing via drones in the Middle East, North Africa and South Asia is a routine feature of the worldwide campaign by US, UK and allied countries' campaign against Islamic extremism. Since the beginning of the millennium, the upsurge in international terrorism has propelled a radical global revision of anti-terrorism laws, in which proscription plays a central role, funnelling decision-making powers upwards into the hands of the executive and away from the legislature and the judiciary. This is a feature common to the four countries considered in this chapter: Australia, Canada, the UK and US. Referred to here as Anglosphere states (Bennett 2004, 2007), they share a political, legal and institutional framework built on common law principles, a shared language and a commitment to liberal democratic ideas stemming from the Westminster style of government.

Across a range of public policy issues, the Anglosphere countries are known frequently to share programmes, ideas and evidence with one another in a process of policy transfer (see Dolowitz and Marsh 1996; Dolowitz and Marsh 2000; Legrand 2012). In the counter-terrorism sphere, these countries have developed a mutual understanding of the 'problem' of terrorism and a shared determination of how it should be tackled. As such, my comparison of these four countries proceeds not only from their common institutional and legal frameworks, but also because the raft of laws enacted therein were drafted with international harmonisation in mind.

Gauging the effectiveness of proscription powers is a puzzle. While the powers have been employed to ban a growing number of terrorist organisations, supported by legislation that defines terrorism generously, the reality is that in Australia, Canada, the UK and the US there are relatively few known instances where individuals have been charged, much less prosecuted and convicted, for membership thereof. As a result, we might wonder whether proscription powers are effective in facilitating law enforcement agencies' disruption of terrorism, or if in fact, 'the rarity of terrorist attacks, and accompanying state secrecy, impede assessment of effectiveness' (Lum *et al.* 2006, p. 491). It is, however, timely to consider this question of effectiveness since there are few signs of governments slowing their efforts to proscribe organisations deemed a threat. In fact, after the murder of a British soldier in Woolwich in 2013, the British Home Secretary Theresa May spoke in support of further extending proscription laws:

> We do need to look at the powers. We do need to look at the laws. We do need to look, for example, at the question of whether perhaps we need to have banning orders to ban organisations that don't meet the threshold for proscription.
>
> (26 May 2013)

The central claim of the following pages is that democratic oversight mechanisms of proscription frameworks have been deliberately weakened by governments to widen government discretion, or scope of action, driven by a concern for expedience rather than effectiveness. To do this, I begin by setting out the conceptual and normative underpinnings of proscription and considering the question of effectiveness. Specifically, I draw attention to the deployment of proscription by government as a means to signal a group's illegitimacy and to create a hostile operating environment for it. Further, these objectives are set against wider concerns pertaining to democratic freedoms.

The chapter then considers the origins and current status of the powers available to the governments of Australia, Canada, the UK and the US to outlaw terrorist organisations. Here we review the specific national and historical contexts of laws designating organisations, terrorist or otherwise, as threats to national security. It explores the common features of these legal frameworks, and draws attention to the wide discretion granted to the executive by the drafting of the laws.

A third section reviews the known usage of these laws in the respective jurisdictions. After the introduction of the new anti-terrorism legislation post-9/11, proscription was deployed widely and frequently. Since then, additions to the lists of designated organisations have been piecemeal. Nevertheless, the laws have been influential on other forms of non-terrorist legislation pertaining to organised crime in Australia and national security in the UK.

The objects of proscription

It is crucial to consider whether proscription is effective in order to satisfy concerns that laws should not sit on the statute books without justification, and further that they should not be used for purposes counter to their stated purpose. While violent extremism may well pose a threat to society, proscription laws represent a serious challenge to the core principles of a free society.

Even before al Qaeda dramatically reshaped the worldview, and with it domestic freedoms, of Western countries in 2001, legislators were aware of the rise of extremist organisations mobilising on an international footing. In the late 1970s and 1980s, a series of high-profile terrorist attacks ratcheted up public awareness of international political conflict. The siege at Iran's London embassy in 1985 and the attacks on Israeli athletes at the Munich Olympics both represented an expanding theatre of conflict for extremist groups willing to attack overseas targets connected to domestic conflicts. Indeed, this internationalisation of violent extremism was in part responsible for the revision and consolidation of Britain's anti-terrorism legislation in 2000. The subsequent attacks of September 11, 2001 supported the growing sense that violent extremism was becoming a pervasive threat to the Western world as a whole. The British Prime Minister David Cameron has claimed of Islamic violent extremism that, 'This terrorism is completely indiscriminate and has been thrust upon us'.[1] And as Jenkins argues, 'The attacks on a Bali nightclub that killed 180 people of various nationalities support the growing sense that international terrorism is a threat to all nationalities' (2003: 421). The targeted and discriminating nature of politically-motivated terrorism is, it seems, trumped by an indiscriminate religiously-motivated terrorism from which no nationality is safe. The attacks of September 11, 2001, the 2002 Bali bombings, and the July 7, 2005 bombings in London all contributed to a growing sense that the Western way of life, its civil society and political institutions are threatened by an uncontained extremism that does not discriminate between military and non-military, government or civilian targets. This indiscriminate international (Islamist) threat has thereby been painted as a pervasive enemy of the global community:

> The work of the Catholic theologians [Aquinas and Augustine] drew upon traditions stretching back to the ancient world that would have considered terrorists to be hostis humani generis, the enemy of all mankind, who merited virtually no protections under the laws of war.
>
> (John Yoo, 7 June 2012, *Wall Street Journal*)

The sentiment that terrorists are 'the enemy of mankind' and undeserving of the state's legal protections has been cemented by senior officials in the UK and Australia who have sought to deprive those suspected of violent extremism of their nationality. In the UK, the Nationality, Immigration and Asylum Act 2002 (NIAA), empowers the Home Secretary to deprive a person of their British citizenship if they pose a threat to the UK or British overseas territory, with the caveat that she can only do so if that person holds a second citizenship. In January 2014 the Home Secretary proposed legislation, currently under consideration in Parliament,[2] that seeks to remove that caveat entirely and, if passed into law, will enable the UK government to deprive a naturalised person of their citizenship 'even if to do so would have the effect of making the person stateless' (*Immigration Bill*, s.66). In support of this, the former Australian foreign minister, Senator Bob Carr, revealed in October 2013 that during his tenure he too sought legal advice on banning those who had fought in the Syrian conflict from returning to Australian shore, again rendering them stateless. Carr argued that the government should promote the message: 'You won't be allowed back into Australia if you defy Australian law and fight in Syria'.[3]

Justifications for proscription

Arguments in support of proscription tend to link together three related claims of what proscription can achieve: material, ideational and symbolic effects that diminish the terrorist threat and signal the limits of society's tolerance. In support of the UK's TA 2000, for instance, the then Home Secretary Charles Clarke MP argued, 'It is important for society to state that certain activities are simply [...] beyond the pale; [...]. The legislation is a powerful symbol of that censure and is important' (Standing Committee D, 20 January 2000). This sentiment was echoed by the Australian Attorney-General, Robert McClelland, who wrote: 'a primary objective of proscription is the expression of clear public revulsion towards the activities of terrorist organisations' (McClelland 2004: 266). The symbolism of proscription is associated with ideas of what is, or is not, legitimate political activity. Indeed, while the revision of the UK's anti-terrorism legislation was under consideration in 1998, the Home Office issued guidance to the proposed laws setting out the objectives of proscription:

> Whilst the measures may not in themselves have closed down terrorist organisations, a knock on effect has been to deny the proscribed groups legitimate publicity and with it lawful ways of soliciting support and raising funds .. perhaps more importantly the provisions have signalled forcefully the Government's, and society's, rejection of these organisations' claims to legitimacy.
>
> (Home Office 1998, 4.7)

From this perspective, the objective of proscription is simultaneously symbolic and material: the intended effect of banning terrorist organisations is material insofar as the government seeks to undermine groups' efforts at 'soliciting support and raising funds', and this is both justified and reinforced via a symbolic rejection of such groups' 'claims to legitimacy'. These determinations of the utility of proscription are echoed by the US State Department, which states that proscription 'Stigmatizes and isolates designated terrorist organizations internationally' and 'Deters donations or contributions to and economic transactions with named organizations'. These two objectives are apparent, too, in the introduction of post-9/11 anti-terrorism legislation by the Australian government:

> proscription contributes to the creation of a hostile operating environment for groups wanting to establish a presence in Australia for either operational or facilitation purposes. It also sends a clear message to Australian citizens that involvement with such organisations, either in Australia or overseas, will not be permitted. Proscription also communicates to the international community that Australia rejects claims to legitimacy by these organisations.
> (Combined government submission, 2007, p. 2 cited in Parliamentary Joint Committee on Intelligence and Security 2007)

Similarly, in the days following the September 11th attacks, the Minister of Justice and Attorney General of Canada, Anne McLellan argued before the Canadian Parliament's Standing Committee on Justice and Human Rights that the state required enhanced powers to combat organisations concerned in terrorism:

> We must be able to disable organizations before they are able to put hijackers on planes or threaten our sense of security as we have seen in recent days with the scare of anthrax. We must have mechanisms in place to go after terrorist organizations and put them out of business.
> (McLellan 2001)

If we consider the rationales provided by Anglosphere governments for proscription, two guiding ideological and material aims emerge: First, an operational aim which is to create a 'hostile operating environment', 'isolate' and 'disable organisations'; and, second, an overarching ideological aim to 'stigmatize' organisations and signal a general rejection of their 'claims to legitimacy'. The authors of the legislation seek not only to diminish the ability of organisations bent on violence from carrying out their aims, but to preclude the opportunity for such groups to form at all. These objectives are not readily amenable to empirical scrutiny, although that is not always a necessary condition for good public policy.

It is further clear that the authors of the relevant legislation have drawn heavily on 'like-minded' countries. The Australian government, for example, has stated that 'Australia's proscription regime is consistent with widespread international practice, with the United States, the United Kingdom, Canada and

New Zealand all having some form of proscription' (2007: 25). Likewise, the Canadian Minister of Justice, Anne McLellan, observed: 'We have taken into account international law and the laws of other countries such as the United States and the United Kingdom and we have adopted safeguards within individual measures'. Yet, since their inception in 2001, this suite of anti-terrorism measures in place across the Anglosphere and elsewhere have attracted considerable disquiet amongst academics and others for their impact on fundamental rights. Muller, for example, describes the shift in anti-terrorism legislation as a 'dangerous political and human rights lacuna in the international legal system' (Muller 2008: 130). In a review of the Australian Security Intelligence Organisation Legislation Amendment (Terrorism) Act 2003, Michaelsen (2005: 178) concludes that 'In effect, these provisions abandon several fundamental principles of the rule of law: they dilute the prohibition of arbitrary detention, they obliterate the right to habeas corpus, they remove the right to silence, and they reverse the onus of proof'. Blackbourn (2008: 65) meanwhile argues that the UK's TA 2000 represents 'the extension of law enforcement powers to the detriment of civil liberties'. Canada's proscription framework attracts similar critique from Dosman, who writes:

> While offering the benefits of alacrity, comity with intelligence-sharing partners, and domestic control, the process of listing by Schedule raises significant procedural and substantive concerns.
> (Dosman 2004: 14)

Not all share this dim outlook. Waddington (2005: 371) finds that 'Civil libertarian political analyses are excessively pessimistic', arguing that 'the 20th century witnessed a general advance in civil liberties' (ibid.: 372). Other proponents of restrictive anti-terrorism laws recruit the 'lesser evils theory' to situate the erosion of liberal democratic values alongside the deleterious effects of terrorist attacks on society. In his critique of the impact of anti-terrorism practices on human rights, Gearty explains that those holding to the 'lesser evils' discourse assert that to fight back against the threats of terrorism, we must sometimes commits acts of evil or harm. This 'lesser evils' discourse thus holds that 'these actions are nevertheless justified, both as necessary (to save ourselves) and as less evil than what our opponents do...' (Gearty 2007: 351).

Anti-terrorism legislation in the Anglosphere

The framing of modern proscription powers owes much to the frantic drafting of new anti-terrorism laws in the aftermath of the al Qaeda attacks of September 11, 2001. In the turmoil of uncertainty following 9/11, the United Nations (UN) acted as the chief stimulus for the reform of anti-terrorism statutes across the world (Scheppele 2006). Just two weeks after the attacks, the UN passed Security Council Resolution 1373. Although the UN made no attempt to define terrorism in the Resolution, and would not do so until 2004,[4] it nonetheless provided that member states enact legislation to tackle the threat posed by a seam of seemingly ubiquitous violent Islamic extremist organisations. The Resolution stipulated that Member States should freeze financial assets connected to persons directly or indirectly connected to terrorists, designated by the UN's 1267 Committee, and enact or modify domestic criminal legislation to prevent persons within the state from providing financial or other support to terrorists (see Dosman 2004: 9–10).

While UN Resolutions have no binding legal force, they nevertheless impose a 'normative obligation' on Member States (Saul 2005: 142–143) and the response to Resolution 1373 was immediate. States moved quickly to draft new legislation to comply with the UN's stricture: Australia passed The Charter of the United Nations (Anti-Terrorism Measures) Regulations 2001 and The Security Legislation Amendment (Terrorism) Act 2002; Canada passed Anti-Terrorism Act 2001; the UK amended the TA 2000 with the Anti-Terrorism, Crime and Security Act 2001; and the US enacted the Uniting and Strengthening America by Providing Appropriate Tools Required to Intercept and Obstruct Terrorism Act 2001 (USA PATRIOT Act).

Proscription in the United Kingdom

Of the legislation considered in this chapter, the TA 2000 is the only statute to result from a deliberative process of legal revision rather than the rapidly engineered laws sparked by 9/11. The TA 2000 was the culmination of a long-standing review of the domestic and international terrorism threats to the UK and marked a significant new phase in laws tackling political violence (Walker 2006). The TA 2000 consolidated and updated into a permanent statute the array of sundry anti-terrorism powers that had developed incrementally over the course of the twentieth century in the UK's engagement with terrorism connected to Northern Ireland. Previously, the anti-terrorism powers available to policing and security agencies were defined in two parallel instruments, separated by their geographical application: the Northern Ireland (Emergency Provisions) Act 1973 (EPA: reenacted 1976, 1984, 1989), which applied only to Northern Ireland; and the Prevention of Terrorism (Temporary Provisions) Act 1974 (PTA: reenacted 1978, 1991, 1996), which applied to mainland Great Britain. These Acts were calibrated to facilitate the state's pursuit and punishment of the sophisticated threat from dissident Irish Republican groups. The legislation relaxed evidential requirements and commissioned so-called 'Diplock courts', jury-less trials presided by a single judge, for cases connected to terrorism (Bamford 2004: 747).

These two pieces of legislation were reviewed by Lord Lloyd in 'The Inquiry Into Legislation Against Terrorism 1996'. Lord Lloyd recommended that the government scrap the EPA and PTA and draft a permanent unified statute to remove the territorial distinction and consolidate the powers therein. The ensuing Terrorism Act 2000 provided a new definition of terrorism and created a range of associated offences. In addition, activities that fell within the definition of terrorism triggered the availability of a host of investigation and detention powers to policing and security agencies.

Notwithstanding the deliberative process that preceded the first iteration of the TA 2000, the UK also introduced additional powers to the TA 2000 after 9/11 via the Anti-Terrorism, Crime and Security Act 2001. The 2001 amendment equipped the government with the power to indefinitely detain without trial non UK-nationals deemed a terrorist threat until they could be deported or otherwise depart the UK. After the London bombings of 7 July 2005, the Terrorism Act 2006 was passed by Parliament to further augment the already-powerful powers contained in the TA 2000, including criminalising the glorification of terrorism.

The provisions for proscription in the TA 2000 place the onus of power on the Home Secretary. The Home Secretary is empowered to lay an order before Parliament to proscribe an organisation if she believes it to be 'concerned' in terrorism. The statute stipulates that an organisation is regarded as concerned in terrorism if it prepares for, commits or participates in an act of terrorism; promotes or encourages terrorism; or 'is otherwise concerned in' terrorism. If an organisation meets these criteria, the Home Secretary has discretion to consider a range of other factors and proceed with proscription 'if he believes that it is concerned in terrorism' (TA 2000 Pt.II S.3(4)). These include:

> the nature and scale of an organisation's activities; the specific threat that it poses to the UK; the specific threat that it poses to British nationals overseas; the extent of the organisation's presence in the UK; and the need to support other members of the international community in the global fight against terrorism.

If the Home Secretary, having given consideration to the criteria above, decides to proceed with proscription she may lay an order before Parliament for the organisation's proscription. This order – which cannot be amended by Parliament – may include multiple organisations and is subject merely to a vote to pass or reject the order by the House of Commons and House of Lords. At the time of writing, 60 international terrorist organisations and 14 domestic terrorist organisations have been proscribed to date under the TA 2000.

Proscription in Australia

In 1950 the Australian government sought to outlaw the Communist Party of Australia with the Communist Party Dissolution Act 1950, which was successfully challenged and struck down by the High Court of Australia. Prior to this, the *Unlawful Associations Act 1916* had been introduced to tackle a radical labour organisation: Industrial Workers of the World (IWW) (see Lynch *et al.* 2009: 28). Within a few months of the Act passing, 103 workers had been imprisoned under the legislation for their membership of the IWW. Yet, subsequent prosecutions were frustrated when members of the IWW reformed the organisation under a different name, a contingency not anticipated by the drafters of the legislation. As a consequence, the Unlawful Associations Act 1917 was passed, which provided the Governor-General with the power to declare an organisation to be unlawful without having to amend the legislation (for a comprehensive overview of proscription laws in Australia, see Lynch et al. 2009).

Australia's response to the 2001 UN Resolution was to explicitly incorporate into domestic law the list of individuals and entities identified by Resolution 1373 as concerned in terrorism. The Charter of the United Nations (Anti-Terrorism Measures) Regulations 2001 was introduced in Australia on 15 October 2001. The next year, Australian legislators drew up a comprehensive revision of the Criminal Code, drawing from the newly-defined range of terrorist offences in the UK and US (Hocking 2003: 356; Lynch et al. 2009). The Security Legislation Amendment (Terrorism) Act 2002 amended the Criminal Code Act 1995 and created a host of new criminal offences connected to terrorism. Under Subdivision 2 of Div 102, it is a criminal offence to be a member (informally or formally) of a terrorist organisation, to direct the activities of a terrorist organisation, to train to receive training from a terrorist organisation, to provide or receive funds from a terrorist organisation. Further, the Act makes it a criminal offence to knowingly associate with a member of a terrorist organisation on more one occasion.

Under these powers, the Attorney-General may make a regulation to designate a terrorist organisation at her own initiative, subject to a period in which Parliament may disallow the regulation. In addition, the legislation was initially limited to organisations that had been identified by the United Nations Security Council as terrorist. This provision was removed by the Criminal Code Amendment (Terrorist Organisations) Act 2004 (Cth), which gave the Attorney-General the power to designate any organisation for which she is satisfied reasonable grounds exist to believe that the organisation is concerned in terrorism.

Proscription in Canada

In response to UN Resolution 1373 the Canadian Parliament passed the Anti-Terrorism Act (ATA 2001), which received Royal Assent on 18 December 2001. Prior to the ATA, regulations were already in place to enact UN counter-terrorism listings: the United Nations al Qaida and Taliban Regulations (UNAQTR) (1999) and the Regulations Implementing the United Nations Resolutions on the Suppression of Terrorism (RIUNRST). The ATA 2001 is structured by a three-tier approach to eradicating the threat: (i) measures to identify and prosecute terrorists; (ii) powers to state agencies to investigate and pre-empt terror plots; and (iii) stronger provisions countering the dissemination of hate propaganda (see Jenkins 2003: 422–423).

Under a new Bill S-7 s.83.28(10), passed in April 2013, the right to remain silent has been annulled under certain circumstances. This legislation empowers security agencies to compel individuals to provide testimony in terrorism investigations, even if the individual has not been charged with an offence. The new legislation defines terrorism as an act, actual or intended, committed with 'a political, religious or ideological purpose, objective or cause' that intends to intimidate or threaten the public, or seeks to influence any government or international organisation, and intentionally causes harm to or endangers the public or seeks to disrupt 'an essential service, facility or system'. According to Roach, this definition 'was clearly inspired by' the UK's TA 2000 in requiring a religious or ideological motivation connected to an expansive range of consequential harms that stretch beyond violence to the public (2005: 513).

The ATA also introduced executive proscription of terrorist 'entities' to the Criminal Code. Under the Criminal Code (C46), the Canadian Governor-in-Council may list an entity if, having received a recommendation from the Solicitor General, he or she is satisfied that;

(a) the entity has knowingly carried out, attempted to carry out, participated in or facilitated a terrorist act; or (b) the entity is knowingly acting on behalf of, at the direction of or in association with an entity referred to in (a).

In contrast to the UK and Australian legislation, it is not an offence per se to be a member of a proscribed organisation, although greater criminal liabilities are introduced for offences connected to membership and 'the effect of listing is to make it risky under the law for anyone to deal with the entity in question' (Wispinski 2006: 17).

Proscription in the United States

In the 1950s, Senator Joseph McCarthy famously led efforts to rid the US of the spectre of communism. McCarthyism, as these efforts came to be known, came to symbolise the excesses of an institutionalised paranoia relating to 'reds under the bed'. During this era, various legal instruments were used to tackle and proscribe organisations associated with communism: the Smith Act of 1940, the Internal Security Act of 1950 and the Communist Control Act of 1954, though the latter were used to mixed effect. Until the attacks of September 11, 2001, the US had a raft of legal instruments in place to address terrorism. The Immigration and Nationality Act 1952; Omnibus Diplomatic Security and Antiterrorism Act of 1986; Anti-Terrorism Act of 1987 (targeting the PLO); Federal Courts Administration Act of 1992 (which defined terrorism); and the Antiterrorism and Effective Death Penalty Act of 1996, which targeted fundraising by terrorist organisations and banned US companies from conducting financial transaction with states sponsoring terrorism. After the 9/11 attacks, the US hurriedly introduced the USA PATRIOT Act 2001, which amended the powers available to authorities in the Foreign Intelligence Surveillance Act of 1978 (FISA), the Electronic Communications Privacy Act of 1986 and the Immigration and Nationality Act (INA).

On 23 September 2001, almost immediately after the attacks of 9/11, President George W. Bush signed into law Executive Order 13224, which authorised the US government 'to designate and block the assets of foreign individuals and entities that commit, or pose a significant risk of committing, acts of terrorism' (US Department of State 2001). The process of designating a foreign terrorist organisation (FTO) is administered by the Bureau of Counter-terrorism in the Department of State, which monitors extremist organisations worldwide. If an organisation is deemed to fall within the provisions of the INA, the Bureau of Counter-terrorism prepares an administrative record, 'typically including both classified and open sources of information', which is submitted to the Secretary of State. Under section 219 of the INA, the INA empowers the Secretary to designate an organisation if she finds that (i) the organisation is a foreign organisation, (ii) the organisation is either engaged in terrorist activity or has the capacity or intention to engage in terrorist activity; (iii) the terrorist activity 'threatens the security of United States nationals or the national security of the United States' (Sec 219 (1) a,b,c). If the Secretary of State believes an organisation satisfies these criteria, she must consult with the Secretary of the Treasury and the Attorney-General before the designation is made final. Once an organisation is determined to warrant designation, the Secretary of State must notify Congress of her intention. If, after seven days, Congress has not opted to review the decision, the designation takes effect. Designated organisations have thirty days to seek judicial review of the designation, after which designation cannot be challenged for two years.

Common features of proscription legislation in the Anglosphere

At present, there are 74 organisations proscribed in the UK under the TA 2000. Fourteen of these are connected to Northern Ireland, and were already proscribed in the UK prior to the introduction of the Terrorism Act. The remaining 60 have all been added to the list since the introduction of the TA 2000, two of which for glorifying terrorism under the Terrorism Act 2006. In Australia there are 19 organisations currently proscribed, and in the US 59 organisations designated as Foreign Terrorist Organisations. Of these, 24 were designated prior to 9/11. In Canada, 53 organisations are listed as terrorist entities. Of the Anglosphere countries, the Australian government has been the most restrained in its deployment of proscription powers: since 2002, only 19 organisations have been listed there as terrorist organisations.

The legal instruments outlined above share some distinctive procedural features. Here I draw attention to four, linked to the fiat of unilateral decision-making by the executive. First and foremost, the decision to initiate a proscription is held by a single individual. While Australia initially opted directly to incorporate the UN's list of terrorist organisations, rather than undertake an independent process of designating organisations, it subsequently joined Canada, the UK and the US in providing the Attorney-General (the Secretary of State in the UK and the US) with the power to determine which organisations pose sufficient threat to warrant proscription. This represents an executive fiat insofar as no other institution or individual, including the courts or the legislature, is able to initiate proceedings to outlaw a group.

Secondly, and contributing to the strength of the executive fiat, is the information contributing to the decision-making. For the Anglosphere, the legislation of these countries merely requires the executive to be 'satisfied' (Australia, Canada), or 'believes' (UK, US) that the organisation under consideration is concerned in terrorism. Importantly, across all these countries, no other body or individual is empowered to scrutinise the evidence supporting the determination prior to proscription's commencement; there is no oversight of this information, nor is the executive required to disclose his or her reasoning, although the Australian Attorney-General does so voluntarily.

Third, legislatures are not provided with the dossier of evidence supporting the decision to proscribe. Without the ability to review this information, the legislatures are thereby constricted in their capacity to scrutinise or, indeed, challenge the proscription order. Since 2001, none of the proscription orders made in the Anglosphere states have been resisted by their respective legislatures. While the requirement for proscription to be supported, or at least not opposed, means that proscription remains theoretically within the ambit of democratic decision-making, in practice the procedure all but precludes meaningful scrutiny and opposition to the Attorney-General/Secretary of State order. This is reinforced by a procedure that is geared towards the presumption of complicity in terrorism.

Fourth, the process by which executive proscription orders are approved by the legislature, as they must in each country except Canada, is weighted heavily against scrutiny. In the UK, Parliament is unable to amend an order or scrutinise the information contributing to the Home Secretary's decision. Further, the Home Secretary is able, and has done so in the majority of orders, to make an order for multiple organisations at once. In 2001, the presentation of 20 organisations in a single order, which Parliament was powerless to amend, prompted Lord Archer to lament the abuse of process that meant Parliament was unable to 'oppose the inclusion of any one organisation without opposing the entire order'. In the US, the proscription gains legal force merely a week after it is made unless Congress resists the order.

These common features of proscription laws point in the same direction. Proscription laws have been drafted and adapted to widen the discretionary power of the executive at the expense of legislative or judicial oversight. Proscription orders made by the executive have never been resisted by legislatures, and only rarely reversed by the judiciary, the effect of which is to make proscription an executive fiat which, according to David Anderson, 'is in practice irreversible' (2013: 65).

The application and assessment of proscription

The Anglosphere countries have walked their anti-terrorism powers in step with one another and have done so with little regard to evaluating the effectiveness of these powers. Few other policy areas have so egregiously escaped empirical scrutiny, especially in a straitened financial climate in which all other arms of government have been compelled to deliver better value for money. It hardly needs to be said that this is an issue of some importance. Lum *et al.* (2006: 490) underline the importance of empirically-informed action in this space: 'evidence-based counter-terrorism policies are those policies which not only show promise in achieving outcomes sought, but at the same time do not cause harm'. In this section, we consider two related issues: the evaluation of the effectiveness of proscription frameworks and the impact of proscription legislation on targeted organisations and society at large.

Evaluating the impact of anti-terrorism powers

For public policy theorists, determining the effect, and by extension, the success of policy is a thorny issue. The operations and outcomes of policies and programmes cannot be easily extricated and isolated from the tide of social forces, economic fluctuations, domestic and international politics and laws (Marsh and McConnell 2010: 582). Given the continued acceptance and growing support for widening proscription powers against groups and individuals, it is surprising that proscription powers, in concept and in application, have attracted little critique in mainstream politics, civil society or academia. In a meta-analysis of published research findings pertaining to terrorism, an approach known as a Campbell Collaborative systematic review, Lum *et al.* (2006) reviewed over 20,000 pieces of literature relating to terrorism, and managed to find just seven that attempted to provide a rigorous review of the effectiveness of any counter-terrorism programme. So the overriding challenge in assessing the effectiveness of counter-terrorism measures is the paucity of data pertaining to operational or programme outcomes, criminal charges or prosecutions. There are two possibilities why this is so: evidence is difficult to acquire, or officials are reluctant to collect it.

In support of the former, Lum *et al.* (2006: 511) suggest that the paucity of evaluations might be the result of the relatively rare instances of terrorist attacks, 'the difficulty in detecting intervention effects of major programs', the ambiguity of how terrorist threat is defined, the secrecy shrouding counter-terrorism efforts, and the difficulty in establishing 'clear standards of accuracy and reliability'. In a review of the first five years of the proscription laws in Australia, the Inquiry into the proscription of 'terrorist organisations' under the Australian Criminal Code, found that 'Australia has listed nineteen organisations but so far proscription has not been an element in any of the prosecutions for terrorist organisation offences' (Jull 2007: iii). More recently, this question of effectiveness was directly addressed by Australia's Independent National Security Legislation Monitor, Brett Walker. In his Annual Report of 2012, Walker put forward an equivocal view of measuring effectiveness, claiming that in the absence of a terrorist attack on Australian shores, 'it can be said that Australia is most fortunate to lack the means of rigorous empirical examination' (2012: 3). Walker's perspective illustrates the methodological complexity involved in gauging the effectiveness of a measure designed to forestall, diminish, prevent or avoid an infrequent event from occurring:

[Australian security agencies] have been effective, in the sense that terrorist offences resulting in actual violence have not occurred. They have also been effective in the sense that prosecutions have been well conducted, with (as it happens) convictions secured. It should not be regarded as a logical extension of that observation that the CT Laws themselves are effective. A more realistic statement is that Australia's agencies, working within the CT Laws, have been effective.

The success or otherwise of policy is problematised further by the difficulty involved in discerning the independent effects of the various anti-terrorist measures at play at any one time. Marsh and McConnell write that public policy evaluation is frequently stymied by, 'significant methodological difficulties posed by lack of information and the problem of attempting to identify the causal effect of a policy, compared to other independent variables, such as overlapping policies, media influences, economic forces, and so on' (2010: 582). This is illustrated by the UK's attempt to provide a comprehensive package of counter-terrorism measures CONTEST, which integrates four Ps of action: 'Prevent, Pursue, Protect, and Prepare'.

To the second possibility, that officials are reluctant to enact monitoring of counter-terrorism outcomes across the world, there seems to be a manifest ambivalence towards reviewing effectiveness. In her review of the UN's anti-terrorism measures, Bianchi describes the prospect of assessing implementation of the measures as a 'daunting task', and notes that lawyers, 'lack adequate parameters to objectively judge the efficacy of states' implementing measures as well as their consistency with other obligations incumbent on them' (Bianchi 2006: 884). This is echoed in Lum *et al.*'s meta-review of literature examining counter-terrorism measures, in which they find that 'we currently know almost nothing about the effectiveness of any of these programs' (Lum *et al.* 2006: 510).

More recently, the UK Independent Reviewer of Terrorism Legislation sought to determine the extent to which counter-terrorism laws had resulted in substantive prosecutions. In his report on the Terrorism Acts in 2012, he found that the UK government does not collate complete data on all offences brought in prosecutions of individuals under the sections 11 to 13 of the TA 2000: only 'principal offences' are recorded and reported. Since membership of a terrorist organisation might be a lesser charge than the principal offence in a prosecution, the Reviewer thus concluded it was 'impossible to know the full extent' to which proscription laws criminalising membership of a terrorist organisation had been used.

In Canada, too, during debate over proposed anti-terrorism provisions contained in Bill C-36, the Solicitor General of Canada Lawrence MacAulay argued in support of the need for designating terrorist organisations, stating:

> To defeat terrorists, we also need to choke off their money supply. This bill goes a long way towards achieving that. We're going to designate certain terrorist groups, make it easier to freeze their assets, prosecute those who

give them financial support, and deny or remove charitable status from those who provide resources to terrorist groups.[5]

Yet these aims have not been demonstrably achieved. Senate and Commons Committees from the Canadian Parliament delivered two much-delayed reviews of the provisions and operations of the ATA 2001 in March 2007. Neither committee sought to evaluate whether Canada's efforts in targeting the financing of terrorism or deregistering charities connected to terrorism had been effective, leading Kent Roach to comment: 'The performance of the committees again raises the issue of where, if anywhere, the efficacy of the state's national security activities will be reviewed' (Roach 2005: 18).

Diminish or displace? Unintended consequences of proscription

As already argued, the consequences of proscription are poorly understood. Governments have been reluctant to explore, at least as far as in public domain knowledge, the impact of this power on the operational effectiveness of targeted groups. Yet there are many indications that proscription may have two significant unintended consequences: (i) proscription incentivises targeted organisations to transform their structure; and (ii) legitimises and potentially emboldens the targeted organisations.

The claim that proscription potentially leads to groups transforming rather than disbanding stems from Van Dongen (2011), who argues that proscription may have two 'substitution' effects. First, he claims that proscription may result in 'geographical substitution', which suggests that 'Eradication of a terrorist movement in one country may divert the people and the resources to movements in other countries'. (Van Dongen 2011: 366). Second, he suggests the possibility of a 'function substitution' effect, 'which means that terrorism does not really disappear, but rather turns into different forms of aggression' (2011: 366). In the modern era, it is all too easy for ideas to propagate though the Internet. Only minimal effort is required for a would-be extremist to access the ideas of banned organisations. A ban on organisations, which based on territorial law, is easily circumvented by virtual networks active in cyberspace. Indeed, as Van Dongen suggests, it is possible that proscription merely incentivises organisations to adopt less perceptible modes of operations; diminishing the capacity of communities and, perhaps, security agencies to identify emerging threats.

The second issue concerns the emboldening effect that proscription may have on targeted organisations. Three examples underline this possibility. First, in the 1970s the UK's policy of internment was deemed partly responsible for increased sympathy for Irish Republicanism: the IRA commander Jim McVeigh subsequently claimed that internment was 'among the best recruiting tools the IRA ever had' (cited in Blackbourn 2008: 69). Second, writing on the conflict in Sri Lanka involving the Tamils and the LTTE, Nadarajah and Sriskandarajah claim that 'proscriptions may even have consolidated the resolve of the Tamil diaspora organisations to support the Tamil nationalist project and the LTTE'

(2005: 97; see also Walker 2000: 15). Finally, and more recently, ahead of the designation of the Nigerian Islamic extremist organisation, Boko Haram, there were clear concerns of the possibility that proscription may only act to benefit the group. At a Hearing of the US House of Representatives Subcommittee on Africa, Global Health, and Human Rights in July 2012, US Ambassador Johnnie Carson suggested that designating Boko Haram a terrorist organisation, 'would serve to enhance their status, probably give them greater international notoriety amongst radical Islamic groups, probably lead to more recruiting and probably more assistance'. The concern that designation could strengthen the arm and image of Boko Haram has been echoed widely in the media (see Taylor 2013)[6] and, reportedly, within the US Government itself.[7] According to Nnamdi Obasi, an analyst at the International Crisis Group, designation 'could also further radicalise the movement and push it to strengthen international linkages with other Islamist groups'.[8]

There is a dissonance between the efforts of governments dedicated to constructing proscription frameworks and the apparent apathy toward their effectiveness. While the introduction of New Public Management three decades ago injected heightened measures of scrutiny for many government portfolios in the Anglosphere, it is apparent that anti-terrorism policies have remained relatively immune from such scrutiny. Although we should keep in mind that proscription frameworks are largely based on historical antecedents, this is an inadequate justification for the continuing reliance on such a severe and largely untested approach to combating violent extremism. As argued here, there are considerable and growing concerns around the unintended, and perhaps perverse, consequences of proscribing organisations.

Conclusion

Alongside other powers now available to Western governments, such as control orders, detention without trial, and the suspension of *habeus corpus*, proscription is among the most severe measures available to liberal democratic governments. For security officials charged with protecting the state and society from the destructive ambitions of violent extremists, proscription can be used symbolically to signal the government's condemnation of unwelcome ideologies and to offer a means to suppress the group's activities. Yet it is nevertheless apparent in both political and academic discourse that proscription powers sit uncomfortably in modern liberal democracies. Liberal democracy is underpinned by a marriage of individual rights and freedoms, protected by and upheld within a system of representative government. The proscription of organisations by virtue of their (actual or potential) ideas and actions is an *ex ante* interruption of, at least, freedoms of association and freedoms of expression; two of the most treasured freedoms of liberal democracy.

It is important to recognise that proscription is a long-standing instrument of government and not a modern product of the war on terrorism. As described in the introduction to this chapter, designating and banning enemies of the states reaches back into centuries of state traditions and the core tenets of proscription represent an extension of this past. It is abundantly clear that, for example, contemporary decision-making around proscription remains highly centralised. Almost every stage of the proscription process is weighted in favour of the preferences of the executive. The decision to initiate proscription and the scrutiny of information relevant to the order rest with the Attorney-General or Secretary of State in the four countries considered here. Moreover, since the executive in the Canadian, UK and US government withholds the information underpinning the decision to proscribe an organisation, these legislatures' capacity to scrutinise a proscription order is considerably diminished.

While these characteristics of proscription frameworks are concerning in and of themselves, this is further compounded by egregious reluctance to consider whether proscription manages to achieve its aims of signalling society's abhorrence of the proscribed organisations and hindering its operations. We might question whether the use of such a severe power as proscription should occur without at least some enquiry as to its effects. Indeed, a number of scholars have drawn attention to an array of unintended consequences that that proscription might bring about, including many that risk entrenching rather ameliorating violent extremism. Together, the range of concerns associated with proscription frameworks in the Anglosphere point to a severe deficit in our understanding of the relationship between proscription orders and their attendant outcomes. To adequately safeguard liberal democracy and the rule of law, it is imperative to that we not only render explicit the decision-making process around proscribing organisations and their ideas but also enhance our understanding of its consequences.

Notes

1 Cameron, D. PM's Speech at Munich Security Conference, 5 February 2011. Retrieved from http://webarchive.nationalarchives.gov.uk/20130109092234/http://number10.gov.uk/news/pms-speech-at-munich-security-conference/, accessed 10 January 2014.
2 As of the time of writing, April 2014.
3 Reported in *The Australian*, 28 October 2013. 'Carr considered banning Syria fighters from returning to Australia'. www.theaustralian.com.au/national-affairs/politics-news/carr-considered-banning-syria-fighters-from-returning-to-australia/story-fn59nqld-1226747831076#sthash.VLLxWLhZ.dpuf.
4 The UN passed resolution 1566 in October 2004, which provided the definition of terrorism as: 'criminal acts, including against civilians, committed with the intent to cause death or serious bodily injury, or taking of hostages, with the purpose to provoke a state of terror in the general public or in a group of persons or particular persons, intimidate a population or compel a government or an international organization to do or to abstain from doing any act'.
5 MacAulay, L. Evidence to the Standing Committee on Justice and Human Rights, Parliament of Canada, 18 October 2001. Retrieved from: www.parl.gc.ca/HousePublications/Publication.aspx?DocId=652657&Language=E&Mode=, accessed 23 February 2014.
6 www.washingtontimes.com/news/2013/apr/28/for-boko-haram-us-tries-to-handle-with-care-nigeri/?page=all.

7 'Nigeria: US "to name Boko Haram as a terrorist group"', 13 November 2013. Retrieved from www.bbc.co.uk/news/world-africa-24922833, accessed 18 December 2013.
8 Quoted in 'Boko Haram: Is terror designation a badge of honour?', 15 November 2013. Retrieved from www.bbc.co.uk/news/world-africa-24959207, accessed 20 December 2013.

References

Bamford, B. (2004) 'The United Kingdom's "War against Terrorism"', *Terrorism and Policical Violence*, 16 (4), pp. 737–756.
Bennett, J.C. (2004) *Anglosphere: The Future of the English-Speaking Nations in the Internet Era*: Rowman & Littlefield (Non NBN).
Bennett, J.C. (2007) *The Anglosphere Challenge: Why the English-Speaking Nations Will Lead the Way in the Twenty First Century*: Rowman & Littlefield.
Bianchi, A. (2006) 'Assessing the effectiveness of the UN Security Council's anti-terrorism measures: the quest for legitimacy and cohesion', *European Journal of International Law*, 17 (5), pp. 881–919.
Blackbourn, J. (2008) 'Counter-Terrorism and Civil Liberties: The United Kingdom Experience, 1968–2008', *JIJIS*, 8, pp. 63.
Dolowitz, D. and Marsh, D. (1996) 'Who Learns What from Whom: A Review of the Policy Transfer Literature', *Political Studies*, 44 (2), pp. 343–357.
Dolowitz, D.P. and Marsh, D. (2000) 'Learning from Abroad: The Role of Policy Transfer in Contemporary Policy-Making', *Governance*, 13 (1), pp. 5–23.
Dosman, E.A. (2004) 'For the Record: Designating Listed Entities for the Purposes of Terrorist Financing Offences at Canadian Law', *U. Toronto Fac. L. Rev.*, 62, p. 1.
Gearty, C. (2007) 'Terrorism and Human Rights', *Government and Opposition*, 42 (3), pp. 340–362.
Harding, L. (2014) 'David Miranda's Detention: A Chilling Attack on Journalism', *Guardian*, 2 February 2014. Available at: www.theguardian.com/world/2014/feb/02/david-miranda-detention-chilling-attack-journalism, accessed 4 February 2014.
Hocking, J. (2003) Counter-Terrorism and the Criminalisation of Politics: Australia's New Security Powers of Detention, Proscription and Control. *Australian Journal of Politics & History*, 49 (3), pp. 355–371.
Jenkins, D. (2003) 'In Support of Canada's Anti-Terrorism Act: A Comparison of Canadian, British, and American Anti-Terrorism Law', *Sask. L. Rev.*, 66, p. 419.
Jull, D (2007) 'Foreword', *Inquiry into the proscription of 'terrorist organisations' under the Australian Criminal Code. Parliamentary Joint Committee on Intelligence and Security*. Commonwealth of Australia: Canberra.
Legrand, T. (2012) 'Overseas and over Here: Policy Transfer and Evidence-Based Policy-Making' *Policy studies*, 33 (4), pp. 329–348.
Lum, C., Kennedy, L.W. and Sherley, A. (2006) 'Are Counter-Terrorism Strategies Effective? The Results of the Campbell Systematic Review on Counter-Terrorism Evaluation Research', *Journal of Experimental Criminology*, 2 (4), pp. 489–516.
Lynch, A., McGarrity, N. and Williams, G. (2009) 'Lessons from the History of the Proscription of Terrorist and Other Organizations by the Australian Parliament', *Legal Hist.*, 13, p. 25.
McClelland, R. (2004) 'The Legal Response to Terrorism: A Labor Perspective', *University of New South Wales Law Journal*, 27 (2), pp. 262–269.

McLellan, A. (2001) Evidence to the Standing Committee on Justice and Human Rights. Parliament of Canada. Thursday, 18 October 2001. Available at: www.parl.gc.ca/HousePublications/Publication.aspx?DocId=652657&Language=E&Mode=1, accessed 21 June 2013.

MacAulay, L. (2001) 'Evidence to the Standing Committee on Justice and Human Rights, Parliament of Canada', 18 October 2001. Retrieved from: www.parl.gc.ca/HousePublications/Publication.aspx?DocId=652657&Language=E&Mode=, accessed 23 February 2014.

Marsh, D. and McConnell, A. (2010) 'Towards a Framework for Establishing Policy Success', *Public administration*, 88 (2), pp. 564–583.

Michaelsen, C. (2005) 'Antiterrorism Legislation in Australia: A Proportionate Response to the Terrorist Threat?', *Studies in Conflict & Terrorism*, 28 (4), pp. 321–339.

Muller, M. (2008) 'Terrorism, Proscription and the Right to Resist in the Age of Conflict', *Denning LJ*, 20, p. 111.

Nadarajah, S. and Sriskandarajah, D. (2005) 'Liberation Struggle or Terrorism? The Politics of Naming the LTTE', *Third World Quarterly*, 26 (1), pp. 87–100.

Parliamentary Joint Committee on Intelligence and Security (2007) 'Inquiry into the proscription of "terrorist organisations" under the Australian Criminal Code', The Parliament of the Commonwealth of Australia, Commonwealth of Australia.

Roach, K. (2005) 'Canada's Response to Terrorism', in Victor Ramraj, Michael Hor, Kent Roach (eds), *Global Anti-Terrorism Law and Policy*, Cambridge University Press. Available at SSRN: http://ssrn.com/abstract=1177282, accessed 1 February 2014.

Saul, B. (2005) 'Definition of "Terrorism" in the UN Security Council: 1985–2004', *Chinese Journal of International Law*, 4 (1), pp. 141–166.

Scheppele, K.L. (2006) 'The Migration of Anti-Constitutional Ideas: The Post-9/11 Globalization of Public Law and the International State of Emergency', *The migration of constitutional ideas*, 347.

Van Dongen, T. (2011) 'Break It Down: An Alternative Approach to Measuring Effectiveness in Counterterrorism' *Journal of Applied Security Research*, 6 (3), pp. 357–371.

Waddington, P.A.J. (2005) 'Slippery Slopes and Civil Libertarian Pessimism', *Policing & Society*, 15 (3), pp. 353–375.

Walker, C. (2000) 'Briefing on the Terrorism Act 2000', *Terrorism and Political Violence*, 12 (2), pp. 1–36.

Walker, C. (2006) 'Clamping Down on Terrorism in the United Kingdom', *Journal of International Criminal Justice*, 4 (5), pp. 1137–1151.

Wispinski, J. (2006) *The USA Patriot Act and Canada's Anti-Terrorism Act: Key Differences in Legislative Approach*, Parliamentary Information and Research Service: Ottawa.

Yoo, J. (2012) 'Obama, Drones and Thomas Aquinas', Wall Street Journal, 7 June. Retrieved to: http://online.wsj.com/news/articles/SB10001424052702303665904577452271794312802, accessed 22 June 2013.

9 Britain's Prevent programme
An end in sight?

Paul Thomas

Introduction

Britain's Prevent programme, described as being an education and community engagement-based policy approach to terrorism prevention (DCLG 2007a; HMG 2011), has been highly contentious domestically but also influential on policy programmes developed in other Western states similarly facing a significant threat of domestic Islamist terrorism (Neumann 2011). Shaped in reaction to the shocking 7/7 London bombings of July 2005, the importance of this preventative policy has seemed self-evident, given the regular flow of foiled plots and convictions in the following years. The murder of soldier Lee Rigby in May 2013 by two British Islamist extremists represented the first civilian deaths in Britain through Islamist terrorism since 7/7, yet was this comparative 'success' in avoiding further such deaths through Islamist terror actions anything to do with the focus and content of the large-scale Prevent programme? The immediate response of the Coalition government to the Woolwich murder was that Prevent needed more investment and must do better (Travis 2013). However, how can the effectiveness of this terrorism prevention, 'hearts and minds' educational programme be measured? How do we know whether Prevent has made the people of Britain any safer or, indeed, whether, it may have made them less safe? What actually have been the ambitions and consequences of Britain's Prevent programme to date, and is Prevent a temporary phenomenon soon to end or a long-term policy response? The chapter questions whether Prevent, as we have known it, needs to exist (O'Toole *et al.* 2012).

This chapter examines Britain's Prevent programme and its operationalisation to explore these key questions. It argues that, whilst some positive results have inevitably come from such a large-scale programme, Prevent has been conceptually misguided and inherently flawed, so leading to counterproductive overlaps and contradictions with other key policy agendas, particularly 'Community Cohesion', the post-2001 British policy approach to multiculturalism and ethnic integration (Denham 2001). Here it is suggested that Prevent has both significantly securitised the national and local state's relationships with British Muslim communities, so damaging the very 'human intelligence' (English 2009) needed to counter a genuine threat of terrorism and ideologies that support it, and also essentialised and reified Muslim faith identity in direct contradiction to wider policy agendas recognising and even promoting more intersectional, nuanced and contingent forms of identity. These problematic features have been inherent to Prevent and although there have been significant 'turning points' in the life of Prevent, most notably the supposed watershed of the June 2011 Prevent Review, it is argued here that any changes have been superficial and limited. On that basis, the chapter argues that Prevent, in its form and scale at time of writing, must come to an end, with the progressive, stated Prevent ambitions of partnership and education-based anti-extremism work developed in very different and more effective ways.

To develop this case, the chapter first provides a brief overview of Prevent's origins and factual development. It then discusses the stated and apparent ambitions of Prevent and the real, largely negative, consequences that have flowed from the operationalisation of those ambitions. It goes onto discuss the temporalities of Prevent, both the nature and meaning of key episodes in the short life of Prevent, and what this analysis suggests about the longevity of Prevent in a distinct and recognisable form.

The development of Prevent

The overtly critical analysis of Prevent's consequences and impacts developed below needs to acknowledge the essentially reactive nature of Prevent's development. Whilst Prevent was one of the key elements, one of the so-called 'Four Ps', of the original British CONTEST counter-International Terrorism policy (Home Office 2003), it was entirely undeveloped until the 7/7 bombings. Here, whilst aware of domestic Islamist extremists in Britain, MI5 had not expected domestic terror attacks (Hewitt 2008), as the 9/11 and the 2004 Madrid train bombings were interpreted as having both involved foreigners who had come to the countries with the specific goal of carrying out terrorist actions (a wrong interpretation of the Madrid attacks; Atran 2010). This, coupled with a continuing post-Good Friday Agreement concern with Northern Ireland meant that the Police and Security Services had neither good intelligence of, or a developed prevention plan in relation to, Britain's Muslim communities and minorities within them promoting extreme Islamist doctrines. From then on Britain was playing catch-up, as shown by key elements of Prevent. One example of this is the fact that the initial, 'Pathfinder' phase of Prevent funding that commenced in April 2007 was aimed at the 70 local authority areas in England and Wales with 5 per cent or more of their population being Muslim, a clear indication of the lack of reliable intelligence around Islamist extremist activity and its 'hotspots' (DCLG 2007a; Thomas 2012). In the later 2008–2011 iteration that saw a very significant expansion of Prevent, this was extended to all English local authorities with 2 per cent or more of Muslims (a clumsy conflation of mainly Pakistani/Bangladeshi ethnic origins with faith identity; Thomas and Sanderson 2011), but this still did not cover Crawley in Sussex, home of Omar Khyam, the key ringleader of the 'Crevice' bomb plot.

This 2008 onwards expansion of Prevent demonstrated the complexity of the programme. Local Authority activity on Prevent was funded by the Department for Communities and Local Government (DCLG) and saw very significant programmes of largely generalised and rather bland youth and community activity with groups of Muslim young people – the Government boasted of working with over 40,000 young Muslims in the first year alone (DCLG 2008). Local Authorities were initially given very significant latitude over how to use this Prevent funding, with some using it to develop programmes in-house and others dispersing some or all the funding to local Muslim community groups (Lowndes and Thorp 2010). A significant focus for many local authorities and partners was developments and improvements in local Muslim civil society organisations (Thomas 2008), through initiatives such as committee training for Mosques and strengthening of educational processes at Madrassas (after-school Mosque classes for young people). Local Authorities were obliged to rapidly established local multi-agency coordination groups, known as Gold, Silver and Bronze groups to denote the seniority of the staff involved at each level, with these groups developing the local 'Channel' processes that were designed to work with individuals seen as in danger of 'radicalisation'. Local Authorities also had to report to Government on their Prevent work via 'National Indicator 35', the Prevent-specific monitoring channel within national government's overall funding and performance monitoring regime. All local authorities were obliged to establish and operationalise all of these Prevent developments and community-focused activity at very short notice, no matter what concerns or objections they had, as explored further below (Monro et al. 2010; Husband and Alam 2011).

Alongside this was funding from the Home Office via the newly-established Office for Security and Counter-Terrorism (OSCT) for Prevent programmes in Prisons, the Youth Offending Sector and Further and Higher Educational Institutions. Whilst the work with young offenders and adult prisoners involved direct educational programmes, Prevent activity directed at universities and colleges did not contain any direct educational work. Instead, it was concerned with strengthening relationships between the educational institutions and local Police and Counter-Terrorism Units (CTUs), and of heightening scrutiny of student activity on and around campuses. At a national level, Home Office Prevent funding was utilised to develop more polyphonic Muslim representation with the establishment of Muslim Women's and Young People's Advisory Groups, and more 'moderate' forms of religious interpretation and leadership through bodies like the Sufi Muslim Council, the Quilliam Foundation and the Radical Middle Way road show series.

Central to this Prevent activity across all sectors was the Police, with over 300 new Prevent-dedicated Police posts established during 2008–2011. These were split between local-level 'Prevent Engagement Officers' and posts within the new regional CTUs that brought together the former Special Branch apparatus and the significantly expanded Security Service personnel. At the time of writing, the national investment in Prevent, a purely preventative, 'hearts and minds' education and engagement programme, had reached over £200 million since its inception in 2006. The sheer scale of this programme, coupled with the very significant role for Police and Security Service personnel, which includes pivotal positions in the local multi-agency arrangements (Lamb 2012), inevitably attracted controversy. By 2009, evidence started to emerge of an apparent blurring of boundaries between education and surveillance (Kundnani 2009; Dodd 2009), with this including pressure on community and youth workers to provide intelligence to the Police, and even CTU staff getting involved in direct community-based Prevent delivery (Knight 2010). Media coverage of these issues prompted an Inquiry by the Communities and Local Government Select Committee that focused on the relationship between DCLG and the Home Office and the associated tensions between the Prevent and Community Cohesion policy agendas. The resulting report, published just before the May 2010 general election (House of Commons 2010), was highly critical of Prevent's organisation and called for DCLG to solely focus on Community Cohesion.

The incoming Conservative-Liberal Democrat Coalition Government immediately suspended further Prevent funding to local authorities and instituted a review of Prevent. After a long pause, apparently due to disagreements within the Coalition over Prevent's emphasis, the 2011 Prevent Review (HMG 2011) seemed to accept much of the CLG Select Committee's recommendations in that DCLG was removed from Prevent involvement. Alongside this, the number of local authorities funded for Prevent activity was reduced to 28, supposedly on an intelligence-led basis (although this list was very similar to the 28 local authorities having the largest Muslim populations; O'Toole *et al.* 2012), with much closer scrutiny by OSCT and withdrawal of funding from Muslim community organisations seen as counter to Western liberal norms, a stress on values in keeping with the policy direction identified in an earlier speech by Prime Minister Cameron (2011). These 2011 changes were apparently accepted by the Labour opposition and were generally seen as having successfully removed Prevent from the political foreground until the May 2013 Woolwich murder of soldier Lee Rigby raised fresh concerns about both Prevent's effectiveness and the approach taken from 2011 onwards by the Coalition (Boffey and Doward 2013).

Prevent's ambitions

A number of explicit and implicit ambitions can be identified for the Prevent programme. Some of these can be seen as constructive and thoughtful in theory, but problematic in terms of how they could be effectively implemented, monitored and evaluated – to be blunt, what is a programme like Prevent meant to achieve, and what would 'success' or effectiveness look like? Some ambitions of Prevent can be seen as somewhat in tension with each other, particularly between local Muslim community 'responsibility' (McGhee 2010) and the securitised state's desire for control over and knowledge of activities within those communities (Kundnani 2009). Other ambitions of Prevent may have appeared logical in their own terms but blatantly in contradiction to wider and deeper state policy priorities, particularly those around 'Community Cohesion', multiculturalism and the re-evaluated conceptions of identity and citizenship underpinning them. Those blatant contradictions and their very significant and negative resulting impacts are discussed in the 'Consequences' section further on.

Credit has to be given to the British Government for investing significantly in a terrorism prevention programme from 2006 onwards, given the traditional political and media pressure to focus exclusively on repressive interrogation of the broader (Muslim) communities seen as harbouring and even producing terrorists responsible for events such as 7/7 (Gupta 2008). The counterproductive effects of such clumsy crackdowns have been seen previously both historically in Northern Ireland, and within modern British Muslim communities (Hewitt 2008). Arguably, the new Prevent programme also gave the British state the opportunity to develop the more complex and developed channels of dialogue with Muslim communities that they wanted anyway (O'Toole *et al.* 2013).

However, the policy contradictions and lack of clarity about what Prevent was actually trying to achieve and who it was actually aimed at were apparent from the start. The context for this new Prevent initiative was a speech in January 2007 by Deputy Assistant Commissioner Peter Clarke, head of Counter-Terrorism Command at the Metropolitan Police, that Britain was losing the battle for 'hearts and minds' within Muslim communities, and the perception within the Security Services that there was a wider group of people within Muslim communities who held very negative feelings about the British state and some of its key policies, so providing a pool for terrorists to swim in (Thomas 2012). What was not clear here, however, was how big the state viewed this 'pool' as being. In much of the earlier Prevent policy documentation (DCLG 2007 a and b), there was talk of a small minority of extremists and of the state working in partnership with mainstream Muslims, as highlighted in then-DCLG Minister Ruth Kelly's speech to launch the 'pathfinder' phase of Prevent: '*Violent extremism seeks to drive us apart. Together, we will overcome it.*' (DCLG 2007b: 2). However, the accompanying guidance documentation for local authorities charged with launching Prevent spoke of the need for '*demonstrable changes in attitudes amongst Muslims*' (DCLG 2007b: 7). The sheer scale of the number of young Muslims engaged with by Prevent in that 'Pathfinder phase' (DCLG 2008) and the subsequent 2008–2011 expansion suggested both that the state perceived the 'pool' of potential terrorism supporters within Muslim communities was really quite large and that the state had a very limited sense of who those people might be.

State partnership and dialogue with Muslim communities around counter-terrorism was certainly an aim of Prevent, and can be identified in a number of ways in the 2007–2011 phase of the programme. The involvement of the DCLG in Prevent ensured that its national and local implementation was initially connected to broader engagement around cohesion, community regeneration and dialogue with faith communities. The initial latitude allowed to local authorities to use Prevent money as they wanted enabled some to hand over all or some of the money directly to Muslim community groups, and others to work collaboratively with them over the design of Prevent activity (Turley 2009; Lowndes and Thorp 2010; Iacopini *et al.* 2011). This did meet with a mixed response. Many local authorities were reluctant to develop a distinct Prevent programme, both because it clashed with the aims and practice of the Community Cohesion policy agenda, as discussed below, and because the sheer scale of Prevent seemed to target and inherently stigmatise entire Muslim communities (Husband and Alam 2011). Forced to implement the programme anyway, many local authorities used opaque titles like 'Pathfinder' to avoid the Prevent label (Thomas 2008), whilst a significant number of Muslim community groups refused to accept Prevent funding, based on the same concerns of blanket stigmatisation.

Nevertheless, there is significant empirical evidence that Prevent funding in this phase strengthened dialogue and understanding between Muslim communities and their local authorities and Police forces, and also enabled a strengthening in Muslim civil society structures and organisations (Turley 2009; O'Toole *et al.* 2013). On a national level considerable resources were provided for enhanced consultation structures with British Muslims and some success was achieved in developing more polyphonic community representation to government, albeit under an overtly counter-terrorism programme. This state approach has been characterised as: *forcing responsibility for countering extremism onto Muslim communities through a process of devolving responsibility downwards'* (McGhee 2010: 33) but can also be seen as a genuine attempt to develop partnership with 'responsible' Muslims, one consistent with the communitarianist, third-way approach of a Labour government that was pessimistic about its ability to solely produce social change (Levitas 2005). Whether 'responsible' Muslims are the same thing as religiously or politically 'moderate' Muslims has been an inherent tension within Prevent and the 2011 Prevent Review seemed to represent a decisive step towards the state demanding 'moderation' from any potential partners, so arguably undermining the effectiveness of Prevent against stated goals.

What is clear from the above discussion is that Prevent has only been concerned with British Muslims, and has failed to develop any work around right-wing/racist terrorism, or other forms of political extremism (Thomas 2012). This approach has been based on the state's position that Islamist extremism is not only the most serious terrorism threat facing Britain, but is only the only one that is 'international' in scope, so falling under the 'CONTEST' banner. The international links exposed by the far-right 2011 massacre in Norway and the developing, transnational far-right ideologies supporting Breivik's murders have not altered the view of the British state. This has left Britain's Prevent programme as focused only, and on a very large scale, on Muslim communities. This has been greatly problematic in terms of the resulting reactions from both the Muslim communities targeted and the other ethnic/faith communities not covered by this very substantial state funding scheme, as discussed below. It also indicates that the state understands the Islamist terror threat purely in terms of Islamic identity and practice, despite the fact that there is no agreed profile of who is radicalised towards political violence and that the concept of 'radicalisation' itself is increasingly disputed (Kundnani 2012). Here, it can be argued that, whilst this terrorist violence is planned and justified in the name of Islam, religion explains its motivations much less well than understandings of the rupturing experiences of transnationalism and globalisation, or even understandings of nihilistic and far-left political violence (Roy 2004).

These problematic features inevitably lead onto questions of what Prevent is actually trying to achieve. The 'hearts and minds' formulation of Prevent, and its strong focus throughout on young people identifies it as an educational programme. However, analysis of the 2007–2011 phases suggested that very little educational input or dialogue around terrorism, political violence or forms of extremism was actually going on within Prevent programmes (Thomas 2009, 2010). This is not surprising for a number of reasons. Firstly, any such educational work would involve overt discussion of difficult and contentious issues, such as foreign wars, racism, suicide bombing and religion, and it is far from clear that such genuine political education/dialogue with young people is what the state had in mind when establishing Prevent. Evidence shows previous policy attempts to operationalise overt 'anti-racist' educational programmes with White young people in schools and youth projects were undermined by avoidance and lack of confidence within the professional practitioners involved, who felt that they lacked the materials, clarity and organisational support to do such work (Thomas 2011). Despite Prevent's scale, little focus has been put on educational resources or, more crucially, on training and orientation for professional practitioners. The UK Youth Parliament, one of the small minority of Prevent-funded organisations who did engage in such overt and constructive political education work with young people (of all ethnic and faith backgrounds, on a community cohesion basis) offered to develop a national Prevent training programme for youth and community professionals, but the British Government refused to fund it (House of Commons 2010). Here, the evidence up until 2011 is of engagement with Muslim young people, but only very limited educational focus on the actual political, social and religious issues potentially driving any support for violent extremism (Thomas 2012). The more limited and possibly more focused Prevent programmes in funded areas post-2011 may have developed more robust educational content (although we have no evidence for this, as far as I am aware), but they have remained Muslim-only, raising fundamental questions about how mindsets relating to 'other' communities and intolerant social norms in the wider community can be influenced without having meaningful contact with those 'other' lifestyles, beliefs and value systems.

Certainly, Prevent, at least in its 2007–2011 phase, involved overt attempts at social engineering over community leadership and social and religious practices within British Muslim communities. This can be seen in the national prioritisation of new consultation bodies representing Muslim women and young people, and the requirement that local authorities also prioritise such work locally. There was also the breaking off of contact with the Mosque-based Muslim Council of Britain, and the establishment of and support for 'moderate' bodies like the Sufi

Muslim Council and anti-extremist think-tank the Quilliam Foundation (Birt 2009). More specifically, there was considerable focus on religious interpretation, and on the organisation and conduct of religious organisations and places of worship. These included the 'Radical Middle Way' road shows aimed at promoting 'moderate' interpretations of Islam and its place in Western societies to young Muslims, and considerable focus on the organisation and content of Madrassas and of the training and linguistic skills of new Imams recruited by Mosques.

Other fundamental features of Prevent would suggest that it is actually a securitised engagement approach with Muslim communities, much more about intelligence-gathering, facilitation/encouragement of self-policing and possibly even surveillance, rather than 'education' in any meaningful sense (Kundnani 2009; Husband and Alam 2011). Certainly the very large number of new and dedicated Police/Security Service posts focused on Prevent and the pivotal role of the Police and OSCT/regional CTUs in the programme's local and national coordination would support this perspective. The specific and evidenced examples of surveillance and of Police/CTU pressure on educational practitioners to pass on intelligence provided in the *Spooked* (Kundnani 2009) report were flatly contradicted by the then Labour Government. However, more recent research on the role played by the West Midlands CTU in Prevent clearly identifies the Police as the main players in Prevent (Lamb 2012).

Not only have the Police led and dominated decisions over Prevent funding and planning, they have even got involved in direct 'educational' delivery with Muslim young people and communities, a highly questionable blurring of professional boundaries (Knight 2010). Following the 2011 Prevent Review, local autonomy over Prevent largely disappeared, with even the funded areas having to apply regularly to the Police and Security Service officers-led OSCT for funding against specific criteria. Anecdotal evidence suggests refusal of support for any bids involving non-Muslims or research, and personal Ministerial scrutiny of bids, even though the eventual delivery is largely by local authority or third sector youth and community workers. The large-scale, monocultural focus on British Muslim communities and the centrality of the Police and Security Services to all levels and aspects of Prevent make it very hard to avoid the conclusion that it is significantly an intelligence-gathering and surveillance system, operationalised overtly at least partially through 'engagement'. Indeed, Prevent's creator, Sir David Omand, doubted that engagement and intelligence-gathering could or even should be separated within practice (APPGHS 2011) This can be seen most clearly around the Higher and Further Education sector, where Prevent activity has been entirely about Police/CTU liaison with educational institutions and state focus on how those institutions monitor Muslim student activity on and around campuses, rather than any educational engagement with students themselves (Thomas 2012).

The problematic stated and implicit ambitions of Prevent discussed above mean that it has been very hard for politicians to explain, or for the general public to understand, what Prevent is actually for. Indeed, when John Denham took over as DCLG Minister he identified that: '*I found in the CLG, after some very rigorous examinations with officials that there was no understood model of how Prevent was meant to work.*' (O'Toole *et al.* 2013: 57)

This, and the concurrent political scrutiny over the real purpose and content of Prevent (House of Commons 2010), led Denham, a Minister with strong educational and community cohesion credentials (Denham 2001), to offer the clarification to the national Prevent conference held in late 2009 that Prevent was a 'crime prevention programme' (Denham 2009). This was a potentially helpful attempt to answer allegations that Prevent had much wider and more questionable ambitions around surveillance or around altering the leadership and practices of British Muslim communities. However, it was also highly problematic. First, assuming the 'crime' to be prevented was terrorism, why has Prevent engaged with such large numbers of Muslim young people, yet focused so little on political, social and individual/psychological factors likely to make at least some young Muslims be at risk of terrorist involvement, as discussed above? Second, British crime prevention-based youth activities, such as Youth Inclusion Projects managed by local Youth Offending Teams, work with smaller numbers of carefully-targeted young people, often referred by relevant agencies. The 'Channel' programme, one small element of Prevent nationally, would seem to fit the 'crime prevention' understanding reasonably well, but the broader, large-scale Prevent activity to date outlined above simply does not fit any meaningful understanding of that concept. It is highly likely that this stated ambition and formulation was offered by a minister, and a whole government department, deeply unconvinced by Prevent and the role within it that they were being asked to play.

The consequences of Prevent

The shape and content of Prevent outlined previously, alongside the explicit and implicit ambitions analysed, have led to some clear, and largely negative, consequences flowing from this (over) ambitious counter-terrorism programme. In particular, three key consequences of Prevent can be identified. Firstly, there is the very significant contradiction to the broader policy agenda of Community Cohesion and ethnic integration and the damaging overlap with it in terms of 'space' for policy development and implementation. It is argued here and elsewhere (Thomas 2012) that these contradictions and tensions between the two policy agendas have gravely damaged the development of community cohesion practice whilst also undermining the effectiveness of Prevent itself. Secondly, the monocultural and large-scale focus on essentialised Muslims and their reified faith identity by the British state through Prevent has hardened defensive and antagonistic identifications within Muslim communities whilst also promoting 'virulent envy' (Birt 2009) over resource allocation from other ethnic, faith and social class communities. Lastly, it has clearly securitised the British state's relationships with Muslim communities at both national and local levels (Kundnani 2009), something that has grown significantly under the Coalition government and their 2011 Prevent Review. This has given at least the appearance of large-scale surveillance and has inevitably damaged the flow of much-needed human intelligence.

The Prevent/community cohesion tension

The relationship between Prevent and the pre-existing policy priority of community cohesion has been problematic from the start. The problem here is not just an organisational one of demarcation but a much more fundamental, conceptual one relating to Prevent's failure to reflect and work with the analysis and approach of community cohesion, so damaging the effectiveness of Prevent on its own stated terms. The British discursive policy shift from multiculturalism to community cohesion came in the wake of the 2001 northern riots involving young Muslims, but was a direction government wanted to go in anyway (Thomas 2011). Its foregrounding of commonality and shared values, rather than discrete and separate ethnic and faith identifications reflects a growing concern that 'parallel lives' were developing for such separate communities, not just in terms of physical segregation but in terms of lack of shared contact, cultures and identifications (Cantle 2001). Here, there was not only a focus on individual and community agency consistent with wider Labour social policy analysis and prescriptions, but also the perception that the previous phase of 'political multiculturalism' state policy had increasing downsides. These previous policies had of necessity deployed 'strategic essentialism' (Law 1996) to tackle the gross ethnic inequalities and blatant racial discrimination common to Britain of the 1980s and greatly contributed to the significant diminution of those ethnic inequalities and overt racism. However, in their focus on distinct ethnic identifies, such policies both hardened and reified these distinct ethnic/faith identities whilst providing separate, defined spaces for these individual communities. The post-2001 riots analysis, highly relevant to the ambitions of Prevent, was that extreme and oppositional identities and ideologies can develop more easily in culturally segregated communities holding antagonistic attitudes to 'others', an analysis as true of White racism as of extreme strands within Muslim communities.

This analysis from the post-riots Cantle Report (2001) was accepted by government and adopted as a new policy priority (Denham 2001). The resulting national government guidance and funding streams for local authorities focused very much on cross-community contact and work programmes that emphasised common needs and interests. This emphasis on commonality, alongside some sections of the report and some associated political pronouncements that seemed to focus very partially on Muslim responsibility (Travis 2001), was interpreted by some as a lurch back to the coercive assimilationist approach of the 1960s, a denial of difference and of multiculturalist progress itself (Kundnani 2002; Alexander 2004). However, empirical evidence on how community cohesion has been interpreted and implemented on the ground contradicts this (Thomas 2011). Here, community cohesion practice involves acknowledgement and celebration of distinct ethnic and faith identities but also work that emphasises cross-community content and commonality, so seeking to augment distinct identities with stronger forms of shared identity. Such cross-community contact is based upon 'contact-theory' (Hewstone et al. 2007), a social psychology-based approach to prejudice reduction carried out in depth and over considerable time. Such community cohesion-based approaches have strong support from local policy-makers and practitioners (Monro et al. 2010), meaning that when Prevent was announced local authorities in key areas like West Yorkshire fully understood the domestic terrorist threat but did not see why a separate policy programme was needed – for them, the community cohesion programmes they were enthusiastically developing were exactly designed to address and counter prejudices and extremism of all kinds (Husband and Alam 2011).

Moreover, Prevent's monocultural focus on Muslims, interested only in their 'Muslimness,' was understood as directly counter to the policy approach to identity in society inherent to community cohesion. Here more intersectional understandings of individual citizenship based around a human rights framework were being developed in tandem, with the need for more 'cooler' and contingent identifications seen as vital in an increasingly diverse and complex society (McGhee 2006). The scale and width of Prevent's monocultural focus on Muslims as an undifferentiated community remains a flagrant contradiction to the community cohesion policy agenda and is viewed as highly problematic by the ground level policy-makers and practitioners asked to implement it (Husband and Alam 2011).

Beyond this conceptual contradiction were practical and organisational problems for community cohesion flowing from Prevent's rapid and nationally-forced implementation. The demands for local authorities to quickly develop Prevent programmes and the associated multi-agency liaison structures meant that focus on developing community cohesion programmes and structures waned (Monro et al. 2010) and its forward progress stalled – terrorism was simply seen as more urgent and important than community relations, emphasised by the ubiquitous presence of counter-terrorism police and Security Service staff. The relationship between the two policy agendas was identified as problematic by a range of submissions to the CLG Select Committee Inquiry into Prevent (House of Commons 2010), and the eventual Prevent Review of 2011 seemed to accept the Inquiry's recommendations to separate DCLG and the Home Office, Community Cohesion and Prevent. However, by then the damage had been done. The Muslim Participation in Contemporary Governance project identifies a senior civil servant at the OSCT as acknowledging that, because of the sheer power of OSCT, '*so what happened was Prevent took over Cohesion*' (O'Toole et al. 2013: 57), a national process that was replicated at local ground level. This was confirmed in the aftermath of the 2011 Prevent Review, as OSCT control of local Prevent activity became total, whilst the government's long-awaited 'Integration' (their new term for community cohesion) policy document (DCLG 2012) was a grievous disappointment. It washed national government's hands of community cohesion/integration, saying that it was a matter for local government only. All national monitoring, guidance and finding for community cohesion was ended forthwith and the document didn't use the terms 'racism' or 'equalities' at all. Meanwhile, Prevent, focused only on Muslims, sailed onwards.

A suspect community?

Prevent's large-scale and monocultural focus on Muslim communities has not just been contradictory and damaging to community cohesion, but also has done very real damage both to the state's relationship with Muslim communities and relationships between distinct communities. The term 'suspect community', resonant of Britain's previous attitude to those of Catholic Irish origin and living in Britain, has been deployed in relation to the state's approach to British Muslims (Hickman et al. 2010), but this only partially works around Prevent's impact. Some key figures and organisations within British Muslim communities have enthusiastically participated in Prevent (O'Toole et al. 2013), not just seeing it as helpful 'Muslim money' (Lowndes and Thorp 2010), but also as a mechanism for acknowledging and confronting extremist activity and ideologies within their communities. However, the scale of the programme, and its securitised reality discussed below, has undoubtedly fuelled further defensive identifications and feelings amongst British Muslims who have suffered significant, hostile criticisms from both sections of the mainstream media and from overtly Islamophobic political groups like the English Defence League. Such pressure and constant questioning of their individual and collective 'loyalty' to Britain (Thomas and Sanderson 2011) makes it easier, not harder for young Muslims to be attracted to the 'single narrative' of worldwide Muslim grievance and oppression propagated by extreme strands of political Islamism. The overt social engineering of Muslim representation by Prevent described above, the significant and worrying extent of the state's 'internal penetration' of Muslim communities as Stuart Hall (BBC Radio 4 2011) has described it, merely adds to such feelings for some Muslims, exacerbated by Prevent's failure to engage with other forms of extremism, particularly far-right racism and violence. Repeated political calls to ban non-violent Islamist groups like Hizb ut-Tahir without also banning the EDL also add to such perceptions.

Meanwhile Yaha Birt (2009) accurately predicted that the money and focus of Prevent would create 'virulent envy' amongst other ethnic, faith and social communities. The 2001 riots in Oldham, Burnley and Bradford were significantly provoked by the sense within some marginalised White communities that Muslim communities were favoured by government funding streams (Thomas and Sanderson 2013). This was factually wrong but the 'strategic essentialism' (Law 1996) and ethnicised targets of political multiculturalism policies made such racialised interpretations more possible. Such resentment was illustrated in the CLG Select Committee Inquiry process, when representatives of all the other major faiths queued up to give evidence and complain that Muslims were getting state funding for mundane development of faith facilities such as madrassas whilst simultaneously claiming that only Muslims had an 'extremism' problem!

(House of Commons 2010). The large, monocultural and unfocused nature of Prevent between 2007 and 2011 made such grievances from other communities plausible at a time of significant cuts in other policy funding streams.

Policed multiculturalism?

The allegations that Britain's Prevent programme has been little more than an elaborate surveillance scheme devised by the 'spooks' have been aired and argued over elsewhere (Kundnani 2009; House of Commons 2010). The broader point is that such allegations are possible to make, and seem as significantly credible as elements of them do, because of the pivotal role for the Police and Security Service personnel in Prevent design and delivery, both locally via the Regional CTUs, and nationally via the controlling OSCT. It is inescapable that a policy programme apparently about education and community-based engagement has been controlled and sometimes directly delivered by these forces of overt state power – a clear securitisation of the state's relationship with Muslim communities, given the scale and complexity of the Prevent programme. Earlier, the chapter discussed how the Prevent policy agenda has both contradicted and ultimately sidelined the community cohesion/integration agenda that actually offered valuable insights on both the causes of extremism and on how to develop an inclusive and non-stigmatising vehicle for addressing extremism and ideologies that support it. Within Prevent we have seen a growing securitisation and progressively increasing Police/CTU control over the programme, despite continual rhetoric of partnership and multi-agency dialogue (HMG 2011). There is clear evidence that as the local and regional Prevent multi-agency coordination processes developed, the Police became more powerful and used that power to progressively limit local autonomy, so ending the minority of creative attempts to implement Prevent. This is highlighted in an empirical study of the role played by West Midlands CTU and its officers in Prevent:

> The Police seem to have been given the responsibility of delivering Prevent because other local bodies did not process the organisational capability to successfully implement, manage and adapt a programme ... despite Prevent being proposed as a multi-organisational programme, the Police in the West Midlands are the central organisation and undertake the majority of the work relating to Prevent.
>
> (Lamb 2012: 91)

This growing Police/CTU hegemony can be explained partly by their resource dominance – the Police had a great number of dedicated, Prevent-funded posts, whilst local authority Prevent funding was overwhelmingly for activities, rather than posts, with the burden of Prevent liaison therefore falling on hard-pressed policy officers who also had responsibility for wider policy agendas such as community cohesion. However, it can also be explained in terms of 'cultural capital', with the Police/CTU having the monopoly on intelligence and knowledge about ongoing plots and criminal investigation that could only be shared on a 'need to know basis' (Husband and Alam 2011), so establishing a clear cultural dominance and pecking order within Prevent operations. The Prevent Review (HMG 2011) extended this dominance significantly at the national level, cutting out the more partnership-orientated DCLG and making Prevent the sole property of the criminal justice-focused Home Office. As outlined above, this Review also gave the OSCT and its staff total control of all funding to and activities by local authorities.

Other elements of Prevent support such an analysis of securitisation. The Prevent Review put renewed emphasis Channel, the mechanism by which individuals viewed as vulnerable to radicalisation and to even 'grooming' by violent extremists are identified and referred, through multi-agency processes, to individual counselling or appropriate group work programmes. Some of the approach of Channel answers earlier questions levelled at Prevent, in that it works with only small numbers – hundreds, not many thousands, and identifies those individuals on a stated basis of facts and evidence. Channel is also probably the best example of interventions by skilled and confident professional practitioners who feel equipped to engage with complex and sensitive issues attached to 'radicalisation'. However, it involves identifying and intervening with young people, including a significant number aged 14 years old and under (HMG 2011), who have not committed any crime or participated in any identifiable criminal conspiracy. A briefing document prepared for the US Congress on international terrorism prevention approaches (Neumann 2011) admitted that a Channel-type approach would be viewed as completely unacceptable in the US due to civil liberty concerns. Similarly, Prevent's focus on universities has been entirely about monitoring of student activity and behaviour on and around campuses, and liaison between CTU and educational institutions (Thomas 2012). The Coalition government and influential think-tanks have been fiercely critical of British universities for not doing enough to identify and counter violent extremism (House of Commons 2012), yet what they propose seems to raise fundamental challenges to notions of academic freedom and the concept of universities as institutions where difficult and important social, moral and political subjects can be both researched and debated openly and freely. The dangers of such a mindset were demonstrated by the arrest and detention of two research students at the University of Nottingham on the grounds that they had downloaded Islamist extremist material that was both available in the University library and freely available on the Amazon website. Anti-Islamist think-tanks such as the Henry Jackson Society/Centre for Social Cohesion have been significantly influential in fuelling this scrutiny of universities, but the evidence base for actual terrorist recruitment or plots being developed on university campuses is very weak and unconvincing (House of Commons 2012).

Prevent: coming to an end?

Given the issues and tensions around Prevent that have been highlighted here, what is the prognosis for Prevent – is it a temporary phenomenon or a permanent reality? To date, Prevent's development has been unpredictable and uncertain. It existed in name only until the visceral shock of the 7/7 bombings and the realisation that this was a domestic plot (Hewitt 2008). Rapidly operationalised, often despite vehement opposition and concerns from local authorities and respected Muslim community organisations, Prevent was launched without a clear blueprint or developed sense of how its ambitions could be meaningfully operationalised. The chapter has highlighted the opposition and uncertainty about Prevent from local authorities and their parent government department, the DCLG. Here, even if Prevent was not deliberately intended as a Police-led surveillance scheme, the lack of a clear and achievable methodology and strategy, and the associated uncertainty of local government left the Police and Security Service in growing charge.

The inevitable charges of spying (Dodd 2009) could have sunk Prevent, but the continuing reality of foiled plots and convictions has made it very hard for politicians of all parties to step away from a programme that visibly demonstrates to the general public that something (even if it is not the right thing) is being done to stop this threat in the long-term. The 2011 Prevent Review did succeed in cooling off political and media concern about Prevent by downsizing it significantly and ending 'means-based' funding for radical Islamist groups working with vulnerable young people. Many local authorities ceased to receive Prevent funding after 2011 but were still required to have action plans and multi-agency liaison structures as part of their normal, ongoing operations. This 'mainstreaming' approach – Prevent without dedicated Prevent funding – may be the long-term direction of travel, and it will continue to be controlled by the Police/CTU, rather than by those local authorities involved in more organic and nuanced contact with Muslim communities and their varied representatives. However, the immediate response to the May 2013 Woolwich murder focused on whether Prevent was doing enough things or doing them in the right way (Travis 2013; Boffey and Doward 2013), and highlighted the continued political and popular pressure to have a named and visible terrorism prevention programme whilst Britain continues to have an apparent Islamist terror threat. This is a worrying conclusion, as this chapter has argued that the confused ambitions and the monocultural focus of Prevent alongside its contradictory tension with community cohesion have had strongly negative consequences. These have been to undermine and sideline community cohesion work, to further alienate and separate Muslim communities through a reification of simplistic and essentialised faith identity and to overtly securitise the state's relationship with those Muslim communities on a very large scale. Rather than continue, in overt or 'mainstreamed' covert forms, Prevent needs to be ended. Any genuine attempts to create community-based anti-extremism programmes with young people need to draw on the analysis of, and work in harmony with, constructive and non-stigmatising community cohesion practice (Thomas 2011) and the more intersectional and nuanced identities that it seeks to work with and encourage.

References

Alexander, C. (2004) 'Imagining the Asian Gang: Ethnicity, Masculinity and Youth after "the riots"', *Critical Social Policy*, 24 (4), pp. 526–549.

All-Party Parliamentary Group on Homeland Security (APPGHS) (2011) *Keeping Britain Safe: An Assessment of UK Homeland Security Strategy*, London: The Henry Jackson Society.

Association of Chief Police Officers (2009) *Submission to Communities and Local Government Select Committee Prevent Inquiry* (*Prevent* 60, House of Commons, 2010).

Atran, S. (2010) *Talking to the Enemy: Violent extremism, Sacred values and what it means to be human*, London: Allen Lane.

BBC News (2013) *English Defence League rally bomb plotters jailed*, Available at: www.bbc.co.uk/news/uk-22841573. Date accessed: 15 July 2013.

BBC Radio 4 (2011) *Thinking Allowed*, broadcast 16 March.

Birt, Y. (2009) 'Promoting virulent envy – reconsidering the UK's terrorist prevention strategy', *Royal United Services Institute (RUSI) Journal*, 154 (4), pp. 52–58.

Boffey, D. and Doward, J. (2013) Coalition 'has abandoned key fight with extremists', *Observer*, 26 May.

Cameron, D. (2011) *Speech to the Munich Security Conference*, 5 February.

Cantle, T. (2001) *Community Cohesion – A Report of the Independent Review Team*, London: Home Office.

Denham, J. (2001) *Building Cohesive Communities: A Report of the Ministerial Group on Public Order and Community Cohesion*, London: Home Office.

Denham, J. (2009) *Rt. Hon John Denham, MP, Ministerial Speech to National Prevent Conference*, Birmingham, 8 December.

Department for Communities and Local Government (DCLG) (2007a) Preventing *Violent Extremism: Winning hearts and minds*, London: DCLG.

DCLG (2007b) Preventing *Violent Extremism guidance note for Government Offices and Local Authorities in England*, London: DCLG.

DCLG (2008) *Prevent Pathfinder Fund – Mapping of Project Activities 2007/08*, London: DCLG.

DCLG (2012) *Creating the Conditions for Integration*, London: DCLG.

Dodd, V. (2009) 'MPs investigate anti-extremism programme after spying claims' *Guardian*, 19 October.

Eatwell, R. and Goodwin, M. (eds) (2010) *The new Extremism in 21st Century Britain*, Abingdon: Routledge.

English, R. (2009) *Terrorism and how to respond*, Oxford; Oxford University Press.

Gupta, D. (2008) *Understanding terrorism and political violence*, Abingdon: Routledge.

Her Majesty's Government (HMG) (2011) *Prevent Strategy*, London: The Stationery Office.

Hewitt, S. (2008) *The British War on Terror: Terrorism and counter-terrorism on the home front since 9/11*, London: Continuum.

Hewstone, M., Tausch, N., Hughes, J. and Cairns, E. (2007) 'Prejudice, Intergroup Contact and Identity: Do Neighbourhoods Matter?' In M. Wetherell, M. Lafleche and R. Berkley (eds) *Identity, Ethnic Diversity and Community cohesion.*

Hickman, M., Silvestri, S., Thomas, L. and Nickels, H. (2010) *'Suspect Communities':the impact of counter-terrorism on Irish communities and Muslim communities in Britain 1974–2007*, Paper at the British Sociological Association Annual Conference, Glasgow, 7 April.

Home Office (2003) CONTEST: The Government's Counter-Terrorism Strategy, London: The Home Office.
House of Commons Communities and Local Government Committee (2010) Preventing Violent Extremism: Sixth Report of session 2009–10, London: The Stationery Office.
House of Commons Home Affairs Select Committee (2012) Roots of Violent Radicalisation; Nineteenth Report of Session 2010–12, London: The Stationery Office.
Husband, C. and Alam, Y. (2011) Social Cohesion and counter-terrorism: A policy contradiction?, Bristol: Policy Press.
Iacopini, G., Stock, L. and Junge, K. (2011) Evaluation of Tower Hamlets Prevent Projects, London: Tavistock Institute.
Knight, S. (2010) 'Preventing Violent Extremism in Britain', Financial Times Magazine, 26 February.
Kundnani, A. (2002) The death of multiculturalism, London: Institute of Race Relations. Available at: www.irr.org.uk/2002/april/ak000001.html. Date accessed: 15 January 2003.
Kundnani, A. (2009) Spooked: How not to prevent violent extremism, London: Institute of Race Relations.
Kundnani, A. (2012) 'Radicalisation: The Journey of a Concept', Race and Class, 54 (2), pp. 3–25.
Lamb, J.B. (2012) 'Preventing Violent Extremism: A Policing case study of the West Midlands', Policing, 7 (1), pp. 88–95.
Law, I. (1996) Racism, Ethnicity and Social Policy, London: Prentice Hall.
Levitas, R. (2005) (2nd Edition) The Inclusive Society? Social Exclusion and New Labour, Basingstoke: Palgrave.
Lowndes, V. and Thorp, L. (2010) Preventing violent extremism – why local context matters, in Eatwell and Goodwin, 2010, pp. 123–141.
McGhee, D. (2006) 'The new Commission for Equality and Human Rights: Building Community Cohesion and revitalising citizenship in contemporary Britain', Ethnopolitics, 5 (2), pp. 145–166.
McGhee, D. (2010) Security, Citizenship and Human Rights: Shared values in uncertain times, Basingstoke: Palgrave Macmillan.
Meer, N. and Modood, T. (2009) The 'Multicultural state we're in: Muslims, 'multiculture' and the 'civic re-balancing of British Multiculturalism', Political Studies, 57 (3), pp. 473–497.
Modood, T., Berthoud, R., Lakey, J., Nazroo, J. Smith, P., Virdee, S. and Beishon, S. (1997) Ethnic Minorities in Britain – Diversity and Disadvantage, London: PSI.
Monro, S., Razaq, U., Thomas, P. and Mycock, A. (2010) Regional Improvement and Efficiency Partnerships: Community Cohesion and Prevent pilot – A report for Local Government Yorkshire and the Humber, Huddersfield: University of Huddersfield.
Neumann, P. (2011) Preventing Violent Radicalisation in America, Washington DC: National Security Preparedness Group.
O'Toole, T., Jones, S. and DeHanas, D. (2012) The new Prevent: Will it work? Can it work? A working paper from the Muslim Participation in Contemporary Governance Project, Bristol: University of Bristol.
O'Toole, T., DeHanas, D., Modood, T., Meer, N. and Jones, S. (2013) Taking Part: Muslim Participation in Contemporary Governance, Bristol: University of Bristol.
Roy, O. (2004) Globalised Islam: The search for a new Ummah, London: Hurst.
Solomos, J. (2003) (3rd Edition) Race and Racism in Britain, Basingstoke: Palgrave.
Thomas, P. and Sanderson, P. (2011) 'Unwilling Citizens? Muslim Young People and National Identity', Sociology, 45 (6), pp. 1028–1044.

Thomas, P. and Sanderson, P. (2013) 'Crossing the Line: White Young People and Community Cohesion', *Critical Social Policy*, 33 (1), pp. 160–180.

Thomas, P. (2008) *Evaluation of the Kirklees Preventing Violent Extremism Pathfinder: Issues and Lessons from the first year*, Huddersfield: The University of Huddersfield.

Thomas, P. (2009) 'Between Two Stools? The Government's Preventing Violent Extremism agenda', *The Political Quarterly*, 80 (2), pp. 482–492.

Thomas, P. (2010) 'Failed and friendless – the government's Preventing Violent Extremism agenda', *British Journal of Politics and International Relations*, 12 (3), pp. 442–458.

Thomas, P. (2011) *Youth, Multiculturalism and Community Cohesion*, Basingstoke: Palgrave Macmillan.

Thomas, P. (2012) *Responding to the Threat of Violent Extremism – Failing to Prevent*, London: Bloomsbury Academic.

Travis, A. (2001) 'Blunkett in race row over culture tests', *Guardian*, 10 December.

Travis, A. (2013) 'PM rejects knee-jerk response as hawks call for revival of snooper's charter', *Guardian*, 24 May.

Turley, A. (2009) *Stronger Together: A new approach to preventing violent extremism*, London: New Local Government Network.

10 How terrorism ends

Negotiating the end of the IRA's 'armed struggle'

Paul Dixon

Introduction

There is an international debate over whether states should or should not 'talk to terrorists'.[1] Neoconservatives are prominent opponents of negotiations because they interpret 'evil terrorism' in the most demonic way and see negotiations as appeasement and a sign of the state's weakness. 'Talking to terrorists', therefore, encourages terrorists to increase their violence in renewed hope of victory. 'Conciliators' by contrast argue that 'talking to terrorists' can be an effective way of bringing about a peaceful end to armed conflict. Conciliators see the Northern Ireland peace process as a key example of the effectiveness of politics and diplomacy in resolving entrenched and violent conflict because that process did involve extensive talks with Republican and loyalist paramilitaries which resulted agreements in 1998 and 2007 that have led to a more peaceful accommodation.

Since 2007, and the establishment of a stable powersharing government in Northern Ireland, some Neoconservatives have tried to take the 'hard case' of Northern Ireland and attempted to argue that it actually supports their argument for 'nearly never talking to terrorists' (Bew *et al.* 2009; Reiss 2010). They have argued that, by the early 1990s, hard power and the 'dirty war' waged by the British state had effectively 'defeated' the IRA. The peace process was, therefore, an IRA 'surrender process' in which the British Government took an uncompromising fundamentalist stance in negotiations laying down 'clear red lines' and refusing to compromise 'democratic norms'. From this they deduce the lesson that terrorists should not be talked to until they have been defeated through 'hard power' and 'dirty war' and call for a more repressive security policy to deal with Republican Dissidents. For Neoconservatives the world is a morality tale in which good behaviour by states leads to good consequences (Bew *et al.* 2009).

This chapter is a critique of the Neoconservative's attempt to capture the Northern Ireland peace process in the global debate on the role of 'talks' in how to end terrorism. It is argued that 'talks' with 'terrorists' can be a very effective way of ending armed conflict. The IRA was not 'defeated' by the early 1990s but the conflict between the British state and the IRA was stalemated or deadlocked. Because the conflict was stalemated, the peace process was not a 'surrender' but involved difficult, if not tortuous, negotiations between much more equally matched governments and political parties. Governments faced difficult moral dilemmas and compromises in which 'red lines' – for example, on the 'permanence' of the IRA's ceasefire and decommissioning – were crossed and democratic norms were compromised. The peace process was successful precisely because it was generally characterised by an often courageous, 'pragmatic realism' which attempted to combine realism with idealism in order to achieve a more peaceful future for the people of Britain and Ireland.

This chapter will: first, describe the general debate over whether to 'talk to terrrorists'. Second, explain the general Neoconservative position on engaging with terrorists. Third, analyse the Neoconservatives' analysis of the Northern Ireland peace process. Fourth, critique the Orthodox Neoconservative view that the IRA was 'defeated', which is the claim on which their argument is constructed. The conclusion highlights the pragmatic realism of the negotiators of the peace process and their difficult moral choices that they faced. The Neoconservatives' account of the peace process is deeply flawed, but this may be irrelevant if their ability to propagandise their account is successful.

Not (or nearly never) talking to 'terrorists'

The prevailing view is against negotiating with 'terrorists' (Toros 2008: 408). Four periods have been identified in the Western response to non-state terrorism. It is argued that from the late 1960s to the late 1980s Western states and their allies tended to use 'force-based suppression' to counter terrorism. During the 1990s counter-terrorism shifted, with notable exceptions, towards '...fairly widespread adoption of conciliation and law-enforcement-based counter-terrorism strategies. Direct talks with terrorist groups and movements got under way in Northern Ireland, Spain, Israel, South Africa, Sri Lanka and elsewhere' (R. Jackson *et al.* 2011: 229). The identification of so-called 'New War' and 'New Terrorism' combined with the 9/11 attack appeared to suggest the emergence of 'a new and more threatening form of terrorism, one that posed an existential threat to Western societies and the stability of the international system'. Conciliation and law-enforcement was marginalised as wars were launched against Afghanistan and Iraq along with numerous smaller military operations, interdiction and rendition programmes in an attempt to destroy al Qaeda and suppress global terrorism. This was accompanied by counter-terrorism legislation that was criticised for being repressive and restrictive towards human rights. In the fourth phase, new 'counter-radicalization programmes' and 'hearts and minds' approaches to counterinsurgency were added to the state's repertoire for fighting non-state terrorism (Jackson *et al.* 2009).

Opponents of negotiations often take the most hostile possible interpretation of the intentions of 'evil terrorists' in order to justify a belligerent stance. An essentialist interpretation of terrorism may be taken in which terrorists are seen as ideological fanatics, criminals or psychopaths who cannot be conciliated and, therefore, have to be eradicated, militarily defeated or intimidated by force into submission. Some have argued that in 'New Wars' and 'New Terrorism' we are seeing the rise of 'absolutist' or 'irreconcilable' terrorists and the decline of 'old', 'non-absolutist', 'reconcilable' or 'contingent' terrorists. Anthony Coates describes why militarists reject conciliation:

> Conciliation is rejected because the conflict is understood to be an absolute one: there can be no compromise and no reconciliation with an absolute enemy. The ends of war are not negotiable. The moral imperative of this kind of war is not to make peace with an enemy but to destroy him.
>
> (Coates 1997: 57)

There is a zero-sum, 'battle of wills' between the state and terrorists and insurgents in which the state must prevail. Negotiations are only possible after the defeat of terrorism or once the enemy's will to resist has been broken and they realise that the state's triumph is inevitable. Otherwise they can damage the state's credibility and image of determination which is vital in the propaganda war for overcoming the enemy's will to resist (Dixon 2012b: 60, 66–67, 75). The emphasis is on 'hard power' for defeating the terrorists, if necessary through the use of 'repression' and 'dirty war'. In this 'battle for survival' the end nearly always justifies the means. Premature negotiations are dangerous because they damage the state's credibility, are a sign of 'weakness' and encourage the perception that the state is losing. This encourages terrorists to redouble their violent campaign in order to achieve outright victory. Ceasefires to permit negotiations, allow the terrorists to regroup and rearm and can lead to divisions within the state over negotiations, the military may see negotiations as undermining their strategy (Dixon 2012b). Terrorists exploit the benefits of the ceasefire in order to prosecute their war more effectively when they return to violence. Peace processes and negotiations give authority to terrorist organisations because they are now more likely to be seen as legitimate organisations with a political agenda rather than a criminal enterprise. This could encourage the international spread of terrorism. Negotiations imply concessions or the 'appeasement' of terrorist organisations. The 'appeasement' of Hitler at Munich in 1938 becomes a key justification for seeking military rather than diplomatic solutions to political problems. Democracy is corrupted by engaging with terrorists because it demonstrates the effectiveness of the gun in bringing about political change and, by contrast, appears to show the weakness of unarmed, democratic politicians. Agreements reached at the end of negotiations are, therefore, at least partly a reward for the use of violence. This corrupts democracy, creates a dangerous precedent and encourages terrorists around the world. Negotiations with terrorists may not only corrupt democracy but also create divisions within the state and weaken it, preparing the way for terrorists to relaunch their violent struggle in an attempt to defeat the state. Military victories 'appear to offer better chances of a stable peace, as well as better reasons to hope for the development of a more democratic society' (Duyvesteyn and Schuurman 2011: 687).

Talking to non-state terrorists

Publicly, states tend to claim that they will never talk or negotiate with terrorists but in practice they often do. Realists, like Neoconservatives, may also demonise the enemy in the propaganda war but they do not mistake their propaganda for accurate analysis and are more likely to accept that negotiations can be a successful way of ending armed conflict. They seek to avoid talk of 'victory' and 'defeat' because this rhetoric makes agreement between conflicting parties more problematic.

Jonathan Powell, Tony Blair's key negotiator on Northern Ireland, argued that the war had stalemated in Northern Ireland and an inclusive process that included paramilitaries was vital for the peace process to succeed. He goes so far as to suggest that '...on the basis of my experience I think it is always right to talk to your enemy however badly they are behaving' (Powell 2008: 66). It is only the extremes that can build a durable peace. The former Irish Taoiseach (Prime Minister) Garrett Fitzgerald took issue with Powell arguing that prior to the peace process 'contacts' with the IRA were dangerous because they risked giving the IRA the impression that they were winning and gave them the 'oxygen of publicity' (Fitzgerald 2008). There are risks and legitimate fears in talking to terrorist organisations, in particular contexts it is possible they could antagonise rather than ameliorate the security situation, they may also encourage the legitimacy and support for paramilitary organisations and undermine more moderate, democratic political parties. Jonathan Powell's position may be more defensible if it is specified what he means by 'talks' and in what circumstances he thinks them to be appropriate. 'Talking to your enemy' could be anything from private conversations and gossip between the different parties to the conflict and third parties then being relayed to their opponents to public, official peace talks between terrorists and the state.

The decision as to the nature of the talks, level of diplomacy and symbolism is a matter of political judgment that depends on context. The announcement or commencement of formal negotiations in one context could be politically disastrous and escalate violence, whereas in another it may be the path towards a negotiated settlement. 'Contacts' with terrorist organisations may be an easy way to explore the possibility of accommodation and to gather information about the bottom line of opponents. The state can avoid giving legitimacy to terrorist organisations by engaging in deniable contacts, building confidence through reciprocal concessions, and laying out the parameters of an agreement before moving toward public negotiations. There are different ways of 'talking' or 'negotiating with' terrorists. These may range from indirect, unauthorised conversations between terrorists or the state and third parties that are then relayed between the two sides. There could be deniable contacts through 'third parties' who off their own initiative seek to find a negotiated end to violence. Intelligence operatives and civil servants may be used to initiate more official and direct contacts between the state and the terrorist organisation, which may still be to some extent deniable if they are exposed (they may be blamed on 'rogue' or 'maverick' officials acting without official authorisation). The importance and symbolism of talks can be scaled up through more senior state officials, to political representatives and full-blown public and formal talks between the state and terrorist organisation (which may still be accompanied or supplemented by secret negotiations). The United States' practice of using 'terrorist blacklists' can impede attempts to alter the behaviour of 'terrorist' organisations or investigate and explore opportunities for negotiated settlement (Gross 2011).

There are a number of reasons why negotiations are thought to be useful for ending armed conflict. Negotiations and diplomacy have a track record of successfully bringing about peaceful political change. Transitions from authoritarianism to democracy have often been negotiated, confounding Neoconservative expectations, in order to avoid predicted civil war. In South Africa, for example, there was considerably secrecy involved in the negotiated end of 'white' minority rule and although there was terrible violence this was not as bad as the violence that had been anticipated. In Iraq, 'the Arab Awakening' involved the US military negotiating with 'terrorists' who had killed US troops in order to defeat al Qaeda. Negotiations and 'concessions' can meet the legitimate demands of terrorist groups and end the reason for violence. They may also demonstrate the effectiveness of the democratic political process over violence in bringing about some political change. This strengthens the 'moderate' faction of a terrorist organisation in its internal battle with militarist hardliners. Whereas intransigence by the state might strengthen the hand of hardliners who can argue that there is no alternative but 'armed struggle' in order to bring about change.

The process of negotiations can play an important role in changing the attitudes of the parties to the conflict. During violent conflict opponents may be demonised and the attempt to understand a terrorist organisation confused with sympathy for it. Through negotiations politicians and policy-makers on all sides may be educated about their opponent's beliefs, demands and actions. States and parties also become informed about the political constraints and opportunities facing their rivals and, therefore, the likely problems in reaching a negotiated compromise. Terrorists may also become more involved in politics by contesting elections and so the electorate becomes a constraint on what is seen as 'legitimate' violence by the terrorist organisation. States may hope that the terrorists become so entangled and involved in the democratic process that they cannot go back to 'war'.

The distinction between 'absolutist' and 'irreconcilable' and 'non-absolutist' or 'reconcilable' terrorists (or the definition of 'spoilers') does not acknowledge the contested nature of these categorisations or the possibility that terrorists might move between these categories depending on circumstances. Political actors may well take a hardline position in public as a negotiating tactic rather than revealing their bottom line prior to negotiations. Political actors may give ambiguous and contradictory signals that makes it difficult to assess whether a particular terrorist group, or a faction of that group, is genuine about seeking a negotiated end to violence. Advocates of negotiations may also argue that a negotiated end to violent conflict may also prove to be more robust and long-lasting than a victory for one faction.

'Appeasement', as Paul Kennedy points out, can be an inoffensive if not positive term, meaning to cool tensions. The difficulty is distinguishing between a 'good' appeasement policy and a 'bad' one. He points to the history of British diplomatic appeasement of the US, which 'arguably played a massive role in helping to bring the United States to an official pro-British stance as the two great wars of the twentieth century approached' (Kennedy 2010: 9). He argues, 'It is not a crime, or a moral failing, to recognize where and when it may be best to withdraw from a battlefield and to reduce a commitment. Most great statesmen have done that' (Kennedy 2010: 16). The US defeat in Vietnam, for example, did not lead to the other dominoes falling in South East Asia.

The state may also use negotiations in a more aggressive way to divide and defeat terrorist organisations. A peace process may create divisions between factions who favour and oppose negotiations. This could end in a split within the organisation and intelligence may then be forthcoming from the more moderate faction in order to marginalise hardliners. There may also be an opportunity to break the momentum of the terrorist organisation to gain intelligence on it. It may also create a breathing space for the state's security forces to reorganise. Some argue, for example, that the British Government's talks with the IRA 1975–1976 were designed to demoralise and divide the IRA (Dixon 2008: 159–165).

Neoconservatives: nearly never talking to terrorists

The Northern Ireland peace process is a key supporting case for the 'conciliation and law-enforcement' approach to counter-terrorism that was developing in the nineties (Dixon 2008: chapters 8–10). Since 2007, British 'Orthodox Neoconservatives' have challenged this and claimed that by the early 1990s the British state had 'defeated' the IRA and, in effect, the peace process managed the IRA's surrender. The British state set out clear red lines for terrorist participation in the peace process and, therefore, did not compromise democratic norms.

Since at least the invasion of Iraq in 2003, Neoconservatism has become a toxic brand, particularly in Europe. British Neoconservatives who are attempting to influence the political debate or have political ambitions are, therefore, more likely to shy away from the label and conceal their normative position. In addition, defining Neoconservatism is difficult and controversial. Justin Vaisse has argued: 'Discontinuity, heterogeneity, and contradiction are an integral part of neoconservatism, a word that is in danger of losing any precise meaning' (Vaisse 2010: 6–7, 271). It has been described variously as a movement, sensibility, tendency or persuasion.

British Neoconservatives tend not to embrace the term 'neoconservative' because of its association with the Presidency of George W. Bush and the deceptions over the invasion of Iraq. In 2004 Michael Gove, Secretary of State for Education (2010–2014) and one of the few self-proclaimed British Neoconservatives, lamented that 'there are remarkably few British politicians, or writers, on the right who are happy to pin the badge of neoconservative to their coat' (Gove

2004: 279). Douglas Murray, in *Neoconservatism: Why we need it* (2006) noted that leading neoconservatives, such as Blair and Wolfowitz rejected the label,

> ...If we are to get anywhere in identifying neoconservative trends and achievements, we will have to accept that many have been carried out, and will continue to be carried out, by people who would hesitate at being described as neocon.... But just because someone doesn't call himself a neoconservative does not mean that his [*sic*] ideas, outlook, and actions are not neoconservative or neoconservative-inspired.
>
> (Murray 2006: 43–44)

A broad interpretation of British Neoconservatism would embrace Tony Blair and quite a few others in the Labour party. John Kampfner has argued, 'The British neo-cons probably do not acknowledge their own existence' (Kampfner 2003). To avoid identification, British Neoconservatives, therefore, use a number of euphemisms for neoconservative such as 'muscular liberal interventionist', 'liberal interventionist', 'liberal internationalist', 'muscular liberal' and even 'progressive'. The Conservative Party leader and then Prime Minister, David Cameron, distanced himself from the Neoconservatives. Robin Simcox, Research Fellow at the Henry Jackson Society, argued in the Neoconservative magazine, *Weekly Standard*, that while Prime Minister David Cameron's policies are Neoconservative, he 'is at pains not to be tarred with the neoconservative brush. The term in Europe is now synonymous with extreme right-winger with a penchant for civilian deaths – hardly a vote winner'. He argues that Neoconservative's opponents have 'hijacked the term' and Neoconservatives should take it back (Simcox 2011). Other leading British Neoconservatives are thought to include George Osborne (Chancellor of the Exchequer), David Willetts (Minister of State for Universities and Science), Greg Hands MP, Ed Vaizey MP, Nicholas Boles MP and, probably, William Hague (Foreign Secretary).

For the Neoconservatives the US (or UK) is in permanent crisis, whether from the Soviet threat or from terrorism and 'Islamofascism' and this justifies an ever rising security budget. They demand 'moral clarity' in the global battle between 'good' and 'evil'. Evil terrorists must be defeated rather than appeased. Therefore, Neoconservative have opposed peace processes in Northern Ireland and the Middle East. In the Middle East, Ross and Makovsky argue, the Neoconservatives start from the assertion that,

> the Arabs categorically reject Israel, and peace is not possible as a result. The corollary is that if the Arabs prove themselves in terms of accepting Israel, then peace can be possible, but until that point there is no reason for US engagement on peace. Engagement is futile at best and counterproductive at worst, and as a result, disengagement is the right policy prescription.
>
> (Ross and Makovsky 2010: 91)

Irving Kristol, for example, asserted that the Middle East Peace Process was an 'appeasement' process and the reason peace processes in Cyprus and Northern Ireland get nowhere 'is that no mediator can envisage an end situation satisfactory to both parties' (Kristol 1997). Moral relativism leads to negotiations which imply concessions and, therefore, the appeasement of evil. This encourages the insurgents to gain from the legitimacy of negotiations while demoralising the state's forces and encouraging defeatism. The power of the gun over the ballot box is demonstrated and this undermines the effectiveness and electoral appeal of democratic parties. Negotiations should only be contemplated when terrorists have been 'defeated', if necessary by repression and the use of 'dirty war' (Bew et al. 2009: Reiss 2010: 200). Neoconservatives tend to draw a sharp contrast between their 'idealism' and the unprincipled conservative or liberal 'realism' of their opponents. This dichotomy does not do justice to the complexity of Neoconservatism which draws on both idealist and realist traditions. Some argue that the Neoconservative's idealist rhetoric disguises its realist US nationalism and imperialist ambitions (Cooper 2010: 8; Vaisse 2010: 278–279).

Neoconservatives and the Northern Ireland peace process

John Bew, Martyn Frampton and Inigo Gurruchaga's book *Talking to Terrorists: Making Peace in Northern Ireland and the Basque Country* (2009) is an 'Orthodox British Neoconservative' attempt to reinterpret the Northern Ireland peace process as a case favourable to the Neoconservative hostility to negotiating with terrorists (Dixon 2011, 2012, 2012a). Bew and Frampton deny that they are Neoconservatives but are both founding members of the leading British Neoconservative organisation, the Henry Jackson Society, founded in 2005 at Peterhouse College, Cambridge, and participants in Neoconservative networks (Dixon 2011: 655–656; 2012). The Henry Jackson Society was named after the patron saint of Neoconservatives the Democratic Senator Henry 'Scoop' Jackson a Cold War 'liberal', supporter of Israel, 'tough' on Communism, a hawk on the Vietnam War, defender of the defence industry and opponent of Détente in the 1970s. While Bew and Frampton deny that their work is a Neoconservative interpretation of the peace process it is recognised as such by leading right-wing commentators who endorsed its key lesson that terrorist organisations should be defeated before they should be engaged with (Dixon 2012: 305–306).

Three incompatible strands of Neoconservative thought on the peace process are identifiable. The first, is associated with David Trimble, the leader of the UUP, during 1995–2003 (Dixon 2011: 656–657). During this period Trimble negotiated the peace process with a prudence and realism that suggests that this strand is not Neoconservative at all. Trimble assumed that the conflict was 'deadlocked', the IRA were not defeated and that in the negotiation of the peace process he needed to compromise in order to secure the IRA's participation. Trimble sought 'a peace within the realms of the possible' rather than pursuing the 'idealistic' fantasies of complete victory (Dixon 2012: 315–316). After the

DUP overtook the UUP as the dominant party within unionism and became the key unionist negotiators of the peace process, the Trimbleistas shifted towards a more 'idealist', anti-peace process unionism and then an Orthodox Neoconservatism (Dixon 2011).

Neoconservative ideology is most compatible with the second, 'unionist anti-peace process' strand because it opposes 'concessions' or even talking to 'terrorists' (Dixon 2011: 657–659). According to this argument, the IRA was not defeated but was exploiting the peace process to achieve their goals. The British Government, driven by IRA bombs in the City of London in 1992, 1993 and 1996, were involved in a 'surrender process' that by compromising and offering concessions to terrorists without insisting on decommissioning, corrupted core values and democratic norms. The DUP's decision to share power with Sinn Féin in 2007 led to the marginalisation of anti-peace process unionism that became reduced to ultra-hardliners of Traditional Unionist Voice and some on the right of the British Conservative Party. Neoconservatives opposed to the peace process found themselves increasingly discredited by the failure of their alarmist predictions and the manifest success of the peace process in producing decommissioning and relatively stable, democratic government. This situation threatened to leave Neoconservatives unable to use the success of Northern Ireland in the rhetorical battle over how to deal with 'terrorism'. John Bew and Martyn Frampton initially adopted an anti-peace process unionist position and decried the realism and lack of principle demonstrated in the peace process (Dixon 2011: 658–659). Even as late as 2009, Frampton argued that the IRA had *not* been defeated but continued to pursue its ideological goal of a united Ireland by other means.

> [The] ... supposition that Sinn Féin and the wider republican movement have, to all intents and purposes, accepted defeat, runs, as this study will show, contrary to the evidence. Indeed, the 'defeat hypothesis' rests on an understanding of what the Good Friday Agreement represents to the republican movement, which is almost wholly at variance with the way Sinn Féin has acted since 1998.
> (Frampton 2009: 6; see also Bew *et al.* 2009)

The Orthodox Neoconservative interpretation, detailed in Bew *et al.*'s *Talking to Terrorists* (2009) claims that it was the British state's repressive security policy and 'dirty war' that had defeated the IRA by the early 1990s. This explains why the British were able to impose an uncompromising, peace process on the IRA. The peace process was successful because the British laid down consistent, clear 'red lines' for terrorist participation and did not compromise on 'core' issues, and this prevented the corruption of democracy. They conclude,

> ...Ultimately, if talking to terrorists can be said to have had some success in Northern Ireland, this was only when the terrorists had come to accept the rules of the game and agreed to abide by them in the search for a settlement.

This argument is important to Neoconservatives because it seeks to establish that the British Government succeeded without making concessions to violence. The reason that the British talked to 'terrorists' is because the government was negotiating from a position of strength, the 'terrorists' were not on the 'crest of a wave' and it was the IRA that approached the British (Bew et al. 2009: 255, 259, 246). Prior to the 1990s and the defeat of the IRA, British Government talks with the IRA were counterproductive because they encouraged the terrorists to believe that they were winning leading to an increase in violence (Dixon 2012: 309). The British Government did not have to 'appease' the Sinn Féin leadership because Gerry Adams and Martin McGuinness had complete control over the Republican movement. British Governments managed the surrender of the IRA, although this was mismanaged by the Labour government in the post-GFA period (Bew et al. 2009: 250, 164).

Talking to Terrorists emphasises the role of 'hard power' and 'dirty war' in defeating the IRA and forcing them to the negotiating table. The 'dirty war' is usually interpreted as including:

1 An alleged 'shoot to kill' policy by the British state.
2 Some level of collusion between the British state and loyalist paramilitaries who were provided with information to help them target alleged Republicans.
3 The use and abuse of informers within loyalist and Republican paramilitary organisations who were allowed to participate in murder to protect themselves.

These informers are alleged to include Freddie 'Scap' Scappaticci who was in charge of the IRA's internal security department, the so-called 'nutting squad', which tortured and killed those claimed to have been informers. Denis Donaldson is another leading informer who was close to the Sinn Féin leadership and became their key administrator in the Northern Ireland parliament. Roy McShane, one of a pool of drivers for leading Republicans, including Gerry Adams, is also alleged to have been a British agent. There are persistent rumours of other British informers prominent in Sinn Féin. Remarkably Martin McGuinness, Sinn Féin's Deputy First Minister, felt he had to publicly deny being a British agent.

Three reasons are given for Republicans entering a peace process in the 1990s, all of which emphasise the importance of 'hard power': 'war weariness'; a sectarian, loyalist backlash against Republicans; and the growing effectiveness of the security forces. Britain's 'unofficial war' against Republicans had a 'decisive impact' (Bew et al. 2009: 108–110, 247). Frampton argues: '...all that can be said with certainty is that the 'dirty war' largely achieved its aims'. Yet he also argues, 'it seems irrefutable that this 'dirty war' saw agents of the State carry out the most serious violations of human rights, up to and including murder' (Frampton 2008: 96, 89). Bew and Frampton also try to rehabilitate internment without trial in 1971 and argue that the British Government's talks with the IRA in July 1972 were counterproductive and responsible for that year being the most violent of the conflict. Yet there are a number of other developments that are plausible contributors to the violence: the introduction of internment, August 1971; Bloody Sunday, January 1972; the introduction of direct rule, March 1972; as well as the growing ambiguity of British policy from the Autumn of 1971 and the loyalist backlash, are among other plausible contributors to the violence in 1972. The decision to talk to the IRA in 1972 came a few weeks before 'Operation Motorman' which led to a major decline in violence (Dixon 2012a: 309–310).

The hardline attitude of Neoconservatives towards the Northern Ireland peace process is also apparent in their approach to 'Islamic terrorism' in Britain. They have adopted an assimilationist, British nationalist perspective on the threat from 'Islamic terrorism' which has attacked diversity and multiculturalism as a threat to national cohesion and security. They argue for an uncompromising British nationalist stance which does not accommodate 'sectarian realities'. Clear moral boundaries are to be set and there is a reluctance to engage with political Islamists. This is hardly in keeping with the spirit of the peace process in Northern Ireland where 'terrorists' have been actively engaged, where there were legal political parties that were closely linked to paramilitary organisations, and where 'terrorists' are now in government and there is explicit recognition of diversity and Irish identity.

Defining defeat

The language of 'defeat' and 'victory' can inhibit negotiations and accommodation. This is because it can be politically difficult for a political or military leader to enter into negotiations when their opponent is claiming that such negotiations represent their victory. President Obama avoided discussion of 'defeating' the Taliban in Afghanistan because that '...suggested an unconditional surrender – total capitulation, victory, winning in the fullest sense of the word, utterly destroying the Taliban.' Yet the President could also not be seen to 'lose' the war (Woodward 2010: 145, 146, 166–167). The 'defeat' claim is important to Neoconservatives in order to reject the efficacy of politics, diplomacy, negotiation, compromise, 'soft power' and moral 'greyness' in favour 'hard power' and 'dirty war'. Terrorists should only be talked to when they have been defeated. The state then adopts an uncompromising 'negotiating' stance in which moral clarity leads to the establishment of clear 'red lines' and a 'robust insistence on democratic norms'. Bew and Frampton are careless in their use of terms and claim simultaneously that the IRA was 'defeated', the conflict was in 'stalemate' or 'deadlock' and that the IRA 'won' (Dixon 2012: 311–312). This flexibility allows them to attempt to present contrasting interpretations of the peace process to suit different audiences.

The claim of Neoconservatives that the IRA was 'defeated' is an inaccurate description but also politically provocative. Words are used precisely and carefully in order to more accurately convey meaning. If the term 'defeat' is used when a more accurate term is 'stalemate' then the wrong 'lessons' are likely to be drawn from the Northern Ireland conflict. The term defeat suggests that the opponent is beaten or destroyed (Dixon 2012: 310–311). An argument could be made that the British 'defeated' the IRA because they 'frustrated' them or prevented them from achieving their aim. But in this case, it could be argued, that many governments and parties to the conflict failed to achieve their aims or were frustrated and, therefore, they were all 'defeated'. In which case it seems that any peace process that involves negotiations and compromise involves the 'defeat' of the participants. This not only seems to be a misleading use of the word 'defeat', but it is also a provocative definition that is unlikely to encourage negotiation and compromise because these are defined as 'defeat'. Whether or not we 'objectively' believe that the IRA was defeated by the early 1990s is not necessarily that important if key actors to the conflict did not perceive the IRA to have been defeated (including the IRA themselves) and there is little or no evidence that they did. Indeed, the tortuous negotiation of the peace process is difficult to understand if it is assumed that the IRA had been 'defeated' or 'destroyed'.

Political leaders tend to want to claim that they have 'won' in negotiations in order to satisfy their supporters and voters. 'Victory' can be turned into 'defeat' if opponents manage to persuade the audience that a party or leader was 'defeated'. In the 'zero sum' politics of Northern Ireland, triumphalist claims of victory may appease one leader's supporters but damage the ability of opposition leaders to manage theirs. This is why Sinn Féin's attempt to present compromise as victory during the peace process had an adverse effect on the UUP leader's ability to bring its supporters behind the Good Friday Agreement. Militarists – both Republican Dissidents and Neoconservatives – have used the claim that the IRA were defeated to attack Sinn Féin and destabilise the peace process. The Republican leadership were anxious, therefore, that their entry into a peace process would not be portrayed as defeat and this is partly why they objected to demands for decommissioning. The British Prime Minister, John Major, observed that the Republican's moderating rhetorical shifts were accompanied by an escalation of IRA violence and the reassertion of fundamentalist positions: 'The IRA leadership had their own perverted logic. For them, an offer of peace needed to be accompanied by violence to show their volunteers that they were not surrendering' (Major 1999: 433). Patrick Mayhew, Secretary of State for Northern Ireland, rejected triumphalist claims of victory and defeat, 'There is no victory and no defeat. This military language is out of place. What is needed is the language of trust' (*Irish Times* 21 September 1995). The Good Friday and St Andrews Agreements were deliberately designed to be open to multiple interpretations so that each leader could claim victory to their supporters (Mowlam 2002: 231; Dixon 2008: 314–319). As Mo Mowlam said, the GFA is a package, 'There are no winners or losers' (*News Letter* 20 May 1998).

Challenging the 'defeat thesis'

Three groups argue that the IRA were defeated: Neoconservatives; Republican Dissidents and elements of the security forces. Neoconservatives argue the IRA were defeated to oppose talking to terrorists. Republican Dissidents seek to undermine the Sinn Féin leadership by claiming that it has 'surrendered' to the British state and call for Republicans to fight the armed struggle to victory. Elements in the security forces claim victory to enhance their influence in ongoing power struggles within the state and to demand more repressive security policies. Some claim victory for the old Royal Ulster Constabulary in order to criticise the reformed Police Service of Northern Ireland. The Army claims success in Northern Ireland to boost its claims to be able to defeat insurgency. The intelligence services claim victory to emphasise their ongoing role in containing terrorism. Significantly, claims that the IRA was defeated have tended to increase only after 2007, when it became more obvious that the IRA had not achieved a united Ireland. The security forces certainly played their role in containing the Republican threat but it is the complex and morally difficult political negotiations and diplomacy that more convincingly explains the success of the peace process (Dixon 2008). This explains why the peace process was not an IRA 'surrender process', but involved tortuous negotiations, the compromising of democratic norms and a high degree of uncertainty as to the intentions of the Republican leadership and its ability to deliver their movement. The successful outcome represented the triumph of politics and diplomacy over the gun (Blair 2010; Powell 2008).

A more sophisticated case that the IRA was 'defeated' is possible but not advanced by Neoconservatives. This case is that a faction of the SF/IRA leadership acknowledged that they had been 'defeated' but needed the British Government, Irish nationalists and the US to act as if they were not defeated and not use the language of victory in order to maximise the IRA leadership's chances of bringing a united Republican movement into the peace process. The 'defeat' theory is not particularly plausible because of the lack of evidence to support it and the compelling arguments against that can be arrayed against it.

First, if the key actors involved in the peace process, including the Republican leadership, did not believe they had been defeated and acted on that perception, then does it make much sense to describe the IRA as having been defeated? The governments and parties to the peace process did not believe the IRA had been defeated and therefore accepted that the IRA's ceasefire was not permanent and that they might go back to 'war', which they did in 1996–1997 (even after 1997 their ceasefire was a 'necessary fiction') (Dixon 2008: 292–293). In 1989, Peter Brooke, the Secretary of State for Northern Ireland, made a public overture to Republicans. He said that the security forces could contain the IRA but he found it 'difficult to envisage' their military defeat. This was in line with an influential view in British counterinsurgency thinking that the army could only 'hold the ring' until a political settlement was found. If the terrorists decided 'that the game had ceased to be worth the candle' then it would be possible that the British Government could sit down and talk with Sinn Féin. The accounts of leading British and Irish politicians involved in the peace process, John Major, Tony Blair, Peter Mandelson, Jonathan Powell, Albert Reynolds and Bertie Ahern make it clear that they did not believe that the IRA were defeated (Dixon 2008: 216–219; 242–243). Michael Ancram, Conservative

Junior Minister and Minister of State in the Northern Ireland Office 1993–1997, has argue that the Conservative Government's analysis was:

> First, that the war could not be won. Second, that there could be no long-term solution to the problem we were confronting without the eventual involvement of those we were fighting. Third, that even as the fighting continued, we needed to find a means of engaging them. And fourth, that this could only be done by opening dialogue.
>
> (Ancram 2007: 23)

Until very late in the peace process senior British policy-makers were unsure of whether the IRA would relaunch their 'armed struggle'. According to Blair, from the GFA to October 2002 the IRA '...were going to wait to see if the Unionists delivered their side of the bargain, and until then the IRA would hold the use of force in reserve' (Blair 2010: 189). David Trimble is one of the heroes of the peace process because he did not act as if the IRA had been defeated but as if the 'armed struggle' had reached 'deadlock'. This explains the UUP leader's courageous leadership in attempting to support the attempt of the Adams/McGuinness leadership to bring a united Republican movement into a peace process and reach accommodation. During his negotiation of the peace process the UUP leader did not claim that the IRA were defeated, 'Undoubtedly, the IRA were not winning. They could do damage but they could not "drive the British out".' By 2004, Trimble was still not convinced the IRA would make the transition to purely peaceful methods (Millar 2004: 62, 63–64; Dixon 2011: 656–657; 2012a: 315–316). If the IRA had been defeated then Trimble would have looked foolish for having made any 'concessions' to Sinn Féin. He argues that 'concern was real enough', 'about a serious split in the republican movement' and 'that decommissioning became the lightning-rod issue going forward'. Although the Republicans manipulated this concern to their advantage, Trimble was worried enough that he was prepared to enter an executive without decommissioning in December 1999. It was only with the benefit of hindsight that Trimble argued that the Real IRA split in 1997 was 'relatively modest in import' and that 'the Adams/McGuinness leadership was secure' (Trimble 2009: 90–91).

Neoconservatives have claimed that Danny Morrison, a leading Republican and confidante of Gerry Adams, illustrates their view that the IRA was 'defeated'. Morrison has confirmed that the IRA 'could fight on forever without necessarily winning' but that if it had escalated its campaign and was defeated it would not be able to negotiate. Morrison's concern seemed to be that if the IRA entered a peace process, 'People would have to feel that a settlement was just and that their opponents were making compromises also.' He could not see a weak IRA ever halting the campaign but Republicans could 'cash in the chips in return for substantial changes' (Alonso 2007: 158, 139; Morrison 1999: 235, 262, 277). If the IRA had been defeated, the peace process would have been about managing their surrender and few if any painful concessions, such as on decommissioning and reform of the police, would need to have been made.

Second, security force claims that the enemy has been defeated or is on the verge of defeat have been used as a rhetorical device to pressure politicians into adopting the military's prescriptions. The security forces claimed that the IRA was close to defeat in 1971–1972 and 1975–1976. This 'strategy of optimism' is traceable back to Robert Thompson in Vietnam and has been used to deflect responsibility for defeat from the military and onto politicians. It is also used to bolster arguments for greater resources and powers for the security forces in dealing with armed threats. The 'strategy of optimism' has recently been criticised because of its unrealistic claims that victory is just around the corner in Afghanistan (Dixon 2012c: 14–15, 96, 97).

Third, there is evidence that the peace process was emerging before the 1990s, when Neoconservatives claim that the IRA were defeated, indicating that the peace process emerged from a situation of stalemate rather than defeat. Republican Dissidents argue that the IRA was defeated any time from the mid-1970s until the early 1990s, but usually from the mid-1980s. There is strong evidence that Gerry Adams was beginning to seek a way out of the 'armed struggle' from the early to mid-1980s before the early 1990s when Neoconservatives claim the IRA was defeated. These developments included:

- Sinn Féin's shift to a more political and electoral path in 1981–1982;
- the Sinn Féin leadership beginning to look for a way out of the 'armed struggle' in 1982;
- the Anglo-Irish Agreement 1985;
- British contacts with Sinn Féin 1986;
- Sinn Féin's decision to end abstentionism to taking seats in the Irish parliament in 1986 and subsequent ideological developments;
- Irish Government contacts with Sinn Féin;
- SDLP/Sinn Féin talks 1988;
- Brooke's interview and speeches 1989 and 1990;
- the revival of the British Government/Sinn Féin back channel in 1990 and
- the end of the Cold War with its impact on British strategic calculations and US attitudes.

Fourth, the Republican movement has always been penetrated by informers. The IRA have adopted counter-measures and penetration has not prevented the IRA from running a highly effective military campaign. The British state did have some well-placed informers in the IRA but this needs to be set in the context of the history of the Republican movement's problems with informers *prior* to the early 1990s. Republicans had always been infiltrated and were always on their guard against betrayal. The IRA declared amnesties to reduce the threat of informers to their organisation and in the late 1970s reorganised into a cellular structure to inhibit penetration. By the early 1980s the IRA had been so penetrated that a member was as likely to be killed by his own organisation as they were by the British (McGladdery 2006: 58; *Observer* 24 July 2005). The 'Supergrass Trials' of the early 1980s may well have provided the security forces with further knowledge about the IRA. At least 450 people were charged on the basis of their evidence, and, according to Urban, the IRA leadership were brought 'close to panic' (Urban 2001: 135). On his release from jail in 1986 Brendan Hughes found the IRA 'riddled' with British spies but he also apparently believed that the IRA and the British could not defeat each other (Moloney 2010: 263, 261).

Fifth, there is a lack of contemporaneous evidence that the British Army or the RUC believed that the IRA had been defeated. The security forces (British Army, RUC and MI5) have an organisational interest in asserting that the IRA was defeated in order to bolster their reputation and power. General Sir James Glover's secret report on the IRA in 1978, frankly described the effectiveness of the IRA and doubted that the IRA would be defeated (*The Times* 6 June 2000). A 'Senior British Army Officer', believed to have been the General Officer Commanding Northern Ireland 1990–1993, General Sir John Wilsey, presented a 'depressingly realistic assessment of the IRA' in late 1991. He described the IRA as,

> better equipped, better resourced, better led, bolder and more secure against our penetration than at any time before.... They are an absolutely formidable enemy. The essential attributes of their leaders are better than ever before. Some of their operations are brilliant in terrorist terms.
>
> (*The Times* 11 January 1992)

After the IRA ceasefire in 1994, the military perceived the IRA and Republican Dissidents to be a serious threat and were critical of the British Government's attempts to 'demilitarise' Northern Ireland. A 'senior British security source' told *The Times* that the IRA's terrorist capability had increased 'significantly' since the Good Friday Agreement (*The Times* 11 February 2000). There is also contemporary evidence that senior officers in the RUC did not believe the IRA had been defeated and acknowledged the difficult task the Adams leadership had in bringing the Republican movement to political accommodation (Dixon 2008: 242–244). There appears to be little evidence that MI5 considered the IRA to have been defeated and plenty to the contrary. For example, Hollingsworth and Fielding find the IRA 'running rampant' between October 1992 and April 1993, planting more bombs than at any other time during the 20 years of hostilities (Hollingsworth and Fielding 2000: 4; Andrew 2010; Urban 1996).

Sixth, the IRA's bombing campaign during the 1990s suggested that the IRA was not so penetrated that it could not operate effectively. Although penetrated by informers, from 1989–1997 the IRA launched a bombing offensive against England. There were 204 bombings and seven shootings during this period resulting in the deaths of 11 civilians, 15 British Army and police personnel with 718 injured (McGladdery 2006: 229, 215–216). The IRA bombed: Downing Street (February 1991); the City of London (1992, 1993, 1996) and Manchester (1996). It is estimated that the bombings caused over £2 billion worth of damage and caused considerable concern in the City of London. In Northern Ireland, the

End of the IRA's 'armed struggle' 203

winding down of the violence between the British and the IRA, in the early 1990s, may well have been an effect of the emerging peace process, rather than signalling the defeat of the IRA. This was exemplified by the Derry initiative in the early 1990s, which led to the IRA and British Army making reciprocal gestures in order to build trust and wind down the conflict (Moloney 2002, chapter 13).

Afghanistan

Neoconservatives have attempted to capture the Northern Ireland case and use it to justify a hardline stance in the global debate against 'talking to terrorists' whether Hamas, Hezbollah, the 'Sunni' militias in Iraq, al Qaeda or the Taliban. The Neoconservative Henry Jackson Society published 'Succeeding in Afghanistan' (2010), which argued that negotiations with the Taliban could only take place from a position of strength. Since the Taliban believed that they were winning a properly resourced counterinsurgency strategy would need to be implemented to create the conditions for success (Grant 2010). This was coupled with an argument that there should be no talk of withdrawal dates and deadlines because this encourages the Taliban and undermines NATO. The war should be won and, it was claimed, the Taliban had no desire to negotiate (Cannon 2010). The designation of the Haqqani network, which is allied with the Taliban, as a 'terrorist' organisation by the US makes future US negotiations with the Haqqani illegal (*Guardian* 8 September 2012).

Neoconservatives explicitly draw on the 'lessons of Northern Ireland' to justify their highly sceptical position on negotiating with the Taliban over Afghanistan. John Bew and Martyn Frampton echoed this line in 'We Should Talk to the Taliban Only from a Position of Strength not Weakness' for *The Spectator* (27 July 2009). Northern Ireland, they argued, demonstrated that terrorists should be talked to only from a position of strength and not when terrorists are on 'the crest of a wave'. They supported a surge in Afghanistan and argued that talk of withdrawal sends the wrong message. The International Centre for the Study of Radicalisation and Political Violence (ICSR), based at Kings College London, published *Talking to the Taliban: Hope over History?* (2013) by John Bew, Ryan Evans, Martyn Frampton, Peter Neumann and Marisa Porges. The authors refer to Northern Ireland as part of 'a wealth of experiences from previous conflicts which echo the four lessons that we have identified based on the decade of failed engagement with the Taliban' (Bew *et al.* 2013: 51). These claims are based on the work of John Bew and Peter Neumann, both directors of the ICSR, and Martyn Frampton. The ICSR, it has been argued, are part of the nexus of institutions demonstrating '...that the organisational lines between academia and the military/government have been at minimum blurred, perhaps even erased altogether' (Miller and Mills 2010: 214).

Peter Neumann's *Britain's Long War: British Strategy in the Northern Ireland Conflict, 1969–98* (2003) argues that the IRA was 'defeated' because they did not win but implies that the British Government could have militarily defeated the IRA if it had chosen to in the early 1990s (Neumann 2003: 155, 157; elsewhere he seems to argue that there was a stalemate, Neumann 2007). Neumann argues that the Northern Irish peace process is the best example of how negotiations can be successfully conducted. But he declares that governments should only begin formal negotiations after the terrorist group has declared a permanent cessation of violence and 'terrorists agree to play by democratic rules' (Neumann 2007). The IRA's 1994 ceasefire was not permanent and even for some time after the Good Friday Agreement the IRA was allegedly involved in murder, so-called 'punishment beatings and shootings', gun-running, breaking into police stations, spying and robbery. Prime Minister Tony Blair confirms in his memoirs, '...we had to pretend this was an orderly and structured transition. So there were fudges, things said and done that had little intellectual or political consistency except that of seeing us through each set of obstacles' (Blair 2010: 189). The lessons of Northern Ireland for Iraq, according to Neumann, were that 'If the coalition wants to succeed in making Iraq a "beacon of democracy", its military campaign has to be determined by the principles of honesty, fairness, and – most importantly – perseverance' (Neumann 2004: 27).

The ICSR's *Talking to the Taliban* (2013) distilled four lessons from Northern Ireland for Afghanistan. These are so demanding that they rule out the prospect of success for negotiations (the subtitle '*Hope over History*' suggests a pessimistic view of the prospects for talks):

1 *Speak with one voice* – since there are always multiple partners in peace processes, often with conflicting interests if not also internal conflicts, this recommendation may well be unrealistic. Although the attempt to reach consensus may be useful.
2 *Make sure you have a clear strategic rationale* – to support this they claim that 'the talks process in Northern Ireland, which supporters of negotiations with the Taliban frequently reference, was a masterpiece in clarity and purpose...' (Bew *et al.* 2013: 51). This is misleading because, as has already been pointed out, the peace process was marked by a series of documents – not least the Good Friday Agreement itself – that were deliberately designed to be 'constructively ambiguous' so they could be presented in different ways to divergent audiences.
3 *Potential spoilers needs to be 'inside the tent'* – during the peace process anti-peace process Neoconservatives and Orthodox Neoconservatives were highly suspicious of Republicans and wanted to exclude them from the peace process. Republican dissidents are now potential spoilers but Neoconservatives do not want them 'inside the tent'.
4 *Recognise the needs of the 'silent majority'* – they argue for 'transparent' negotiations and securing a deal with armed groups has to be balanced 'by making sure it does not come at the expense of the fundamental interests and needs of the "silent majority"' (Bew *et al.* 2013: 52). The peace process in Northern Ireland was anything but transparent. The process was driven

by elites and deception was used because significant sections of the public, perhaps even a 'silent majority' during the referendum campaign on the Agreement in 1998, were opposed to many of the necessary compromises.

The report was highly sceptical of the success of any talks and regretted the shift from a more ambitious counterinsurgency strategy to 'defeat' the Taliban to a more limited counter-terrorism operation and withdrawal (*Daily Telegraph* 19 July 2013). President Obama had avoided use of the term 'defeat' in Afghanistan because it set the bar of success very high. Instead he rejected the victory/defeat goal to allow for a more flexible and, if necessary, modest strategy (Woodward 2010).

Conclusion

States tend to publicly oppose negotiating with terrorists. But if they do negotiate then they may want to claim that they are setting down 'clear red lines' and assert that they have not violated democratic norms. This is because states are concerned that negotiations, concessions and compromise with terrorist organisations give them legitimacy and encourage the belief that violence is an effective route to political change and undermines democracy.

Neoconservatives and realists may agree that the public presentation of a peace process should minimise the possible damage to 'democratic and human rights norms'. Where they differ, is that Neoconservatives claim to believe their own propaganda, accept the most hardline interpretation of the enemy's intentions and insist on the state adopting an intransigent position and pursuing a military victory, which is likely to scupper any prospect of a negotiated settlement. Realists, by contrast, recognise the contrast between the state's and 'enemy's' public, 'front stage', position in the 'propaganda war' and the possibilities for pragmatism and compromise that may exist 'behind the scenes' and which can be explored through 'contacts' with opponents. They will entertain the possibility that opposition leaders are operating under constraints and so may interpret their mixed messages in a more subtle and less hostile way.

Orthodox Neoconservatives favour military solutions to conflict and have attempted to claim that the lesson to be drawn from the Northern Ireland case is to 'nearly never talk to terrorists' unless they have been defeated. They claim that during the peace process the British Government tended to act with 'moral clarity' by managing the IRA's surrender and not compromising democratic norms.

The Neoconservatives' loudly proclaimed 'idealism' and 'moral clarity' disguises their own realist practice. In Northern Ireland they believed that it was military force and the 'dirty war', including serious violations of human rights, that was successful in bringing about the defeat of the IRA: the peace process was a consequence of that defeat and enabled the British Government to dictate terms to the IRA. Neoconservatives have been prepared to support non-state 'terrorists' whose aims they agree with (Contras, Cuban exiles, MEK in Iran) and have had an interesting symbiotic relationship with Republican Dissidents. Neoconservatives emphasise the threat from dissidents to justify unspecified and potentially counterproductive 'tougher' security measures to 'defeat' them. These would probably be privately welcomed by Republican Dissidents because of their potential to generate greater support for them.

There is little empirical support for the Orthodox Neoconservative position and, indeed, it contradicts other strands of Neoconservative thought. Orthodox Neoconservatives have simultaneously attempted to combine contradictory strands of Neoconservative thinking one of which claims the IRA are winning and the other that the IRA have lost. There is little evidence that the IRA was defeated and, therefore that 'dirty war' was effective, or that the peace process was conducted in the uncompromising way advocated by orthodox Neoconservatives. The Orthodox Neoconservative morality tale suggests that the ideal conduct of the British state produces ideal results, with bad behaviour producing bad results.

Those who insincerely support a peace process have used crude and essentialist interpretations of conflict, coupled with a pessimism about the inflexible nature of political opponents, to justify a hardline approach to talks that are likely to prevent negotiation and accommodation. Neoconservatives tend to over-moralise politics (seeing their moral position as the only appropriate one) and ignore the constraints that confront potential negotiating partners. They prefer to take at face value the 'evil', 'terrorist' leadership's most hardline statements and actions. A Neoconservative insistence that: terrorists are not talked to until they have been 'defeated'; on 'clear red lines' for negotiations, and a resolve that 'democratic norms' are not compromised would most likely have led to the failure of the Northern Ireland peace process. As Ian Lustick has pointed out in regard to the Middle East, a peace process should be strategic, dynamic and ambiguous in order to create the scope for politicians who are committed to the principles underlying the agreement to be flexible and manoeuvre against anti-peace process rivals (Lustick 1997: 61, 62).

Realists may argue that the state is fighting a propaganda war against terrorists and, therefore, should publicly oppose negotiating with terrorists. They may even argue that a peace process must be publicly presented in such a way so as to minimise the damage of compromise with terrorists to democratic norms. However, realists are more aware of the difficult circumstances in which peacemaking actually takes place and are more willing to make and defend the difficult moral compromises that may be necessary to achieve a peaceful accommodation. The dominant negotiating style during the peace process was not the fundamentalist, idealist stance of orthodox and anti-peace process Neoconservatism with its prescription of no compromise or no surrender. This would have made any peace process, let alone accommodation, problematic to say the least. David Trimble's pragmatic realist negotiating style reflected much more the dominant negotiating style of the pro-Agreement governments and parties that successfully reached accommodation. Paradoxically, the inaccurate claim that the IRA was defeated diminishes the prominent role of David Trimble by failing to acknowledge the difficult circumstances and calculations that he and others faced in negotiations. It was because the IRA had not, in any meaningful sense of the word, been 'defeated' that various actors were negotiating a morally difficult, compromise accommodation.

Political actors deployed various 'political skills or lying and manipulation' in order to reassure their supporters and voters while bringing them towards an accommodation (Dixon 2002). The Conservative Government did explore backstage contacts with Republicans while the IRA's violence continued and then deceived in order to cover this up. The Conservative then Labour Government's flexible approach to decommissioning illustrates their willingness to take a pragmatic approach to advancing the peace process. Initially decommissioning was to have taken place before even contacts between Sinn Féin and British officials. This position was salami sliced away so that IRA decommissioning did not take place until after prisoner releases had been completed and Sinn Féin were sitting in government. The Conservative Government accelerated the pace of the peace process after the IRA broke its ceasefire in February 1996. This prompted criticism that the governments had only moved in response to violence. Senior Labour figures publicly admitted that they deployed a pragmatic realism and even deception in driving the peace process forward which involved uncomfortable compromises with paramilitaries. Mo Mowlam acknowledged, 'Yes, it was an imperfect peace, but surely that is better than no peace at all?' (Mowlam 2002: 269) The British Prime Minister only recognised that 'constructive ambiguity' and deception had facilitated the peace process but that this had increasingly become an impediment (Mowlam 2002: 269; Blair 2010; Powell 2008). The Labour Government's pragmatic realist style during the peace process, however, can be contrasted with its attitude to counter-terrorism after 9/11 (Guelke 2007).

The realism of the British Government's and the UUP's approach helps to explain the appeal and success of the DUP's 'idealist' stance. Anti-peace process unionists and dissident Republicans did have a point when they criticised the deceptive means by which leading actors drove the peace process forward, although this loudly-proclaimed piety and idealism often concealed their own brutal and violent political practice. The DUP was an electorally successful party because it took advantage of this populist, anti-political view of 'politicians as liars', and used it to their electoral advantage. Once dominant, they shifted towards a more realist narrative to justify powersharing with Republicans.

The incoherence of Neoconservative accounts of the peace process is not difficult to demonstrate. The problem is that Neoconservatives are part of powerful networks – comprising politicians, businesses, 'think-tanks' and academics – that attempt to shape perceptions and 'create their own reality' by persuading the world that their account of reality is true.

Note

1 I am very grateful to the editors for their feedback on this chapter. I, alone, am responsible for the arguments expressed.

References

Alonso, R. (2007) *The IRA and Armed Struggle* (Abingdon: Routledge).
Ancram, Michael (2007) 'Dancing with Wolves: the Importance of Talking to Your Enemies', *Middle East Policy*, XIV, (2), Summer.
Andrew, Christopher (2010) *The Defence of the Realm: The Authorized History of MI5* (London: Penguin).
Bew, J., Frampton, M. and Gurruchaga, I. (2009) *Talking to Terrorists: Making Peace in Northern Ireland and the Basque Country* (London: Hurst).
Bew, J., Evans, R., Frampton, M., Neumann, P. and Porges, M. (2013) *Talking to the Taliban: Hope over History?* (London: The International Centre for the Study of Radicalisation and Political Violence (ICSR) at Kings College).
Blair, Tony (2010) *A Journey* (London: Hutchinson).
Cannon, Peter John (2010) 'Afghanistan on a knife edge', Henry Jackson Society, 23 July.
Cooper, D. (2010) *Neoconservatism and American Foreign Policy: A Critical Analysis* (London: Routledge).
Dixon, P. (2001) 'British Policy towards Northern Ireland 1969–2000: Continuity, Tactical Adjustment and Consistent "Inconsistencies"', *British Journal of Politics and International Relations*, 3, 3.
Dixon, P. (2002) 'Political Skills or Lying and Manipulation? The Choreography of the Northern Ireland Peace Process', *Political Studies*, 50, 3.
Dixon, P. (2004) '"Peace Within the Realms of the Possible?" David Trimble, Unionist Ideology and Theatrical Politics', *Terrorism and Political Violence*, 16 (3).
Dixon, P. (2008) *Northern Ireland: The Politics of War and Peace* (Basingstoke: Palgrave, 2nd edn).
Dixon, Paul (2011) 'Guns First, Talks Later: Neoconservatives and the Northern Ireland Peace Process', *Journal of Imperial and Commonwealth History*, 39, 4.
Dixon, Paul (2012a) 'Was the IRA defeated? Neoconservative Propaganda as History' *Journal of Imperial and Commonwealth History*, 40.
Dixon, P. (2012b) 'Beyond Hearts and Minds: Perspectives on British Counterinsurgency', in P. Dixon (ed.) *The British Approach to Counterinsurgency: From Malaya and Northern Ireland to Iraq and Afghanistan* (Basingstoke: Palgrave Macmillan).
Duyvesteyn, I. and Bart Schuurman (2011) 'The Paradoxes of Negotiating with Terrorist and Insurgent Organisations', *Journal of Imperial and Commonwealth History*, 39, 4.
Fitzgerald, Garret (2008) 'Powell wrong about talking in the midst of terror campaign', *Irish Times*, 29 March.
Frampton, Martyn (2008) 'Agents and Ambushes: Britain's "Dirty War" in Northern Ireland' in S. Cohen (ed.) *Democracies at War Against Terrorism: A Comparative Perspective* (Basingstoke: Palgrave).
Frampton, Martyn (2009) *The Long March: The Political Strategy of Sinn Féin, 1981–2007* (Basingstoke: Palgrave).
Frampton, Martyn and John Bew (2009) 'We should talk to the Taliban only from a position of strength not of weakness', *The Spectator* Blog, 27 July, available at: http://blogs.spectator.co.uk/coffeehouse/2009/07/we-should-talk-to-the-taliban-only-from-a-position-of-strength-not-weakness/
Gove, Michael (2004) 'The very British roots of Neoconservatism and its lessons for British Conservatives' in Irwin Stelzer (ed.) *The Neocon Reader* (New York: Grove Press).
Grant, George (2010) 'Succeeding in Afghanistan' (London: Henry Jackson Society).
Gross, J. (2011) 'Proscription Problems: The Practical Implications of Terrorist Lists on Diplomacy and Peacebuilding in Nepal', *Praxis: The Fletcher Journal of Human Security*, 26.

Guelke, Adrian (2007) 'The Northern Ireland Peace Process and the War against Terrorism: Conflicting Conceptions?' *Government and Opposition*, 47, 2.

Hollingsworth, Mark and Nick Fielding (2000) *Defending the Realm: MI5 and the Shayler Affair* (London, Andre Deutsch).

Jackson, R., Jarvis, L., Gunning, J. and Smyth, M. (2011) *Terrorism: A Critical Introduction* (Basingstoke: Palgrave).

Kampfner, J. (2003) 'The British Neocons', *New Statesman*, 12 May.

Kennedy, Paul (2010) 'A Time to Appease', *The National Interest*, July/August.

Kristol, I (1997) 'Conflicts That Can't Be Resolved', *Wall Street Journal*, 5 September.

Lustick, Ian (1977) 'The Oslo Peace Process as an Obstacle to Peace', *Journal of Palestine Studies*, vol. 27, no. 1.

Major, J. (1999) *John Major: The Autobiography* (London: HarperCollins).

McGladdery, G. (2006) *The Provisional IRA in England: The Bombing Campaign 1973–1997* (Dublin: Irish Academic Press).

Millar, F. (2004) *The Price of Peace* (Dublin: The Liffey Press).

Miller, D. and Mills, T. (2010) 'Counterinsurgency and terror expertise: the integration of social scientists into the war effort', *Cambridge Review of International Affairs*, 23, 2.

Moloney, Ed (2002) *A Secret History of the IRA* (London: Penguin).

Moloney, Ed (2010) *Voices from the Grave* (London: Faber).

Mowlam, Mo (2002) *Momentum The Struggle for Peace, Politics and the People* (London: Hodder and Stoughton).

Morrison, D. (1999), *Then the walls came down: A Prison Journal* (Cork: Mercier Press).

Murray, Douglas (2006) *Neoconservatism: Why We Need It* (New York: Encounter Books).

Neumann, Peter (2003) *Britain's Long War: British Strategy in the Northern Ireland Conflict, 1969–9* (Basingstoke: Palgrave).

Neumann, Peter (2004) 'Iraq: Lessons from Northern Ireland', *History Today*, 54, 2, February.

Neumann, Peter (2007) 'Negotiating with Terrorists', *Foreign Affairs*, 86, 1.

Powell, J. (2008) *Great Hatred, Little Room: Making Peace in Northern Ireland* (London: The Bodley Head).

Reiss, Mitchell (2010) *Negotiating with Evil: When to Talk to Terrorists* (New York: Open Road).

Ross, Dennis and Makovsky, David (2010) *Myths, Illusions, and Peace: Finding a New Direction for American in the Middle East* (New York: Penguin).

Schmitt, Gary (2009) 'Peace, It's Wonderful: But Winning it is Hard Work', *Weekly Standard*, 14, 45.

Simcox, Robin (2011) 'David Cameron's Bad History', *Weekly Standard*, 14 March.

Toros, Harmonie (2008) 'We Don't Negotiate with Terrorists!': Legitimacy and Complexity in Terrorist Conflicts', *Security Dialogue*, 39, 4.

Trimble, D. (2009) 'Belfast Talk' *American Interest*, November/December.

Urban, M. (1996) *UK Eyes Alpha: The Inside Story of British Intelligence* (London: Faber).

Urban, M. (2001) *Big Boys Rules: the Bestselling Story of the SAS and the Secret Struggle against the IRA* (London: Faber).

Vaisse, Justin (2010) *Neoconservatism: The Biography of a Movement* (London: The Belknap Press).

Woodward, B. (2010) *Obama's War* (London: Simon and Schuster).

11 From counter-terrorism to soft-authoritarianism
The case of Sri Lanka

Neil DeVotta

Introduction

When Sri Lanka gained independence in 1948 it was considered a model colony that had a great chance of becoming a postcolonial success story. The island had been granted universal franchise in 1931 and, notwithstanding ethnic differences, Sinhalese and Tamils elites from the majority and minority communities, respectively, had banded together to successfully negotiate independence from the British. Yet within eight years Sinhalese elites resorted to linguistic and religious nationalism, which exacerbated relations between the groups, and gradually led to civil war (DeVotta 2004).

Civil wars justify counter-terror practices, and the longer the conflict the more draconian these practices can become. While authoritarian states experiencing civil wars may resort to crackdowns without much constraint –because the populace has little say in how policy gets conducted in such states – democratic states can gradually embrace and justify similarly brutal counter-terror strategies the longer the conflict lasts. The upshot is that ethnic conflicts end up compromising democracy and over the long term can lead to authoritarianism (Horowitz 1993). Sri Lanka represents such a case.

The country was a commendable democracy in its first decade following independence. Pro-Sinhalese ethnocentric policies slowly but surely pushed it into an illiberal orbit. The extrajudicial and extraconstitutional methods that were adopted to end the civil war in turn have made it easier for the current Mahinda Rajapaksa administration to institute authoritarian practices that have caused democracy to become further compromised. In short, Sri Lanka has regressed from liberal democracy to illiberal democracy to soft-authoritarianism, and the ethnic conflict and attendant counter-terror strategies are a major reason for this democratic deficit. The continued militarisation, notwithstanding the civil war having ended in 2009, and the Rajapaksa family's determination to create a political dynasty suggest that this democratic erosion is likely to continue.

Soft-authoritarianism here refers to a regime that manipulates features of democracy to maintain legitimacy even as it operates in illiberal ways, thereby undermining democratic institutions and the rule of law, so as to perpetuate power. Unlike 'hard authoritarian' states that get ruled by *diktat* (Illarionov

2009), soft authoritarian regimes blend aspects of electoral democracy with authoritarianism. Typically, these are regimes that craftily design electoral competition to suggest opposition forces can come to power but rig the system to ensure their defeat (Way and Levitsky 2010; Diamond 2008).

The argument made here is that the counter-terror strategies Sri Lanka's civil war justified have in turn contributed to the current soft-authoritarian dispensation. The literature on exceptionalism provides a basis for situating this argument theoretically. Exceptionalism refers to how a country or society can undergo an 'exceptional' period of crisis or transformation that makes institutionalised norms, rules, and laws irrelevant. It is a milieu that is conducive to superimposing radical change that established social orders may otherwise oppose. For instance, exceptionalism can easily foist illiberal policies on even liberal societies by utilising arguments concerning security, territoriality and sovereignty. Thus the 'war on terror' following the terrorist attacks on 9/11 allowed the Bush Administration to justify detention sites like Guantanamo Bay and Abu Ghraib and illiberal practices such as extraordinary rendition and mass surveillance as exceptions to extant norms (Neal 2006: 31; Aradau and Van Munster 2009: 688). The exceptions can be instituted via extrajudicial and extra-constitutional means or by simply creating new laws that overturn extant laws (Ericson 2007). Good laws are thus easily defenestrated by bad laws utilising arguments about crises and exceptional times. With the state bearing primary responsibility for ensuring security and sovereignty, such bad laws are easily legitimated and institutionalised. When this takes place in relatively democratised societies, the inevitable result is a move toward illiberalism and democratic erosion.

Exceptionalism is rooted in fear and insecurity, promotes superordination/inclusion and subordination/exclusion in societal relations, and predisposes people to violence (Huysmans 2006). In countries where ethnic contestation is rife, it is easy for those controlling the levers of state power to manipulate exceptionalism and subjugate legitimate opposition (be it ethnic or ideological nemeses). This is because ethnic civil wars enable opponents to be demonised and trivialised by portraying them as racist, rapacious, predatory, outsiders, and traitorous. The subsequent us/sons-of-the-soil versus them/interlopers mentality in turn sets up a narrative that can be mined to institute exceptional policies – ethnic or otherwise. Sri Lanka's trajectory of democratic erosion is a classic example of such exceptionalism.

Exceptionalism is also concerned with how illiberalism leads to authoritarianism – especially when untrammeled executive power undermines the rule of law (Huysmans 2008: 167). In this regard, too, Sri Lanka stands out. Indeed, the exceptionalism that undergirded the island's ethnocentric and counter-terror policies is part of the same narrative and logic that are being used now to legitimise soft-authoritarian politics.

The essay's first section provides a brief overview of how Sri Lanka's civil war evolved. It thereafter evaluates the strategies that the Sri Lankan Government under President Mahinda Rajapaksa adopted to defeat the LTTE, while the third section discusses how many of these strategies continue to be used as part of the government's attempt to perpetuate its power. In short, Sri Lanka vanquished the LTTE and reaped a democratic deficit. And all indications suggest that this democratic deficit is deepening under Rajapaksa family rule. The essay concludes by arguing that the triumphalism following the defeat of the LTTE among most Sri Lankans is misplaced since the military victory that unleashed such triumphalism has also enabled the current climate of repression. While the literature makes it debatable whether civil wars definitively contribute to authoritarianism (Fortna and Huang 2012), in Sri Lanka's experience it is indisputable that the island's civil war has indeed contributed to authoritarianism.

Overview of Sri Lanka's civil war

Most consider Sri Lanka's civil war to have begun in 1983, after the anti-Tamil pogrom in July that year convinced many Tamils that seceding from the island and setting up their own state in the predominantly Tamil northeast was their best option. The pogrom itself was sparked when a Tamil rebel group, the Liberation Tigers of Tamil Eelam (LTTE), ambushed an army patrol and killed 13 soldiers, whose remains when brought to Colombo caused enraged Sinhalese mobs to attack Tamils and their homes and businesses. The mobs, some which used electoral lists to target Tamils, were encouraged by politicians from the ruling United National Party (UNP), certain members of the military, and some among the Buddhist clergy.

One can point to multiple influences that contributed to Sinhalese-Tamil animus that led to the civil war. British attempts at dividing and ruling, which led to the minority Tamils being overrepresented and empowered within the state bureaucracy, and the British colonial regime backtracking on its promises to protect and foster the majority community's Buddhist religion, which typically depended on some state subventions, even as it tolerated and promoted proselytism certainly contributed to Sinhalese Buddhist hostility. Tamil demands for equal representation between all minorities and the majority Sinhalese in the pre-independence legislature also caused ethnic tension. The passage of the Sinhala Only Act of 1956 and the manner in which the island's two main political parties, the UNP and Sri Lanka Freedom Party (SLFP), thereafter went about trying to outbid each other on who could best protect Sinhalese interests at the expense of the Tamils not only led to anti-Tamil riots but also sundered the possibility for peaceful ethnic coexistence (Horowitz 1985; DeVotta 2004).

The ensuing tensions led to the army being deployed in the predominantly Tamil Northern Province starting in 1961, a development that most Tamils associated with military occupation. The ham-handed manner in which some army personnel interacted with Tamils during this time hardly endeared the military to Tamil civilians. Such tension only increased as the relatively polyethnic armed forces became a mainly Sinhalese Buddhist armed force – given the state's calibrated attempts to hire mainly Sinhalese Buddhists into the military and bureaucracy. This combined with successive governments' other manifold ethnocentric policies only hardened Tamil opinion against the government.[1] Over time, marginalised and disempowered Tamil youth especially began clamoring for a separate state (*eelam*) and their rise came at the expense of moderate Tamil politicians. The various separatist youth groups may have numbered over 40 at its high point, but the LTTE eventually ruthlessly eliminated and co-opted all groups so as to become the face of Tamil separatism and the sole representative of Sri Lankan Tamils (Wilson 2000).

The military stationed in the Northern Province at this time did not have to design counter-terror strategies since there was no terrorism to counter. This more or less was the situation well into the 1970s, despite Tamil groups robbing banks to purchase weapons and attacking police stations. The distinction between (counter)insurgency and (counter-)terrorism is useful in this context, given that the Tamil rebellion until the early 1980s was more of an insurgency. While insurgencies and terrorism both involve violence and while governments are eager to equate insurgencies with terrorism, insurgencies tend to usually be associated with nationalist movements while terrorism tends to be transnational in nature (Boyle 2010). Thus counterinsurgency strategies often seek to win the 'hearts and minds' of the populace so as to vitiate support for insurgencies even as the state seeks to neutralise the insurgents, whereas counter-terror strategies mainly focus on 'offensive measures' geared toward eliminating terrorists (ibid. 342). Confusion tends to ensue when terrorists and insurgents band together for ideological or opportunistic reasons, as has been the case in especially Afghanistan (Kilcullen 2009).

In Sri Lanka's case, the LTTE ambush in July 1983 was the largest assault against the Sri Lankan military up to that point in time, and it signalled an escalation in the quest for *eelam*. The anti-Tamil pogrom that followed likewise convinced many Tamils that separatism was the only solution to the Tamils' plight, which is why thousands of Tamil youth living and working amidst Sinhalese in the south fled to the northeast determined to fight for *eelam*. The Sri Lankan government had passed the Prevention of Terrorism Act of 1979, although it is debatable if the Tamil rebels deserved the label at the time. This changed by the mid 1980s when the thousands of Tamils who fled abroad following the 1983 pogrom formed a potent diaspora that financially contributed towards and lobbied their host countries for *eelam*, the rebels extended their operations especially into India and the Indians (who were experiencing tense relations with the Sri Lankan government over the latter's pro-Western policies) clandestinely supported the rebels so as to destabilise Sri Lanka, and the LTTE adopted tactics like suicide bombing and mass killings in their fight against the island's military.

The Prevention of Terrorism Act had permitted the security forces to arrest, imprison and leave incommunicado without access to a lawyer anyone thought to be connected to separatism, and this led to thousands of Tamils being caught in its dragnet. The torture many endured only made them hell-bent to secede. Consequently, the mid 1980s saw rampant violence on both sides. When Tamil militants attacked innocent Sinhalese villages in border areas, military personnel likewise retaliated against Tamil civilians (Swamy 1994). The tit-for-tat attacks led to hundreds of innocent Sinhalese and Tamils being killed. The Northern Province soon became a no-go zone for civilians in the south and army checkpoints and high security zones (HSZ) soon proliferated across the northeast.

A second brutal uprising between 1988 and 1990 by the Janatha Vimukthi Peramuna (People's Liberation Front, JVP),[2] a Sinhalese outfit that sought to topple the government, led to government-sponsored paramilitary groups killings thousands of JVP cadre and supporters even as the Indian Peace Keeping Force (IPKF), which India superimposed on Sri Lanka as part of the 1987 Indo-Lanka Accord to end the island's ethnic conflict, battled the LTTE in the northeast. While the Sri Lankan government almost wiped out the JVP, the IPKF withdrew after having fought India's longest war. A bloodied LTTE nevertheless emerged as a force to be recognised and thereafter became the sole representative of the Tamils. Thanks to monies raised voluntarily and forcibly among the Tamil diaspora, the LTTE quickly built a conventional armed force and sea wing, which helped with smuggling weapons and transporting cadre. During its final years the group also created a crude air wing.

The LTTE's ruthless nature, which partly manifested itself in suicide terrorism, helped justify a culture of impunity within the military, and this led to some among the military raping, torturing, disappearing and killing Tamils who were not even connected to the LTTE. In this context, it is debatable if the Sri Lankan military ever seriously pursued a counterinsurgency strategy, because while Sri Lanka's military stationed in the northeast operated, in the main, within the rule of law until the civil war broke out, their main goal was to pacify Tamils, not win them over.

Indeed, with Sinhalese Buddhist ethnocentrism well embedded by the time the LTTE reigned supreme among Tamil separatists, it was second nature for the mainly Sinhalese Buddhist military to lord over Tamils. If anything, except for the well-known anti-LTTE Tamils that were allied with the government, all Tamils were automatically suspected of being pro-LTTE. Thus one could argue that much of the abuse that was heaped on Tamils especially in the northeast post-1983 was part of a counter-terror policy – even if that was not articulated as such at the highest levels of the military (Whitaker 2007).

Peace talks ensued at various points during the civil war but failed to take hold because the LTTE's leader Velupillai Prabhakaran was only interested in separatism and the Sri Lankan Government failed to institute meaningful devolution that will have allowed Tamils to operate in the northeast with sufficient autonomy. The island's civil war endured in this fashion until the SLFP's Mahinda Rajapaksa won the presidency in November 2005 and the government soon thereafter decided it would fight the LTTE to the finish irrespective of what it cost in lives and money.

This chapter seeks to analyse how the Mahinda Rajapaksa Government went about defeating a foe that most experts determined could not be eliminated militarily and how the mechanisms used to do so continue to influence the island's politics in the post-war era. After all, the LTTE fought the Indian army – to this day the longest war the Indians have waged – and not just survived but came out

From counter-terrorism to soft authoritarianism 215

on top; for in the end it was the Indians who retreated. The group thereafter consolidated its status by creating a conventional army, navy and (eventually) crude air force. Its diaspora supporters were so sophisticated and widespread that the group often operated like a multinational entity. Yet within three years of the final phase of the civil war that began in July 2006, the LTTE was militarily wiped out.

Counter-terror strategies typically come at the expense of citizens' individual liberties, and Sri Lanka was no exception. Sri Lankans in general and the Sinhalese Buddhist majority specifically tolerated successive governments' extrajudicial and extraconstitutional malpractices because they felt they were necessary to defeat the terrorist threat the LTTE represented. In any case, such malpractices hardly affected the majority Sinhalese Buddhist community, since the troubling practices were mainly directed at Tamils who were considered sympathetic toward the LTTE's separatist quest. But the culture of impunity that these malpractices instituted became ingrained and post-civil war it continues unabated. Indeed, the very forces that were used to defeat terrorism and the tactics employed as part of the state's counter-terrorism strategy are now being channelled to institute a soft-authoritarian dispensation designed to create a Rajapaksa dynasty. From that standpoint, the end of Sri Lanka's civil war has not brought about a more peaceful era. On the contrary, it has led to a climate where democracy has been severely compromised and authoritarianism, sustained using the very mechanisms that were utilised to defeat the LTTE, is on the ascendant.

Counter-terrorism and the LTTE's defeat

Sri Lanka's civil war had reached a stalemate by the time the Mahinda Rajapaksa government came to power. A Norwegian peace process had halted fighting between the combatants even as Sinhalese Buddhist nationalists especially vilified the Norwegians for being partial toward the LTTE. The LTTE had continued to rearm and recruit during the ceasefire, which it had done during prior ceasefires as well, and the group continued assassinating intelligence personnel and Tamils suspected of collaborating with the government and military. All concerned believed that LTTE leader Velupillai Prabhakaran was fanatically committed toward securing a separate state and that it was a matter of time before the conflict recrudesced. Consequently, the new government quietly went about recruiting and training soldiers even as it began procuring weapons from various countries. The new Secretary of Defense Gotabhaya Rajapaksa, who is the president's brother, and the then Army Commander Sarath Fonseka both played crucial roles in this regard. Their determination to wipe out the LTTE was sealed after the group tried and failed to assassinate Sarath Fonseka and Gotabhaya Rajapaksa in April and December 2006, respectively.

It is possible to note five overarching strategies that the government embraced to defeat the LTTE (DeVotta 2009). First, the military indiscriminately bombed suspected LTTE locations without regard to noncombatant casualties. In short, it refused to differentiate strictly between LTTE combatants and Tamil civilians. The policy apparently was to create as much carnage among all those associated with the LTTE. After adopting conventional capabilities the LTTE had forced civilians to march with it whenever retreating – since this allowed for a steady source of recruitment and labor; permitted its cadres to mingle among civilians and use them as human shields; helped the group create and superintend institutions affecting the populace, which made it easy to propagandise a de facto state; and forced the international community to focus on the Tamils' plight. The LTTE's ability to operate among the population helped legitimate its claim that it was fighting to protect the lives and rights of the Tamils, and this had restricted prior governments from targeting certain LTTE areas. Not so the Rajapaksa Government.

As LTTE areas shrank, the military ceaselessly bombed rebel positions. The Sri Lankan Government had forced most NGOs and media to leave LTTE areas by cancelling visas and refusing to renew their mandates before the last phase of the war. The goal was to ensure that the final phase of the war took place without independent observers. Despite such independent entities barred from the war zone, human rights organisations – thanks to some access to the conflict area and video footage from the LTTE's media outlets and Tamils trapped within the conflict area – came up with sufficient evidence to accuse the Sri Lankan military of perpetrating war crimes. Despite claiming that no human rights violations were committed when defeating the LTTE, the Sri Lankan government categorically refused independent monitors access to the battle zone for extended periods of time following the war, suggesting there may have been much it wanted concealed. Indeed, the evidence suggests that the military deliberately targeted civilians and hospitals within the very no-fire zones the government itself designated so as to inflict maximum casualties (Weiss 2011; U.S. Department of State 2009). The bombing of LTTE areas without regard to collateral damage has led to claims that between 40,000 and 70,000 civilians were killed during the final phase of the war.

Second, the indiscriminate counter-terrorism policy was extended to target Tamils in other ways throughout the island. For example, killer squads operating from white vans systematically eliminated those suspected of sympathising with the LTTE or considered potential recruits. According to the United Nations Working Group on Enforced and Involuntary Disappearances, more people 'disappeared' in Sri Lanka in 2006 and 2007 than in any other country (Nanjappa 2008). While the government denied being involved in the disappearances, in some instances those who were abducted from white vans were thereafter located within the precincts of the Terrorist Investigation Division and Criminal Investigation Division. Being abducted in this fashion became so common that Sri Lankans began referring to those who had disappeared as being 'white vanned'. The Sinhalese population tolerated this activity because those mainly targeted were Tamils and because people felt such draconian practices were necessary to eradicate LTTE spies living in Colombo and the island's south.

This state-sanctioned practice of terrorising Tamils who were nearly all automatically considered LTTE sympathisers allowed security personnel and paramilitary groups, including anti-LTTE Tamil militants, to operate amid a culture of utter impunity – extorting, raping, disappearing and murdering with abandon (Human Rights Watch 2008; U.S. Department of State 2008). Tamils evidencing leadership abilities, especially in the northeast, were also systematically assassinated (University Teachers for Human Rights(a) 2007). In the northern city of Jaffna, military and paramilitary forces resorted to 'routine shooting safari[s] on motorbikes' in broad daylight (University Teachers for Human Rights(b) 2007). Such repression, coupled with omnipresent checkpoints, cowed the Tamil populace and circumscribed their movements, making it easier for the government to control them. This also affected the LTTE's mobility, which explains the absence of suicide bombings in the south during the latter stage of the conflict.

Third, the government sought to muzzle the media by cracking down on outlets that criticised its malpractices or reported on military casualties. This took place even as the state owned media and the newly-created Media Center for National Security conducted an effective propaganda campaign that inflated LTTE battle deaths and underreported military casualties so as to maintain soldiers' morale and public support for the war. Associated with this was a policy that brutally attacked media that reported on corruption related to military procurement or violations pertaining to human rights. The message sent out was that those who criticised the military were traitors, while those who supported it were patriots. The public was encouraged to fete war heroes, which led to roads being named after them (including in the northeast where some of these soldiers perished) and schools and temples honoring them. This war hero culture led to military personnel also being featured on posters, cutouts, streamers and television, with even private channels being pressured to screen pro-military music videos and teledramas. Operating in tandem with the traitor-patriot narrative, it also caused fearful journalists and their media to resort to self-censorship. With the president being the Minister of Defense and his brother being the Secretary of Defense, critiquing them (and the Rajapaksa family in general) also became off limits.

Consequently, many journalists who critiqued aspects of the war or questioned the military's and government's narrative regarding the war were branded traitors; some were given death threats; others were assaulted, kidnapped, or imprisoned on false charges; or murdered. According to the island's Free Media Movement, between November 2005 (when Mahinda Rajapaksa became president) and June 2008 alone over 100 journalists were attacked and over two dozen forced to flee abroad (Mallawarachi 2008). Amnesty International also reported that 14 media persons were killed between 2006 and mid 2009 (Amnesty International 2009). The threats and harassment against journalists were so severe that many stopped reporting or succumbed to self-censorship, all of which caused the international organisation Reporters Without Borders to rank Sri Lanka as the most dangerous democracy for journalists in 2008. State-sponsored propaganda combined with the brutal media crackdown was so successful that most Sri Lankans did not know the full extent of the carnage that

Tamil civilians experienced as the war ended. That in turn made it easier for the government to sell the notion that subsequent allegations of war crimes were part of a Western conspiracy to undermine Sri Lanka, Buddhism, the Sinhalese and the military.

Fourth, the military set up a number of guerrilla units that targeted LTTE commanders even as small infantry units attacked LTTE positions using multi-pronged artillery assaults and air raids, which forced the LTTE to defend its territory on multiple fronts. On past occasions the military had been forced to spread thin following the capture of LTTE-controlled territory, which allowed the rebels to reorganise and retake lost lands. This time around the military recruited aggressively, adding nearly 3,000 soldiers every month, and ensured there were sufficient personnel to retain captured LTTE-controlled territory. This forced the rebels to operate in a continually circumscribed space and made it easier for the military to target LTTE forces and Tamil civilians.

Fifth, notwithstanding international pressure, the Rajapaksa government opposed international investigations into human rights violations during its counter-terrorism operations. It argued that such probes infringed on the country's sovereignty. Officials characterised those calling for investigations or ceasefires as foreign busybodies, minions of neocolonial powers set on discrediting Sri Lanka, part of a Western and UN conspiracy to brand the island a 'failed state', and LTTE stooges. This put pressure on the government's critics and purchased sufficient time for the military to wrap up the war in a comprehensive manner.

The LTTE accepted defeat on May 17 2009. Prabhakaran's body was presented to the media two days later. Sri Lanka's long-standing war ended in a complete victory for the government despite many local and foreign experts saying the LTTE were too formidable to be defeated.

The Sri Lankan military has since held a number of seminars for foreign military officials on how to defeat terrorism; and the government often retaliates against charges of human rights violations by claiming that countries like the United States that have been overly critical of it but have failed to defeat terrorists in Iraq and Afghanistan should stop vilifying Sri Lanka's military and instead take tuition from its armed forces. It is clear, however, that no democratic society with a functioning media and a moral aversion to vicarious punishment could replicate Sri Lanka's success in defeating terrorism.

The understandable triumphalism that followed the LTTE's defeat also saw President Rajapaksa being proclaimed the country's savior. Some suggested he ought to be crowned king. Indeed, soon after the war ended the president's brother Basil Rajapaksa bragged that 'an era of "ruler kings" has begun' (*The Economist* 2010: 49). It appears that way given how the Rajapaksa family has consolidated its power within the country. It has done so by not merely banking on the defeat of the LTTE, but by perfecting the extraconstitutional and extrajudicial practices it used to defeat the LTTE.

The next section elaborates on how the civil war's end has catapulted the island toward a soft-authoritarian dispensation. It does so by evaluating how the island's First Family dominates politics partly by undermining checks and balances, the ways in which the country is being militarised (more so than it was during the civil war), and the continuing assault on civil society and media.

The turn to soft-authoritarianism

If the manner in which the LTTE unravelled was unprecedented, so has the manner in which the Rajapaksa family has arrogated power (especially) since the civil war ended. On the one hand, South Asia is noted for its political families, with Sri Lanka's Bandaranaikes – S.W.R.D. Bandaranaike, Sirimavo Bandaranaike, and Chandrika Bandaranaike Kumaratunga – having led the region in making political dynasties fashionable. On the other hand, no family –dynasty or otherwise – has asserted so much control in so little time as the Rajapaksas. While Mahinda Rajapaksa's uncle and father laid the foundation for his own long rise, the president's siblings and extended family are so fully involved in the country's affairs that governance in Sri Lanka is now synonymous with family rule. This is best illustrated by looking at how the Rajapaksa family dominates Sri Lanka's politics.

The First Family

President Rajapaksa is also the Minister of Defense and Urban Development, Finance and Planning, Ports and Highways, and Law and Order, which places approximately 78 government institutions under his direct control.

Basil Rajapaksa, his brother, is Minister of Economic Development, which includes the Board of Investment and the Tourist Promotion Bureau. Basil is also chairman of the Presidential Task Force, thus controlling all development in the Northern Province. Furthermore, Basil now heads the recently created *Divinegume* (Improving Lives) Department, which combined three entities providing development aid to low income households and which was the reason behind the president ordering the first woman chief justice impeached (see below).

Their brother Gotabhaya is the Defense Secretary in charge of the armed forces, police and coast guard. He also oversees immigration and emigration, the Land Reclamation and Development Corporation, and the Urban Development Authority. These three brothers among them control nearly 100 government departments that account for between 60–70 per cent of the budget.

Another brother, Chamal, is Speaker of Parliament. With the government having bribed and cajoled members of the opposition into joining its side and, consequently, enjoying a two-thirds majority, he ensures that the First Family's wishes hold sway within the legislature.

The president's 27-year-old son Namal and two cousins are also members of Parliament, while nearly 130 relatives occupy prominent government posts. The Rajapaksas want to perpetuate their rule by hook or by crook and create a family dynasty. And notwithstanding disagreements within the family, Namal is being groomed to succeed the president.

No development since the end of the civil war has highlighted Sri Lanka's democratic regression, its current authoritarian trajectory, and the Rajapaksas' determination to perpetuate their power and try to build a political dynasty than the passing of the 18th Amendment to the constitution in September 2010. The 18th Amendment abolished presidential term limits, which allows President Rajapaksa to run for office for a third term (in or before November 2016). More troubling, it effectively nullified the 17th Amendment, which Parliament passed unanimously in 2001.

Although not fully enforced, the 17th Amendment was drafted by the Organization of Professional Associations and created an independent 10-person Constitutional Council (including three members from minority communities) with sole powers to appoint and dismiss commissioners superintending elections, police, public services, finance, human rights, and bribery and corruption. The Constitutional Council's permission was also required to appoint the chief justice and other justices on the Supreme Court, president and judges of the Court of Appeal, members of the Judicial Services Commission (excepting its chairman), attorney general, inspector general of police, auditor general, parliamentary commissioner for administration (or ombudsman), and secretary general of Parliament.

The 18th Amendment abolished the Constitutional Council and now allows the president to appoint persons to all the above offices after merely taking into consideration 'observations' from the prime minister, speaker and leader of the opposition. With the prime minister handpicked by the president (and with both his brothers Basil and Gotabya Rajapaksa often mentioned as likely candidates for the post), his brother (Chamal Rajapaksa) as speaker, a thoroughly demoralised opposition, and a two-thirds majority in a supine governing coalition, there is arguably no elected leader in the world who enjoys such untrammelled powers as does President Rajapaksa.

One major way soft authoritarian leaders ensure a veneer of democracy is by maintaining a defanged opposition (which they use as ineffective competition and to legitimise their rule). Mahinda Rajapaksa has been a maestro at doing so. Consequently, nearly every party in the opposition is now weak and divided, with the president playing a major role in ensuring such division. It is legal for parliamentarians elected through one party to cross over to another party and still keep their seats, and the government has bribed and coerced numerous politicians in the opposition to join its ranks by providing them ministerial portfolios or threatening legal action over real and manufactured violations. All this has led to Sri Lanka having what must be the world's largest cabinet – a total of 107 cabinet ministers, senior ministers, deputy ministers and project ministers in a parliament of 225 members. The UPFA currently has nearly 160 MPs that are part of its coalition, which means that nearly two-thirds of the government's parliamentarians are now ministers of some sort.

Another recent development that confirmed the government's authoritarian trajectory was the impeachment of the country's first woman chief justice in January 2013. Chief Justice Shirani Bandaranayake, like her predecessors and fellow justices, initially contributed to verdicts that bolstered the executive presidency at the expense of other institutions. Yet when she ruled that the *Divinegume* Department (which under the guise of development allows Basil Rajapaksa to control an additional $600 million to expand the First Family's patronage system) violated aspects of the constitution, the president set up a Parliamentary Select Committee (PSC) comprised of politicians from the ruling coalition that found her guilty of financial and official misconduct, leading to her impeachment. This was done despite the Supreme Court ruling that the PSC had no right to investigate a senior judge; the Appeals Court ordering parliament to abandon the impeachment process; and civil society organisations, clergy members, foreign governments and various international bodies likewise objecting forcefully. The president disregarded such entreaties and removed the Chief Justice, even as pro-government goons brandishing poles gathered outside her official residence to make sure she relinquished her post. Prior to this parliamentarians associated with the government supported the impeachment of the Chief Justice by signing a blank sheet of paper devoid of the impeachment motion, thereby highlighting how checks and balances have ceased to operate within government.

Sri Lanka's judiciary has been gradually compromised since the 1978 constitution concentrated powers within the executive branch, but blatant interference in the judiciary's affairs has reached new heights under the Rajapaksa Government. For instance, increasingly those being appointed to the Supreme Court and Appellate Court are persons who have worked in the Attorney General's Office and carry over an 'executive mindset' to their interpretation of the law. The present government has gone out of its way to shower retired judges with perks ranging from ambassadorships to high-ranking posts in government institutions even as it has provided lucrative opportunities for spouses of sitting justices. This has, predictably, affected the courts' independence. 'Telephone justice' (where judges are called and told how to rule) is also commonplace within the Appellate Court and Supreme Court. All this coupled with the general lack of judicial independence have led even senior lawyers to advise clients to settle disputes out of court even when they felt their clients had a good case in hand. Judges are especially intimidated by politicians and, consequently, rarely rule against them or those who are closely associated with them, which in turn allow such persons to operate with impunity.

Chief Justice Bandaranaike's impeachment parallels the manner in which Army Commander Sarath Fonseka was treated after the war ended. Fonseka had the gumption to run against President Rajapaksa in the presidential election following the war's end and was soon thereafter imprisoned for over two years using dubious charges. Security personnel dragged him out of his office when arresting him. Notwithstanding his vanity and arrogance, Fonseka was – is – considered a national hero for having devised the military strategy that ultimately defeated the LTTE. His humiliation was designed to send a message to all those who may flirt with challenging the government, just as Chief Justice Shirani Bandaranayake's impeachment has sent a clear message to judges who may consider obstructing the government's agenda. Their experience and the impotent opposition when juxtaposed with the Rajapaksas' control over the country clearly highlight the degree to which the island's checks and balances have been vitiated since President Rajapaksa came to power.

Militarisation

Leaders bent on authoritarianism are good at feeding the military knowing full well that how the soldiers turn in a crisis could determine their fate (Barany 2013). The Rajapaksas are no different. Sri Lanka did experience a clumsy military coup in 1962 headed mainly by Christian officers that unsurprisingly failed (Horowitz 1980), but the predominantly Sinhalese Buddhist military that has taken shape since then has stayed staunchly loyal to its civilian rulers.

Sinhalese Buddhists ardently believe that Sri Lanka is the designated sanctuary of Buddhism and the Sinhalese are Buddha's chosen people to preserve and propagate his doctrine. In this context the LTTE attempt to sunder the island was unacceptable and it led to Buddhist clergy and Sinhalese Buddhist nationalists supporting to the hilt a military solution to the conflict (as opposed to a political solution). Promoting a military solution meant promoting the military and the Rajapaksas, who are consummate Sinhalese Buddhist nationalists, supported and defended the military because doing so was consistent with their ethnoreligious ideology and because they appear to believe that feeding the military would make the military partial toward them.

Gotabhaya Rajapaksa served in the military and the First Family has succeeded in using his knowledge and links to the armed forces to create a powerful nexus between itself and the military. Thus officers whose loyalty to the Rajapaksas was in doubt have been forced into retirement or provided sinecures (i.e. positions within state corporations and ambassadorships) even as loyalists have been further empowered. For instance, the Northern and Eastern Provinces have long been run by retired military officers. But now many retired military personnel have been recruited to work within government at various levels, and increasingly at even lower levels – especially in the north and east. The government appears to signal that military personnel and their families are more patriotic than average citizens – as when it encourages military personnel to have more children or provide military families incentives to move to the predominantly Tamil Northern Province so as to change the region's demographics. With some leaders of the military potentially vulnerable to accusations of war crimes, such a pro-military culture amidst the perpetuation of the Rajapaksa regime is a welcome development.

As noted above, the growth in the military's size and lethal capabilities was necessitated by the need to defeat the LTTE, and Defense Secretary Gotabhaya Rajapaksa and former Army Commander Sarath Fonseka ensured that this happened expeditiously. Consequently, the military (army, navy and air force) now numbers around 300,000, making Sri Lanka's armed forces one of the largest per capita in the world. If the police and paramilitaries are included, the country has over 400,000 personnel under arms (*The Island* 2014). What is especially striking is that the government has refused to demobilise the armed forces. On the contrary, it has continued to recruit members into so-called Civil Defense Forces and used them to build and renovate temples, schools, water tanks, roads and bridges.

The government's point that it cannot summarily fire poor soldiers from rural families now that the war is over is understandable. Just as Sri Lanka relies heavily on remittances from citizens working abroad, this soldiery contributes its own form of remittance to some of the country's most destitute areas. Since most are Sinhalese Buddhists who disproportionately support the SLFP and are from areas that usually support the SLFP, getting rid of them is also not politically smart. Much of Sri Lanka's political violence (especially during elections) and serious criminal activity are associated with military deserters and there is genuine concern that thousands of battle-hardened jobless veterans could turn to a life of crime that can destabilise society, and this argument has also been used to justify not demobilising the military.

But thousands of military personnel cannot be left idling; and so Sri Lanka's military has increasingly gotten involved in governance and development. The military's development activities include building roads and bridges; refurbishing schools, rundown buildings and sports stadiums; supervising private companies that collect trash in Colombo; and conducting compulsory training for university entrants. The military has also been used to demolish buildings with no titles and to forcibly evict long-standing occupants of those buildings. When dengue fever spread in Colombo and some other areas, the military was used to clean clogged drains and eradicate mosquito breeding grounds. When the Commonwealth Heads of State Meeting was held in Colombo in November 2013, it was military personnel who were used to spruce up the city.

More troubling for private entrepreneurs, the military is also increasingly involved in commercial activities. These range from small to large scale and include farming and selling vegetables; operating travel offices; conducting whale and dolphin watching tours and a canal boat service; running restaurants and guesthouses; and (in Northern Province) overseeing businesses ranging from tea stalls to barber salons. It now also operates hotels, cricket stadiums, golf courses and construction companies. All three armed forces have been asked to bid on construction contracts, which will harm commercial enterprises unable to compete with military entities whose standard overhead costs get subsidised by the state. Additionally, Rakna Arakshaka Lanka Ltd., a firm operating under the Ministry of Defense, now oversees security at the airport, Port's Authority, state institutions and universities. Some university students have strongly protested against the firm's presence on campuses, claiming it monitors their activities and seeks to stifle their criticism of the government, to no effect.

The defense secretary especially justifies maintaining a large military by claiming the LTTE could recrudesce – although he has also claimed that a large military is necessary to maintain democracy (*The Economist* 2012: 46). As per civil society members and clergy in the Northern Province, nearly one in eight persons in Jaffna and one in four persons in areas that the LTTE long controlled is a soldier. It is not just the predominantly Tamil northeast that is now being militarised to greater levels, but the south as well. Gotabhaya Rajapaksa has ordered an army presence in every district in the country, and new mini army camps have been built (or are in the process of being built) throughout the island. For instance, while there was during the war hardly any major military camp in Hambantota, a town and district in the south where the Rajapaksa family has long commanded broad support, there are now nearly two dozen mini camps in operation. Basil Rajapaksa has argued that such military camps are necessary to maintain the island's unity and that only those supporting terrorism would seek to reduce defense allocations (*Asian Tribune* 2011).

As noted above, such arguments extend a patriot-traitor narrative that was created right after Mahinda Rajapaksa became president. This narrative prohibits any criticism of the military and its leaders – and this includes civilian leaders like the defense secretary and president – even as it promotes a *ranawiru* (war hero) culture throughout the country (Hewamanne 2009). The self-censorship that accompanied that culture during the civil war continues to the point where some journalists claim that the political climate post-civil war is less tolerant than it was during the war.

The real reason for maintaining such a large military was perhaps made clear when army personnel recently attacked citizens protesting in Weliweriya, a predominantly Sinhalese Buddhist town just over an hour from Colombo. Authoritarian governments are averse to public protests and seek to crush them before they get out of hand. This lesson is their major take away from the Arab Spring. In Sri Lanka's case, what transpired in Weliweriya proves an apt example in this regard. The basis for the protest was government inaction despite people in Weliweriya repeatedly complaining that toxic chemicals from a nearby factory producing gloves were polluting their water supply. The well-orchestrated army crackdown saw protesters being fired at and brutally beaten (Bastians 2013). Many Sri Lankans felt that if the army could take such action in a town located only about an hour from Colombo, in a mainly Sinhalese district that is considered a SLFP stronghold, and where Basil Rajapaksa won elections handily, it could go much further when dealing with the country's utterly disempowered minorities especially in the northeast.

With the military now playing a dominant role in the everyday life of the country many feel the armed forces can be used to intimidate political opponents and prevent a transfer of power following an opposition victory. Weliweriya may thus be a harbinger of what is to come in Sri Lanka. This scenario is hardly farfetched when one considers how those loyal to former army Commander Sarath Fonseka have been systematically purged and officers loyal to the president and his family promoted in their place and the extent to which surveillance cameras, phone tapping and Internet monitoring have expanded.

If a militarised culture is a situation where people are fascinated with the military, weapons and war and they go about their lives surrounded by military symbols and a military presence without considering this to be unnatural or problematic (Enloe 2000: 2), then areas outside Sri Lanka's northeast could be said to have reached such a stage. The more the military becomes associated with the regime and involved in the economy, the more difficult it would be for Sri Lanka to transition to a democratic post-Rajapaksa government.

Assaulting civil society and media

Governments that preceded the Rajapaksa regime did harass civil society; and censorship during the previous Chandrika Kumaratunga government hurt media freedom and led to the *Sunday Leader* newspaper being shut down for a while. But past governments' ire was with particular segments of civil society and media and not their entire communities. The Rajapaksa Government, however, considers civil society an adversary, and this has led to think-tanks and NGOs being intimidated, obstructed, monitored, threatened and vilified as anti-national, anti-patriotic, pro-LTTE and parasitic. The upshot is that the space permitting civil society activity in Sri Lanka has shrunk drastically, and current trends suggest that it could shrink further.

For instance, a few years ago academics and civil society activists who signed a letter protesting the death threats levelled at the director of the Centre for Policy Alternatives (CPA) were visited and questioned in their offices and homes by members of the Criminal Investigation Department – as a way of letting them know their whereabouts were well known to the intelligence services. The former head of Transparency International's (TI) house was bombed apparently due to TI's investigations into election violations and corrupt procurements within the military. The government partly harasses civil society groups by requiring them to submit to onerous registration and auditing procedures. Similarly, members of the CID make unannounced visits to NGOs and inquire about details and programmes to keep staff off balance and in a reactive mode. In some instances, the government writes to foreign funders to confirm financial sources. Currently civil society actors operate under the belief that their phone lines are tapped.

NGOs that work in the north face even greater scrutiny and suspicion, for they are automatically considered pro-LTTE. The Rajapaksa regime considers most prominent civil society organisations, including foreign NGOs, to be pro-Tamil and pro-minority, which in turn automatically makes them anti-government. In this context, Tamil civil society especially feels marginalised since it operates in a climate of fear and must avoid being branded pro-LTTE. The NGO Secretariat now comes under the Ministry of Defense, which likes to argue that many NGOs operate at cross purposes with Sri Lanka's national interests. Some NGOs that flocked to the island following the December 2004 tsunami made a mockery of relief work and took advantage of Sri Lankan hospitality and customs. Thereafter, it was clear that NGO activity needed to be regulated to an extent. Yet what has been taking place recently under the guise of regulation is strict government control of NGO activity. Thus foreign NGO staffs are now given three-year visas while UN staffs are allowed four-year visas. Many have been refused visas and sent out of the country. By refusing and threatening to refuse NGO personnel visas, the government has managed to get NGOs to comply with its dictates, and this divides the NGO community by making it harder to coordinate activities. The Ministry of Defense has said it would like donor agencies to coordinate aid through it, which is a way to ensure tighter restrictions on civil society.

The media too continue to operate in fear, with nearly all private media having dealt with some combination of intimidation, attack, arson and the killing and disappearance of journalists. The January 2009 death of Lasantha Wickrematunge, editor of the *Sunday Leader*, is supposedly still being probed. By some counts nearly two dozen journalists have been killed since Mahinda Rajapaksa became president. Self-censorship is pronounced and many academics and civil society activists have stopped writing critically. Lawyers defending media outlets in cases that pit them against the government have been branded traitors, causing some to suspend their services.[3]

The government refuses to advertise the affairs of state corporations in media it considers hostile. It also puts pressure on private entities not to advertise in such media. With the government increasingly getting involved in the affairs of private companies (such as banks and insurance corporations) and thereafter planting government representatives on these companies' boards, these outfits are also forced to not advertise in certain media. The government has also encouraged businessmen close to the regime and politicians associated with the regime to buy up media that operate independently to the point where there are currently just two newspapers in English that operate with any semblance of independence.

Media in turn know where not to tread. Criticising the president too directly is considered dangerous, especially if done so in the vernacular press. Some criticism is tolerated within the English language press since the vast majority who read the English publications do not vote for the government to begin with and since it allows the government to point to such criticism when defending itself against allegations of muzzling the media. But criticising the military and even hinting at corruption within the military is totally avoided in all media. None today dare report critically on the defense secretary. Some journalists refuse to write about him; and some editors refuse to publish stories on him (*The Economist* 2012: 46). The government has a stable of dependable allies to attack those who write against it. The government also resorts to various investigations and law suits to force critics into line. Furthermore, the president personally gifts journalists – including those belonging to the non-state media – laptops and approves loans from state banks for duty free vehicles so as to cultivate ties with media personnel (*Colombo Telegraph* 2014).

Increasingly the Rajapaksa Government has been using the private media for propaganda purposes, which is new. This started during the last phase of the civil war and was especially obvious following the war victory, when videos and songs promoting the military and president were aired repeatedly for weeks on end. Private media were apparently compelled to air such programmes and the president's and defense secretary's speeches, going by how often they repeated airing the same programme. It now appears that such media have, in the main, opted to endear itself to the First Family so as to ensure state patronage and avoid being harassed – for compromised journalism is ultimately preferable to loss of life and limb.

Conclusion

Notwithstanding pre-independence ethnic squabbling between Sinhalese and Tamils concerning political representation, Sri Lanka started out as a commendable democracy. As noted, universal suffrage was instituted in 1931 – just three years after it was introduced in Britain. Many considered the country the most likely to succeed among those states that were part of the post-World War II decolonisation process (Wriggins 1961). The country's two main political parties kept alternating in power so that by 1960 the island had passed the two turnover test, which Samuel Huntington (1991) used as a gauge to determine democratic consolidation. Then it embraced ethnocentrism, which culminated in civil war.

The defeat of the LTTE engineered by the Rajapaksa brothers has certainly provided the president a lasting legacy. Yet over four years later a second soft-authoritarian legacy that is destroying democratic institutions is in the making. Indeed, the craving for power and control; disregard for the rule of law; intolerance of opposition; and tolerance of impunity, venality, and predatory politics that undergird Rajapaksa rule are corrupting and undermining already mediocre institutions (DeVotta 2014). A culture of impunity especially is hard to compartmentalise, and in Sri Lanka's case it has spread among the ruling elite and those with links to this elite. Presidential immunity and patronage have only exacerbated this culture of impunity. So has corruption at the highest levels of government, with bribery being rampant and conducted without fear. It is now the norm for the powerful and those connected to such persons to violate speed limits, not pay traffic fines, not appear in court, use the police to get rid of evidence, intimidate witnesses to retract testimonies and coerce judges to rule in their favour. All this has weakened Sri Lanka as a viable democratic state.

Sri Lankan politicians long claimed that the country did not have an ethnic problem; it merely had a terrorist problem. It was a convenient way of glossing over their support for creating an ethnocentric state that promoted the majority community's interests at the expense of minorities and national cohesion. The fact is that their actions spawned a civil war that compromised the island's democracy and in turn laid the conditions for the current soft-authoritarian dispensation. The draconian strategies that were packaged into a counter-terror policy may have effectively eliminated the LTTE, but they are now being furthered to superimpose authoritarianism. This is not what those who eagerly looked forward to a post-civil war era bargained for, although it perhaps evidences how challenging it can be for states to disengage from institutionalised extraconstitutional and extrajudicial processes. The longer such processes last, the harder it becomes to change course. Sri Lanka's civil war lasted nearly three decades, and that too after Sinhalese-Tamil animus festered for a quarter of a century. Rectifying the wreckage that ethnocentrism, the civil war and counter-terrorism have collectively unleashed on the island will be a daunting yet necessary task if Sri Lanka is to become a decent democracy once again.

Notes

1 The grievances include Tamil civil servants being forced to learn Sinhala to be promoted and Tamils not hired into government service after the Sinhala Only Act came into effect; Sinhala civil servants being stationed in Tamil areas to ensure linguistic hegemony; Tamil students being required to score higher to enter universities; quota systems being introduced to increase the number of Sinhalese students from especially rural areas; successive governments avoiding the development of Tamil areas (especially irrigation development); international aid that was earmarked for Tamil areas being diverted to Sinhalese areas; successive governments aggressively pursuing Sinhalisation (and ethnic flooding) of the Eastern Province; the military's deployment in the Northern Provinces leading to humiliating practices; Sinhala only being introduced to the court system in northeast (later revoked); the 1972 constitution incorporating Sinhala as the sole official language, branding the island a unitary state, and giving Buddhism the foremost place; and anti-Tamil rioting in 1956, 1958 and 1977.
2 The JVP's first attempt took place in 1971.
3 For instance, lawyers defending the *Sunday Leader* newspaper against the Defense Secretary's charges of defamation were branded 'traitors' on the Defense Ministry webpage and also by the former Prime Minister in Parliament.

References

Amnesty International (2009) 'Sri Lanka human rights'. Available at: www.amnestyusa.org/all-countries/sri-lanka/page.do?id=1011241 (last accessed 5 July 2009).

Aradau, C. and Van Munster, R. (2009) 'Exceptionalism and the "war on terror": criminology meets international relations', *British Journal of Criminology*, 49/5, 686–701.

Asian Tribune (2011) Available at: www.asiantribune.com/news/2011/12/01/sri-lanka-2nd-reading-budget-adopted-majority-91-votes (last accessed 2 December 2011).

Barany, Z. (2013) 'Armies and revolutions', *Journal of Democracy* vol. 24, no. 2, pp. 62–76.

Bastians, D. (2013) 'Death by a thousand cuts', *Daily FT*, 8 August 2013. Available from: www.ft.lk/2013/08/08/death-by-a-thousand-cuts/ (last accessed 15 January 2014).

Boyle, M.J. (2010) 'Do counterterrorism and counterinsurgency go together?', *International Affairs*, 86/2, 333–353.

Colombo Telegraph (2014) 'Expose: media heads to bow; Rajapaksa gives 547 journos interest free car loans', 20 January. Available at: www.colombotelegraph.com/index.php/expose-media-heads-to-bow-rajapaksa-gives-547-journos-interest-free-car-loans/ (last accessed 25 January 2014).

DeVotta, N. (2004) *Blowback: linguistic nationalism, institutional decay, and ethnic conflict in Sri Lanka*, Stanford University Press, Stanford.

DeVotta, N. (2009) 'The liberation tigers of Tamil eelam and the lost quest for separatism in Sri Lanka', *Asian Survey*, 49/6, 1021–1051.

DeVotta, N. (2014) 'Parties, political decay, and democratic regression in Sri Lanka', *Commonwealth and Comparative Politics*, 52/1, 139–165.

Diamond, L. (2008) 'The democratic rollback: the resurgence of the predatory state', *Foreign Affairs* 87/2, 36–48.

Enloe, C. (2000) *Maneuvers: The international politics of militarizing women's lives*, University of California Press, Berkeley.

Ericson, R.V. (2007) *Crime in an insecure world*, Polity Press, London.

Fortna, P.F. and Huang, R. (2012) 'Democratization after civil war: a brush-clearing exercise', *International Studies Quarterly* 56/4, 801–808.

Hewamanne, S. (2009) 'Duty bound? Militarization, romances, and new forms of violence among Sri Lanka's free trade zone factory workers', *Cultural Dynamics* 21/2, 153–184.

Horowitz, D. (1985) *Ethnic groups in conflict*, University of California Press, Berkeley.

Horowitz, D. (1993) 'Democracy in divided societies', *Journal of Democracy*, 4/4, 18–38.

Human Rights Watch (2008) *Recurring nightmare: state responsibility for 'Disappearances' and abductions in Sri Lanka*. Available at: http://hrw.org/reports/2008/srilanka0308/ (last accessed 2 July 2008).

Huysmans, J. (2008) 'The jargon of exception—on Schmitt, Agamben and the absence of political society', *International Political Sociology*, 2/2, 165–183.

Huysmans, J. (2006) *The politics of insecurity: fear, migration and asylum in the EU*, Routledge, London.

Illarionov, A. (2009) 'Reading Russia: The *Siloviki* in charge', *Journal of Democracy* 20/2, 69–72.

Kilcullen, D. (2009) *The accidental guerrilla: fighting small wars in the midst of a big one*, Hurst, London.

Levitsky, S. and Way, L.A. (2010) *Competitive authoritarianism: hybrid regimes after the cold war*, Cambridge University Press, New York.

Mallawarachi, B. (2008) 'Sri Lankan journalists cite intimidation', *Lanka Academic*. Available at: www.theacademic.org/. (last accessed 22 June 2008).

Nanjappa, V. (2008) 'Rights group flays Sri Lanka on "disappearances"'. Available at: http://im.rediff.com/news/2008/mar/06ltte.htm. (last accessed 15 July 2008).

Neal, A. (2006) 'Foucault in Guantanamo: towards the archeology of the exception', *Security Dialogue*, 37/1, 31–46.

Swamy, M.R.N. (1994) *Tigers of Lanka: from boys to guerrillas*, Konark Publishers Pvt Ltd., Delhi.

The Economist (2010) 'Beating the drum', 18 November, p. 49.

The Economist (2012) 'My brothers' keepers,' 11 February, p. 46.

The Island (2014) 'What a shame!' 22 January. Available at: www.island.lk/index.php?page_cat=news-section&page=news-section&code_title=42 (last accessed 24 January 2014).

University Teachers for Human Rights (2007a) *Can the east be won through human culling*, Special Report No. 26. Available at: www.uthr.org/SpecialReports/spreport26.htm. (last accessed 3 August 2007).

University Teachers for Human Rights (2007b) *Slow strangulation of Jaffna: trashing General Larry Wijeratne's legacy and enthroning barbarism*, Special Report No. 28 Available at: www.uthr.org/SpecialReports/spreport28.htm. (last accessed 4 December 2007).

U.S. Department of State (2008) *Sri Lanka: country reports on human rights practices—2007*, Bureau of Democracy, Human Rights, and Labor. Available at: www.state.gov/g/drl/rls/hrrpt/2007/100620.htm (last accessed 12 March 2008).

U.S. Department of State (2009) *Report to Congress on incidents during the recent conflict in Sri Lanka*, U.S. Department of State, Washington, D.C.

Weiss, G. (2011) *The cage: the fight for Sri Lanka and the last days of the Tamil Tigers*, The Bodley Head, London.

Whitaker, M.P. (2007) *Learning politics from Sivaram: the life and death of a revolutionary Tamil journalist in Sri Lanka*, Pluto Press, London.

Wilson, A.J. (2000) *Sri Lankan Tamil nationalism: its origins and development in the nineteenth and twentieth centuries*, University of British Columbia Press, Vancouver.

Index

7/7 *or* July 7th 2005 London bombings 19, 152, 157, 169, 170, 173, 183
9/11 11, 16, 41, 43, 44, 45, 109, 152, 155, 156, 159, 170, 188, 211

Adams, Gerry 196, 200, 201, 202
Afghanistan 11, 14, 16, 17, 20, 22, 24, 27, 188, 197, 201, 203–5, 213, 218
Allende, Salvador 45
al-Awlaki, Anwar 19
al Qaeda 4, 5, 11–28, 69, 86, 152, 155, 188, 191, 203
al Qaeda in Iraq (AQI) 20, 21
al Qaeda in the Arabian Peninsula (AQAP) 16, 19, 23–4
al Qaeda in the Maghreb (AQIM) 19, 20, 21, 23, 24
al-Shabaab 12, 16, 19, 20, 22, 23, 25, 27
al-Wuhayshi, Nasir 12
al-Zawahiri, Ayman 12, 20, 21
Anglosphere, the 150–1
Anti-Terrorism Act 2001 (Canada) 156, 158
Arab Spring 18, 20, 21, 224
Aradau, Claudia 61, 124, 211
Australia 50, 143, 150–63

Bali bombings 2002 152
Basque Country 91, 94–5, 97–8, 101
bin Laden, Osama 20, 21
Blair, Tony 124, 138, 144, 193, 199, 200, 204, 207
Blakeley, Ruth 79
Boko Haram 12, 20, 23, 24, 27, 165
borders 58
Breen Smyth, Marie 79
Breivik, Anders 43, 174
Brigate Rosse 48, 49
British Empire 47–8, 53

Bush, George W. 3, 11, 13, 16, 159, 192, 211

Cameron, David 18, 152, 172, 193
Campbell, David 46
Canada 150, 151, 154–6, 158, 160–1, 164–4
Carr, Bob 153
Central Intelligence Agency (CIA) 17, 44, 45
Channel Programme (UK) 52, 171, 177, 182
citizenship 50, 56, 69, 86, 94, 109, 110, 112, 113, 150, 153, 173, 179
Clarke, Charles 153
Cold War 17, 25, 47, 194, 201
community cohesion 2, 8, 169, 172, 173, 174, 175, 177, 178–83, 197, 227
community policing 6, 85, 86
CONTEST (UK) 3, 57, 69, 70, 83, 130, 146, 163, 170, 174; Prevent strand 7–8, 50, 51, 52, 83, 130, 163, 169–83; Pursue strand 7, 83, 130, 163
control orders 109, 117, 144, 145, 165
counter insurgency 13–14, 22, 23, 26, 28, 188, 199, 203, 205, 213, 214
counter-terrorism: as colonial policing 47; effectiveness of 14, 18, 80, 82, 83, 110, 112, 123, 151, 161–3, 165, 169, 172, 174, 177, 178, 187; 'hard' versus 'soft' 77; Legislation 41–2, 47–50, 60–2, 64, 70, 77–8, 95, 116, 120, 130–46, 150–66; pre emptive 5, 25, 28, 41, 50, 54, 57, 130–46, 158; purposes of 152, 141
Crenshaw, Martha 80, 81
criminal law 130, 131, 133–4, 135, 136, 138, 146
critical terrorism studies (CTS) 78
Croft, Stuart 51, 68

232 Index

Cronin, Audrey 4, 80, 81

de Menezes, Jean Charles 121–3, 126
democracy 42, 63–4, 96, 97, 99, 101, 165–6, 189, 191, 195, 204, 205, 210–11, 215, 220, 223, 227–8
Department of Communities and Local Government (DCLG), UK 51, 171, 172, 173, 177, 179, 182, 183
deportation 63, 130
deradicalisation 49, 50, 96
detention, pre-charge 6, 47, 77, 109, 113, 114, 121–2, 157, 165, 182

East African Embassy bombings 1998 67
Edkins, Jenny 44
Ethniki Organosis Kyprion Agoniston (EOKA) 47, 48, 53
European Union (EU) 15, 79
Euskadi Ta Askatasuna (ETA) 6, 91, 94–5, 97–8, 100, 101, 102
exceptional (ism) 3, 57, 60–3, 131, 211
extraordinary rendition 47, 188, 211

Federal Bureau of Investigation (FBI) 67

Gearty, Conor 109, 155
Geneva Conventions 80
Guantanamo Bay 53, 211
Gunning, Jeroen 78, 79

Hamas 15, 16, 17, 203
Haqqani Network 21, 22, 203
Hezbollah 15, 17, 203
Horgan, John 4, 49
human rights 6, 24, 26, 77, 96, 99, 130, 138–40, 146, 155, 179, 188, 196, 205, 216, 217, 218, 220
Huysmans, Jef 61, 211

identity 4, 5, 8, 46, 56–70, 170, 173, 174, 177, 179, 183, 197
Independent Reviewer of Terrorism Legislation 132, 134, 144, 145, 161, 163
intelligence 7, 8, 15, 16, 19, 26, 81, 85, 124, 125, 126, 138–46, 155, 159, 169, 170, 172, 176, 178, 181, 190, 192, 199, 225
intercept evidence 138, 146
internment 46, 47, 164, 196, 197
Irish Republican Army (IRA) 8, 48, 66, 67, 164, 192, 194–207
Iranian Embassy Siege 1985 152

Iraq 12, 14, 17, 19, 25, 45, 188, 191, 192, 203, 204, 218
Islamophobia 115, 116, 117, 126, 180
Israel 15, 16, 188, 193
Italy 47, 49, 53

Jabhat al Nusra 20
Jackson, Richard 2, 3, 4, 62, 65, 78, 79, 84, 109–12, 119, 124, 125, 126, 188
Jenkins, Brian 22, 28, 79

Klein, Naomi 45

Lacan, Jacques 5, 41, 42
Lambert, Robert 50, 85
Liberation Tigers of Tamil Eelam (LTTE) 8, 164, 211–19, 221–5, 227

MacAulay, Lawrence 163
McCarthyism 159
McGuinness, Martin 196, 200
Madrid bombings (2004) 19, 96, 170
Mali 18, 19, 20, 23, 25, 27
Mandela, Nelson 137
Mau Mau emergency 1952–1960 47
media, and terrorism 17, 21, 48, 111–12, 117–21, 125–6, 165, 216–19, 225–7
Movement for Tawhid and Jihad in West Africa (MUJAO) 20, 23
Mueller, John 1, 25, 44
Munich Olympics attacks 1972 152

Nationality, Immigration and Asylum Act 2002 (UK) 153
National Military Strategic Plan for the War on Terrorism 2006 (US) 16
National Security Strategy 2002 (US) 15
National Strategy for Combating Terrorism 2003 (US) 14
National Strategy for Counterterrorism 2011 (US) 25
negotiations (with terrorists) 2, 8, 61, 64, 80, 81, 187–94, 196–9, 203–7
neoconservatism 8, 192–7, 198, 199, 200, 201, 203–6
New Zealand 155
Northern Ireland 8, 47, 53, 63, 64, 67, 69, 187–207; peace process 61, 194–203, 204

Obama, Barack 3, 5, 16, 22, 25–6, 197, 205
old v new terrorism 3, 63, 188–9
ontological security 124

Orientalism 58, 59
othering/otherness 57, 59, 66, 87

Pact in favour of freedoms and against terrorism 2000 (Spain) 95, 101
Pakistan 12, 16, 15, 17, 20, 21, 22, 24, 50, 114, 115
Palestine Liberation Organization (PLO) 16, 65, 159
policy transfer 7, 151
postcolonialism 5, 8, 57–9, 61, 65, 210
precautionary principle 124
precursor offences 130–46
Prevention of Terrorism Act 1976 (Sri Lanka) 213
Prevention of Terrorism Act 1974 (UK) 62, 70
Prima Linea 48, 49
proscription 2, 7, 130, 150–66
Protection of Freedoms Act 2012 (UK) 3
psychoanalytic theory 42, 43

radicalisation 19, 21, 41, 46, 50, 51, 52, 53, 54, 121, 165, 171, 174, 175, 182
Regulation of Investigatory Powers Act 2000 (UK) 138
Rigby, Lee 151, 169, 172, 183
rule of law 9, 22, 26, 64, 65, 96, 130, 134, 146, 155, 166, 210, 211, 214, 227

Saudi Arabia 15, 50
security studies 60
securitization 8, 51, 56–70, 85, 181, 182
Shapiro, Michael 56, 58, 59, 63, 69
Schmid, Alex 78, 79
'shock and awe' 44–5
Somalia 12, 16, 18, 20, 21, 22, 23, 25, 26, 27
sovereignty 41–2, 46–53, 211, 218
Spain 6, 91–102, 188
Sri Lanka 2, 8–9, 164, 188, 210–28
stop and search 77, 82, 114–17
surveillance 77, 94, 119, 139, 142, 143, 159, 172, 176, 177, 178, 181, 183, 211, 224

suspect community 50, 60, 63, 86, 109, 180
Syria 12, 16, 18, 19, 20, 21, 23, 153

Taliban 12, 17, 21, 197, 203–5
temporality: constructions of 56–70
terrorism: definitions 14, 78, 79, 137, 144, 156, 159, 191; discourse 41–54, 56–70
Terrorism Act 2000 (UK) 82, 114, 132, 135, 156, 160
Terrorism Act 2006 (UK) 132, 136, 137, 157, 160
Terrorism Prevention and Investigation Measures (TPIMs) 109, 130, 131, 141–2, 145, 146
terrorism studies 79
trauma 44, 45, 98
Trimble, David 194, 200, 206
Tsarnaev, Tamerlan and Dzhokhar 19
Tzu, Sun 44

United Nations 11, 13, 155, 158, 216; Security Council Resolution 1373 155, 156, 158
Uniting and Strengthening America by Providing Appropriate Tools Required to Intercept and Obstruct Terrorism Act 2001 (USA) 156, 159

Van Munster, Rens 61, 124, 211
victims of terrorism 93–7

Walker, Clive 109, 140, 156, 165
War on Terror 2, 3, 4, 11, 14, 16, 17, 23, 26, 47, 80, 165, 211
waterboarding 79
Westminster model, the 150
Wilkinson, Paul 78, 80

Žižek, Slavoj 5, 41, 42, 46, 48

eBooks
from Taylor & Francis

Helping you to choose the right eBooks for your Library

Add to your library's digital collection today with Taylor & Francis eBooks. We have over 50,000 eBooks in the Humanities, Social Sciences, Behavioural Sciences, Built Environment and Law, from leading imprints, including Routledge, Focal Press and Psychology Press.

Choose from a range of subject packages or create your own!

Benefits for you
- Free MARC records
- COUNTER-compliant usage statistics
- Flexible purchase and pricing options
- 70% approx of our eBooks are now DRM-free.

Benefits for your user
- Off-site, anytime access via Athens or referring URL
- Print or copy pages or chapters
- Full content search
- Bookmark, highlight and annotate text
- Access to thousands of pages of quality research at the click of a button.

Free Trials Available

We offer free trials to qualifying academic, corporate and government customers.

ORDER YOUR FREE INSTITUTIONAL TRIAL TODAY

eCollections

Choose from 20 different subject eCollections, including:

- Asian Studies
- Economics
- Health Studies
- Law
- Middle East Studies

eFocus

We have 16 cutting-edge interdisciplinary collections, including:

- Development Studies
- The Environment
- Islam
- Korea
- Urban Studies

For more information, pricing enquiries or to order a free trial, please contact your local sales team:

UK/Rest of World: **online.sales@tandf.co.uk**
USA/Canada/Latin America: **e-reference@taylorandfrancis.com**
East/Southeast Asia: **martin.jack@tandf.com.sg**
India: **journalsales@tandfindia.com**

www.tandfebooks.com